Black Motherscholarship Within and Beyond the Academy

Crystasany R. Turner · Meghan L. Green
Editors

Black Motherscholarship Within and Beyond the Academy

Reconceptualizing Radical Futurity

Springer

Editors
Crystasany R. Turner
Milwaukee, WI, USA

Meghan L. Green
Chicago, IL, USA

ISBN 978-3-031-99757-0 ISBN 978-3-031-99758-7 (eBook)
https://doi.org/10.1007/978-3-031-99758-7

This Springer imprint is published by the registered company Springer Nature Switzerland AG
The registered company address is: Gewerbestrasse 11, 6330 Cham, Switzerland

"To the Unseen"
Personal and collective,
Unique and familiar,
With you and for you.

We embody the fullness—
Of empathy and strength,
Of pain, reflection,
Isolation, healing, and joy—
All that echoes in the quiet.

We remember
Our divine purpose and positioning on this earth,
Calling forth sacred pieces of ourselves
To share, to heal, to liberate.
We root ourselves
In community and sisterhood,
In spiritwork,
In the generations who've gone before—
Those who resisted,
Who reclaimed what was stolen,
Who made the invisible visible
Through love and unwavering truth.

We honor our mothers—
Tender and radical.

Our collective children—our babies—
Born of blood and of spirit,
Cradled by lullabies turned battle cries.
You are the worlds we dream.
You are the future we build.

To the Thousands Unseen,
Whom we may never meet—
You are the reason we write.

Foreword

"I am sick and tired of being sick and tired."

—Fannie Lou Hamer

Fannie Lou Hamer once declared, *"I am sick and tired of being sick and tired."* Her words were a public indictment of systemic neglect and a bold refusal to acquiesce to the conditions designed to ignore, abandon, and disempower Black people—that same exhaustion, and the determination that rises from it, courses through this collection like lifeblood. *Black Motherscholarship Within and Beyond the Academy* is a collective indictment and a sacred offering. It testifies that Black women are no longer content to survive the academy—we are here to transform it.

Like many other Black women committed to racial and gender justice, Hamer found courage in collective truth-telling— testifying in her own tongue and with persistence. Her insistence on standing in the collective truth mirrors the power of this text. This book does not ask permission to speak the unspoken. Instead, the editors of the collection intuitively know that silence would be a betrayal of all the mothers, scholars, and daughters who came before them.

The editors were able to artistically present a mosaic of experiences and stories that demonstrate the psychic and spiritual toll of navigating spaces never meant to hold us, while simultaneously uplifting the revolutionary nature of Black mothering as scholarship, praxis, and prophecy. In every story uplifted, I see the manifestation of bell hooks' *engaged pedagogy*, a pedagogy that insists learning must be a practice of freedom, grounded in love, healing, and community. hooks taught us that the classroom could be a space of possibility. This book reminds us that *so can the womb, the kitchen, the protest line, the dissertation committee, and the bedtime story.*

What Drs. Crystasany R. Turner and Meghan L. Green have curated here is not simply a scholarly contribution; it is a constellation of offerings from Black women who refuse to sever any part of themselves for the sake of academic legibility. This is not performance. This is presence. This is not survival. This is *fortitude*. Fortitude forged through generations of women who carried us on their backs while pushing open the doors of schools, community centers, birthing rooms, and lecture halls.

In this collection, you will find mothering/daughtering/sisterhood as resistance, as disruption, as love, as grief, as joy, as methodology. We are reminded of the following question: How do we dare to, like our ancestors and Black feminist writers before us, find the courage, in the face of white supremacy patriarchy capitalism imperialism, to speak the unspeakable, to write the unwriteable, and to hold the impossible contradictions of Black womanhood with tenderness and rigor? And, how do we protect our families and community members while raising our voices?

We see the ethics of care bloom through the pain of a mother's loss of a child and the celebration of birth. We see care in the informal networks of other mothers and sister scholars. We see healing in the refusal to bifurcate mind and body, reason and emotion, the academy and the home. Each essay is a balm and a blueprint, a love note and a strategy manual.

Black motherscholarship has always existed—in the whispered prayers of enslaved foremothers, in the notebooks of Harlem Renaissance poets, in the organizing kitchens of civil rights matriarchs, in the side-eyes of faculty meetings where one more microaggression dares to appear. But to name it, to archive it, to theorize it? That is revolutionary. That is *radical futurity*.

These pages are alive with the voices of Black women who have chosen to create new maps, and in the editors' words, "maroon communities" of care. They are building *homeplaces* where the work of raising free Black children and free Black minds is not oppositional, but deeply intertwined.

As I reflect on my own journey as a Black feminist scholar, I feel the pulse of every chapter in this book beating in time with the questions I've carried my entire career: How do we teach and love in ways that refuse racial and gender domination? How do we heal while organizing against oppressive systems? How do we mother and daughter ourselves and each other when the world insists we do neither?

How to ask and re-ask these questions in community is our next frontier in Black feminist praxis. This book reminds us to pause long enough to name our losses, joys, ancestors, and babies. It is a human right to grieve and love without apology. And so this book becomes a living archive, a sacred ledger of what it means to care radically, to research with heart, and to mother with political clarity. Drawing upon the legacies of Hamer, Davis, hooks, Shakur, Collins, and so many unnamed foremothers, this work is situated firmly in the Black feminist tradition—and it moves us forward.

We dream. We breathe. We desire.

To the reader, you are not merely reading a book. You are being invited into a collective—a collective of thinkers, caregivers, educators, daughters, aunties, and mamas. A collective that holds space for Black women educators' full range of emotions, a collective that does not separate love from educational justice or care from educational theory.

We love together.
We heal together.
We fight together.
We live together.

Venus E. Evans-Winters, LCSW, Ph.D.
University of San Diego
San Diego, CA, USA

Acknowledgements

"Let Our Work Speak For Us"
As we grapple with what it means to operate from a space of wholeness,
We sought out to honor the fullness of ourselves in every aspect of our lives.
Holding space for memories that were personal and collective, unique and familiar.
We recognized that *we* are the ones most capable of holding our stories, and
Unsettling the binary understanding of trauma and healing.
This book is Spirit work.

We watered ourselves with/in Spirit,
Creating an expansive sphere of being and knowing.
Each piece offering glimpses into the galaxies of our existences while
Supporting a future one cannot fully see.
This book is our homeplace.

A reclamation of the liminal space
Between worlds of heartache and promise.
A cry into the unknown, reaching out the Unseen.
We are community mothers who resist the silencing and invisibility of mother work.
This book is our faith in the love we have for each other.

Ethical Considerations in Autoethnographic Work

This manuscript includes chapters where motherscholars engage in autoethnographic storytelling that centers their lived experiences alongside those of their children.

In such instances, the inclusion of children's names, voices, and images is intentional and ethically guided. These narratives are constructed through ongoing familial dialogue, with informed agreement from the children involved. While Institutional Review Board (IRB) approval is not typically required for self-reflective, autoethnographic research, all contributors have approached these decisions with deep care, cultural awareness, and a commitment to honoring children's autonomy and well-being.

We offer this context as guidance for others in the field who may engage in motherscholarship or family-centered inquiry and encourage all scholars to approach similar work with transparency, respect, and a clear ethical framework.

Contents

Editors and Contributors

About the Editors

Crystasany R. Turner is an Assistant Professor of Inclusive Early Childhood Teacher Education at the University of Wisconsin-Milwaukee. Rooted in Black feminist epistemologies, her research and scholarship highlight the perspectives of Black women educators and their cultural knowledge as manifested in their care and education of Children of Color. Her teaching and research focus includes Black feminist epistemologies, early childhood education for social justice, and spirit-centered pedagogies. Her work interrogates imbalanced social power, institutional inequities, and systemic oppression affecting diverse children and families. Dr. Turner's scholarship has been published in *Race Ethnicity and Education*, the *Journal of African American Women and Girls in Education*, the *Journal of Teacher Education*, and the *Bloomsbury Encyclopedia of Social Justice in Education* amongst others.

Meghan L. Green is an Assistant Professor of Raciolinguistic Justice in Early Childhood Teacher Education at the Erikson Institute. As an arts-based qualitative researcher, she uses multiple modes of creative representation to reflect on her positionality and to craft her story as a cis Black queer woman engaging in critically informed research methodologies within this time and space. Her scholarship centers Black feminist thought and endarkened feminist epistemology within early childhood settings, specifically highlighting the diverse lived experiences of Black early childhood educators through arts-based qualitative inquiry methods including, autoethnography, endarkened narrative inquiry, photovoice, and poetic inquiry. Her scholarly works have been published in journals such as the *International Journal of Qualitative Methods*, the *Journal of African American Women and Girls in Education, Early Childhood Education Journal*, "Ethnic Studies Pedagogies", and *Equity & Excellence in Education.*

Contributors

Yetunde Alabede Michigan State University, East Lansing, MI, USA

Danille Elize Arendse Department of Psychology, University of Pretoria, Pretoria, South Africa;
The Harriet Tubman Institute, York University, Toronto, ON, Canada

Eboni N. Bango Texas A&M University, College Station, TX, USA

Daphanie N. Bibbs University at Buffalo, Buffalo, NY, USA

Dionne L. Davis Texas State University, San Marcos, TX, USA

Jemilia S. Davis University of North Carolina at Chapel Hill, Chapel Hill, NC, USA

Talia R. Esnard The University of the West Indies, St. Augustine, Trinidad and Tobago

Tasleem Firdausee Western Michigan University, Kalamazoo, MI, USA

Lakya Goss Michigan State University, East Lansing, MI, USA

Javiera Green University of Illinois Urbana-Champaign, Urbana, IL, USA

Meghan L. Green Erikson Institute, Chicago, IL, USA

Melissa A. Green The Open University, Milton Keynes, UK

Salandra Grice-Johnson Sam Houston State University, Huntsville, TX, USA

Brooke Harris Garad Butler University, Indianapolis, IN, USA

Brandy D. James Ball State University, Muncie, IN, USA

Kristina Johnson Yates Indiana University – Indianapolis, Indianapolis, IN, USA

Larissa Malone University of North Carolina Wilmington, Wilmington, NC, USA

Lynnette Mawhinney Rutgers University-Newark, Newark, NJ, USA

Jendayi Mbalia University of Wisconsin-Milwaukee, Milwaukee, WI, USA

Ann Marie Mobley University of South Florida, Tampa, FL, USA

LoRen Modisa University of South Alabama, Mobile, AL, USA

Jamie Lulamae Moore College of the Sequoias, The Puente Project, Visalia, CA, USA

Eghosa Obaizamomwan-Hamilton Stanford University, Stanford, CA, USA

Allyce Pinchback-Johnson Pinchback Consulting, Pittsburgh, PA, USA

Laura Krystal Porterfield Rutgers University-Newark, Newark, NJ, USA

Sacha Sharp Indiana University School of Medicine, Indianapolis, IN, USA

Atiya Kai Stokes-Brown Coastal Carolina University, Conway, SC, USA

DeLisha Tapscott Purdue University, West Lafayette, IN, USA

Crystasany R. Turner University of Wisconsin-Milwaukee, Milwaukee, WI, USA

Michele Turner Institute for Equity and Transformational Change, Madison College, Madison, WI, USA

Tiffany S. Wiggins University of North Carolina at Chapel Hill, Chapel Hill, NC, USA

Regina Gavin Williams North Carolina Central University, Durham, NC, USA [illegible] Sharma [illegible] University [illegible] Medicine, Indianapolis, IN, USA

[illegible] Stokes [illegible], SC, USA

[illegible], IN, USA

[illegible]

[illegible]

[illegible]

[illegible], USA

“They Never Leave You”: Bearing Witness and Holding Space for Radical Healing, Reclamation, and Love

Crystasany R. Turner and Meghan L. Green

Abstract This chapter explores the creation of spaces where Black Motherscholars can embrace the fullness of their identities as women, mothers, scholars, individuals, and members of a collective. Through reflective dialogue and shared storytelling, we engage in a process of radical healing, navigating the complexities of grief and joy, brokenness and wholeness, loss and reclamation. This work serves as both a personal and communal act of resistance, honoring the narratives of Black women who traverse the intersections of motherhood and academia. By centering our experiences as knowledge production, we affirm that our stories are not only valid but essential to shaping transformative spaces of belonging. In holding space for ourselves and others, we weave a tapestry of intergenerational and interdisciplinary connection, fostering a web of communal support, empathy, and resilience. Ultimately, this chapter situates Black mothering within and beyond the academy as both an individual journey and a collective movement toward liberation, healing, and intellectual reimagining.

Keywords Black mothering · Radical healing · Storytelling · Communal support

We are two Black mothers who occupy space in the ostensible ivory tower. Integral to our work as academics and teacher educators is our grappling with what it means to operate from a space of wholeness, where we can honor the fullness of ourselves in every aspect of our lives, including our scholarship (Turner & Allen, 2022; Turner & Green, 2023). As follows, the idea for this book was conceived after a conversation at a conference where we, Meghan and Crystasany, sat with another sisterscholar sharing stories about our various experiences and challenges with fertility, birthing, and mothering.

C. R. Turner (✉)
University of Wisconsin-Milwaukee, Milwaukee, WI, USA
e-mail: crturner@uwm.edu

M. L. Green
Erikson Institute, Chicago, IL, USA
e-mail: mgreen@erikson.edu

C. R. Turner and M. L. Green (eds.), *Black Motherscholarship Within and Beyond the Academy*, https://doi.org/10.1007/978-3-031-99758-7_1

As we each took turns sharing the traumatic birthing experiences of our children and experiences of pregnancy loss, it became evident that our stories were at once personal and collective, unique and familiar. During a discussion recalling this initial conversation as the conception of these volumes, Meghan reflected on her son who was lost. She commented that these experiences "…never leave you. It just always impacts how you move"—a sentiment that we let resonate in silence. Many times, within the urgency culture and plantation-like labor extraction of educational systems, we are not permitted this time to pause and reflect on our human experiences. Instead, we must make ourselves "okay" and simply continue to show up— to perform. Not only is this performance required in our professional spaces, but for many of us who are already mothers, partners, daughters and community members, we must continue to show up in these spaces as well.

Now, in our reflections as we sit to write this introduction, we imagine, *how can we foster spaces in which we can hold the fullness of our identity as women, mothers, scholars, individuals, and members of a collective? How can we simultaneously navigate grief and loss, brokenness and wholeness, healing and joy?* Through our sister talks, we now realize this book is a reclamation of stories as our theories and sense-making, an act of radical healing of both ourselves and others, and a conduit to connect us with a larger community of intergenerational, interdisciplinary Black women who also navigate the complexity of their lives as motherscholars. As we hold this space for our narratives and the stories of other Black motherscholars, we weave a web of communal support, empathy, and strength through the knowledge that we are at once exquisitely exceptional and part of a larger experience of Black mothering within and beyond the academy.

A Reclamation

Generations of Black women scholars have illuminated the multidimensional impact of gender and race on Black women and mothers in institutions of higher education. Their work illustrates the various ways Black women's voices are underrepresented, misrepresented, and all together silenced as we counter normative views and dominant understandings of knowledge production (Turner & Green, 2023). Similarly, our voices have been disregarded in conversations of the health and well-being of our own bodies, as scores of Black women discuss feelings of being silenced or deemed invisible. In her poem titled *Ivory Towers, Bassinets, and Wheelchairs Oh My!*, Dr. Brandy James recalls her birthing experiences as doctors, specialists, and researchers dismissed her pleas for better care and her intuitive knowledge of "something wrong" during her delivery.

The constant disregard and silencing of Black women's voices in institutional spaces (educational, medical, etc.) has shown Black women that *we* are the ones most capable of holding our stories. If we, our children, and communities are to have a voice in creating our futures, we must reclaim authority of our narratives and (re)member our divine purpose and positioning on this earth. Endarkened feminist narrative praxis (Turner, 2026) tells us that as we reclaim and share our Narratives,

> it allows Black women to cultivate meaning from an ever-shifting collective consciousness and, in turn, increases their collective cultural funds of knowledge. With language and expression as vehicles of empowerment, this reflective and purposeful dialogue aids in the exchange of resistance and navigational strategies encouraging Black women's persistence against the onslaught of social inequities.

In (re)membering her son's existence and (re)claiming his narrative, Meghan described how this reflective process began as an internal conversation. "That [was] the way to keep this memory of my child alive, you know what I'm saying? Everybody else could forget, but I will never forget."

In reclaiming our stories through personal reflection and dialogue, we are able to hold and (re)member those sacred aspects of ourselves and share with others as we see fit. "The act of using one's voice requires a listener and thus establishes a connection. For African American women the listener most able to pierce the invisibility created by Black women's objectification is another Black woman" (Collins, 2000, p. 104). Within the soft, vulnerable space we created for our narratives of pain, reflection, isolation, healing, and joy, we imagined how we could make space to hold and honor the aspects of our lives that are not given space—"It's almost like where's the line with sympathy and empathy?" Our process of reclamation included moments of reflection on how to transition fluidly between loss and creation and nurturing homeplaces that uplift the complexity of our lived experiences.

An Act of Radical Healing

In our conversation, Crystasany reflected on how the loss of her last baby is something she still struggles with. Of course it has to do with the physical loss of a child; but the real struggle is against all the thoughts of "why?".

> Despite the doctor's words that normalize and downplay the loss of my baby, I often fight feelings of guilt that shadow those relentless questions. 'Why didn't I carry myself and my child stronger? Why do I work so much? If I could let go a little in my activism, would I have my baby with me now to care for and to love? How am I supposed to keep going as if I am okay?'

With these questions still spinning in Crystasany's head, Meghan shared that when going through the loss of her son, "writing was cathartic" for her. Through her writing, Meghan was able to hold space for the memory of her son, keeping his name present in family conversations.

> It was so healing to write. I had to shift my idea of what loss was; and that was the biggest lesson: that maybe it wasn't that there was a physical loss. There are so many other ways that I feel like this child's spirit has been with me for almost 17 years now.

For Crystasany, witnessing Meghan's strength and vulnerability in claiming her story, and giving voice to her son's name and the testimony of his existence was a balm. Not only was Meghan's writing foundational to her own healing, but her storying provided a sort of map for Crystasany's healing journey.

This journey highlights the connections between joy and pain, unsettling the binary understanding of trauma and healing. Healing, whether from the loss of a child or experiences of institutionalized misogynoir, is not represented by a straight line towards one destination; rather, it should be (re)conceptualized as a constellation of experiences. These experiences were never meant to leave us completely, but instead serve as reminders of where we have been, our present circumstances, and glimpses of where we are heading.

A Conduit

Crystasany recalls that in her loneliest moments, when her soul and spirit are exhausted, she often finds herself returning to a practice passed on to her by a senior Latina scholar.

> *Stand up, close your eyes.*
> *Root your toes into the earth*
> *and let your Self be grounded in the ancient mother.*
>
> *From the top of your head, open your third eye*
> *To gaze on the beauty of Divine Spirit.*
> *Lengthen your spine with the energy of a thousand generations*
> *Who were born, lived, and died for you to stand here today.*
>
> *Hear the call of a thousand generations,*
> *Your children and your children's children*
> *Longing for you to complete your divine purpose.*
>
> *Reach to your sides and stretch your hands*
> *Toward those who walk beside you all around the earth.*
> *Thousands of Unseen, who you may never meet.*
> *Know that they are there and walk with you on this journey.*

This book is the embodiment of generations of stories lived and told by Black women. It started as a call— a cry into the unknown, reaching out to the Unseen. Fighting sentiments of isolation and our own exceptionalism as mothers, activists, scholars and women, we searched for sisters who shared our experiences of Mothering within and beyond the walls of the academy. Carrying our children and our communities with grace and dignity in a world in which "we were never meant to survive" (Lorde, 1978, p. 31), we persist and we thrive as an act of resistance.

Despite the inimical environments in which we find ourselves, we have learned the lessons of our ancestors—to root ourselves in community and sisterhood. We create homespaces and maroon communities of care that provide us with the safety and strength to regenerate. We have learned to water ourselves with/in Spirit, while we labor and dream of a better world for ourselves, our children, and our children's children. Our call for our sisters, the Unseen, was answered across the nation and around the world. Women of Africa, the Caribbean, the United Kingdom and scores of Black women across the diaspora galvanized to share their stories of revolutionary mothering and dreams of radical futurity.

> **Crystasany:** That's why I know that this is sacred work. This is spiritwork. In a similar way that you and me sharing our stories was healing, I hope that we can create a space of healing and reciprocity for our sister scholars—the women who we are just learning about through this project. That is my prayer for this book.

Within this work, we lean on the Spirit and the wisdom of our ancestors who prepared the Blackprint for navigating our activism, scholarship, and diverse forms of motherhood in institutional spaces. Our stories become the conduit through which we forge intergenerational connections, make meaning, and continue the work of social transformation (Green & Green, 2023).

Epistemological Mothering

The present edited volume venerates Black motherscholars' multifaceted ways of being and knowing across time and space. Epistemological mothering amongst Black women manifests in similar ways. Authors in this text engaged with several onto-epistemological frameworks which center Black women's knowledge and praxis traditions including, but not limited to, Black feminist thought (Collins, 2000); womanism (Walker, 1983); intersectionality (Crenshaw, 1989); critical race feminism (Wing, 2015); and Caribbean feminist approaches (Carty, 1988; Reynolds, 2005).

Our pro-Black stance in this book "focuses on the agency, resistance, everyday lives, and joy of Black people" (Boutte & Compton-Lilly, 2022, p. 323). While gathering narratives to feature in this book, we received pushback from other Women of Color, questioning why we chose to highlight the experiences of *Black* mothers. We acknowledge and honor the generations of Fierce Mothering (Gámez, 2015) of our Latina, Indigenous, and Asian sisters; and our centering of Black mothers takes nothing from their stories. Yet, citing the inordinately high rates of Black maternal (CDC, 2022) and fetal death and the scores of Black mothers who have suffered pregnancy loss and fertility struggles due to the premature weathering (Geronimus, 1992; Wallace & Harville, 2013) of our bodies and spirits within institutional spaces, we find it essential to center the Black woman's experience to speak back to the rampant anti-Blackness that permeates every Western social institution. As such, we stand in solidarity with Women of Color in the academy across racial and ethnic social locations as we confront anti-Blackness directly and unapologetically.

Intersectionality rests on the communal experiences of Black women in the United States and abroad (Crenshaw, 1991). We find the strength and wherewithal to persevere against common threats to our humanity in our shared encounters with various forms of oppression. We then take the knowledge we have garnered from these lessons and band together to support the liberation of marginalized people across demographics. Through delving into the complexities of physical and emotional violence against Women of Color, Crenshaw (1991) found that an either/or position regarding identity politics was insufficient and advocated instead for the use of a both/and perspective—asserting that there is "the need to account for multiple grounds of identity when considering how the social world is constructed" (p. 1245).

Carbado and Harris (2019) examined the similarities and differences between intersectionality and two other prominent theoretical frameworks: (a) *anti-essentialism* and (b) *dominance theory*. They contended that there are times when labels and categories that are often considered *essentialist* serve a necessary purpose. Although racial categories, such as African American or Black, for example, can be examples of *essentialist* labels because of the monolithic assumptions therewithin, the terms can also be useful when describing or organizing the referenced group of people. Intersectionality, as a theoretical framework, allows us to center the lived experiences of Black women while providing "generalizable theory about power and marginalization" (Carbado et al., 2013, p. 305).

Somewhere in between this and that, Black motherscholarship exists in the liminal space between worlds of heartache and promise. Black motherscholars have never been just one thing. Our circumstances in the academy have always been complex and messy, allowing for multiple vantage points and divergent lived experiences. Our goal in the present work was never to present a monolithic landscape of Black motherscholarship, but instead we sought to offer an expansive sphere of being and knowing as a means of reclaiming our places as authorities of our own lives. As we write and edit this volume, collectively we bestow glimpses into the galaxies of our existences.

(Re)Storying the Social History of Black Mothering

Related to our grappling with essentialism and monolithic notions of Blackness, womanhood and mothering, we challenge portrayals of mothering and motherhood within dominator culture that have historically been "inextricably tied to whiteness, the 'private,' and to blood-related relationships" (Pitts, 2014, p. 142). We resist notions of intensive mothering, which "serves the interest of men, capitalism, the state, the middle class, and whites" (Bell, 2004, p. 48). In alignment with the Black feminist understanding of the interconnectedness of our personal, professional and civic lives, we recognize our roles as mothers and othermothers manifest throughout our public and private spheres. As such, we conceptualize motherscholarship not only as the state of being both a mother and a scholar, but as a means of honoring the invisible labor and love put into developing another individual mentally, socially, and spiritually within the institutional settings as well as in the home.

Within educational settings, Black women often take on the role of othermothers and role models for the students in our care. Black women in the home and in the classroom prepare our children for the realities of racialization and gendered oppressions (Hughes & Chen, 1999; Suizzo et al., 2008). Black mothers and othermothers often share pieces of cultural knowledge rooted in our own racialized experiences with our children— acting as cultural translators to prepare the next generation for race-based challenges (Griffin & Tackie, 2016).

Even in predominantly white academic spaces, such as teacher education programs, we continue to care for the children of white folks as we prepare them to work in classrooms with our Black and Brown youth. We align our understanding of these forms of activist mothering and carework with Hidalgo and colleagues (2022) who remind us that,

> "Mothering and activism are complementary endeavors. As mothers and activists, we labor intensely, knowing we may never see the fruit of our efforts. Our work is a leap of faith, an act of hope, and an investment in a future tantalizingly different from the one we know". (Hidalgo et al., 2022, p.123)

The motherscholars whose voices are represented in this book are educators, activists and community mothers who resist the silencing and invisibility of motherwork both within and beyond the academy. In this writing, we draw on Patricia Hill-Collins' (1991) conceptualization of "motherwork," which accounts for the intersectional experiences of Black motherhood and the historical and present abuses of Women of Color in the United States. With this Black feminist understanding of the labor of motherhood, we can honor the nuances of Black motherhood in all of its joy, fears, pain, and beauty. The act of *mothering* extends beyond the label habitually ascribed to white, middle-class women regardless of their participation in the tasks of raising their children (Gumbs, 2016). Mothering venerates the innovative essence of supporting a future one cannot fully see. It is the labor that sustains communities through chosen blood, sweat, and tears. Both Collins (1991) and Gumbs (2016) call for us to (re)member that radical mothering is labor that provides a space for creative autonomy and transformation towards constructing the worlds we desire.

Reflections of Methodologies

Black feminism empowers Black mothers and othermothers to name their own reality through "parables, chronicles, stories, counterstories, poetry, fiction and revisionist histories" (Ladson-Billings & Tate, 1995, p. 56). In accordance, the narratives of the Black motherscholars in these volumes represent a revisionist perspective of dominant discourses of Black womanhood, motherhood, scholarship and activism. Through the use of critical methodologies rooted in endarkened feminist modes of inquiry and our cultural ways of knowing, the authors of these chapters speak back to discourses of gendered racism and the exploitation of our bodies, minds and spirits (Dillard, 2000).

Our goal throughout this project was to highlight Black motherscholarship that utilized data collection and analysis techniques that were "an embodiment of our lived experiences across cultural contexts" (Evans-Winters, 2019, p. 120). Chapter authors employed methodologies grounded in culturally situated communal storying traditions—i.e. duoethnography, collaborative or collective autoethnography, and kitchen table talks—and created vulnerable, yet familiar, spaces as Black mother-scholars to build community and support each other through professional networks (Evans-Winters, 2019; Kinloch et al., 2020).

While many of the Black motherscholars featured in these volumes found that autoethnography offered them a means to provide both windows into human experience and mirrors to reflect meaning about our time in the world, some reflected on the need to craft research methodologies that spoke to a greater sense of wholeness and more accurately described our experiences and understandings of the world. For example, some authors utilized art-based qualitative methodological frameworks such as autohistoria-teoría (Anzaldúa, 1987, 2015) and duo-nkwaethnography (Allen-Handy, 2021) to evoke the healing nature of self/communal-reflective work.

Conceptualizing Radical Futurity

The process of worldbuilding requires imagining contexts that currently do not exist. As Black motherscholars, we sit in spaces that we know were never created with our wellbeing in mind. Instead of begrudgingly requesting those spaces to shift towards principles of justice and equity, we take it upon ourselves to create new possibilities of wholeness and affirmation outside of institutional norms. The first step in radical futurity is healing modern day iterations of misogynoir. We believe the social liberation of Black women predicates humankind's collective freedom, because our "freedom would necessitate the destruction of all the systems of oppression" (Combahee River Collective, 1977).

Waiting for saviors has never suited Black women's goals for liberation, and we have never fully trusted the interlocking systems of racialized and gendered oppression to be anything other than what they were designed to be—sites of spirit murder. Collins (2015) wrote, "no one else sets you free; rather, you empower yourself when your particular freedom struggle is part of a broader social justice project" (Collins, 2015, n.p.). The transformative potential of Black worldmaking, grounded in Afro-futurist ideals, resides in our pursuits of Black liberation and self-determination. Afrofuturism speaks to remembering what was; surviving what is; and dreaming of what could be (Toliver, 2021). Dreaming of new horizons requires that we step out on faith—the faith that our creations will be closer to the liberatory futures we envision and faith in our ability to provide for communal needs. Radical futurity requires faith in the love we have for each other.

Because institutions do not have the capacity to love us, how do we rectify feelings of dissonance in organizations in which our mere presence disrupts business as usual? Within our documentation and theorizing of Black women's positioning within the academy and beyond, we recognize that satisfaction at dismantling anti-Blackness and misogynoir in the ivory tower does not serve us. While language and understanding of historical and current systems of oppression are necessary; our liberation is birthed in our dreams. As Gloria Anzaldúa (1987) reminds us, "Nothing happens in the 'real' world unless it first happens in the images in our heads."

As such, this volume of narratives serves as an onto-epistemological hush harbor (Neal-Stanley, 2023). Within the sacred space of our hush harbor, we can reflect and make-meaning of our experiences, and (re)member the ancestral wisdom of things that "appeared to be wholly new, never before seen…followed, almost immediately, by the sense that it was always there, that we…knew it was always there, and have always known it was as it was…though we have now for the first time recognized, become fully cognizant of, our knowledge" (Morrison, 1994). Within this (re)membering, we subvert oppressive hegemonic ideologies and instead create futures that honor the body, minds, and spirits of Black women within our cultural epistemologies and ways of being.

Within our dreaming of radical futurity, we imagine, *what would it look like for Black women to operate in institutional spaces that can honor our wholeness in all the complex intersections of our identities? How can institutions support Black women in creating homeplaces for us and our children. What would it mean for institutions to build trusting relationships with communities by acknowledging that no one is unharmed by the terrorism of white supremacy?* These and many others are the questions we confront in the pages to come. These are the queries that began with our ancestors and are built upon within radical Black spaces as we (re)center Black joy (Muhammad, 2023; Stewart, 2021), Black possibility (Warren, 2021), and Black dreams (Kelley, 2022).

Organization of Chapters

The first half of this book is organized to take readers on a journey through various vantage points and diverse lived experiences of Black motherscholars. We begin this work paying homage to our shared ancestors, acknowledging that without their labor and freedom dreams (Kelley, 2022) we would not occupy the spaces we are today. Next, we offer diverse perspectives illustrating the experiences of Black motherhood in the academy today in three parts including: *Historical Perspectives of Black Motherscholarship, Theorizing Motherhood,* and *Critical Counter Narratives.* Each part represents a unique perspective into the lives, practices, and theorizing of Black motherscholars.

In the second half of the book, we move from the current depictions of Black motherscholarship to co-imagining what a more liberatory future for Black mother academics and our children could look like through the four following parts:

Centering Our Children's Voices, Motherscholar Identity Formation, and *Motherscholars in Community.* These chapters illustrate what radical futurity could look like as we co-imagine and co-create a more just and liberatory future for Black motherscholars.

Part I: Historical Perspectives of Black Motherscholarship

In this first part, the authors trace the contributions of Black motherscholars throughout local, national, and international history and their impact on academia and social justice movements. Chapter 2, ***Looking Back to Move Forward: Unpacking Maternal Misogynoir in the Academy***, by Dr. Crystasany R. Turner, uses the lens of plantation politics to conceptualize *maternal misogynoir*—drawing parallels between the reproductive exploitation of Black women during enslavement and their experiences within academia. Chapter 3, ***For Black Women Who Have Reconsidered Flipping School Boards When Letters and Lawsuits Weren't Enough: A Divine and Ancestral Throughline of Black Education Activism***, by Dr. Allyce Pinchback-Johnson, highlights historical and contemporary educational activism led by Black women— such as Dr. Barbara Sizemore's efforts in Pittsburgh Public Schools and the recent successes of Black Women for a Better Education—connecting these movements through an endarkened feminist epistemology. Finally, Chapter 4, "***They Are a Burden to You***"***: Reflecting on Mothering as Decolonial Love in Academia in South Africa*** by Dr. Danille Elize Arendse, employs autoethnography to reflect on moving away from colonial conceptions of the academic mother towards inclusionary notions of mothers as full citizens of the academy.

Part II: Theorizing Motherhood

The chapters of this part examine, challenge, and (re)story societal perceptions and representations of Black motherhood to recenter the epistemic authority of Black women theorizing their scholarship and carework. Chapter 5, ***I Know it in My Knower: Testaments of Spirituality within Critical Race Mothering*** by Larissa Malone, Ph.D., explores spirituality within the framework of critical race mothering, highlighting its role in confronting injustices. Through counternarratives, it validates the spiritual identity of Black mothers and challenges the expectation for scholars to suppress their spiritual identity. In Chapter 6, ***Madness and Black Motherhood: Reimagining Scholarship for a Radical Future,*** Dr. Javiera Green explores literary depictions of Black motherhood in Toni Morrison's *Beloved* (1987) and *The Unsettled* (2023) by Ayana Mathis and examines how conceptualizations of madness impact knowledge-making processes in the discipline of Black motherscholarship.

Chapter 7, ***A Duty of Care: Re-Envisioning Academia Through the Intersectional Lenses of Gender, Race, Disability, and Black Feminist Praxis*** by Mel

Green, challenges traditional academic norms by radically reevaluating perceptions of disability and Blackness, advocating for a subversion of dominant, stereotypical views. Grounded in Critical Race Theory, Chapter 8, ***Black While Mothering: Retaining Scholarship, Motherhood, and Presence*** by Dr. Eghosa Obaizamomwan-Hamilton, reframes the experiences of Black motherscholars as acts of refusal within oppressive systems, aiming to redefine their roles and contributions within academia. Chapter 9, ***Black Motherhood, Adoption and Academia: One Black Mother Scholar's Journey Building Family*** by Dr. Atiya Kai Stokes-Brown, highlights how Black motherscholars navigate the responsibilities of academic life with motherhood, focusing specifically on the experiences of a Black motherscholar navigating the adoption and foster care systems.

Part III: Critical Counter Narratives

The chapters of this part collectively delve into the complex experiences of Black motherscholars, highlighting the multifaceted identities and roles of Black motherscholars as academics, caregivers, activists, and community leaders. In Chapter 10, ***Ivory Towers, Bassinets, and Wheelchairs Oh My!,*** Dr. Brandy James utilizes poetry and storytelling to creatively unlock some of the guarded spaces in Black disability educational studies and Black motherhood disability discourse. Chapter 11, ***Backing our Babies: The Praxis of Three Black Muslim Motherscholars at Home and in the Academy*** by Lakya Goss, Yetunde Alabede, and Tasleem Firdausee, engages three Black Muslim graduate students in kitchen-table talk. Using critical narrative analysis, it expands discourse on mothering, Black feminist theories, and spirituality in academia, shedding light on how Black Muslim motherscholars navigate the complexities of their intersecting identities within predominantly white academic spaces. Chapter 12, ***Self-Efficacy in the Brilliant Black Girl: Exploring the Impact of Exceptionalism on Academic and Professional Success*** by Dr. LoRen Modisa, explores the implications of exceptionalism on the lives of Black motherscholars. Guided by parent racial socialization and academic identity development theories, this chapter sheds light on the complexities of the burden associated with being a talented Black woman.

Chapter 13, ***Academic Mothering for Black Women in the Caribbean: A Matricentric Caribbean Feminist Approach*** by Dr. Talia Esnard, utilizes matricentric Caribbean Feminist approach and narrative inquiry to assess the status and scope of scholarship on academic mothers in the Caribbean and calls for a contextualized understanding of motherscholarship across geographic and social locations. This part closes with Chapter 14, ***I Have My Sister's Back: Cultivating Counterspaces in the Academy to Keep Black Motherscholars Safe,*** by Drs. Dionne L. Davis and Ann Marie Mobley who share a collaborative autoethnography to examine the emotional complexities experienced by Black motherscholars, drawing on Black feminist thought to analyze historical conceptions of Black motherhood and institutional practices.

Part IV: Centering Our Children's Voices

Analyzing the practices of communal care adopted by Black motherscholars through fostering sisterhood, maroon communities, and joy as resistance, these chapters and creative pieces emphasize the need for radical healing, community support, and reimagined futures. Chapter 15, ***The Unrelenting Duality of Black Motherhood: A Dialogical Examination of the Role of the Radical Black Motherscholar*** by Dr. Jendayi Mbalia, focuses on the role of the Radical Black Motherscholar, showcasing the tension between preparing children for an unjust world and fostering dreams of liberation. In Chapter 16, ***On My Mama!': A Duoethnography of Black Mother Scholars' Contributions Towards Liberatory Education for Black Children,*** authors Eboni N. Bango and Dr. Salandra Grice-Johnson use Black Gaze theory to address how Black motherscholars continue to take up space and interject their liberatory approaches towards true educational equity for Black children.

Part V: Motherscholar Identity Formation

The chapters in this part delve deeper into Black motherscholars' intimate thoughts on how they integrate multiple identities into their personal and professional lives. Chapter 17, ***"Torn Between Ways": Exploring (Non)Dualities through Visual Duo-Nkwaethnography as Black MotherScholars*** by Drs. Laura Krystal Porterfield and Lynnette Mawhinney, employs photovoice and video diaries to explore the everyday experiences of Black motherscholars. Emphasizing the intersectionality of race, gender, and class within academia. It highlights the inherent dualities and tensions faced by Black motherscholars amidst systemic barriers.

Chapter 18, ***White Shadows: The Path to Awareness*** by Dr. Michele Turner, recounts the author's journey as a Black mother navigating racialized experiences in undergraduate spaces and offers reflective insights into race, education, and personal transformation. In Chapter 19, ***We Ain't Going If She Can't Come with Me: The Story of a Black Single Mama Who Walked Across EVERY Stage with her Daughter,*** author Daphanie N. Bibbs, M.Ed. uses autoethnography to examine her personal experiences as a Black single mother scholar navigating predominantly white institutions. Chapter 20, ***Interrogations of the Mythical Norm: Using Endarkened Poetic Inquiry to Queer Black Motherscholarship*** by Dr. Meghan L. Green, utilizes endarkened poetic inquiry to talk back to the mainstream discourse of higher education and explore how she understands her positionality as a Black queer motherscholar inside/outside of academia.

Part VI: Motherscholars in Community

The chapters in this part collectively explore the collaborative efforts of Black motherscholars in community-based research, activism, and advocacy. They emphasize the importance of community, resilience, and intersectional support networks. Chapter 21, ***Visionary Daughters: The Generational Shift from Mothering to Daughtering for Early Career Community College Faculty*** by Dr. Jamie Moore, illustrates how the historical struggle of Black women for educational access intersects with contemporary challenges in academia, particularly in California Community Colleges. Using Black feminist autotheory, this chapter explores how Black women faculty navigate caregiving burnout amidst shifting equity movements, proposing visionary daughtering as a path to reclaim autonomy within academia. Chapter 22, ***We All We Got! Kinship as Resistance: Reimagining the Academy through Black Women's Othermothering*** by Dr. DeLisha Tapscott, highlights the significance of fictive kinship and othermothering practices among Black women scholars, advocating for inclusive policies and practices that integrate these relational dynamics into academia.

In Chapter 23, ***Beyond Surviving: On Black Motherscholars Thriving in Wellness,*** Drs. Tiffany S. Wiggins, Regina Gavin Williams, and Jemilia S. Davis utilize collaborative autoethnography to explore the nuanced lives of three Black women at the intersection of faculty expectations, practitioner roles, and parenting demands—all while striving for holistic wellness. Chapter 24, ***Blackademic Mamas in Chat: Using Endarkened Feminist Epistemology to Explore How Black Mothers Navigate Academic Socialization***—by authors Sacha Sharp, Ph.D., Brooke Harris Garad, Ph.D., and Kristina Johnson Yates—gleans inspiration from bell hooks' "Sisters of the Yam". Describing the formation of a Black Academic Mamas group, this chapter illustrates how this virtual space provided social, emotional, and professional support for navigating personal and professional lives.

Competing Interests The authors have no conflicts of interest to declare that are relevant to the content of this manuscript.

References

Allen-Handy, A. (2021). Extracting life-giving strength from my Roots. *The Journal of Intersectionality, 5*(1), 70–88.

Anzaldúa, G. (1987). *Borderlands/La frontera: The new mestiza.* Aunt Lute Books.

Anzaldúa, G. E. (2015). *Light in the dark/Luz en lo oscuro: Rewriting identity, spirituality, reality.* In A. Keating (Ed.), Duke University Press.

Bell, S. (2004). Intensive performance of mothering: A sociological perspective. *Qualitative Research, 4*, 45–75.

Boutte, G. S., & Compton-Lilly, C. (2022). Prioritizing pro-blackness in literacy research, scholarship, and teaching. *Journal of Early Childhood Literacy, 22*(3), 323–334.

Carbado, D. W., & Harris, C. I. (2019). Intersectionality at 30. *Harvard Law Review, 132*(8), 2193–2239.
Carbado, D. W., Crenshaw, K. W., Mays, V. M., & Tomlinson, B. (2013). Intersectionality: Mapping the movements of a theory1. *Du Bois Review: Social Science Research on Race, 10*(2), 303–312.
Carty, L. E. (1988). *Political economy of gender inequality at the University of West Indies* (Doctoral dissertation, University of Toronto, Toronto, ON, CA).
Centers for Disease Control and Prevention. (2022). Working together to reduce Black maternal mortality. *Health Equity Featured Articles.*
Collins, P. H. (1991). The meaning of motherhood in black culture and black mother-daughter relationships. In P. Bell-Scott, B. Guy-Sheftall, J. J. Royster, J. Sims-Wood, M. Decosta-Willis, & L. Fultz (Eds.), *Double stitch: Black women write about mothers and daughters* (pp. 42–60). Beacon Press.
Collins, P. H. (2000). *Black feminist thought: Knowledge, consciousness, and the politics of empowerment*. Routledge.
Collins, P. H. (2015). No guarantees: Symposium on black feminist thought. *Ethnic and Racial Studies, 38*(13), 2349–2354.
Combahee River Collective. (1977). The Combahee River Collective Statement. United States. [Web Archive] Retrieved from the Library of Congress. https://www.loc.gov/item/lcwaN0028151/
Crenshaw, K. (1989). Demarginalizing the intersection of race and sex: A black feminist critique of antidiscrimination doctrine, feminist theory and antiracist politics. *u. Chi. Legal f.*, 139.
Crenshaw, K. (1991). Mapping the margins: Intersectionality, identity politics, and violence against women of color. *Stanford Law Review, 43*(6), 1241–1299. https://doi.org/10.2307/1229039
Dillard, C. B. (2000). The substance of things hoped for, the evidence of things not seen: Examining an endarkened feminist epistemology in educational research and leadership. *International Journal of Qualitative Studies in Education, 13*(6), 661–681.
Evans-Winters, V. E. (2019). *Black feminism in qualitative inquiry: A mosaic for writing our daughter's body*. Routledge.
Gámez, G. (2015). *But some of them are fierce: navigating and negotiating the terrain of motherhood as formerly incarcerated and convicted women.* Arizona State University.
Geronimus, A. T. (1992). The weathering hypothesis and the health of African-American women and infants: Evidence and speculations. *Ethnicity & Disease*, 207–221.
Green, M. L., & Green, P. H. (2023). Witnessing the pedagogical impact of ethnic studies through an intergenerational collaborative. *Ethnic Studies Pedagogies, 1*(1), 165–171.
Griffin, A., & Tackie, H. (2016). Through our eyes: Perspectives from black teachers. *Phi Delta Kappan, 98*(5), 36–40.
Gumbs, A. P., Martens, C., & Williams, M. (Eds.). (2016). *Revolutionary mothering: Love on the front lines.* Pm Press.
Hidalgo, L. A., Vega, C., Cisneros, N. A., & Reyes, J. M. (2022). Fierce mothers: The cords that bind us. *Feminist Formations, 34*(1), 122–146.
Hughes, D., & Chen, L. (1999). The nature of parents' race-related communications to children: A developmental perspective.
Kelley, R. D. (2022). *Freedom dreams: The black radical imagination.* Beacon Press.
Kinloch, V., Penn, C., & Burkhard, T. (2020). Black lives matter: Storying, identities, and counternarratives. *Journal of Literacy Research, 52*(4), 382–405.
Ladson-Billings, G., & Tate, W. F. (1995). Toward a critical race theory of education. *Teachers College Record, 97*(1), 47–68.
Lorde, A. (1978). A litany for survival by Audre Lorde. *Recuperat el, 3.*
Morrison, T. (1994). Playing in the dark: Whiteness and the literary imagination. *Modern Philology, 92*(2), 267–271.
Muhammad, G. (2023). *Unearthing joy: A guide to culturally and historically responsive teaching and learning*. Scholastic.

Neal-Stanley, A. M. (2023). The fugitive spirit of historical Black women teachers: Theorizing hush harbors as praxis. *Curriculum Inquiry*, 1–25.
Pitts, M. (2014). Nineteenth-century motherwork: Ideology, experience, and agency in autobiographical narratives by black women. *Patricia Hill Collins*, 142–159.
Reynolds, T. (2005). *Caribbean mothers: Identity and experience in the UK*. Tufnell press.
Stewart, L. (2021). *The politics of Black joy: Nora Zeale Hurston and neo-abolitionism.* Northwestern University Press.
Suizzo, M. A., Robinson, C., & Pahlke, E. (2008). African American mothers' socialization beliefs and goals with young children: Themes of history, education, and collective independence. *Journal of Family Issues, 29*(3), 287–316.
Toliver, S. R. (2021). *Recovering black storytelling in qualitative research: Endarkened Storywork.* Routledge.
Turner, C. R. (2026). Endarkened Feminist Narrative. In *The Bloomsbury Encyclopedia of Social Justice in Education: Language, Literacy, Culture, and Youth* (Vol. 6). Bloomsbury Publishing.
Turner, C. R., & Allen, K. R. (2022). "She's a friend of my mind": A reflection of Black sisterhood in academia. *Race Ethnicity and Education*, 1–18.
Turner, C., & Green, M. (2023). "My representation is performative": Black women's reflection of academia through collaborative autoethnographic poetic inquiry. *Journal of African American Women and Girls in Education, 3*(1), 31–48.
Walker, A. (1983). *In search of our mothers' gardens: Womanist prose.* Houghton Mifflin Harcourt.
Wallace, M. E., & Harville, E. W. (2013). Allostatic load and birth outcomes among white and black women in New Orleans. *Maternal and Child Health Journal, 17*, 1025–1029.
Warren, C. (2021). *About centering possibility in black education.* Teachers College Press.
Wing, A. K. (2015). Critical race feminism. In *Theories of race and ethnicity: Contemporary debates and perspectives* (pp. 162–179).

Crystasany R. Turner is an Assistant Professor of Inclusive Early Childhood Teacher Education at the University of Wisconsin-Milwaukee. Rooted in Black feminist epistemologies, her research and scholarship highlight the perspectives of Black women educators and their cultural knowledge as manifested in their care and education of Children of Color. Her teaching and research focus includes endarkened feminist narrative, early childhood education for social justice, and spirit-centered pedagogies. Her work interrogates imbalanced social power, institutional inequities, and systemic oppression affecting diverse children and families. Dr. Turner's scholarship has been published in "Race Ethnicity and Education", the "Journal of African American Women and Girls in Education", the "Journal of Teacher Education", and the "Bloomsbury Encyclopedia of Social Justice in Education" amongst others.

Meghan L. Green is an Assistant Professor of Raciolinguistic Justice in Early Childhood Teacher Education at the Erikson Institute. As an arts-based qualitative researcher, she uses multiple modes of creative representation to reflect on her positionality and to craft her story as a cis Black queer woman engaging in critically informed research methodologies within this time and space. Her scholarship centers Black feminist thought and endarkened feminist epistemology within early childhood settings, specifically highlighting the diverse lived experiences of Black early childhood educators through arts-based qualitative inquiry methods including, autoethnography, endarkened narrative inquiry, photovoice, and endarkened poetic inquiry. Her scholarly works have been published in journals such as the "International Journal of Qualitative Methods", the "Journal of African American Women and Girls in Education", "Early Childhood Education Journal", "Ethnic Studies Pedagogies", and "Equity and Excellence in Education".

Historical Perspectives of Black Motherscholarship

Looking Back to Move Forward: Unpacking Maternal Misogynoir in the Academy

Crystasany R. Turner

Abstract Through the lens of plantation politics, this chapter introduces the term *maternal misogynoir* to conceptualize the unique forms of oppression Black women face due to their identity and role as mothers. The analysis draws parallels between the reproductive exploitation of Black women during enslavement and their experiences within academia, emphasizing enduring legacies of commodification, systemic control, devaluation, and redistribution. Three central elements of maternal misogynoir within academic institutions are discussed: institutional control over reproductive and personal choices, stereotyping as modern Mammies, and the emotional and psychological toll on Black motherscholars. By naming these experiences through the framework of *maternal misogynoir*, the chapter seeks to make visible the experiences of Black motherscholars and inspire dialogue, resistance, and collective transformation.

Keywords Black motherscholars · Maternal misogynoir · Plantation politics · Neoliberalism

The term "Sankofa," from the Akan people of Ghana, translates to "it is not taboo to fetch what is at risk of being left behind." It embodies the idea of (re)membering and (re)claiming what was lost, stolen, or forfeited in the past to create a better future (Dillard, 2016). In this book, as we asked authors to envision "radical futurity" for Black motherscholars, I felt compelled to ground our aspirations for equitable futures in remembering our foremothers—women who fought and survived so that we could persist and thrive in the institutional spaces we now occupy.

This chapter invites readers to (re)member the lives of our African foremothers, forcibly brought to the Americas to serve the evil desires of white colonizers. By recalling their narratives and the ways they resisted the exploitation of their bodies, minds and spirits, we gain deeper insights into modern-day iterations of the same struggles they endured. Through this act of (re)membering and (re)claiming our

C. R. Turner (✉)
University of Wisconsin-Milwaukee, Milwaukee, WI, USA
e-mail: crturner@uwm.edu

C. R. Turner and M. L. Green (eds.), *Black Motherscholarship Within and Beyond the Academy*, https://doi.org/10.1007/978-3-031-99758-7_2

ancestral power, we can transform academic institutions into more liberatory spaces for Black motherscholars, our communities, and our children.

Although white historians have described the lives of enslaved Africans as some of "the happiest, and, in some sense the freest people in the world," (see Fitzhugh, 1966), the accounts of hundreds of enslaved ancestors tell a starkly different truth (Berry & Gross, 2020; Jennings, 1990). Similarly, today universities tout diversity and inclusion policies and posit tenure and promotion as the standard of "success" within the academy. However, countless narratives of Black women and other People of Color within the space depict stories of isolation, dehumanization, limited power, lack of support, stereotyping, tokenization, microaggressions, and marginalization (Benjamin, 1997; Berry & Mizelle, 2006; Collins, 1990; Gregory, 2001; Louis et al., 2016; Green & Mabokela, 2001; Pittman, 2010; Turner, 2002; Turner & Green, 2023).

Saidiya Hartman (2008) conceptualizes the afterlife of slavery as the ongoing social, political, and economic conditions of inequality, violence, and racism that stem from the historical institution of slavery and persist into the present. Hartman (2008) argues that the legacy of slavery—embedded in the structures of modern society and the enduring psychological, cultural, and material losses—impacts the lives of Black people through persistently positioning Black lives as disposable. She goes on to state that "[t]he theft, regulation and destruction of black women's sexual and reproductive capacities would also define the afterlife of slavery" (Hartman, 2008, pg. 166). With this understanding, I argue that modern day academic institutions—from which they fought so hard to exclude Black women—now operate as neoplantations. Like the historical plantations of transatlantic slavery, where Black women were exploited, appropriated, and commodified for their physical labor and reproductive capabilities, Black women's labor and motherwork in academia often reflect these enduring patterns of systemic racism and gendered oppression (Dancy et al., 2018; Hills, 2019; Omalade, 1994).

Zora Neal Hurston admonished, "If you are silent about your pain, they'll kill you and say you enjoyed it." Therefore, contrary to notions that Black women, mothers, scholars, and activists, have been silent within these unjust conditions, various Black feminist scholars have documented and interrogated systemic racism, sexism, and unbalanced power in higher education and beyond. Following their example, this chapter is written to lay bare the methods in which the academy and institutions founded and maintained by white supremacy uphold legacies of exploitation of Black motherscholars' intellect and labor through what I call *maternal misogynoir*.

Neoliberalism, Plantation Politics and Black Women's Reproduction

The enslavement, maltreatment, and exploitation of millions of African women, men, and children was justified through white supremacist capitalism, which conflates production with value (Hersey, 2022). Squire et al. (2018) explains that "Neoliberalism is marketization and commodification of goods for capitalistic gain" (p. 11). Within neoliberal institutions seeped in anti-Black settler colonialism (Dancy et al., 2018), Black motherscholars are subjected to capitalist values, hyper-individualism, and the commodification of their intellectual labor for the gain of those in power. As a result, we are expected to maximize productivity (publishing, teaching, and service) within scarcity and urgency cultures (Hersey, 2022).

A core aspect of this neoliberal, capitalist agenda is the dehumanization and objectification of human bodies (particularly People of Color) for increased profitability (Dancy et al., 2018; Hersey, 2022; Squire et al., 2018). In Antebellum plantations, slave codes governed every aspect of the structural and procedural lives of enslaved Africans to effectively commodify their labor and reproductive capacities (Berry & Gross, 2020; Durant, 1999; Morgan, 2018). The codes restricted the enslaved Africans' movement, education, relationships, and behavior to ensure compliance with the economic objectives of the institution of slavery and upheld racial and social hierarchies. Critical scholars, historians, and sociologists have drawn parallels between these systems and how modern institutions of higher education still aim to regulate and constrain Scholars of Color within the academy through neoliberal ideals and plantation politics (Dancy et al., 2018; Durant, 1999; Squire et al., 2018).

Similarly, within this examination of Black motherscholars' positioning within the academy, the framework of "plantation politics" allows me to draw correlations between the way "old ideologies and tools for oppressing and marginalizing people of color are connected to newer strategies of repression and policing within universities" (Squire et al., 2018, pp. 2–3). The idea is that there is nothing new under the sun; instead, white supremacy continues to adapt and recreate itself within modern times to maintain power within the status quo.

For example, in both slavery and modern-day academia, Black women's reproduction is framed within structures that exploit their bodies and labor for the benefit of broader systems (Hartman, 2008). Hersey (2022) discusses how within the terrorism of white supremacist capitalism, the human body exists only to make profit. During slavery, Black women's physical reproductive capacities were seen as a financial investment essential to the expansion of the institution (Berry, 2017; Berry & Gross, 2020; Hartman, 2008; Jennings, 1990). Black women's bodies were central to the economic infrastructure of slavery; and "subjection was anchored in black women's reproductive capacities" (Hartman, 2008, p. 168). Black women's potential to procreate was central to slavery's economic infrastructure, with enslavers insuring and commodifying their reproductive ability to increase the labor force thus making Black bodies a "well-thought out" enterprise (Berry, 2017, p. 89).

In modern academic institutions, Black women's physical reproduction is no longer directly commodified. Instead, it is our intellectual labor and carework that is commodified through grant work, institutional service, leading DEI initiatives, caring for Students of Color, etc. Ironically, our physical reproduction of offspring is now seen as antithetical to this intellectual labor and therefore indirectly controlled and penalized through embedded structural inequities. As such, Black mothers in the academy face limited maternity leave, inadequate childcare support, and implicit biases against parenting, which disproportionately hinder their career advancement. These institutional barriers and systemic burdens on Black motherscholars reflect the adaptation of plantation politics to continue exploiting Black women's labor to benefit white patriarchal capitalism.

Theorizing Maternal Misogynoir

Anti-Blackness within academia has been well-documented, as Scholars of Color recognize the academy was created by white men for the intellectual and epistemic reproduction of white men (Thelin, 2004). United States Ivy League colleges were built on the backs of enslaved Black folks as,

"Black people erected the buildings, cooked the food, and cleaned the dormitories and yet were not understood as laborers, but as property. Colonizers advocated (from college campus podiums) for the inhumane treatment of Black people everywhere, and violence was a common experience for the enslaved on college campuses" (Dancy et al., 2018, p. 182).

It follows that institutions created and maintained by white patriarchy and anti-Blackness continue to propagate ideologies of *misogynoir*—the anti-Black racist misogyny that Black women experience (Bailey & Trudy, 2018). This is illustrated in various forms of institutional and individual oppressions including Black women's assumed academic incompetence; lower teaching evaluations; overburdened and uncompensated service expectations; and reduced opportunities to gain tenure and promotion (Agathangelou & Ling, 2002; Chávez & Mitchell, 2020; Cromartie & Hinnant-Crawford, 2021; Hills, 2019; Ladson-Billings, 1997; Turner, 2002).

While the violence of misogynoir has been documented within the ongoing disparities in Black women's access to equitable education, healthcare (CDC, 2022; Hunt, 2021; Lui et al., 2024), employment (Collins, 2000); housing (Grossman et al., 2024), and the criminal justice system (Richie, 2012); there is need for language to conceptualize the experiences of Black women who hold the social role and identity of *mother*. hooks (1994) teaches us that by naming our experiences, individuals can make the invisible visible, confront systems of domination, and create spaces for dialogue, resistance, and collective understanding. For this, I offer the language of *maternal misogynoir*—addressing the unique forms of misogynoir experienced by Black women due to our identity and experiences of mothering.

Institutional manifestations of maternal misogynoir have been well documented throughout history as Black mothers have been persistently relegated to the margins of social reform and legislative protections (Collins, 2000; Turner & Turner, 2022). In the medical field, the effects of maternal misogynoir are evident in the exorbitant maternal fetal death rate in the United States. Childbirth is statistically the most dangerous time in a Black woman's life, as U.S. Black birthing individuals are 243% more likely to suffer a pregnancy-related death than their white counterparts (Centers for Disease Control and Prevention [CDC], 2022; Hunt, 2021). Further, reports of mistreatment in childbirth were even higher among birthing individuals who were unmarried, publicly insured, or from the LGBTQIA community (Liu et al., 2024)—illustrating the intersectional experiences of Black mothers based on race, class, and sexuality.

Within the area of socioeconomics, discriminatory policies and legislation have consistently encumbered Black mother's access to equitable childcare and social welfare (Cahan, 1989; Collins, 2016; Cunningham & Osborn, 1979; Turner, 2024; Turner & Turner, 2022). White anthropologists and politicians persistently blame Black mothers in "female authoritarian households" with high rates of "illegitimate children" for welfare dependency, a "Culture of Poverty", and other issues within Black communities (see Lewis, 1966; Moynihan, 1965). In the 1970s, the myth of the "Welfare Queen" relied on racist, sexist, ageist, and classist stereotypes of Black mothers as deceitful individuals who collected excessive welfare benefits through fraud. This harmful narrative was used to justify legislative policies—such as the Family Support Act, which created the Job Opportunities and Basic Skills (JOBS) program, and the Personal Responsibility and Work Opportunity Reconciliation Act—that ultimately excluded and further marginalized Black mothers (Turner, 2024; Turner & Turner, 2022).

This language has been echoed in modern political rhetoric during debates about welfare reform when politicians, such as Eric Hovde, the 2024 Republican challenger for the U.S. Senate in Wisconsin, consistently blamed single mothers for social decline and a "culture of dependency" (Becker, 2024)—perpetuating stereotypes of Black mothers as "irresponsible" or overly dependent on government support. As such, evidence of maternal misogynoir litters the history of the United States within every social-political institution. For the purpose of this chapter, I will focus on delineating the manifestations of maternal misogynoir within the academy and institutions of higher education.

Maternal Misogynoir in the Academy

"Black women occupy a complex, paradoxical relationship to America. We are at once marginalized and ostracized, yet our very being has been exploited to help create and maintain white supremacy" (Berry & Gross, 2020, p. 2). During slavery, Black women's bodies were sites of dual exploitation: as laborers and reproducers. Jennings (1990) argued that "Female bondage was worse than male bondage because the female slave was both a woman and a slave in a patriarchal regime" (p. 45). This is to say that while slavery was horrible for Black men,

> Female bondage was more severe than male bondage because these women had to bear children and cope with sexual abuse in addition to doing the work assigned to them, work that was often similar in type and quantity to that of male slaves. When it was profitable to exploit women as if they were men in the work force, slaveholders regarded female slaves, in effect, as genderless. (Jennings, 1990, p.46)

Similar to the dual objectification of Black women on the plantation, Black women scholars hold dual roles within the modern neoplantations of higher education. Not only do Black women faculty carry teaching, service and research loads, we bear the added labor of academic mothering within gendered regimes that "remain structured largely on the male lifestyle"—characterized by fewer caregiving responsibilities and greater freedom to focus solely on professional achievements (Armenti, 2004, p. 78).

Using the lens of plantation politics, we can draw connections between Black women's reproduction during enslavement and within academic institutions as well as how this reflects the enduring legacy of commodification, systemic control, devaluation, and redistribution. In the following sections, I will describe three elements of maternal misogynoir evidenced within the academy including: institutional control over reproduction and personal choices, stereotyping as modern Mammies, and emotional and psychological strain.

Reproductive Control and Exclusion

Historically, enslaved Black women were denied agency over their own bodies—with their reproductive capacities commodified and controlled (Berry & Gross, 2020; Collins, 2000; Hartman, 2008; Jennings, 1990). In contemporary academia, similar patterns emerge as women's reproductive choices are often skewed by the choice to *either* pursue academic "success" *or* to be a "good mother" (Sutherland, 2008). Notably, much of the research around motherhood, maternity, and parental leave in academia has been conducted from a heteronormative, white feminist perspective (i.e., Armenti, 2004; Castañeda & Isgro, 2013; CohenMiller, 2014; Grenier & Burke, 2008; Lynch, 2008; Ward & Wolf-Wendel, 2012)—illustrating how white patriarchal capitalism in neoliberal institutions harms everyone (Hersey, 2022). In this work, researchers found tensions emerge due to the demanding nature of academic labor, ambiguity and inconsistency in parental-leave policies, slowed advancement, income disparities, and tension between family and professional goals (Conley & Carey, 2013; De Casanova & Brown, 2013).

As a result of these systemic inequities, women who enter graduate school as mothers, or become mothers during their studies, often face little to no institutional support and experience alienation from fellow graduate students (Kulp, 2020). Social and professional networks, essential for social-emotional and academic success, are often inaccessible to these women. Additionally, motherscholars frequently encounter caregiver bias—or a "motherhood penalty"—from non-mother administrators and colleagues, who may perceive them as less competent or less committed to their work (Budig, 2014). This bias leads to further disparities in hiring, promotion, and salary recommendations (Correll et al., 2007).

While these inequities affect motherscholars across race and ethnicity, Black motherscholars have the additional pressures of our Blackness, which signifies our outsiderness within predominantly white institutions (PWIs). Institutional anti-Blackness and misogynoir often cause Black motherscholars to feel deep isolation, lack of support, and the need to prove their worth in order to gain a sense of belonging (Agathangelou & Ling, 2002; Chávez & Mitchell, 2020; Cromartie & Hinnant-Crawford, 2021; Hills, 2019; Ladson-Billings, 1997; Turner, 2002; Turner & Allen, 2024). Often overcompensating with exemplary productivity and credentials, Black women scholars try to demonstrate their belongingness in response to the white and male gaze (Cromartie & Hinnant-Crawford, 2021). In these conditions, becoming a mother and/or prioritizing motherwork can present a profound risk to the Black woman's academic career, as it may amplify existing biases and further marginalize her within a system already rife with inequities.

Because of these realities, some women choose to forego motherhood entirely to prioritize their academic careers, while others delay motherhood until they have completed graduate school or secured a tenure-track position (Abetz, 2019; Hoffman et al., 2020; Kulp, 2020; Martin, 2021). This delay or avoidance of motherhood reflects a modern form of institutionalized reproductive control, as women are often sent the message that motherhood is incompatible with academic success and productivity. Inequitable policies and administrative biases leading to "motherhood penalty" are subversive manifestations of maternal misogynoir in that they directly affect hiring and promotion practices—excluding Black motherscholars from consideration for leadership roles, tenure opportunities, and intellectual recognition. The lack of representation then excludes them from shaping the policies and structures that directly impact their lives and work—reinforcing cycles of erasure and systemic inequity. As a result, institutions maintain the status quo by failing to challenge entrenched systems of inequality and exclusion (Patton & Haynes, 2018). By intertwining control over reproductive choices with exclusion from power, academia replicates oppressive hierarchies rooted in plantation politics, marginalizing Black motherscholars and denying us full participation within the academy.

The "Modern Mammy"

Black women have historically been relegated to caregiving roles, often for white families, while their own children and families were neglected or separated from them (Collins, 2000; Hartman, 2008). Now, in the academy, the role of Black women is still often rigidly defined as caregivers—a role that is simultaneously the source of our exploitation and society's indifference to our abilities, intellect, and talents. This remarkable and resilient labor of care has, paradoxically, been shaped by systems of slavery, anti-Black racism, entrenched sexism, and societal disregard for Black women's humanity (Hartman, 2008).

Morgan (2018) explains that "Enslaved people had to be understood as dispossessed, outside of the normal networks of family and community, to justify the practice of mass enslavement" (p. 1). Therefore, white America's insistence on exploiting Black women's domestic labor and forced child care necessitated that they distinguish Black womanhood from the humanity of white women. For this, white Americans developed various tropes—such as the promiscuous "Jezebel," the domineering "Sapphire," and the nurturing, asexual Mammy figure— to dehumanize Black women and justify our exploitation (Collins, 2000; Davis, 2018). The Mammy, often depicted as a strong-bodied, older woman is an idealized figure of a caregiver: amiable, loyal, maternal, non-threatening, and obedient. Among the domestic labor that the Mammy performed, she also nurtured—even nursed—the children of white folks.

The work of Barbara Omolade (1994) discusses the "mammification" of Black women professionals where the legacy of Black women's domestic work is now woven into their professional lives. Tasked with the labor of the "modern Mammy", "Black women professionals are expected to fix systems which are in crisis due to underfunding, infrastructure deterioration, and demoralized staff." (Collins, 2000, p. 72). Hills (2019) uses the term "academic mammying" to describe behaviors and outcomes "prompted by the burdensome levying of undue expectation (or under-expectation) on black women scholars' performance, embodiment, and competence". This language is helpful in understanding Black women's "invisible" labor when "called upon to attend to the failures of Whites, or 'clean up behind,' through interim positions, promotion following scandal, and committee leadership" (Dancy et al., 2018, p. 183).

Moreover, Black women faculty are frequently expected to provide "emotional labor" or mentorship disproportionately, nurturing colleagues and students while balancing their own professional demands. Some Afrocentric researchers have discussed the beauty of "mothering the mind" (Collins, 1990) through motherwork and othermothering. Other research has found a direct connection between successful Black women mentors and the development of a "pipeline" for future Black women academics (Bernard et al., 2000; Evans & Cokely, 2008). Craddocks (2013) found that Black women senior faculty suggested academic mother/mentoring provided understanding and affirmation of the marginalizing experiences they had faced themselves.

These are all meaningful examples of the ways Black motherscholars form networks of solidarity and support to continue forging the way for the next generation of students and motherscholars (Bernard et al., 2000). However, when institutions misappropriate Black motherscholars' cultural understanding of collectivism (Collins, 2000; Sacks, 1989) and othermothering (Bernard et al., 2000; Collins, 2000; Turner, 2024) to justify the labor of "modern Mammies," it leads to Black motherscholars shouldering disproportionate amounts of "invisible labor". This devaluation of Black women's institutional motherwork—both coerced and freely given—is rooted in faulty logic that suggests if Black women are caregivers by nature (not skill) and their work is motivated by love (not money), then academic mothering must not be "real work" and therefore does not merit recognition or compensation (Turner, 2002).

Not only are Black motherscholars positioned as caregivers and overachievers in their professional roles, they balance the dual expectations of being breadwinners and caretakers in their personal lives. Yet, Mammies are depicted as "inherently" nurturing and excessively strong—dehumanizing the lived realities of Black motherscholars. "This narrow understanding of motherhood and mothers' role in supporting the social economy cannot fully appreciate the weight of Black women's motherwork or the various ways we cope with the daily pressures of maintaining our households, children, families, and communities" (Turner, 2024, p.110). In previous work, my sister scholar and I discussed how "[a]s Black women, wives, and mothers who are also scholars, we cannot exuviate our various social roles, responsibilities, and identities at the door of the institution. Instead, we carry the fullness of ourselves, our families, and our communities into our work, which influence our scholarship and are in turn influenced by our scholarship" (Turner & Allen, 2024, p.11).

Institutional and cultural expectations pressure Black women to exhibit strength, repress vulnerabilities, and prioritize caregiving responsibilities over self-care—causing Black motherscholars physical, emotional, and psychological stress. Black women's narratives of the *Superwoman Schema* (Woods-Giscombé, 2010), the *Strong Black Woman Syndrome* (Nelson et al., 2016), and *Sojourner's Syndrome* (Lekan, 2009) all illustrate the negative effects on Black women's mental health and physical well-being while carrying intersectional roles and responsibilities in our professions, family lives, communities, and activism. As such, the devaluation of our motherwork through the lack of institutional supports that honor the interplay of Black motherscholars' various identities is an enduring form of maternal misogynoir in the academy. Still despite the institutional and social devaluation, "the forms of care, intimacy, and sustenance exploited by racial capitalism […] are not reducible to or exhausted by it. These labors cannot be assimilated to the template or grid of the black worker, but instead nourish the latent text of the fugitive. They enable those 'who were never meant to survive' to sometimes do just that." Hartman, 2008, p. 171).

Emotional and Psychological Strain

Maternal misogynoir in academia creates significant emotional and psychological strain on Black women by compounding the challenges of navigating both anti-Black racism and sexism within a predominantly white and male-dominated environment. Not only are Black women severely underrepresented in higher education—as only 3% of all full-time faculty (NCES, 2019)—they often face inequitable pathways to tenure (Agathangelou & Ling, 2002), hostile campus climates (Dancy et al., 2018; Hills, 2019), gendered racism, and criticism from students about their experiences in the classroom (Gregory, 2001; Thomas, 2020; Turner, 2002). The constant need to overcompensate for biases, such as the "motherhood penalty" or perceptions of incompetence, can lead to feelings of isolation, anxiety, and burnout. Additionally, the lack of institutional support—manifested in inadequate childcare policies, limited maternity leave, and exclusion from leadership opportunities—reinforces a sense of erasure and undervaluation.

For Black women, this emotional toll can be exacerbated by the expectation to excel under the scrutiny of the white and male gaze, which demands relentless productivity to counteract stereotypes (Cromartie & Hinnant-Crawford, 2021). Yet the need for more productivity creates a dilemma as motherscholars often experience guilt for not living up to the expectations of being a "good mother"—despite providing economic nurturing for their children and families (Ashencaen Crabtree & Shiel, 2019; Guy & Arthur, 2020). Black mothers are further burdened by systemic inequities, institutional and interpersonal hostility, and exclusion from decision-making spaces, amplifying their feelings of alienation and marginalization.

In her writing mourning the loss of countless Black women scholars, activists, educators, and mothers, Myesha Priest (2008) described Black women within institutional spaces.

> They are overburdened with departmental duties, admissions and funding committees, advising and mentoring, and outreach and community service. They are hobbled by the lack of institutional and financial support for their work, by issues of retention and mentorship, and by extreme isolation, overwork, and exhaustion.

Research documents the manifestations of race-related stress (Utsey, 1999), internalized racism (Williams & Mohammed, 2013), and the weathering (Geronimus, 1992) of the minds, spirits, and bodies of Black women as a result of prolonged exposure to grind culture (Hersey, 2022) in white patriarchal spaces. In her study on the health of African-American women and their infants, Arline Geronimus (1992) introduced the weathering hypothesis which connects these stressors to the disproportionate rates of Black infant mortality. She described, "the ways in which socioeconomic in-equality, racial discrimination, or race bias in exposures to environmental hazards may affect differentially the health of women who will become mothers, not only in absolute terms, but also interactively with each other and increasingly as women age." This is to say that the longer Black women are exposed to socio-economic distress and race-related stressors, the higher the risk of premature births or infant mortality.

The persistent emotional, intellectual, psychological, political, and physical violence against Black women and our children is arguably the most insidious form of maternal misogynoir as the noxious environment of neoliberal, white patriarchal spaces slowly poisons Black women's bodies, minds, and spirits—diminishing our wombs into the tombs of our unborn.

For Our Children

Through inequitable policies that ignore the intersectional needs of Black motherscholars and maintain institutional cultures seeped in white patriarchal values and norms, institutions of higher education perpetuate patterns of institutionalized maternal misogynoir by controlling Black mothers' reproductive and personal choices, stereotyping them as modern Mammies, and inflicting emotional and psychological strain. These interconnected elements not only perpetuate systemic inequities but demonstrate institutional allegiance to plantation politics and the exploitation of Black women's labor and bodies.

As I conclude this reflection on the historic and modern-day methods of maternal misogynoir, I draw a final connection between plantation politics and the urgent need for institutional change in higher education. In 1662, the *Partus Sequitur Ventrem* Act (literally translated "offspring follows belly"), dictated that children would be slave or free "according to the condition of the mother" (Morgan, 2018, p. 1). This legal precedent represents the foundation of systemic reproductive control and established generations of oppression for Black women and children for the benefit of white enslavers. It shows that capitalist institutions are not merely satisfied with exploiting Black women's bodies and intellect for their gain—they want our children as well. Thus, our fight for liberatory practices in the academy is not just a matter of justice for ourselves; it is a charge to liberate ourselves in the service of our children and our children's children.

We will no longer settle for Black women merely surviving in institutions that devalue our motherwork and exploit our professional labor. We reject the academic norms that misappropriate our cultural ways of being through the logic of mammification, serving neoliberal interests rather than our communities. Instead, we imagine a transformation rooted in justice and joy. We demand space to breathe, to build, and to birth new worlds where our children are not afterthoughts. We call for the agency to live and voice our truths within institutions that honor the fullness of our identities as both mothers and scholars.

Competing Interests The author has no conflicts of interest to declare that are relevant to the content of this chapter.

References

Abetz, J. S. (2019). "I want to be both, but is that possible?": Communicating mother-scholar uncertainty during doctoral candidacy. *Journal of Women and Gender in Higher Education, 12*(1), 70–87.

Agathangelou, A. M., & Ling, L. H. (2002). An unten (ur) able position: The politics of teaching for women of color in the US. *International Feminist Journal of Politics, 4*(3), 368–398.

Armenti, C. (2004). Women faculty seeking tenure and parenthood: Lessons from previous generations. *Cambridge Journal of Education, 34*(1), 65–83; Castaneda, M., & Isgro, K. (Eds.). (2013). *Mothers in academia.* Columbia University Press.

Ashencaen Crabtree, S., & Shiel, C. (2019). "Playing mother": Channeled careers and the construction of gender in academia. *SAGE Open, 9*(3), 2158244019876285.

Bailey, M., & Trudy. (2018). On misogynoir: Citation, erasure, and plagiarism. *Feminist Media Studies, 18*(4), 762–768. https://doi.org/10.1080/14680777.2018.1447395

Becker, A. (2024, March 20). *Republican Eric Hovde blamed societal problems on single moms in his first Senate bid. will he do it again?*. The 19th. https://19thnews.org/2024/03/eric-hovde-wisconsin-single-mothers/?utm_source=chatgpt.com

Bell, M. P., Berry, D., Leopold, J., & Nkomo, S. (2021). Making Black Lives Matter in academia: A Black feminist call for collective action against anti-blackness in the academy. *Gender, Work & Organization, 28*, 39–57.

Benjamin, L. (1997). *Black women in the academy: Promises and perils.* University Press of Florida.

Bernard, C., Bernard, W. T., Epko, C., Enang, J., Joseph, B., & Wane, N. (2000). "She Who Learns Teaches": Othermothering in the Academy. *Journal of the Motherhood Initiative for Research and Community Involvement.*

Berry, D. R. (2017). *The price for their pound of flesh: The value of the enslaved, from womb to grave, in the building of a nation.* Beacon Press.

Berry, D. R., & Gross, K. N. (2020). *A Black women's history of the United States* (Vol. 5). Beacon Press.

Berry, T. R., & Mizelle, N. D. (2006). *From oppression to grace: Women of color and their dilemmas within the academy.* Stylus.

Budig, M. J. (2014). The fatherhood bonus and the motherhood penalty: Parenthood and the gender gap in pay. *Third way, 2.*

Cahan, E. D. (1989). *Past caring: A history of US preschool care and education for the poor, 1820–1965.* National Center for Children in Poverty. https://psycnet.apa.org/record/1990-97267-000; Castaneda, M., & Isgro, K. (Eds.). (2013). *Mothers in academia.* Columbia University Press.

Castañeda, M., & Isgro, K. (2013). Introduction: Speaking truth to power to change the ivory tower. *Mothers in Academia*, 1–14.

Centers for Disease Control and Prevention. (2022). Working together to reduce Black maternal mortality. *Health Equity Featured Articles.*

Chávez, K., & Mitchell, K. M. (2020). Exploring bias in student evaluations: Gender, race, and ethnicity. *PS: Political Science & Politics, 53*(2), 270–274. https://doi.org/10.1017/S1049096519001744

CohenMiller, A. S. (2014). *The phenomenon of doctoral student motherhood/mothering in academia: Cultural construction, presentation of self, and situated learning (Doctoral dissertation).* The University of Texas.

Collins, P. H. (2000). *Black feminist thought: Knowledge, consciousness, and the politics of empowerment.* Routledge.

Collins, P. H. (1990). Black feminist thought in the matrix of domination. *Black Feminist Thought: Knowledge, Consciousness, and the Politics of Empowerment, 138*, 221–238.

Collins, P. H. (2015). No guarantees: Symposium on black feminist thought. *Ethnic and Racial Studies, 38*(13), 2349–2354.

Collins, P. H. (2016). Shifting the center: Race, class, and feminist theorizing about motherhood. In *Mothering* (pp. 45–65). Routledge.

Conley, C. S., & Carey, D. C. (2013). Academic mothers on leave, on the line: Toward improving parental-leave policies and practices. In *Mothers in academia* (pp. 200–212).

Correll, S. J., Benard, S., & Paik, I. (2007). Getting a job: Is there a motherhood penalty? *American Journal of Sociology, 112*(5), 1297–1338.

Craddock, K. T. (2013). Mothering and mentoring. *Journal of the Motherhood Initiative for Research & Community Involvement, 4*(1).

Cromartie, S., & Hinnant-Crawford, B. N. (2021). *Ain't I a scholar? Black women & misogynoir in the academy.*

Cunningham, C., & Osborn, D. K. (1979). A historical examination of blacks in early childhood education. *Young Children, 35*(3), 20–29.

Dancy, T. E., Edwards, K. T., & Earl Davis, J. (2018). Historically white universities and plantation politics: Anti- Blackness and higher education in the Black Lives Matter era. *Urban Education, 53*(2), 176–195.

Davis, S. M. (2018). Taking back the power: An analysis of Black women's communicative resistance. *Review of Communication, 18*(4), 301–318.

De Casanova, E., & Brown, T. M. (2013). Making it work: Success strategies for graduate student mothers. In *Mothers in academia.* Colombia University Press E-book.

Dillard, C. B. (2016). Turning the ships around: A case study of (re)membering as transnational endarkened feminist inquiry and praxis for black teachers. *Educational Studies, 52*(5), 406–423.

Durant Jr, T. J. (1999). The slave plantation revisited: A sociological perspective. In *Plantation society and race relations: The origins of inequality* (pp. 3–15).

Evans, G. L., & Cokley, K. O. (2008). African American women and the academy: Using career mentoring to increase research productivity. *Training and Education in Professional Psychology, 2*(1), 50.

Fitzhugh, G. (1966). *Cannibals all! Or, slaves without masters.* Harvard University Press.

Geronimus, A. T. (1992). The weathering hypothesis and the health of African-American women and infants: evidence and speculations. *Ethnicity & Disease*, 207–221.

Green, A. L., & Mabokela, R. (2001). *Sisters of the academy: Emergent Black women scholars in higher education.* Routledge.

Gregory, S. T. (2001). Black faculty women in the academy: History, status, and future. *The Journal of Negro Education, 70*, 124–138.

Grenier, R. S., & Burke, M. C. (2008). No margin for error: A study of two women balancing motherhood and Ph. D. studies. *The Qualitative Report, 13*(4), 581–604.

Grossman, T., Hassmer, S., & Johnson, K. (2024, May 1). *Housing discrimination still remains a reality for many women and LGBTQIA+ people.* National Women's Law Center. https://nwlc.org/resource/housing-discriminationstill-remains-a-reality-for-many-women-and-lgbtqia-people/

Guy, B., & Arthur, B. (2020). Academic motherhood during COVID-19: Navigating our dual roles as educators and mothers. *Gender, Work & Organization, 27*(5), 887–899.

Hartman, S. (2008). *Lose your mother: A journey along the Atlantic slave route.* Macmillan.

Hersey, T. (2022). *Rest is resistance: A manifesto.* Hachette UK.

Hills, D. D. W. (2019). "Admirable or Ridiculous?": The burdens of black women scholars and dialogue in the work of solidarity. *Journal of Feminist Studies in Religion, 35*(2), 5–21.

Hoffman, R., Mullan, J., Nguyen, M., & Bonney, A. D. (2020). Motherhood and medicine: Systematic review of the experiences of mothers who are doctors. *Medical Journal of Australia, 213*(7), 329–334.

hooks, b. (1994). *Teaching to transgress: Education as the practice of freedom.* Routledge.

Hunt, J. (2021). Maternal mortality among black women in the United States. *Ballard Brief, 2021*(2), 6.

Jennings, T. (1990). "Us Colored Women Had to Go Though A Plenty": Sexual Exploitation of African-American Slave Women. *Journal of Women's History, 1*(3), 45–74.

Kulp, A. M. (2020). Parenting on the path to the professoriate: A focus on graduate student mothers. *Research in Higher Education, 61*, 408–429.

Ladson-Billings, G. (1997). For colored girls who have considered suicide when the academy's not enough: Reflections of an African American woman scholar. *Learning from our lives: Women, research, and autobiography in education*, 52–70.

Lekan, D. (2009). Sojourner syndrome and health disparities in African American women. *Advances in Nursing Science, 32*(4), 307–321.

Lewis, O. (1966). The culture of poverty. *Scientific American, 215*(4), 19–25. http://www.jstor.org/stable/24931078

Liu, C., Underhill, K., Aubey, J. J., Samari, G., Allen, H. L., & Daw, J. R. (2024). Disparities in mistreatment during childbirth. *JAMA Network Open, 7*(4), e244873–e244873.

Louis, D. A., Rawls, G. J., Jackson-Smith, D., Chambers, G. A., Phillips, L. L., & Louis, S. L. (2016). Listening to our voices: Experiences of black faculty at predominantly white research universities with microaggression. *Journal of Black Studies, 47*(5), 454–474.

Lynch, K. D. (2008). Gender roles and the American academe: A case study of graduate student mothers. *Gender and Education, 20*(6), 585–605.

Martin, L. J. (2021). Delaying, debating and declining motherhood. *Culture, Health & Sexuality, 23*(8), 1034–1049.

Morgan, J. L. (2018). Partus sequitur ventrem: Law, race, and reproduction in colonial slavery. *Small Axe: A Caribbean Journal of Criticism, 22*(1), 1–17.

Moynihan, D. P. (1965). The Negro family: The case for national action (No. 31–33). US Government Printing Office.

National Center for Education Statistics (NCES), U.S. Department of Education. (2019). *Status and Trends in the Education of Racial and Ethnic Groups 2018* (NCES 2019-038), Degrees Awarded.

Nelson, T., Cardemil, E. V., & Adeoye, C. T. (2016). Rethinking strength: Black women's perceptions of the "Strong Black Woman" role. *Psychology of Women Quarterly, 40*(4), 551–563.

Omolade, B. (1994). *The rising song of African American Women.* Routledge.

org.ezproxy.lib.uwm.edu/https://doi.org/10.1080/15358593.2018.1461234

Patton, L. D., & Haynes, C. (2018). Hidden in plain sight: The Black women's blueprint for institutional transformation in higher education. *Teachers College Record, 120*(14), 1–18.

Pittman, C. T. (2010). Race and gender oppression in the classroom: The experiences of women faculty of color with white male students. *Teaching Sociology, 38*(3), 183–196.

Priest, M. (2008). Salvation is the issue. *Meridians, 8*(2), 116–122.

Richie, B. (2012). *Arrested justice: Black women, violence, and America's prison nation.* NYU Press.

Sacks, K. B. (1989). Toward a unified theory of class, race, and gender. *American Ethnologist, 16*(3), 534–550.

Settles I. H., Jones M. K., Buchanan N. T., Dotson K. (2020). Epistemic exclusion: Scholar(ly) devaluation that marginalizes faculty of color. *Journal of Diversity in Higher Education.*

Squire, D., Williams, B. C., & Tuitt, F. (2018). Plantation politics and neoliberal racism in higher education: A framework for reconstructing anti-racist institutions. *Teachers College Record, 120*(14), 1–20.

Sutherland, J. A. (2008). Ideal mama, ideal worker: Negotiating guilt and shame in academe. In E. Evans & C. Grant (Eds.), *Mama, PhD: Women write about motherhood and academic life* (pp. 213–221). Rutgers University Press.

Thelin, J. (2004). *A history of American higher education.* Johns Hopkins University Press.

Thomas, V. (2020). "How Dare You!" African American faculty and the power struggle with White students. *Journal of Cases in Educational Leadership, 23*(4), 115–126.

Turner, C. S. V. (2002). Women of color in academe: Living with multiple marginality. *The Journal of Higher Education, 73*(1), 74–93.

Turner, C. (2024). Othermothering: A black feminist history of communal early childhood education in America. *Journal of African American Women and Girls in Education, 4*(2), 108–127.

Turner, C. R., & Allen, K. R. (2024). She's a friend of my mind: A reflection of Black sisterhood in academia. *Race Ethnicity and Education, 27*(7), 1107–1124.

Turner, C. R., & Turner, M. (2022). A sociohistorical critique of the systemic disenfranchisement of Milwaukee's Black women childcare providers. *Urban Education, 60*(4), 1090–1123

Turner, C., & Green, M. (2023). "My representation is performative": Black women's reflection of academia through collaborative autoethnographic poetic inquiry. *Journal of African American Women and Girls in Education, 3*(1), 31–48.

Utsey, S. O. (1999). Development and validation of a short form of the Index of Race-Related Stress (IRRS)—brief version. *Measurement and Evaluation in Counseling and Development, 32*(3), 149–167.

Ward, K., & Wolf-Wendel, L. (2012). *Academic motherhood: How faculty manage work and family.* Rutgers University Press.
Williams, D. R., & Mohammed, S. A. (2013). Racism and health: Pathways and scientific evidence. *American Behavioral Scientist, 57*(8), 1152–1173.
Williams, R. Y. (2004). *The politics of public housing: Black women's struggles against urban inequality.* Oxford University Press.
Woods-Giscombé, C. L. (2010). Superwoman schema: African American women's views on stress, strength, and health. *Qualitative Health Research, 20*(5), 668–683.

Crystasany R. Turner is an Assistant Professor of Inclusive Early Childhood Teacher Education at the University of Wisconsin-Milwaukee. Rooted in Black feminist epistemologies, her research and scholarship highlight the perspectives of Black women educators and their cultural knowledge as manifested in their care and education of Children of Color. Her teaching and research focus includes endarkened feminist narrative, early childhood education for social justice, and spirit-centered pedagogies. Her work interrogates imbalanced social power, institutional inequities, and systemic oppression affecting diverse children and families. Dr. Turner's scholarship has been published in "Race Ethnicity and Education", the "Journal of African American Women and Girls in Education", the "Journal of Teacher Education", and the "Bloomsbury Encyclopedia of Social Justice in Education" amongst others.

For Black Women Who Have Reconsidered Flipping School Boards When Letters and Lawsuits Weren't Enough: A Divine and Ancestral Throughline of Black Education Activism

Allyce Pinchback-Johnson

Abstract In the 1970s, Pittsburgh scholar-activist Dr. Barbara Sizemore spearheaded a successful political effort in Pittsburgh Public Schools (PPS) to secure a five-person board majority committed to improving outcomes for Black children. Between 2021 and 2023, Black Women for a Better Education (BW4BE) ran school board candidates and ultimately secured a five-member school board majority. The historical throughline between these efforts toward educational activism with a focus on successfully educating Black children was, until recently, intentionally erased. This chapter employs an endarkened feminist epistemology focused on Black women's ways of knowing to chronicle the divine, ancestral connection between Dr. Sizemore and BW4BE's work.

Keyword Endarkened feminist epistemology · Black educational activism · Ancestral connections

Since its 1835 inception, Pittsburgh Public Schools (PPS), a mid-sized urban school district in Pittsburgh, Pennsylvania, has blatantly disregarded and ostracized Black caregivers and community members who have attempted to address concerns about the educational experience of Black students. Until recently, the only moderately successful strategy was political activism led by Black woman scholar-advocate, Dr. Barbara Sizemore, nearly fifty years ago to secure a school board majority.

In the 1970s, Dr. Barbara Sizemore, Professor and Interim Chair of the Department of Black Community, Research, and Education at the University of Pittsburgh, conducted a study about higher achieving, predominantly Black elementary schools in PPS. She found that the commonality between these schools was a set of routines established by school leadership that created an environment of high expectations for teachers and students (Sizemore, 1987). However, Dr. Sizemore's research was

A. Pinchback-Johnson (✉)
Pinchback Consulting, Pittsburgh, PA, USA
e-mail: allyce@pinchbackconsulting.com

C. R. Turner and M. L. Green (eds.), *Black Motherscholarship Within and Beyond the Academy*, https://doi.org/10.1007/978-3-031-99758-7_3

not popular among district leadership. In her paper entitled, "The Organization-A Viable Instrument for Progress," she candidly discussed the strong resistance she faced from PPS administrators when trying to conduct this study. Dr. Sizemore also contended that "the school officials were really embarrassed about the high performance of [high-achieving Black] schools because the performance raised questions about the lower achieving schools." Dr. Sizemore was not shy about sharing these stark differences with the Black caregivers of children in low-achieving schools and encouraging them to share their concerns with district leadership (Sizemore, 1987, p. 4).

Dr. Sizemore's study also mobilized the PPS school board—in particular, her husband Dr. Jake Milliones. Through savvy political organizing, in which they demonstrated to the Black community the power of politics to enact change in PPS, they were able to flip the seats of several school board members who had been apathetic to low Black student achievement, build alliances with current school board members, gain a board majority, and fire the superintendent (Sizemore, 1987). This was a newly viable, yet effective strategy given that PPS had just moved from a judge-appointed school board to a democratically elected school board in 1977 (Benic, 1976). Dr. Richard Wallace was appointed as PPS superintendent in 1980 and ushered in an era of enlightenment during his twelve-year tenure, with a strong focus on curriculum, instruction, assessment, and equity that moved achievement for Black children in unprecedented ways (Sizemore, 1987). PPS became a national model for urban schooling, garnering interest from all over the country (Fondy, 1988; Guydon, 1988).

Dr. Wallace retired from PPS in 1992. By then, Dr. Milliones had left the school board for Pittsburgh City Council and other transitions had occurred on the school board, leaving the future of district governance and leadership in jeopardy. The next superintendent was a traditionalist who dismantled many of Dr. Wallace's programs and resegregated the district through the creation of neighborhood-based K-8 programs, stripping PPS of the progress it made on increasing Black student achievement. This national movement of school resegregation in the 1990s was chronicled by Orfield and Yun (1999), who pointed to several Supreme Court Cases (*Milliken v. Bradley*, *Milliken v. Bradley II*, *Dowell*, *Freeman v. Pitts*, *Jenkins*) that effectively allowed local school boards to revert to segregated school districts.

Dr. Sizemore went on to start the Advocates for African American Students, who filed a lawsuit with the Pennsylvania Human Relations Commission (PHRC) against the district in 1992 due to its inability to educate Black students at high levels. PPS and the Advocates reached a Conciliation Agreement in 2006 outlining over ninety areas of improvement. Due to the lack of adequate progress made on the Conciliation Agreement by 2012, the district and the Advocates entered a Memorandum of Understanding (MOU) which called for two additional years of monitoring. Citing a continued lack of substantial progress, in 2015, the parties entered a five-year MOU (which expired August 31, 2020). The October 2020 PHRC report on the progress of the MOU stated that there is still a large disparity between the outcomes of Black and white children in PPS, which resulted in the establishment of a new five-year MOU in 2022 set to expire in 2027 (Cunningham, 2020).

The Formation of Black Women for a Better Education

My doctoral dissertation sought to explain why Black Women for a Better Education's (BW4BE) power shifting efforts to gain a majority on the PPS board was a necessary step in improving outcomes for Black children in the district. This approach was further validated by the Black scholars and activists of the 1970s who utilized a similar approach to oust apathetic school board members and an ineffective superintendent, ushering in an era of promising transformation for Black PPS students.

I co-founded BW4BE with a group of Black mothers, educators, district partners, and concerned community members in May 2020. BW4BE began as organic conversations between a few Black women in the Pittsburgh region. We came together out of frustration with the district's subpar response to COVID-19 and the subsequent remote learning rollout, a reflection of the myriad organizational inadequacies and shortcomings in PPS. BW4BE has a shared leadership model in which every member plays a role in content development and decision making. We operate as a united front, in alignment with the sisterhood that runs deep with Black women.

In June 2020, BW4BE sent a letter to the PPS board calling for the nonrenewal of the superintendent's contract based on concerns about organizational management and student achievement. Despite gathering over sixty signatures on the letter, promoting a teacher-led petition calling for the nonrenewal of the superintendent's contract (that received over 2,000 signatures), and mobilizing dozens of people to testify at the PPS board public hearing, the board voted (seven in favor, two opposed) to renew the superintendent's contract for four more years.

Despite the initial setback, since 2020 BW4BE has raised public awareness about issues in PPS among thousands of people in the Pittsburgh region through an ongoing series of town hall meetings, white papers, and social media engagement. Our work has received several accolades; and we are regularly called on as subject matter experts by the media and those looking to increase their knowledge of the education system. Building on this momentum, BW4BE ran a slate of five candidates for school board in 2021, three of whom were elected. Through the mobilization of Black women and white allies, BW4BE has kept the public pressure on PPS, which coupled with state findings of ethics violations by the superintendent, led to his resignation in October 2021. We ran another slate of three candidates in May 2023, two of whom were elected. As of the PPS board reorganization in December 2023, we have a board majority of five BW4BE-supported candidates. Additionally, we received significant grant funding from a local foundation in Fall 2023 to build our internal infrastructure through paid part-time staff and an advisory committee, composed of several of our founding members, as well as other Black women community members who have joined BW4BE through the years. This has allowed us to enhance our programming offerings, strategize on how to transform the district with our board majority, and capture the story of Advocates' decades-long fight on behalf of Black children in PPS.

In addition to co-founding BW4BE, I am a Black woman, mother, parent of a PPS alumnus, taxpayer, and former employee of the district. My five years in PPS central office provided an intimate insider perspective of the district. Additionally, I was trained as a racial equity affiliate for PPS, which bolstered my knowledge of the 1992 lawsuit, the Conciliation Agreement, and the subsequent MOUs.

As much as I thought I knew about the decades long struggle between the Advocates and the district, I only recently learned, through my doctoral research, about their prior success in securing a school board majority that replaced an inadequate superintendent with one who moved the needle for Black PPS students. This revelation came as a bittersweet surprise, as it provides precedent for and validation of BW4BE's power shifting efforts, along with the stark reality that nearly fifty years later, this type of Black community-led political activism that upsets district power structures is still necessary. On this journey, it has become abundantly clear that there is a divine, ancestral throughline between Dr. Sizemore's educational activism and BW4BE's power shifting efforts.

Black Activist Mothering

Black motherhood is a multifaceted, women-led, interdependent act. The concept of community mothering or "othermothering" is rooted in West African communal practices but became a necessity during slavery when Black mothers were sold away from their children (Edwards, 2000, p. 88). This practice evolved to include political, education, and community activism as Black women carried out their work from a place of motherhood, which shows up in the form of "church mothers" and "community mothers" (Edwards, 2000, pp. 88–89). For Black women, activism is tied to motherhood, often having to balance the nurturing nature of childrearing with preparing for and protecting their children from an oppressive culture.

Edwards (2000) posited that Black motherhood stands in contrast to the Eurocentric concept of motherhood, which is male-dependent, apolitical, and home-based. It grew out of necessity for Black women, as they were often forced into advocacy and activism through their own experiences with racism and oppression, and the desire to mitigate those experiences for their children (p. 89). Further, the femininity of Black womanhood was stripped away by slavery, given that Black women were expected to perform the same roles as Black men and treated differently than white women. Therefore, care, a trait associated with motherhood, was not ascribed to Black women. On the contrary, Black mothers demonstrate the ultimate care for their children through their advocacy and activism on their behalf. The desire for their children to survive and thrive in an oppressive world is a form of resistance rooted in care.

Sakho's (2017) work introduced the "Black Activist Mothering", an intersectional framework informed by Black feminist thought and critical race theory that described how Black women as mothers showed up in community work as resistors and transformers, building on Townsend Gilkes' (1983) work on "going up for the oppressed.". Sakho's (2017) Black Activist Mothering framework further operationalized endarkened feminist epistemology, the theoretical framework that underpins this case study (and will be discussed further in the next section), through three tools she offered to connect her lived experiences to theory and practice: Gumbo Ya Ya (a translation tool), Veil Walking (a navigational tool), and Holding Space (a facilitation tool).

Theoretical Framework

In exploring Black research methods for data analysis, I was particularly emboldened by Dr. Cynthia Dillard's (2000) endarkened feminist epistemology approach, which allows researchers to articulate how reality is known when based in the historical roots of Black feminist thought. (p. 662). The utilization of an endarkened feminist epistemology, in which research is viewed as a responsibility, "answerable and obligated to the very persons and communities being engaged in the inquiry" is a useful approach for Black women researchers to show up as our most authentic selves (Dillard, 2000, p. 664).

Dillard (2000) went on to explain that narrative research, which is commonly used in Black, indigenous, and other marginalized communities (but often excluded from qualitative research more broadly), "illustrate[s] the relationships of power, the contexts of opportunity (or lack thereof) and…highlight[s] the epistemological roots and their consequent local meanings…in the lives of Black women researchers more generally" (p. 664). She explored the utilization of life notes as a form of narrative research that "[embodies] the meaning and reflections that consciously attend to a whole life as it is embedded in sociocultural contexts and communities of affinity" (p. 664). Dillard (2000) continued, representing data in this way "[gestures] towards the confluence of the aesthetic, female, cultural sensibilities which are often stifled in traditional modes of representation and discourses mostly because they require (but rarely receive) translation from one context to the other which denaturalizes, reduces, and diminishes their richness and meaning" (p. 664).

Methodology

Dr. Sizemore was a torchbearer and a truth teller. The forthright, unapologetic candor of her scholarship, shared in ways only Black women can, was the inspiration for how I crafted my case study about BW4BE for my doctoral dissertation entitled, *For Black women who have reconsidered flipping school boards when letters and lawsuits weren't enough: A case study on the power shifting efforts of Black Women for a Better Education (BW4BE)* (Pinchback-Johnson, 2024). This case study chronicled the unique and special circumstances in which BW4BE was formed, the connections to other Black-led community-based educational reform efforts in PPS, and the success in securing a PPS board majority, while providing readers with ideas on how to shift power in school districts through school board elections.

Stake (2005), as cited in Mertens (2015), contended that a case study is more about an object of study than a specific methodology, making it an effective approach to making meaning of complex phenomena. Case studies allow readers to bring their existing knowledge of similar cases, without losing sight of the unique elements of that case. BW4BE's advocacy for the nonrenewal of the previous superintendent's contract and our success in securing a PPS board majority was in essence a series of change ideas implemented over a three-year period. The story of these efforts and the implications for how they can transform outcomes for Black children was best told through a case study. This allowed us to not only document our work, but to share our learnings as an inspiration for other Black caregivers and concerned community members who want to shift power in their respective school districts on behalf of Black children. Our work is undergirded by the sisterhood we have built upon as Black women committed to education justice, as well of a set of conditions that catalyzed transformation (i.e., the previous superintendent's shortcomings, a global pandemic, and an intimate knowledge of/connection to PPS), which makes our situation both unique and universal.

Data Collection

Data collection for this case study included artifact analysis, interviews with the eight candidates BW4BE endorsed for the PPS board, and a sister circle with BW4BE founding members (including myself). There were a number of artifacts produced by or about BW4BE that I analyzed during this process, including the initial letter we sent to the PPS board in June 2020 calling for the nonrenewal of the superintendent's contract; the series of publications we wrote prior to the May 2021 primary election about the current state of PPS and our aspirations for the future; local media coverage of BW4BE; recordings of our town hall meetings and events; and BW4BE social media posts. These artifacts clarified how BW4BE came on the scene, the approach to our work, how and why we centered Black children in the work, the issues we elevated, our shared leadership model as Black women, and how we addressed criticism for calling out the superintendent.

I conducted 60-min interviews with each of the slate members. Interviewees were asked why they chose to run for school board, why they sought the endorsement of BW4BE, and how they have (or would if they did not win their election) leveraged the power of a board majority to transform outcomes for Black children in PPS.

Sister circles have origins in the Black church and women's club movement (Neal-Barnett et al., 2011). They are structured in a way that decolonizes research by bringing the researcher and participants into community, unlike a traditional focus group where the researcher serves as a neutral facilitator. I conducted one sister circle with a group of six founding BW4BE members (including myself) that was recorded for future transcription and analysis. I solicited the support of a peer facilitator for the sister circle so that I could fully participate. The goal of the sister circle was to recount the history and relevant context that led to the inception of BW4BE, discuss the successes and challenges of our programming, reflect on our power shifting work of obtaining a board majority, and look ahead to the future of BW4BE.

I assigned each person a pseudonym that characterized their approach to the work based on my assessment of what they shared, and what I know about them as my friends and collaborators in Table 1.

To introduce the six founding members and eight school board candidates into my narrative about BW4BE, I created my own version of life notes for each of them. I share a couple excerpts below.

Education Nerd, a married parent of two college-aged PPS graduates, works for a local family foundation with a focus on K-12 education, STEM, and civics...Due to redlining, Education Nerd's family was limited to where they could buy a home but considers her family the winner of the "public school lottery" given that the neighborhood had an "excellent [PPS] elementary school led by an amazing educator." This "phenomenal experience [was] the very foundation of everything that [her] educational life was built on," and informs her understanding of "what great school can do for kids."

Hereditary Activist attended a small PPS elementary school with "some of the most beautiful, wonderful teachers that you could have ever had, including [her] mom who taught [her] for two years." From there she went to international studies-focused middle and high schools and completed the IB [International Baccalaureate] program. As she recalled, "I had a really strong experience at Pittsburgh Public Schools and had some of the best educators and administrators." Hereditary Activist uses her own experience as a reminder "what the district is capable of...and [wants] to hold them to that standard for everyone. If the district was all bad or mediocre,

Table 1 BW4BE founding members and PPS board slate members

Name	Role
Arts educator	2023 BW4BE PPS board slate member
Career educator	2023 BW4BE PPS board slate member
Community advocate	2023 BW4BE PPS board slate member
Converted teacher	2021 BW4BE PPS board slate member
Creative problem solver	2021 BW4BE PPS board slate member
Education nerd	BW4BE founding member 2021 BW4BE PPS board slate member
Hereditary activist	BW4BE founding member
Lifelong liberator	2021 BW4BE PPS board slate member
Master wayfinder	BW4BE founding member
Parent advocate	BW4BE founding member
Risk taker	BW4BE founding member
Servant leader	2021 BW4BE PPS board slate member
Systems disruptor	BW4BE founding member

fine, but they're not. They know how to do it well in certain settings for certain kids; so there's really no excuse why everybody can't get that level of education."

Our BW4BE founding members had a range of experiences with PPS as students, mothers, employees, advisory council members, and partners. Additionally, we each brought extensive education, expertise, and a unique skill set to the work. Like Dr. Sizemore, we brought our whole selves to bear in this struggle for education justices as fellow Black woman scholar-activist mothers.

Data Analysis

Traditional approaches to research, in which the researcher is disconnected from the knowledge they are seeking to maintain objectivity, is not only a fallacy given that "all research is social construction and a cultural endeavor," but contradictory to Black woman ways of knowing and being (Dillard, 2000, p. 662).

As a Black woman, mother, and researcher connected to PPS as an alumna, former employee, parent, and co-founder of BW4BE, my lived experience with PPS and the trajectory of my life are inextricably linked to the district. While traditional research contexts might view this entanglement as biased, I, along with Dillard, argued that it was a "legitimate and powerful…specialized body of knowledge" (p. 664.). Therefore, I presented the story of BW4BE as a five-part narrative of our founding, our activism to shift power in PPS through the disruption of district and board leadership, our community agitation, awareness raising, and capacity building efforts; and most importantly, the interconnected journeys of six founding members and eight BW4BE-endorsed PPS board candidates through my version of life notes.

Findings

As previously discussed, BW4BE's work is an extension of the 1970s political activism led by Dr. Barbara Sizemore and the over thirty-year struggle of the Advocates. The divine, ancestral connection between BW4BE and Dr. Sizemore can be characterized in three ways: Dr. Sizemore and BW4BE as Bold Leaders, Dr. Sizemore and BW4BE as Mothers and Othermothers, and Dr. Sizemore and BW4BE as Spiritual Beings.

Dr. Sizemore and BW4BE as Bold Leaders

One commonality between Dr. Sizemore and BW4BE was the boldness and audaciousness with which we called for transformational change in PPS. Dr. Sizemore went toe-to-toe with an ineffective superintendent on behalf of Black children and led the charge to have him removed. She spearheaded the effort for Black caregivers to sue PPS. BW4BE operated with that same boldness when we called for the non-renewal of the previous superintendent's contract and ran candidates for the school board.

Educational outcomes have been perennially poor for Black children in PPS since its inception (A+ Schools Pittsburgh, 2022, 2023; Sizemore, 1987; Tyack, 1974). Instances of Black activism on behalf of our children—both those of the Advocates and BW4BE—have been disregarded, abandoned, and erased. People with power remain willfully ignorant about PPS (unless it involves their own children), lack motivation to speak out against colleagues and friends about their role in perpetuating these outcomes, and are unwilling to take the political hit of countering legacy institutions who hold their reelection or reappointment in the balance. Career Educator shared their appreciation for BW4BE's willingness say things that were unpopular:

[BW4BE] came out when it wasn't popular to say things that a lot of people knew but for whatever reason weren't willing to say; and people who would publicly say one thing like, "oh, we've got to support this, that, or the other", but behind the scenes would show doubt…Taking unpopular stances on important issues, staying the course, and adjusting of course based upon where the push back comes from, to me, is both a talent and a blessing that our city needs to embrace.

Additionally, as Systems Disruptor rightly pointed out, advocacy in our region has conflated information with action and outputs with outcomes. She shared,

So much in Pittsburgh advocacy is always looking at giving people access to information. But I think what [BW4BE] did was we didn't give people just access to information; we gave them access to change a system. We've got to bridge the access to information in the systemic change and activate that. And that's what Pittsburgh is not used to. Like this is literally just analysis paralysis.

Like the Advocates who faced ostracization and retaliation for suing PPS, BW4BE persisted despite the pushback because the urgency of improving PPS for Black children outweighed the criticism and risk. Kakli (2011) and Cooper (2007) pointed to the same type of determination and resolve in the Black mothers they highlighted in their work. The individual activism of the mother and activist highlighted in Kakli's (2011) portraiture was situated in race-based activism and was catalyzed by her experience as a mother. This is connected to Cooper's (2007) work, which characterized Black mothers' desire for the success of themselves and their children as a "maternal responsibility" given the constant devaluing of Black people by American society. All of us went to great lengths on behalf of our children.

Dr. Sizemore and BW4BE as Mothers and Othermothers

Another important connection between Dr. Sizemore and BW4BE is the divine, ancestral throughline between our educational advocacy efforts that is situated in the Black mothering tradition. Many of our founding members and PPS board slate members came from families who throughout generations emphasized the importance of education and went to tireless lengths for their children and grandchildren to receive a high-quality education. Several of them shared stories about the roles their mothers and foremothers played in shaping their educational trajectories.

For example, Master Wayfinder's mother "was always concerned about where [she and her siblings] went to school," and they often attended schools outside of their neighborhood. When she was in fifth grade, her family moved to a new state where they did not know anyone except her uncle. Her mother really wanted her to attend a certain school, so she knocked on a random stranger's door and asked her to use her address for a small fee each month. The woman agreed. Master Wayfinder commended her mother for "[swallowing] her pride for her kids to get the education that they deserved…and [humbling] herself" to a stranger who could have reported them.

Risk Taker's interest in public education is inspired by her multiple family members who were educators, including her grandmother (who lived to be 108), who was a "master teacher." She shared a story of how for years, her "amazingly tenacious" grandmother petitioned the Carnegie Libraries of New York for books for her small southern town, until "they got so sick of her…and showed up with crates and crates and crates of books," allowing her grandmother to build "one of the best libraries in the region."

In her study of 14 Black mothers in Los Angeles, Cooper (2007) described their school choices and educational advocacy as "motherwork", which was characterized by a desire to ensure their children's survival, improving their children's life outcomes by seeking power, and fostering a positive racial identity in their children. Black mothers viewed education as a means of survival and upward mobility for their children. Similarly, Dr. Sizemore's work in PPS to identify and replicate high-achieving Black schools in the district because "change was what was necessary to narrow the achievement gap between African-American students and White students in the Pittsburgh elementary schools" was a form of motherwork (Sizemore, 1987, p. 4). Like the mothers and ancestors of our founding members, she was relentless in her pursuit of high-quality education for all children because it was critical for their survival and well-being.

Dr. Sizemore and BW4BE as Spiritual Beings

Dillard (2000) contended that "spirituality is intimately woven into the ethos of an endarkened feminist epistemology, with a critical assumption that research is the pursuit of intellect, spirituality, and purpose focused on knowledge production, truth telling, and truth making" (p. 672).

Gumbo Ya Ya

Sakho (2017) stated, Gumbo Ya Ya as a sense making tool; then, allows for critically thinking about multiple stories including master narratives across space, place and time simultaneously while in concert with an event. While not necessarily documented, we, Black women as mothers, cultivate our intellectual and political development by invoking Gumbo Ya Ya, to make sense of our lived experiences by "layering multiple and asymmetrical stories (p. 10).

Even before I fully understood the extent of the Advocates' 1970s political activism that leveraged the PPS board to bring a transformational leader, I realized there was a deeper connection to BW4BE's work. Education Nerd was a PPS student during the time Dr. Sizemore was conducting her research in the district. The school she attended was the highest achieving Black school in the district (Sizemore, 1987). Education Nerd is both a founding member of BW4BE and a current PPS board member. Hereditary Activist was in kindergarten at PPS in 1992, the same year Dr. Sizemore and the Advocates filed the lawsuit. She also worked at PPS for five years before co-founding BW4BE. Parent Advocate served on the EAP and was told she "seemed to be the only one who embodied Barbara [Sizemore's] spirit." To me, these occurrences are not happenstance, but versions of Gumbo Ya Ya, in which stories converge across time, place, and space.

Several of the BW4BE founding members reflected on the spiritual aspects of BW4BE's work and their call to advocacy on behalf of Black children rooted in legacy. Dream Fulfilled shared that she felt "magnetically attracted to strong Black women spaces, including [BW4BE]." Risk Taker called it the generational fortitude to educate and save our children. Master Wayfinder reminded us of the ever-present voice of Black women in the education advocacy space. Hereditary Activist referred to her participation in BW4BE as an "extension of [her] legacy." Parent Advocate shared,

So it's just like this unction, this calling. I look at it as all spiritual warfare. You know, I have centered myself. I have resigned to say this is what I'm supposed to do on this earth in this way. And I feel lucky that I had a collective passion and was introduced to these women in different ways, and still even though I haven't seen you all in a while [prior to the sister circle], I feel still honored that you called me, [Hereditary Activist] and very much a part of this group.

Lifelong Liberator, whose pseudonym is reflective of their dedication to the ongoing Black struggle, was a catalyst for BW4BE's advocacy efforts. We were able to operationalize their call for new district leadership through the letter and provide much-needed support for them on the school board as the lone PPS board incumbent unapologetically committed to Black student achievement. Our partnership with and support of Lifelong Liberator as our elder was in some ways a passing of the torch.

Veil Walking

Veil Walking is a way in which Black women navigate this journey of Black Activist Mothering across space, place and time. Sakho (2017) explained it as follows:

When we Veil Walk, we are carrying messages and possibilities back and forth between individuals, systems, structures, and histories. This means that when we work the borders, gaps, margins and liminal spaces we are passing through veils on a quest not only to transport and translate knowledge from the dominant world back to these uneven and inequitable spaces but also, to carry that rich thick counter-knowledge from the bottom up and across systems of power" (p. 11).

Dr. Sizemore veil walked between university scholar and community activist, elevating best practices in Black PPS student achievement while actively leveraging the school board to appoint new leadership when her scholarship and advocacy was disregarded. The Advocates veil walked between traditional methods of district caregiver engagement and a lawsuit against PPS when they were not granted the same level of privilege as white parents for the same type of advocacy. They were admonished as poor Black caregivers for their audacity to sue the school district. Similarly, BW4BE reverted to power shifting efforts when fact-based advocacy for new district leadership was ignored. In each case, we utilized methods of the dominant culture (i.e., litigation, civic engagement, and the electoral process) to put power in the hands of marginalized Black people in service of their children. This ethereal navigation between the socially constructed white world and our Black world was referred to by Dubois (1903, as cited in Sakho, 2017) as our "double consciousness," and sits at the intersection of "personal or intrapsychic and…institutional or structural level of social interaction" (Winant, 2004, as cited in Sakho, 2017).

Holding Space

Sakho described Holding Space as "the willingness to honor a multiplicity of truths with a level of vulnerability that resists judgment while at the same moment holding inequity and injustice accountable or unapologetically enacting spiritual militancy" (Sakho, 2017, p. 11).

Education Nerd reflected on how BW4BE has expanded the conversation about education in the region:

[BW4BE] has made the conversation more nuanced and forced people to think in ways that they hadn't necessarily thought before. And even if they don't recognize out loud that they have done that…[We have been able to] poke holes in these ideas that are commonly held beliefs about what Black kids need for to get a good education.

BW4BE not only reenergized a conversation about public education in Pittsburgh, but it also helped people to see the possibilities for advocacy and activism to address myriad issues that disproportionately impact Black people in this region. As Creative Problem Solver shared,

We can talk about the very tangible effects of Black Women for a Better Education…But I think there are some indirect positive consequences that come from

Black Women for a Better Education being created. Something like this empowers people to notice when something does not work and decide to move. And I think that's powerful…When you can see a group of people mobilize, organize and act, it gives other people a very clear vision of what that looks like so that they can do it for themselves.

While we are adamantly against anyone and anything that does not have the best interests of Black children in mind, the ways in which we get there are multifaceted. We understand the role of Black people as both oppressors and liberators in PPS. We see charter schools as a benefit and a detriment to our children. We want PPS to become a better district while we also ponder how to facilitate a mass exodus of Black children from a system that has constantly failed them. As Black women, who are constantly on the margins of society, we hold space for this discomfort while creating a safe space for others to join us there alongside our ancestors and elders in the fight for educational justice in PPS.

Recommendations

In defining the responsibility Black women researchers have to their community and its well-being when conducting educational inquiry, Dillard (2000) shared, "to know something is to have a living relationship with it, influencing and being influenced by it, responding to and being responsible for it" (p. 673). As a Black woman researcher and co-founder of BW4BE, I am responsible for the Black children I birthed, I raise, and those in my community. I offer the following recommendations for those aspiring to join this journey.

Lead with Facts

Partner with local organizations and universities and/or submit right-to-know requests to obtain district data. Build your intellectual capital around district systems, operations, and power structures. Creating the BW4BE Learning Institute allowed us to build a cadre of educational thought leaders and prospective board members who were highly knowledgeable about our district.

Keep the Needs of Black Children Centered

If the focus is on what is best for students, then you are moving in the right direction. Be unafraid to speak up against any adult, system, or structure knowingly harming children. Be reminded that holding Black adults in positions of power in educational systems to a lower standard because they are Black, especially at the expense of Black children, is a perpetuation of racism.

Build a School Board Bench

Identify people who are interested in running for the school board. Build their education knowledge base. Connect them to members of your community who are interested in education and/or major election influencers. Ask them to run for the school board. When they tell you "no", ask them again. Raise money for them. Canvas for them. Introduce them to other people who will support their campaigns. Support them in refining their talking points.

Operate as a Protective Collective

BW4BE has been called everything but our name. Our motivations have been questioned. The attacks have been personal and professional. That is why the sisterhood has been so important. We understand each other. We can show up as our authentic selves. We speak as a group. We make collective decisions. Our individual strengths create a powerful whole.

Take Care of Yourself

Since we started BW4BE, our founding members have had babies, changed jobs, lost loved ones, moved into new homes, and battled illness. This is all while living through a pandemic in one of the worst cities in America for Black women (Goodkind et al., 2019). Find time for genuine self-care. Take naps. Close your laptop and love on your children; the work will be there tomorrow. Do not let these systems kill you any faster than they already are.

Closing Thoughts

When I worked at PPS I would often say, "our people perish from lack of context." During that time, I had long conversations with my mother about the cycles of reform and the revolving door of administrators she experienced in her thirty-eight years with the district. With every new person came a new idea, with no assessment of how the previous plans worked before implementing something new. While there were initiatives the district should have abandoned, there were just as many others that were successful but cast to the side with a change in leadership.

The 1970s political activism of the Advocates is a clear example of this. PPS was quick to "celebrate" the thirty-year anniversary of the 1992 lawsuit (though perennially failing outcomes are no cause for celebration), with no mention of how those same Advocates mobilized this city to elect effective board leadership who in turn hired a superintendent who made PPS a national model for urban education (Fondy, 1988; Guydon, 1988). The erasure of the transformational activism of the Advocates who fought for equity in PPS not only prevents us from learning from their success, but it dishonors their legacy.

Co-creating BW4BE with my friends and sisters has been a life-altering experience for me. It is surreal that a few text messages about PPS's response to the pandemic turned into a movement that has the potential to impact Black families in the region for generations to come. But at the same time, it is not surprising because our group of founding members are bold, smart, and passionate Black women who have been making waves in Pittsburgh for decades. We are thankful to Dr. Sizemore for her scholarship, the courage to stand up to PPS, and her brilliance to leverage the political and legal systems to move the needle for Black children in our district. This journey has further illuminated the divine, ancestral connection we have to Dr. Sizemore, each other, and our foremothers in the education justice movement. As Education Nerd put it,

I believe in the power of the Black woman. I don't think that there's a creature on earth as a segment of the population that's more effective. And when I can be in community with brilliant Black women who just get shit done, I will do that. I will do that every time.

Competing Interests The author has no conflicts of interest to declare that are relevant to the content of this manuscript.

References

A+ Schools Pittsburgh. (2023). Report to the Community on Public School Progress in Pittsburgh. https://www.ourschoolspittsburgh.org/report-to-the-community

A+ Schools Pittsburgh. (2022). Report to the Community on Public School Progress in Pittsburgh. https://www.ourschoolspittsburgh.org/2022-report-to-the-community

Benic, T. (1976, April 28). Elected school board passes by big margin. *Pittsburgh Post-Gazette.*

Cooper, C. W. (2007). School choice as 'motherwork': Valuing African-American women's educational advocacy and resistance. *International Journal of Qualitative Studies in Education, 20*(5), 491–512.

Cunningham, M. (2020). Pittsburgh Public School District Memorandum of Understanding Report. Commonwealth of Pennsylvania Human Relations Commission. https://www.pittsburghcurrent.com/wp-content/uploads/2020/11/2020-Equity-MOU-Report_PHRC_PPS.pdf

Dillard, C. B. (2000). The substance of things hoped for, the evidence of things not seen: Examining an endarkened feminist epistemology in educational research and leadership. *International Journal of Qualitative Studies in Education, 13*(6), 661–681.

Edwards, A. E. (2000). Community mothering: The relationship between mothering and the community work of Black women. *Journal of the Motherhood Initiative for Research and Community Involvement*.
Fondy, A. (1988, March 21). City schools get top rating [Editorial]. The Pittsburgh Press.
Gilkes, C. T. (1983). Going up for the oppressed: The career mobility of Black women community workers. *Journal of Social Issues, 39*(3), 115–139.
Goodkind, S., Jacobs, L., Branson, E., & Miller, E. (2019). Pittsburgh's Inequality across gender and race. *Gender Analysis White Paper*. City of Pittsburgh's Gender Equity Committee.
Guydon, L. (1988, January 12). Hawkins lauds Pittsburgh schools. *Pittsburgh-Post Gazette.*
Kakli, Z. (2011). Doing the work: A portrait of an African American mother as an education activist. *The Urban Review, 43*(2), 175–195.
Mertens, D. (2015). *Research and Evaluation in Education and Psychology.* Sage Publications, Inc.
Neal-Barnett, A. M., Stadulis, R., Payne, M. R., Crosby, L., Mitchell, M., Williams, L., & Williams-Costa, C. (2011). In the company of my sisters: Sister circles as an anxiety intervention for professional African American women. *Journal of Affective Disorders, 129*(1–3), 213–218.
Orfield, G., & Yun, J. T. (1999). Resegregation in American schools.
Pinchback-Johnson, A. L. (2024). *For Black women who have reconsidered flipping school boards when letters and lawsuits weren't enough: A case study on the power shifting efforts of Black Women for a Better Education (BW4BE).* [Unpublished doctoral dissertation]. University of Pittsburgh.
Sakho, J. R. (2017). Black activist mothering: Teach me about what teaches you. *Western Journal of Black Studies, 41*(1/2), 6–19.
Sizemore, B. (1987). Developing effective instructional programs.
Tyack, D. B. (1974). *The one best system: A history of American urban education.* Harvard University Press.

Dr. Allyce Pinchback-Johnson is a founding member and Executive Director of Black Women for a Better Education (BW4BE), whose mission is to ensure that Black children have access to the high-quality education they need and deserve. Through their efforts, BW4BE has raised awareness of key issues in public education in Pittsburgh, and their political action committee (PAC) has successfully secured a five-member majority on the Pittsburgh Public Schools (PPS) board of directors. Allyce is also the Founder and Lead Consultant of Pinchback Consulting, which focuses on helping people and organizations become smarter and better at their work through strategic planning, capacity building, and project management.

"*They Are a Burden to You*": Reflecting on Mothering as Decolonial Love in Academia in South Africa

Danille Elize Arendse

Abstract As a first-generation Black academic woman and mother, there are still remnants of the past in post-Apartheid South Africa that continue to permeate the present. In this chapter, I use autoethnography to draw on various experiences I had while completing my postdoctoral fellowship. In this chapter, I argue against glorifying resilient mothering in academia as a norm but rather endorsing mothering as a site of resistance within the academy. Mothering in academia is thus a form of decolonial love, moving away from colonial conceptions of the academic mother towards inclusionary notions of mothers as full citizens of the academy.

Keyword Autoethnography · First generation academic · Decolonial love

Introduction

> …the kind of love that I was interested in, that my characters long for intuitively, is the only kind of love that could liberate them from that horrible legacy of colonial violence. I am speaking about decolonial love'. (Moya, 2012, p. 14)

As a Black woman who willingly entered mothering, the intersection of race, gender and mothering has become interlocked in my experiences of academia and my postdoctoral fellowship experience. In this chapter, I use autoethnography to draw on various experiences I had while completing my postdoctoral fellowship. These experiences range from relocating within South Africa to an unexpected pregnancy and giving birth whilst completing my postdoctoral fellowship. The major themes in my narrative include my experiences as a Black mother in the academy, my embodied self in the academy, and mothering as decolonial love. These reflections allow me to argue that the Black mother may be forced to be resilient to navigate and succeed in the academy; but this should not be glorified as the true essence of the Black mother

D. E. Arendse (✉)
Department of Psychology, University of Pretoria, Pretoria, South Africa
e-mail: danille.bester@up.ac.za

The Harriet Tubman Institute, York University, Toronto, ON, Canada

C. R. Turner and M. L. Green (eds.), *Black Motherscholarship Within and Beyond the Academy*, https://doi.org/10.1007/978-3-031-99758-7_4

lies in her ability to embody decolonial love. I further argue for the decolonizing of the university, so it may become an inclusionary space.

African scholars have repeatedly faced circumstances that seek to diminish their impact on knowledge production due to their colonial past. Thus, the narratives formed about Africa and Black people tend to advance colonially rooted epistemes and inflict ontological violence on Black people, who continue to suffer the effects of coloniality in the present (Arendse, 2021, 2022; Radcliffe, 2017). In South Africa, those who previously suffered under colonialism and Apartheid, are still engaging in this struggle for their humanity to be recognised. Thus, despite South Africa having reached the end of colonialism and Apartheid in 1994, Black people still face the afterlife of these oppressive regimes of control and power.

In South Africa, colonialism and Apartheid promoted the division of races, through racist science which ultimately led to the dehumanizing of Black people (Adhikari, 2006; Arendse, 2021, 2022; Lugones, 2010; Mendez, 2015). Colonialism in South Africa, therefore, promoted white supremacy while informally separating races. During the colonial period, several censuses (1865, 1875, 1880, 1890 and 1921) were done to socially control the population, and this resulted in the labelling of people by racial classification. This legal system, which became known as the Populations Registration Act of 1950 during Apartheid, identified four race groups, namely: White, Black, Coloured, and Indian. During Apartheid South Africa, Black was defined as a person of native African origin while Coloured was understood to be a person of mixed origin/ancestry, thus they were perceived as neither native nor white. Despite the end of Apartheid, South Africa currently still adheres to the Populations Registration Act of 1950 (Adhikari, 2006; Arendse, 2021, 2022). The legal classification of Coloured was created with contempt for racial mixing and to encourage the 'divide and conquer' system during the Apartheid era. As a result, the history and experiences of those labelled as Coloured have remained contentious even in post-Apartheid South Africa. More importantly, Coloured women are continuously tied to sexual shame, negative representations and stereotypes (Adhikari, 2006; Arendse, 2021, 2022).

Since there is a lack of studies in South Africa focused on the experiences of Black mothers in the university (Maluleke et al., 2023), this chapter addresses this need by reflecting on my position as a Black mother as a postdoctoral fellow. A postdoctoral fellowship is considered a transitory space after the completion of a PhD and the fostering of research interests that will position an emerging scholar within academia. The completion of a postdoctoral fellowship is not a necessity but rather a position of learning and expanding one's research capabilities. Having said this, occupying a postdoctoral fellowship does not spare one from negotiating institutional hurdles and economic barriers. Although South Africa is in a post-Apartheid era, there are still remnants of the past that continue to permeate the present.

Laws on Education Promulgated During Apartheid

There were two significant laws promulgated during Apartheid that continue to plague Black people. These laws were the Bantu Education Act of 1953 and the Extension of University Education Act of 1959. Both sought to limit educational prospects for Black people at school and university. The apartheid government was intent on keeping Black people uneducated and depriving them of educational opportunities. This is well captured in a quote by JN Le Roux (National Party politician during 1945) indicated that "We should not give the Natives any academic education. If we do, who is going to do the manual labour in the community?" (Boddy-Evans, 2024). The racist views of educating Black people were furthered by Hendrik Verwoerd, known as the Architect of Apartheid, when he was quoted as saying, "When I have control of Native education, I will reform it so that Natives will be taught from childhood to realise that equality with Europeans is not for them...Education must train and teach people in accordance with their opportunities in life, according to the sphere in which they live" (Tabata, 1980).

The economic circumstances of Black families caused Black girls (inclusive of Coloured) to quit school either because their parents could no longer afford their education, or so that they could assist in generating income for the home or to allow their mother to work while they see to the home and younger siblings (Meer, 1985). Common across all these reasons is the fact that the Black girl is denied education due to severe poverty produced by Apartheid policies. As a result, Apartheid sought to limit the careers of Black women by limiting them to mostly informal labour in rural places with very few being allowed in the formal labour space (Meer, 1985; Mkhize & Msomi, 2016). This meant that Black women were responsible for the upkeep of their homes, families and children, leaving them confined to their homes. This was further entrenched using pass laws that restricted the movement of Black women in particularly white areas in South Africa. Any violation of the pass laws, which at times involved random questioning of Black women, not only left them fearful and humiliated but also deeper into poverty, as they were required to pay steep fines (Kaufman, 2000). Despite white people believing that Black people were intellectually inferior, Black people fought for their liberation and the reform of education. The Congress of South African Students are quoted as saying,

> The education we receive is meant to keep the South African people apart from one another, to breed suspicion, hatred and violence and to keep us backward. Education is formulated so as to reproduce this society of racism and exploitation. (Boddy-Evans, 2024)

The liberation struggle eventually led to a Democratic South Africa in 1994; but 30 years post-Apartheid is not sufficient to truly grapple with the afterlife of the educational disadvantage that Black people had to endure. The consequences of Apartheid have led to Black women being unmarried (Apartheid policies had an impact on Black marriages) with children—leading them to face unemployment, poverty, and economic restriction due to their limited education. This has led to

Black single mothers struggling to maintain an unequal work and family life, often resulting in dire consequences for them, their families, and children (Mkhize & Msomi, 2016).

National Protest Movements and the Experiences of Black Women

Despite the demise of Apartheid, South African higher education had been replicating apartheid logic within the universities which ultimately led to the national protest movements (i.e., #RhodesMustFall and #FeesMustFall) by students that demanded transformation within the university. Part of this national protest movement by students included the promotion of a decolonial agenda within the university as well as the furthering of gender equivalence because women in the academy were still not achieving equality with men. Another significant aspect brought forward was Black women's experiences of isolation and exclusion in the university (Hlatshwayo & Ngcobo, 2023). As expressed by Moolman (in Lewis, 2001, p. 3),

> The passing of a number of progressive laws and the amendment of certain pieces of legislation, theoretically implies the improvement of women's positions in society, yet the reality is that the majority of women continue to face marginalisation and discrimination. (Lewis, 2001, p. 3; Rosen et al., 2024)

Although there has been a transformation in the academy, Black women still face marginalisation and continue to be subjected to oppressive systems due to their racialized and gendered identity. Subsequently, they face prejudice and are susceptible to discrimination (Arendse, 2022; Hlatshwayo & Ngcobo, 2023; Phakeng, 2015). Research has also found that Black women academics still experience racism, sexual harassment, misrecognition, and patriarchy in higher education (Hlatshwayo & Ngcobo, 2023). As Hlatshwayo and Ngcobo (2023), warn,

> the cultural domains, together with the disciplinary and interpersonal domains, seem to align to produce new forms of marginality for Black women academics in relation to the ever-prevailing and deeply ingrained or institutionalised heteronormative and patriarchal structures in higher education that continue to oppress, alienate and colonise them. (p. 179)

There is thus still an imperative to address the colonial state operating in universities that subjugate Black women including Black mothers in the university.

Positionality

In this chapter, I specifically narrate my experiences during my postdoctoral fellowship year in which I was pregnant, subsequently gave birth, and returned to complete my postdoctoral fellowship year. I draw attention to my identity, as I racially identify as a Black woman and culturally as Coloured. My concept of Coloured as an ethnic identity implies that multiple histories and cultures are the result of a diverse ancestry. I reference both identities as the complicated racial dynamics of South Africa require me to situate myself concerning the legal classifications bestowed upon me. Having said this, I endorse Black Consciousness which promotes a shared Black identity, which encompasses those lawfully classified as Black and Coloured during the Apartheid and post-Apartheid period. The philosophy of Black Consciousness seeks to unite all non-White people as they collectively fight oppression and advance Black solidarity. It is through the lenses of Black consciousness that my intricate Blackness as both a Coloured and Black woman can be celebrated (Arendse, 2021, 2022; Biko, 2004). I identify as cisgender with pronouns, 'her' and 'she'. I am currently middle class and speak English, Afrikaans and Afrikaaps[1] languages. I also know limited isiXhosa, isiZulu, and Setswana (African languages in South Africa) words.

Method

The method of autoethnography invites me to speak and to the silencing of my experiences. Although there is not always something inherently wrong when it comes to silence, there are moments when silence is not required (Brant, 2023). It is at this juncture that I break away from silence and decide to speak and to be heard. Autoethnography is a research method that allows the researcher the opportunity to self-reflect on personal experiences they have had and to examine these experiences through a theoretical lens for meaning-making. These experiences are written from a first-person perspective, using 'I', and involve a retrospective analysis of experiences shared by the researcher (Arendse, 2021, 2022; Ellis et al., 2010). The data collection process of my autoethnography journey involved journaling my experiences during my postdoctoral year. I also probed myself in terms of my research question, to guide me in eliciting relevant retrospective observations, ideas, and emotions I had experienced during the postdoctoral year. I then sifted through the different experiences and chronologically formed a story. I then reread my story and added sections that enhanced the meaning which also included sections that I remembered in my re-reading of the narration. Thereafter, I identified themes emerging from the text and critically analysed them using decolonial intersectionality.

My retrospective analysis of my postdoctoral fellowship year, centred on my identity as a Black mother navigating and surviving the academy. A question that arose for me when embarking on this chapter was: *what is the cost of educating a Black mother?* My chapter does not intend to answer this question comprehensively but rather give the perspective of a Black mother who had already achieved a doctoral

[1] Afrikaaps is a language variant found in Western Cape Province, South Africa and predominantly spoken by Coloured people. Its origins lie in colonial South Africa through the enslaved populations.

degree but is still not spared the realities of being a Black mother in the university. More importantly, my chapter provides insight into the complicated identity of Coloured within South Africa that furthers this already difficult situation.

Since the colonial and Apartheid era continues to affect us in the present, I used decolonial intersectionality (Lugones, 2014; Salem, 2014) to interpret my narrative. Decolonial intersectionality can be defined as a feminist theory that incorporates both coloniality and intersectionality, while also paying attention to race and gender as fundamental to experiences. In addition, this framework is critical of binary thinking and contends that racialized people should give voice to their experiences, which are dependent on their environment and interconnecting realities. Within this chapter, I position Apartheid as part of the intersecting realities of oppression that continue to impact identity within South Africa (Arendse, 2021, 2022; Crenshaw, 1994; Lugones, 2014; Salem, 2014).

The Cost of Educating a Black Mother

"*They are a burden to you…*" I still remember how it was said by a relative and the numbness I felt. Then, I had one child and was pregnant with another. I was also starting a postdoctoral fellowship away from home. The odds were against me. Perhaps this was a familiar feeling—never being in a position that didn't require some fight or challenge. "*You better not have any more children…*". These words felt like hits to the chest. What had I done so wrong? Why was it always a choice? Was this the cost I needed to pay for education as a Black mother?

There is a moment that I believe defines you in whatever stage you are in, and these statements were those moments. Perhaps I would have taken it better if the person saying these hurtful remarks were a man—but it was a woman, a Black woman, a Black mother herself. It was in this moment that my imposter syndrome was lurking, ready to show itself again in full attire. What did I think I was doing? Could I even do the postdoctoral fellowship? How would I meet the postdoctoral fellowship obligations while pregnant? Could I manage to publish two papers in one year? I don't even write that well. Those words opened the difficulty of being a first-generation graduate. My journey was just beginning, and it was perhaps a sign to discontinue and cut my losses—to go back to my work and be a mother. It was also at this moment that a defiance arose within me. A fire. A rage. A desire to prove that I could be worthy. I could do it. This ambivalence at this point did not make sense since the obstacles I would need to navigate were uncertain; and my pregnancy, no one could predict how that would go. I allowed my deviance to win.

I would continue with the postdoctoral fellowship. This entailed me leaving my husband and son in Pretoria (a province in South Africa) and relocating to Cape Town (a province in South Africa), which was a two-hour flight apart and a 2000 km (1243 mi.) driving distance. Despite the odds being against me, there was an ease with which the plans unfolded. The universe was conspiring to make it happen. Although Cape Town is home for me in many ways, because most of my family is nearby, I stayed alone. For most of my pregnancy, I was alone in the flat. To my husband, it was a worry; but to me, it was a space of solace. I remember him asking me, "*Is it worth it? You need to answer this for yourself*". These words would plague me every time I encountered a difficulty. I was not afraid to be alone with myself. I had initially expected more involvement from my family, but I soon learned that support would take different forms. Family will not always support you; but there will be others close enough to spur you on, such as the wonderful people I was privileged to befriend at the Centre I did my postdoctoral fellowship. Some of these friendships served to celebrate both my Blackness and my Coloured culture.

I Pushed

During my postdoctoral fellowship, I was determined to participate in everything I could. Whether it meant going home late, working till late, going out to events and seminars, driving at night, travelling till the very last to attend conferences, I would do it all. I didn't want to be treated as if I could not do things because I was pregnant; but instead, I wanted to show that I could keep up. I pushed. I remember as time went on, my stomach got bigger. I felt heavy. At some point, I needed to walk slowly as the weight I was carrying was very heavy. In some ways, it was a physical manifestation of the emotional toll I was undertaking.

To keep my family intact, I used my postdoctoral fellowship funds to book flights so they could visit me every month. I missed my son. He had been breastfeeding (he was already two) and during this period, he subsequently stopped breastfeeding. Since I decided to give birth in Pretoria and use the same gynaecologist as with my first son, I needed to fly home for check-ups almost every month. Although I had a relaxed and healthy pregnancy, on two occasions I was rushed to hospital because I wasn't sure if the baby was moving. Both times, everything was fine. I wasn't sure if it was just my anxiety, the fatigue or the weight of balancing everything.

By the time I needed to leave for maternity, which was the same month I was scheduled for a c-section (due to his size and a previous emergency c-section), I needed my nephew to drive me home as I could no longer safely fly home. This was a two-day drive home, heavily pregnant. I was tired. But I was satisfied. I had published one paper and had confirmation of my second publication. I did it. My colleagues were amazed, and I remember a friend asking me, "*How do you do it? I don't know how you do everything you do.*" It was a compliment; but I didn't feel that it should be one. Additionally, I was the only postdoctoral fellow that had reached the two-publication requirement despite my pregnancy. I should have felt more honored, but instead I just felt grateful and filled with grace. I did not think I was better. In fact, I remember saying to a friend, '*Thank you but this is not something I want to glorify*'. Although it was an achievement, it had come at a cost, unknown to some. Although I was very happy, it was mostly because I could breathe easy again.

"It Was Worth It"

My son was born with a weight of 4 kg (8.82 lbs), it made so much sense. He was born with a clubfoot. This was an additional issue we needed to navigate. Was it my fault? Was it because I insisted on doing the postdoctoral fellowship that he ended up with a clubfoot? It was at this moment that my emotions soared. I didn't have the capacity for WhatsApp, emails…nothing. I just needed to be a mother now. No multitasking. I read up on a clubfoot, and we booked an appointment. I was ashamed. I felt like I had done something wrong. The specialist doctor was so friendly. I felt so emotional, and he was so full of ease. It was like we were having a normal doctor's visit, and he began immediately with the cast on the foot. This would be our life, moving through the different stages of rectifying a clubfoot. I saw other mothers. There was nothing wrong with how they mothered. It was only at a paediatrician's visit that she said to me, "*He was a big baby…you probably felt like he wasn't moving at times because of how he was positioned...he had limited space to move*". It was at this moment that she released me from the guilt that had been stored inside of me.

Prior to my maternity leave commencing, I had agreed to take a shorter maternity leave so that I would not extend my postdoctoral year too far. After two months, I needed to return for a talk and other activities planned. I wasn't ready. Emotionally, I was not yet ready to engage in academic discourse. But I had committed, and I would see it to the end. At one of the conferences I attended, I was voted into the executive committee; and I won a Best Paper Award. It was at this moment, still fatigued from a short maternity, that I had an answer, '*It was worth it*'. What I had been doing was recognized. I felt hope to continue.

Once again, my baby and I left for Cape Town—leaving my home, husband, and older son behind. This time, I needed my mother to assist with looking after my son while I was at university. It was stressful. He was breastfeeding and did not take to the bottle. I would rush home because he would be starving himself and my mother would be stressing. This juggling was becoming impossible. Although I may have appeared intact at university, I was fatigued, stressed, and anxious. The baby needed me, "*When are you coming, this child has been crying for hours*"; but I still had a postdoctoral fellowship to complete. We were in the rat race again. Flying up and down to keep our family unit together, to take the baby for his clubfoot appointments. The madness would end soon, I kept telling myself. And then, while holding the baby and sitting with my laptop, I heard it again "They are a burden to you…". The postdoctoral fellowship year ended, and I had exceeded expectations. It was done.

Discussion

When reflecting on my narrative, three overarching themes emerged, namely: (1) being a Black mother in the academy, (2) my embodied self in the academy and (3) mothering as decolonial love. In the next sections of the chapter, I will unpack these three overarching and subsequent sub-themes concerning my experiences.

Being a Black Mother in the Academy

> "I dream of never being called resilient again in my life. I am exhausted by strength. I want support. I want softness. I want ease. I want to be among kin. Not patted on the back for how well I take a hit." Or for how many. Instead of hearing "You are one of the most resilient people I know," I want to hear "You are so loved." "You are so cared for." "You are genuinely covered." (Shwaikh, 2023)

As a Black mother scholar, I am required to embody multiple identities based on my positioning and the need to fulfil different roles (Arendse, 2022; Maluleke et al., 2023). Through this, I am required to engage in formal (university) labour that leads to paid labour, while the informal (childcare and home) labour results in unpaid labour. Both these spaces require me to move between different aspects of myself—the identity I have as a mother and the identity I have as a postdoctoral fellow. These different forms of labour required from Black mothers are invisible and are often not recognised (Arendse, 2022; Hlatshwayo & Ngcobo, 2023; Rosen et al., 2024; Soja, 1996). When considering the labouring that Black mothers do in the day and at night, they are forced to be resilient if they are to continue to navigate the academy. It is in the management of these different demands that Black women tend to overcompensate and overachieve.

As Rosen et al. (2024) found, Black women were highly motivated to pursue their career objectives despite the obstacles they faced. Furthermore, Black mothers showed high resilience and mental capacity despite their vulnerability to racial trauma, inequality, and institutional barriers (Rosen et al., 2024). Thus, Black mothers have often mentally overcompensated to achieve their goals, because society constantly reduces us to conventional gender roles (Hlatshwayo & Ngcobo, 2023; Maluleke et al., 2023; Rosen et al., 2024). This is evident in my narrative as I balanced between being a mother, and wife and trying to maximise my participation as a postdoctoral fellow, which eventually materialised in my excelling in my postdoctoral year.

The Gendering of Black Mothers

Black women have always been positioned as natural home caregivers; and specifically in South Africa, women are typically still regarded as primary caregivers (hooks,

1990; Maluleke et al., 2023; Rosen et al., 2024). When considering my situation and how I needed to relocate to pursue an opportunity, my distance from home and my child played into the notion that my mothering was inadequate because my 'presence' was limited. This is often how mothering is measured, in that the less time we spend with our children, the worse our mothering skills (Maluleke et al., 2023; Rosen et al., 2024). More importantly, this also emphasizes how colonial structures of family and gender roles are still prevalent in our society; and once we deviate from expected norms, we receive criticism.

There is an inherent and sometimes invisible 'burden' that Black women carry merely by being Black women. So often, the language used against Black women can be oppressive and we sometimes, unconsciously use the very same language to be oppressive towards ourselves as women (and Black women). In my narrative, I illustrate that sometimes Black mothers do not unite and implicate one another by policing each other according to conventional and colonial standards of mothering (Arendse, 2021, 2022; Fanon, 2008). There is a need to resist racism and the colonizing mentality that promotes internalized self-hatred. The choice and will that Black women have is often not reflected in the expected natural role they have as women and mothers. The term, 'burden' brings the humanity and identity of the Black mother into question by assuming that the worth or value of mothering conflicts with their education. It removes the possibility of larger aspirations and potential that connect the Black woman to her role as a mother and an academic. It limits the benefits and possibilities that may be attained and instead focuses on the baggage or deficiency that may occur. As such, the emphasis is placed on the duty of Black mothers to be primarily mothers and insinuates that their need for education is an inconvenience. Thus, the concept of burden inherently takes on a negative connotation and serves to reify gender stereotypes. Since the race and gender of a Black mother cannot be separated from her identity, it constantly informs how she navigates the university, her home, motherhood, and society.

In resistance to my not belonging to myself, I reclaim my agency by being both a mother and a career woman. I have a love for both the children and my career, which allows me to embrace a love that is simultaneously gentle and radical. I see this love as a refusal to be stagnant while also pacing myself. As echoed by bell hooks,

> The purpose of resistance is to seek the healing of yourself in order to be able to see clearly…I think that communities of resistance should be places where people can return to themselves more easily, where the conditions are such that they can heal themselves and recover their wholeness. (hooks, 1990: 385)

Through this mindset, resistance for the Black mother does not require glorifying resilient mothering; but instead, it seeks to endorse the act of mothering as a site of resistance within the academy. The Black mother is thus the community of resistance that bell hooks speaks of (1990; Brant, 2023); and she often, through her own navigation of the academy, creates spaces of safety, dignity, and resistance in the academy, as she is forced to navigate a space that does not always welcome her.

The Language of Solidarity

When considering my husband's question to me, '*Is it worth it*?', the question places more emphasis on interrogating the value of the postdoctoral than emphasising the potential value that may be gained from the experience. Through this, the furthering of education by the Black mother is positioned as a liability for their family. In this way, Black men also enact patriarchy on Black women, and thus the "*liberatory struggles has been undermined by efforts to change that subversive home into a site of patriarchal domination of Black women by Black men, where we abuse one another for not conforming to sexist norms*" (hooks, 1990: 388). Although he may have supported me, he was still endorsing the very system that oppresses Black mothers in the academy. Circumstances such as my husband's remark and other comments within my narrative separate us from one another (both my husband and I in our mutual goals but also Black men and women) and impede on our solidarity, which only serves to feed the interests of white supremacy (Brant, 2023; hooks, 1990). In the same way, that language is used against Black mothers, it can also be used for and by Black mothers for purposes of upliftment and solidarity. Using language to liberate ourselves allows us to take back our power and resist. This means that instead of posing questions such as '*Is it worth it*?', a more empowering question may be, '*What opportunities could you gain from this experience*?' Similarly, '*they are a burden to you*' could be reconstructed as '*they will rely on your wisdom, strength, and compassion to find their path in the future*'. By using language for us, we can give voice to our experiences, while also preventing ourselves from self-silencing. It is through this reorganizing of language that we can dismantle colonial and apartheid epistemology (Brant, 2023). My use of autoethnography is an extension of this expression and allows me to give value to my cultural experiences unique to South Africa.

My Embodied Self in the Academy

As a woman with a legal classification as Coloured, my own positionality as a Black woman is absent, as my appearance dictates that I am Coloured in South Africa. As a result, I continue to be racialised and gendered differently to Black women because of the colonial and Apartheid epistemes associated with my appearance as a Coloured woman. Through this logic, my appearance as a racially diverse woman allows me to endure scorn, derogatory connotations, and stereotypes. My identity is further problematised by claims of having '*no culture*'. Thus, my racialised and gendered identity serves to invisiblize me in some spaces while making me hyper-visible in other contexts. More importantly, the stereotypes that are perpetuated against me only serve to dehumanize me (Arendse, 2021, 2022; Lugones, 2010; Mendez, 2015).

Although my gender and race are not explicit in the narrative as conditions that accompanied my experiences, they are inescapable in South Africa, where race often defines belonging. The academy, thus, acts as a microcosm of South African society, in which I am plagued with conditional citizenship due to my gender and race. My identity as a Black and Coloured mother in South Africa navigating the university space propels me to calls for decolonization for both the academy and my identity. It is also through my embodied experience that I consider that there may have been silent yearnings from my ancestors, Black women, who became Black mothers, desiring to be educated whilst still caring for their home and children.

My narrative brings forth the idea that the Black mother has a body that requires discipline in the space of the academy. Thus, pregnancy is perceived as a negation of this discipline by the university that has capitalist agendas and is reliant on Black labour. This is evident in my narrative that disclosed my requirement of publishing two papers. Black women and I would argue Black mothers in the academy are perpetually oppressed (Brant, 2023; Hlatshwayo & Ngcobo, 2023; Maluleke et al., 2023). The system, university, was never designed for Black mothers; and thus, it does not always cater to or serve us. The university has been complicit in the production and reproduction of colonial knowledge and scientific racism. It is therefore expected that Black women and mothers feel vulnerable within the university, as it has been the source of historical violence and discrimination. The system of capitalism, that is supported by the university, has its basis in racism and coloniality and is responsible for my need to juggle between responsibilities so that I can financially provide for my children, escape poverty, and progress in my career.

Although the university is constructed as a capitalist and colonial structure (Brant, 2023; Hlatshwayo & Ngcobo, 2023), it can also be reconceptualised as a homeplace, a space that is physical but liminal. It then becomes a site for both intellectual and spiritual engagement that seeks to elevate the Black mother and not undermine her. Since this is not the current reality at the university, spaces that celebrate Black mothers should be created so that they can share their knowledge and divine wisdom with others. Such spaces should rely on the wisdom of Black mothers to position themselves politically, socially, psychologically, and ethically. The university should facilitate room for Black mothers to share their experiences with others so that it may inform other young women on how they can navigate both motherhood and academia and not see these spaces as mutually exclusive. Their presence would further the perception that motherhood can be liberating and fulfilling in academia and not be viewed as a career-limiting position.

The university may be a site of colonial reproduction, but it can be imagined as a decolonial site that resists its colonial roots. This reimagined university creates space for resistance, revolution, and reinvention and welcomes the insights of indigenous and African ways of knowing. More importantly, this reimagined university should offer safety to those facing racial trauma, inequality, discrimination, and subjugation, thereby creating a more inclusive space (Brant, 2023).

Mothering as Decolonial Love

Based on my experiences, the concept of decolonial love becomes a necessity. For me, decolonial love means that I must love myself regardless of whether I can exit the systems of oppression created by colonial and apartheid systems, I need to remember my worth and my contribution to knowledge matters. I, therefore, define decolonial love as a radical love that moves us past the grips of colonial and apartheid traumas to a space of self-love and healing. It is through decolonial love that I embrace my contested identity in South Africa and appreciate the intricate Blackness I embody. It is also through such love, that plurality in identity is possible and my identity as both Black and Coloured are expressions of my rich cultural ancestry. As such, in a space such as South Africa where racial identities are still quite enmeshed in Apartheid logic, there is a need to resist the suppression of diverse identities.

In my narrative, my sacrifices to further my education and take hold of an opportunity to further my career is a testament to decolonial love. Although others may perceive me as a poor mother due to their attachment to colonial and apartheid ideas of mothering, my resistance, and continued perseverance are what transformed my mothering into a decolonial praxis. My children and my career are both valuable entities to me; and they do not need to be binaries flung up against each other, since they are interwoven into my life. Having said this, if I do not practice decolonial love, I will be reduced to inhumanity every time words are uttered against me or in opposition to me. Embracing decolonial love makes me aware that when others oppose me, they are perhaps under the illusion of coloniality and apartheid, and they have not yet embraced a decolonial way of being.

Through this conception of decolonial love, we, as Black women, are the very expression of love and abundance; and we need to remind ourselves that we are epistemes that can radically change the university. We do not need to wait for colonial and patriarchal institutions, such as the university, to shed their supremacy and hegemony. Instead, we need to embrace ourselves as knowledge bringers to the university and reclaim our connection to knowledge production. As Butler indicates, "*decolonial love is an act of radical resistance against the hegemony of colonialism and White supremacist patriarchy*" (Butler, 2023: 1389). In this way, we do not seek to conform to a particular norm or endeavour to be perpetual students; rather we exchange knowledge, as we know to give the university as well (Butler, 2023). It therefore moves away from colonially and apartheid-informed notions of who may contribute to knowledge and be the knower.

This is crucial since Black academic women, including students, are characterised as having illegitimate epistemes and are thereby reduced to 'non-beings' in the university (Hlatshwayo & Ngcobo, 2023). Thus, by glorifying the magnitude of obstacles one needs to endure as a Black mother as part of conforming and excelling in the university, we only reproduce colonial and apartheid epistemes of the university. Instead of seeing ourselves as burdensome, we must see our critical contribution to pedagogy in the university. Moreover, decolonial love advocates that we no longer value colonial and apartheid ideas of mothering and the role of women in the university (Butler, 2023). The binary of home and the university as mutually exclusive sites for Black women must be resisted, as our connection to the university and our role therein are fluid. Our experiences are not static and separate but intertwined. I therefore celebrate Black women in all their glory, as we not only embody 'Imbokotho (a rock)' but also decolonial love.

Concluding Thoughts

We must exercise care with ourselves in shaping the university space because for the university to embrace decolonial love, would mean that it needs to relinquish itself of patriarchy, colonialism, and apartheid. This transformation is, however, only possible once we have also resolved our traumas as Black mothers and allowed ourselves the opportunity to reclaim our humanity (Butler, 2023). Therefore, the notion of the Black mother in the academy does not need to take the role of a continuously burdened subject that must overcome challenges and overcompensate by over-achieving academically, but rather towards inclusionary notions of mothers as full citizens of the academy because "*freedom cannot be achieved unless women have been emancipated from all forms of oppression*" (Nelson Mandela).

Competing Interests This work is based on the research supported by the National Institute for the Humanities and Social Sciences (NIHSS). The views expressed in this article are those of the author alone and are not attributable to any institution.

References

Adhikari, M. (2006). Hope, fear, shame, frustration: Continuity and change in the expression of coloured identity in white supremacist South Africa, 1910–1994. *Journal of Southern African Studies, 32*(3), 468–487. https://doi.org/10.1080/03057070600718594

Arendse, D. E. (2021). Culture as a colonial hub: My reflections as a 'coloured' [woman] in post-apartheid South Africa. *Journal of Intercultural Studies, 42*(4), 515–527. https://doi.org/10.1080/07256868.2021.1904233

Arendse, D. E. (2022). Soldier and psychologist by day, PhD student by night. In R. Murambadoro, J. Mashayamombe, & uMbuso Wenkosi (Eds.), *The PhD experience in African higher education* (pp. 115–128). Rowman & Littlefield.

Biko, S. (2004). *I write what I like: A selection of writings*. Picador.

Boddy-Evans, A. (2024, June 25). *Apartheid quotes about bantu education*. Retrieved from https://www.thoughtco.com/apartheid-quotes-bantu-education-43436

Brant, J. (2023). Finding homeplace within indigenous literatures: Honoring the genealogical legacies of bell hooks and Lee Maracle. *Hypatia, 38*, 45–64. https://doi.org/10.1017/hyp.2022.63

Butler, A. (2023). Decolonial love as a pedagogy of care for Black immigrant post-secondary students. *British Journal of Sociology of Education, 44*(8), 1378–1393. https://doi.org/10.1080/01425692.2023.2260113

Crenshaw, K. (1994). Mapping the margins: Intersectionality, identity politics, and violence against women of colour. In M. A. Fineman & R. Mykitiuk (Eds.), *The public nature of private violence* (pp. 93–118). Routledge.
Ellis, C., Adams, T. E., & Bochner, A. P. (2010). Autoethnography: An overview. *Historical Social Research, 12*, 273–290.
Fanon, F. (2008). *Black skin, white masks*. Pluto Press.
Hlatshwayo, M. N., & Ngcobo, B. M. (2023). Are we there yet? An intersectional take on Black women academics' experiences in a South African University. *Journal of Education, 92*, 169–185. https://doi.org/10.17159/2520-9868/i92a10
hooks, B. (1990). Homeplace (a site of resistance). In *Yearning: Race, gender, and cultural politics* (pp. 41–49). South End Press.
Kaufman, C. E. (2000). Reproductive control in apartheid South Africa. *Population Studies, 54*(1), 105–114. https://www.jstor.org/stable/2584636
Lewis, D. (2001). African feminisms. *Agenda, 16*(50), 4–10. https://doi.org/10.1080/10130950.2001.9675989
Lugones, M. (2010). Towards a decolonial feminism. *Hypatia, 25*(4), 742–759. https://doi.org/10.1111/j.1527-2001.2010.01161.x
Lugones, M. (2014). Radical multiculturalism and women of color feminisms. *Journal of Cultural and Religious Theory, 13*(1), 68–80. https://jcrt.org/archives/13.1/lugones.pdf
Maluleke, U., Senekal, J., Munnik, E., & Somhlaba, N. (2023). Balancing dual roles as mothers and students like a walk on a tight rope? Reflections and experiences of student mothers at a South African higher education institution. *South African Journal of Higher Education, 37*(3). https://doi.org/10.20853/37-3-5448
Meer, F. (1985). *Women in the apartheid society* (Reports). United Nations Centre Against Apartheid. https://jstor.org/stable/al.sff.document.nuun1985_04
Mendez, X. (2015). Notes toward a decolonial feminist methodology: Revisiting the race/gender matrix. *Trans-scripts, 5*, 41–59.
Mkhize, N., & Msomi, R. (2016). African single mothers' experiences of work and career in South Africa. *Journal of Comparative Family Studies, 47*(3), 323–342. https://www.jstor.org/stable/44109629
Moya, P. M. L. (2012, June 26). The search for decolonial love: An interview with Junot Díaz. *Boston Review*. https://www.bostonreview.net/articles/paula-ml-moya-decolonial-love-interviewjunot-diaz/
Phakeng, M. (2015). Leadership: The invisibility of African women and the masculinity of power. *South African Journal of Science, 111*(11/12), 1–2.
Radcliffe, S. A. (2017). Decolonizing geographical knowledges. *Transactions of the Institute of British Geographers, 42*, 329–333. https://doi.org/10.1111/tran.12153
Rosen, L. H., Scott, S. R., Shukla, R., Poe, D., & Ahmed, S. (2024). The pandemic and working mothers: Perspectives from American and South African working mothers. *Discover Psychology, 4*(56), 1–15. https://doi.org/10.1007/s44202-024-00165-y
Salem, S. (2014, April 17). Decolonial intersectionality and a transnational feminist movement. *Feminist Wire*. http://thefeministwire.com
Shwaikh, M. (2023). Beyond expectations of resilience: Towards a language of care. *Global Studies Quarterly, 3*(2), 17(1–13). https://doi.org/10.1093/isagsq/ksad030
Soja, E. W. (1996). *Thirdspace: Journeys to Los Angeles and other real-and-imagined places*. Blackwell.
Tabata, I. B. (1980). *Education for barbarism: Bantu (apartheid) education in South Africa*. Unity Movement of South Africa.

Danille Elize Arendse obtained her PhD in Psychology from the University of Pretoria and also holds a BA (psychology), BA Honours degree (Psychology) and MA (Research Psychology) degree from the University of the Western Cape. She joined the SANDF in 2011 as a uniformed member and became employed as a Research Psychologist at the Military Psychological Institute (MPI). She holds a Major rank and has previously taken on the role of Research Psychology Intern Supervisor and Coordinator at MPI. Additionally, she serves as a Research Associate for the Department of Psychology at the University of Pretoria and is an Accredited Conflict Dynamics Mediator. In 2022, she was awarded the Diverse Black Africa research and travel grants from Michigan State University and in 2023, she was awarded the prestigious NIHSS/SU postdoctoral fellowship at the Centre for the Study of the Afterlife of Violence and the Reparative Quest (AVReQ) at Stellenbosch University. She has presented and published papers both locally and internationally and currently practises as a Research Psychologist at MPI. Her research interests include: Coloured identity in South Africa, mentoring, psychometric assessments, military studies, wellbeing, gender, and decolonial research.

Theorizing Motherhood

I Know It in My Knower: Testaments of Spirituality Within Critical Race Mothering

Larissa Malone

Abstract The purpose of this research is to discuss how spirituality is ever-present in Black mother scholarship via a tenet of critical race mothering, an emerging conduit to share mothers' experiences as they navigate a racialized world. Three autoethnographic counternarratives explore spirituality and depict how critical race mothering can be a vehicle to understand, process, and confront racialized injustices. Critical race mothering validates spiritual identity as a powerful asset and implications highlight that the expectation of scholars to quelch their spiritual identity in their research and praxis, deny the power that is located within Black women scholars.

Keywords Critical race mothering · Spirituality · Critical race theory · Black mother scholarship · Autoethnographic counternarratives

One of my earliest memories is witnessing my mother being ushered into a realm that was not of this earth. I recall sitting in a pew early on a Sunday morning. My mother stood next to me with her hands uplifted in worship as tears ran down her face as she swayed along to the choir's soulful melody, that demonstrably resonated with her spirit. She looked uninhibited, transcendent, and simply beautiful. My mother, in this purified state of being, is the first image that appeared in my mind as I sat down to write this essay. I thought it only apropos that I opened with this recollection because it coalesces the power, influence, and legacy of spirituality located within critical race mothering. Spirituality means different things to different people. In this writing, I use the term interchangeably with the religion I practice and the faith I exercise on a daily basis, especially from the aspect of working towards a brighter future through my life's calling of being a critical race motherscholar. I invite readers to adapt this writing to the terms in which you define spirituality and make meaning of it through that lens. While reading, I hope readers will consciously reflect upon memories of mothering and spirituality as I share my positionality, the theoretical development of spirituality within critical race mothering, and discuss three autoethnographic

L. Malone (✉)
University of North Carolina Wilmington, Wilmington, NC, USA
e-mail: malonel@uncw.edu

C. R. Turner and M. L. Green (eds.), *Black Motherscholarship Within and Beyond the Academy*, https://doi.org/10.1007/978-3-031-99758-7_5

counternarratives that explicate the ways that the divine is ever-present in the lives of motherscholars.

My Spiritual Positionality

I am an Afro-Borinquen mother who identifies as a Black woman. Professionally, I have always been in the field of education, first as a Montessori teacher, then as a school administrator, and, currently, as an associate professor in social and cultural foundations at a public institution of higher education in the United States. Personally, I met my husband of over 25 years at the church I attended. We have raised three beautiful girls together that are now all young adults blossoming on their own paths. Although I was raised in church by two Christian parents, it wasn't until my college years that I experienced the joyful freedom in worship that my mother modeled for me in my early years. This blissful state became, and remains, my place of rejuvenation in my adult life. It is this place that I consider my ultimate act of self-care and where I find rest.

It is also the place where I process and receive clear direction for both my professional and personal choices. Yet, for most of my career I did not allow my spirituality to fully enter my critical race scholarship. It wasn't until a colleague exposed me to gospel writings that located race within theology (Cleveland, 2013; Cone, 1969, 1997, 2011; Harper, 2016; Thurman, 1976) that I considered that the opposite may also be true: there is spirituality located within race work. This led me to take a deep dive into the work of Derrick Bell, the godfather of critical race theory, and explicate the faith-based undertones within his work (Bell, 1980a, 1987, 1992, 1996, 2002, 2004). For example, Bell incorporated spiritual nomenclature and metaphorical imagery, critiqued Christianity alongside white supremacy, expressed a deep concern regarding the impact of racism on the human spirit, and capitalized on the strength that faith provides when combatting racism (Malone & Lachaud, 2022). Further, Bracey (2022) connected the existing tenets of critical race theory to religiosity to showcase that spirituality can serve as an act of resistance in a racially unjust world and that critical race theory often operates in the same vein and the same purpose of religion, especially in communities of color.

I learned to lean into spirituality just as much as I did my other identities expressed within my scholarship, such as my gender and race. The expansion of embracing my spirituality in my research endeavors broadened other aspects of my professorship as well. For example, although I've taught education courses on multiculturality and equity for years in teacher certification programs, I previously did not require my students to deeply grapple with how their religious identity influenced how they approached teaching and the ways in which their faith dictated their views on curricula and their future students. Now that I do, my students are typically surprised that spirituality is an identity marker I ask them to consider, although they usually indicate during the classroom introductory questionnaire that 'God' or 'church' is what is most important to them. When we delve into the literature illustrating that most educators are not only white and female (NCES, 2024; Schaeffer, 2024), but most also attend church at a much higher rate than the general population (Slater, 2007), my students begin to make the connection that their race, gender, economic, *and* religious identity shape how they see the world and their presence in K-12 learning environments.

Theorizing Critical Race Mothering

I only recently began to formally write about critical race mothering. Yet, in praxis I learned how to maneuver through the world as a racialized maternal being as soon as I had children. In fact, in many ways, my children and I navigated schooling at the same time, as I was in my master's and doctoral program, contemplating social theories that attempted to explain the experiences of families in school, while mothering school-age children. Yet, much of what I was experiencing as a real-life mother of color was not fully captured in the existent literature; and the literary concepts that did resonate with my lived experience, such as the race and racism experienced by persons of color in the education system, were rarely from the perspective of mothering. To this end, I saw a need to develop critical race mothering, a subfield of critical race theory (Bell, 1992; Delgado & Stefancic, 2001; Ladson-Billings & Tate, 1995), as a mechanism to share the experience of mothers of color as they navigate raising children in a racialized world, namely through educational institutions. Because research is influenced by the researcher's lens (research is me-search), I had critical race education scholars in mind during the conceptualization process of critical race mothering. However, as I moved deeper into theorizing, I realized that critical race mothering needed to be an accessible platform for all mothers of color because collectively, and regardless of profession, our voices are persistently marginalized.

Critical race mothering is inspired by the theory of critical race parenting (DePouw & Matias, 2016; Matias, 2016; Montoya & Sarcedo, 2018), "defined as an educational praxis that can engage both parent and child in a mutual process of teaching and learning about race, especially ones that debunk dominant messages about race" (Matias, 2016, p. 3). Whereas critical race parenting flattens the definition of mothering to include a variety of relationships between an adult and a child claiming, "that fathers and men can, at times, also exhibit maternalism" (Matias, 2016, p. 6), critical race mothering diverges in that it embraces the unique role and positioning of mothering held by women. Further, critical race mothering aims to address the essential question posed by Hudson-Weems (2020, p. 10), "what is the relationship between an Africana woman and her family, her community and her career in today's society that emphasizes, in the midst of oppression, human suffering and death?", through a maternal lens. Further, critical race mothering expands Hudson-Weems' (2020) quandary to all women of color, given the shared experience of existing in a white supremacist culture across marginalized races and ethnicities.

Critical race mothering galvanizes critical race theory tenets to provide insight to counterstories of mothering (Solórzano & Yosso, 2002)—specifically permanence of racism and racial realism (Bell, 1992; Delgado & Stefancic, 2001), the critique of liberalism (DeCuir & Dixson, 2004), interest convergence (Bell, 1980b) and whiteness as property (Harris, 1993)—and also recognizes the contemporary ways women of color mothering has been politicized (Nash, 2021; Roebuck Sahko, 2017). Additionally, based on my experiences, formal and informal research with other mothers of color over the years, and literature on Black mothering (Corley et al., 2020; Huguley et al., 2020; McGee & Spencer, 2015; Robinson & Werblow, 2012, 2013), I have curated the following tenets for critical race mothering: (1) mothering as teacher, (2) mothering as advocate, (3) mothering as spirituality, and (4) mothering as love, and (5) mothering as potentiality. I introduced the meaning of each of the critical race mothering tenets in a previous presentation (Malone, 2023) and will expand upon them in an upcoming publication. Because of limited space and call for focus here, I will only debrief the third tenet of mothering as spirituality in this writing.

Epistemologically, the mothering as spirituality tenet is framed by endarkened feminism (Dillard, 2000) and spiritual (re)membering (Dillard & Neal, 2021), which allows for beliefs and identities of the researcher to shape ideologies, approaches, and a deep mindfulness of and responsibility to the researched. The mothering as spirituality tenet is also informed by the legal field's recognition that harm caused by racism murders the spirit (Love, 2019; Williams, 1991) and that children of color often miss out on "the spiritual uplift and self-assurance" (Bell, 1980b, p. 138) when they are in educational spaces that are not designed with them in mind. The mothering as spirituality tenet is theologically guided by both the work of Cleveland (2022) that helps us imagine, that if we are made in the image of a higher power, then the higher power can and must resemble us, and the work of Cone (1969) that posits that the heavens are as concerned about liberating and empowering persons of color as those that are oppressed. Philosophically, the mothering as spirituality tenet capitalizes upon the dynamic of spirituality identified in Africana Womanism, "which brings into account the power of faith, healing, and the unknown" (Hudson-Weems, 2020, p. 46) and honors "reliance upon the inner spirit or mind" (Hudson-Weems, 2020, p. 46). The development of the mothering as spirituality tenets of critical race mothering is also influenced by the work of Dillard (2006, 2022), Witherspoon and Mitchell (2009), and Witherspoon Arnold et al. (2014), scholarship that centers upon spirituality in education. These writings outline how educators can connect and (re)member the amalgamation of race and spirit and illustrate how educators operationalize criticality in spiritual ways when navigating hostile places.

Critical Race Mothering Autoethnographic Counternarratives

I will now share three autoethnographic counternarratives to testify how the mothering as spirituality tenet is operationalized in the life of a Black motherscholar. As a new empty-nester, I've been reflecting a great deal on the last couple of decades of my life that have mainly consisted of child rearing at the forefront. Through this process, multiple memories arose to the surface of my mind. I began to document specific incidents that occurred, honing in on those related to my work as a critical race scholar. I not only captured the memories from my perspective, but from time to time, I would have conversations with my children. From this, I was not only able to confirm the accuracy of my recollections, but I was also able to weave elements of their perspectives into the narrative that provided a fuller picture. This process, aligned with leading scholarship on qualitative narrative inquiry (Connelly & Clandinin, 1990; Evans-Winters, 2019; Johns, 2020), provided rich stories. I was then able to connect these stories to a variety of literature related to a range of leading topics in education such as multicultural child development and culturally relevant teaching, and in the case of the autoethnographic counternarratives shared here, spirituality, during the process of critical content analysis.

Critical content analysis aims to "locate power in social practices in order to challenge conditions of inequity" (Short, 2017, p. 1). As I read and re-read over the stories I wrote, I was able to extrapolate theoretical truths related to the tenet of mothering as spirituality from seemingly ordinary experiences. Similar to other critical methodologies, critical race analysis works in tandem with a critical theory and has no expectation for the research or the researcher to be politically neutral (Short, 2017). I hope that these narrations not only reveal the power of spirituality within critical race mothering to overcome the endemic bigotry within American schooling but will also encourage others to expressly articulate their spiritual triumphs and struggles that we often mask behind rational, emotional, and physical constructs while practicing Black motherscholarship.

Autoethnographic Counternarrative #1: Is Hate Different from Those We Love?

I typically picked up my daughter from high school during her freshman year to take her to her dance lessons that took place directly after school. Although she attended our local public school, there were many well-respected private schools that were also located within the district boundaries. She knew many of the students in these private schools because some of her friends from middle school elected to enroll in them or because they attended the same dance studio. Earlier that day, I received a message from her superintendent to let parents know that a right-wing church group, known for traveling the country in opposition to LGBTQIA+ rights and individuals, planned to be in the area and was targeting one of the private schools. The organization, categorized as a hate group by the Southern Law Poverty Center, was coming to protest a star student-athlete at the private school that had come out as gay during an public interview earlier that year. The superintendent stated that counter-protests were being planned. In contravention, the school was hosting an in-school assembly celebrating diversity to discourage students from engaging with the protestors. The message ended with the school's commitment to equity and inclusion and a provision of community resources that parents might find useful.

On the drive to dance class, I asked my daughter if she had heard about the protest and counter-protest that were planned for the following day. She had, and, while she didn't know the student, she had friends who did and said he was popular and well-liked. I expressed to her how disgusted I was that this group was coming in from another state to protest a child's identity. I lamented that the group's name went under the guise of 'a church' but they were the antithesis of representing Jesus, who urged us to love our neighbor, not demonize their existence. My daughter, who is typically quite talkative, didn't really say much as I gave my stump speech on the intersection of religion and equity. When I finished speaking, there was a long moment of silence. Then my daughter said quietly, "You know our Bishop does the same thing, right?"

After pausing for a second because I was completely caught off guard by her comment, I automatically jumped into a defensive mode. We had attended our church for over 30 years. It was, without a doubt, our spiritual lifesource and home away from home. My husband and I had met and were married at this church and had since served in ministry and raised our children there. I began to explain to her that our Bishop was from a different generation and 'didn't mean no harm'. She pointed out that he frequently targeted homosexuality in his messages and that it was no different than what the hate group was doing, and, in fact, it might be worse because he was saying it in church that was supposed to be about saving souls. She further rebutted that he often said sexist remarks when he was ministering that were oppressive to women and confined them to archaic roles in church and in society.

As we pulled up to her dance school, I was a little relieved because it meant I had time to sort out my own feelings before we continued the conversation. I loved giving my children the traditional Black church experience. Moreover, I also loved my Bishop who had grown into being a second father to me over the years. However, I did not realize (or at least did not admit out loud) the ways in which our ministry upheld multiple oppressive ideas and how it conflicted with my scholarship, teaching, and service and my own belief system. Additionally, I did not want my daughter to be imprinted with the hypocrisy within our church and be turned off from spirituality forever. She had given me a lot to think about and, post-reflection, it pushed me to challenge all forms of oppression in my spiritual, professional, and home life—regardless of familiarity and tradition. This was the catalyst for me to come to terms that I could not tolerate hate, even from those I loved, and doing so would mean that I would not only have to require more from my own spirituality, but also from my spiritual home.

Autoethnographic Counternarrative #2: Is White Jesus for Us?

Both my husband and I worked in higher education, so our children were obligated to visit our places of employment when they were considering where they would attend college because of the perk of tuition remission. When my eldest daughter was making the college decision, we knew she would have other scholarship options because she was a good student-athlete. However, with her being our first-born, I was worried about her going to a university that was too big where she might get lost in the mix. Thus, in many ways, the institution I worked for at the time, a small faith-based institution that was in a rural environment, really appealed to my desire to keep her safe. I hoped she would consider it as a viable option as she contemplated where she would call home for the next four years.

When she visited my school, she met with two students that gave her a personal tour, as well as representatives of the major she was considering and several members of the athletic department, including her potential coach and athletic director. The school truly rolled out the red carpet for her. I knew that this was partly because she was my daughter and would be a strong asset to their sports program. But I also sensed it was because she was a student of color and the university was working hard on diversifying the student body.

On our drive home, she unequivocally informed me she would not be attending this institution. While she was not at all enthusiastic before she visited the school, her tone let me know that something more was going on beyond the typical teenage malaise. I asked her what made her so adamant that this college was not the school for her. I knew many of the staff she had met on her visit; and they were all very kind, outgoing, people. I questioned her, "weren't they nice to you?" She responded, "Yes, too nice. Like almost creepy nice. Like disconnected from the real world, kind of nice." While she was talking, a scene from the *Stepford Wives* flashed in my mind and I immediately knew what she meant, for I had experienced my own moments of 'too nice' at my institution.

While I was excited at the idea of working at an institution that blended my professional career and my spirituality, I soon realized that their idea of faith was wholly rooted in whiteness. For example, chapel, a service that was open to the entire college community between classes, played traditional white Christian music and the speaker delivered a speech that was void of many of the characteristics of a Black church, such as call and response. The institution not only kept Black culture out, they also perpetually kept white culture in. Many of the students grew up in close proximity to the campus and, although a major metropolitan city was located less than an hour away, most have never traveled to it. It was as if the institution naturally attracted students that grew up in a bubble-wrapped world.

Additionally, almost all the leadership roles were held by white males, many of which had legacy affiliation with the institution that could be traced back multiple generations. In my time there, when issues of race came up, leaders typically defaulted with a colorblind response that "we were all one in Christ", as if acknowledging lived experiences of racism somehow was a contradiction to identifying as a spiritual being. It was no wonder that my daughter could not see herself *at* the institution because she could not see herself *in* the institution. As my daughter continued to talk and I simultaneously reflected on my own experience, I could do nothing but agree with her that this school was not a good fit for her after all. I immediately made peace with her decision.

Autoethnographic Counternarrative #3: How Do I Know What I Know?

Throughout the time of raising my children, there were many spaces where there were unspoken rules. These rules were more prominent in certain spaces more than others, and I really felt the establishment of a 'hidden curriculum' in the independent private school my daughters attended for their elementary and middle years. The school prided itself for its cultural inclusivity on paper but, in reality, had an almost all white staff and student population. We were a double-minority in this elite educational space, in that we were not only racially minoritized, but economically minoritized too. Because of these factors, I often felt like we were two steps behind. I found myself overly dependent on trusting my gut when I sensed there were rules at play that the school assumed I knew, but I didn't because we were neither white nor wealthy.

One example that readily comes to my mind is when one of my three daughters became sick in school and I needed to pick her up during the middle of the day. I arrived at the school ready to gather all my children. After all, the drive from our house to the school was about 30 min. and the school day was about halfway over. However, when I arrived at the school to collect the whole family, the school nurse only brought up my one daughter that I received the call about. I stood there awkwardly for a few seconds and sensed that the expectation was for me to leave my other two children in school to finish out the rest of their studies. I grabbed my sick daughter's hand and the two of us left out of the school's main entrance. When I got in the car, I called my husband and told him what had occurred. He was as puzzled as I was, and exclaimed, "If WE are sick, WE are all coming home, right?" While I agreed with him, I could sense that an individualist orientation (white supremacy culture) vs. collectivist orientation (most non-white cultures) was at play. I could also sense that our family was expected to conform to the dominant culture's mindset. And if it was not for my ability to quickly pick up what the school representative was putting down, it would have made for an awkward interaction.

Another instance of exercising instinctual knowledge occurred at eighth-grade graduation. Traditionally, the head of the middle school said something special about each student during the ceremony. He seemed to take great care in providing customized antidotes for each graduate. As background, neither myself or my daughter were particularly fond of the head of the middle school because of how he treated my daughter, consistently assuming she was on the wrong side of situations. While my daughter would outrightly declare that he did not like her because she was Black though, as a fellow educator, I tried to be more understanding and give him the benefit of the doubt. He and I had met several times, sometimes by his initiation and other times by mine, about her behavior and academic idiosyncrasies throughout her middle school experience. She was one of only two girls of color in her entire grade. I felt strongly in my heart that regardless of what came out of his mouth during meetings, he was secretly upset because my daughter's differences forced him to expand his way of thinking and acquiesce to accommodations he was not used to providing. Yet, I continued to work with him through different issues during her middle school years in hopes our collaboration would raise his level of racial literacy. At graduation though, my premonition, and, more importantly, my daughter's declaration that his antics were rooted in racism, was confirmed when she walked across the graduation stage and he pronounced, "may she learn how to quickly assimilate to her new school environment so that she can have a good high school experience"—blaming her unique race and ethnicity for his inability to create a sense of belonging for her.

I could provide hundreds of examples as a mother that required me to 'know in my knower', an old saying that is often used in traditional Black churches to express one's assured belief in something without the ability to prove it beyond a quickening in the spirit, but the best illustrations come directly from my daughters. Several times throughout their upbringing, and as early as preschool, they would, from time to time, feel uncomfortable with certain people they encountered, whether it be a certain teacher or with a particular friend group at school. Early on, I would contribute their hesitancy to shyness or something of the like, but after the second or third time of finding out later that the people they were hesitant about turned out to regularly practice bigotry, I realized that my daughters had the ability to sense who was not in their corner, even if they were not able to specifically articulate why. I began to trust their intuition, and this aided in our navigation of the complex web of white supremacy in educational institutions.

The Significance of Spirituality in Critical Race Mothering

I chose these stories to share because they each touch upon faith in different ways and across various types of educational institutions to showcase how spirituality is interwoven into the fabric of critical race mothering. Individually, each narrative undergirds the tenet of spirituality in critical race mothering. In the first autoethnographic counternarrative, it was my daughter who pointed out that faith could be used as an excuse for discrimination; and she boldly pointed out that both gender and sexual orientation bigotry regularly occurred not only in schools, but in our chosen place of worship too. In doing so, my daughter illustrated that critical race mothering is a co-construction of how race, racism, and other bigotries infiltrate our lives as we both continue to make meaning of the world around us (Evans-Winters, 2019).

In the second autoethnographic counternarrative, it was clear that my daughter, a young Black woman, felt the faith-based institution of higher education she visited did not include her when they constructed knowledge (Dillard, 2000). Their interpretation of faith included God as a "powerful white man who is for and with powerful white men" only (Cleveland, 2022, p. 15). In the third narrative, I illustrate that without trusting in my cultural intuition, a concept derived by Delgado Bernal (1998) that validates historical, communal, and spiritual ways of knowing as legitimate sources, I would not have been able to navigate educational spaces. Indeed, using spiritual capital, a "set of resources and skills rooted in a spiritual connection to a reality greater than oneself" (Perez Huber, 2009, p. 721), proved to be a necessity while critical race mothering, for both my daughters and myself.

Viewing the autoethnographic counternarratives cross-sectionally, elements of critical race theory as related to mothering are apparent. Elements of racial injustice are present in each of the stories. My heart breaks a bit to look back and see that racism was so very real, almost customary, to my daughters at such an early age. And while their spirits may not have been fully murdered by any one encounter (Williams, 1991), the educational institutions mentioned in the autoethnographic counternarratives did very little to uplift them (Bell, 1980b). Further, in the first autoethnographic counternarrative, church, a spiritual institution, did little to squelch the bigotry of sexism and sexual orientation and actually exacerbated them. Conversely, a positive throughline across the autoethnographic counternarratives is the ability to rely on spirituality to make the unknown known in situations (Hudson-Weems, 2020). This is best seen in the various examples provided in the third autoethnographic counternarratives where faith provided the ability of discernment. Indeed, critical race theory tenets are intertwined with concepts that are intangible and require a large amount of trust in intuition and, critical race mothering as an offshoot, is no different.

Concluding Thoughts

I now return to the essential question that critical race mothering seeks to answer, "what is the relationship between an Africana woman and her family, her community and her career in today's society that emphasizes, in the midst of oppression, human suffering and death?" (Hudson-Weems, 2020, p. 10). To be sure, being a Black motherscholar is complex. Battles are constant and the road is not easy. I am thankful that both my daughters and I recognized that we needed to be in spaces that fully accepted us. I am also grateful that we also recognized that if we found ourselves in spaces that did not, we knew to tap into the spirituality located within us to persevere.

Rarely is consideration made for the spirituality that Black motherscholars regularly exercise, although it is a prominent feature of how women of color navigate predominantly white spaces, inclusive of higher education. This work encourages all educational institutions, and specifically institutions of higher learning where Black motherscholars are employed, to make space for the expression of spirituality in teaching, scholarship, and service and to view spirituality as validate and credible knowledge. Further, it is important for Black motherscholars to share their mothering experiences in their scholarship. I encourage other Black motherscholars to specifically incorporate aspects of spirituality within their mothering scholarship to continue to highlight the importance of this work and expand the conversations surrounding this often overlooked area of research. Lastly, as motherscholars we are often fluent in the institutional language that resonates with those in power. We must make sure that we are providing a voice for all mothers of color, especially those outside the academy, that are struggling with the same issues but may not have the theoretical prowess to support their children's navigation through hostile spaces.

Although decades have passed since the opening memory of my mother worshiping in church, it is still an image that I hold dear to my heart. I remain thankful to my mother for being the first shining example of what it can mean 'to be in this world, and not of this world'. I know these early spiritual experiences shaped who I am today and empower me to continue to be the Black motherscholar that I am intended to be. To be certain, this memory, and others like it, have been the catalyst that has spurred bringing together education, motherhood, and spirituality in order to theorize critical race mothering. It is my ultimate prayer that, through our shared lived experiences, my own daughters will be able to look back on the memories that we made together and see the spirituality that we exhibited as a powerful asset to confront racial injustice.

Competing Interests The author has no conflicts of interest to declare that are relevant to the content of this manuscript.

References

Bell, D. A. (1980a). *Shades of Brown: New perspectives on school desegregation.* Teachers College Press.

Bell, D. A. (1980b). Brown and the interest-convergence dilemma. In D. A. Bell (Ed.), *Shades of Brown: New perspectives on school desegregation* (pp. 91–106). Teachers College Press.

Bell, D. A. (1987). *And we are not saved: The elusive quest for racial justice.* Basic Books.

Bell, D. A. (1992). *Faces at the bottom of the well: The permanence of racism.* Perseus Books.

Bell, D. A. (1996). *Gospel choirs: Psalms of survival in an alien land called home.* Basic Books.

Bell, D. A. (2002). *Ethical ambition: Living a life of meaning and worth.* Bloomsbury.

Bell, D. A. (2004). *Silent covenants: Brown v. board of education and the unfulfilled hopes for racial reform.* Oxford University Press.

Bracey II, G. E. (2022). The spirit of critical race theory. *Sociology of Race and Ethnicity, 8*(4), 503–517. https://doi.org/10.1177/23326492221114814

Cleveland, C. (2013). *Disunity in Christ: Uncovering the hidden forces that keep us apart.* IVP Books.

Cleveland, C. (2022). *God is a Black woman.* Harper One.

Cone, J. H. (1969). *Black theology & Black power.* Harper & Row.

Cone, J. H. (1997). *God of the oppressed.* Orbis Books.

Cone, J. H. (2011). *The cross and the lynching tree.* Orbis Books.

Connelly, F. M., & Clandinin, D. J. (1990). Stories of experience and narrative inquiry. *Educational Researcher, 19*(5), 2–14. https://doi.org/10.3102/0013189X019005002

Corley, N. A., Reeves, P., & Odera, S. G. (2020). "That's just who I am": African American high school seniors and their mothers perspective on academic success. *Child and Adolescent Social Work Journal, 37*(1), 25–37. https://doi.org/10.1007/s10560-019-00621-y

DeCuir, J.T., & Dixson, A.D. (2004). 'So, when it comes out, they aren't that surprised that it is there': Using critical race theory as a tool of analysis of race and racism in education. *Educational Researcher, 33*(5), 26–31. https://doi.org/10.3102/0013189X033005026

Delgado Bernal, D. (1998). Using a Chicana feminist epistemology in educational research. *Harvard Educational Review, 68*(4), 555–582. https://doi.org/10.1177/107780040200800103

Delgado, R., & Stefancic, J. (2001). *Critical race theory: An introduction.* NYU Press.

DePouw, C., & Matias, C. (2016). Critical race parenting: Understanding scholarship/activism in parenting our children. *Educational Studies, 52*(3), 237–259. https://doi.org/10.1080/00131946.2016.1169182

Dillard, C. B. (2000). The substance of things hoped for, the evidence of things not seen: Examining an endarkened feminist epistemology in educational research and leadership. *International Journal of Qualitative Studies in Education, 13*(2), 661–681. https://doi.org/10.1080/09518390050211565

Dillard. C. B. (2006). *On spiritual strivings: Transforming an African American woman's academic life.* State University of New York Press.

Dillard, C. B. (2022). *The spirit of our work: Black women teachers (re)member.* Beacon Press.

Dillard, C. B., & Neal, A. M. (2021). Still following our north star: The necessity of Black women's spiritual (re)membering in qualitative (re)search. *Qualitative Inquiry, 27*(10), 1139–1253. https://doi-org.liblink.uncw.edu/10/1177/1078004211021809

Evans-Winters, V. E. (2019). *Black feminism in qualitative inquiry.* Routledge.

Harper, L. S. (2016). *The very good gospel: How everything wrong can be made right.* Waterbrook.

Harris, C. I. (1993). Whiteness as property. *Harvard Law Review, 106*(8), 1707–1791.

Hudson-Weems, C. (2020). Africana womanism: Reclaiming ourselves. Routledge.

Huguley, J. P., Delale-O'Connor, L., Wang, M., & Parr, A. K. (2020). African American parent's educational involvement in urban schools: Contextualized strategies for student success in adolescence. *Educational Researcher, 50*(1), 6–16. https://doi-org.liblink.uncw.edu/10.3102/0013189X20943199

Johns, C. (2020). *Reflexive narrative: Self inquiry toward self-realization and its performance.* Sage Publications.

Ladson-Billings, G. J., & Tate, W. F. (1995). Toward a critical race theory of education. *Teachers College Record, 97*(1), 47–68. https://doi.org/10.1177/016246819509700104

Love, B. L. (2019). *We want to do more than survive: Abolitionist teaching and the pursuit of educational freedom.* Beacon Press.

Malone, L. (2023). *Resisting numbness and embracing hope: Self-reflexive counternarratives of critical race mothering in suburban schooling* (Conference Presentation). The American Educational Studies Association 2023 Conference, Louisville, KY, United States.

Malone, L., & Lachaud, Q. (2022). FaithCrit: Towards a framework of religio-spirituality in critical race theory. *Journal of Critical Race Inquiry, 9*(2), 93–109.

Matias, C. E. (2016). "Mommy is being brown bad?": Critical race parenting in a post-race era. *Journal of Race and Pedagogy, 1*(3), 1–32.

McGee, E., & Spencer, M. B. (2015). Black parents as advocates, motivators, and teachers of mathematics. *The Journal of Negro Education, 84*(3), 473–490.

Montoya, R., & Sarcedo, G. L. (2018). Critical race parenting in the Trump era: A Sisphean endeavor? A parable. *International Journal of Qualitative Studies in Education, 31*(1), 70–81. https://doi.org/10.1080/09518398.2017.1379621

Nash, J. C. (2021). *Birthing Black mothers.* Duke University Press.

National Center for Education for Education Statistics. (2024). *Racial/ethnic enrollment in public schools.* https://nces.ed.gov/programs/coe/indicator/cge/racial-ethnic-enrollment

Perez Huber, L. (2009). Challenging racist nativist framing: Acknowledging the community cultural wealth of undocumented Chicana college students to reframe the immigration debate. *Harvard Educational Review, 79*(4), 704–720. https://doi.org/10.17763/haer.79.4.r7j1xn011965w186

Robinson, Q. L., & Werblow, J. (2012). Beating the odds: How single Black mothers influence the educational success of their sons enrolled in failing schools. *American Secondary Education, 40*(2), 52–66.

Robinson, Q. L., & Werblow, J. (2013). The power or a single mother: The influence of Black women on their son's academic performance. *Multicultural Perspectives, 15*(4), 202–208. https://doi.org/10.1080/15210960.2013.844605

Roebuck Sahko, J. (2017). Black activist mothering: Teach me about what teaches you. *The Western Journal of Black Studies, 41*(1), 3–16.

Schaeffer, K. (2024). *Key facts about public school teachers in the U.S. Pew Research Center*. https://www.pewresearch.org/short-reads/2024/09/24/key-facts-about-public-school-teachers-in-the-u-s/

Short, K. G. (2017). Critical content analysis as a research methodology. In H. Johnson, J. Mathis, & K. G. Short (Eds.), *Critical content analysis of children's and young adult literature: Reframing perspective* (pp. 1–15). Routledge.

Slater, R. O. (2007). American teachers. *Education Next, 8*(1). https://www.educationnext.org/american-teachers

Solórzano, D. G., & Yosso, T. J. (2002). Critical race methodology: Counter-storytelling as an analytical framework for education research. *Qualitative Inquiry, 8*(1), 23–44. https://doi.org/10.1177/107780040200800103

Thurman, H. (1976). *Jesus and the disinherited.* Beacon Press.

Williams, P. J. (1991). *The alchemy of race and rights.* Harvard University Press.

Witherspoon Arnold, N., Brooks, M., & Arnold, B. M. (2014). *Critical perspective on Black education: Spirituality, religion, and social justice.* Information Age Publishing.

Witherspoon, N., & Mitchell, R. W. (2009). Critical race theory as ordinary theology of African American principles. *International Journal of Qualitative Studies in Education, 22*(6), 655–670. https://doi.org/10.1080/09518390903333871

Larissa Malone Ph.D., is an Associate Professor of Social and Cultural Foundations of Education at the University of North Carolina Wilmington. Dr. Malone's research centers on the minoritized experience in schooling, inclusive of students, parents, and teachers, and has published in The Journal of Negro Education, Educational Studies, and The Journal of Critical Race Inquiry. She is particularly interested in the intersection of education, race, and tangential disciplines, such as religion, geography, social reproduction, and critical race mothering. Her calling in life is to create a more equitable world through the power of education.

Madness and Black Motherhood: Reimagining Scholarship for a Radical Future

Javiera Green

Abstract This chapter explores conceptions of madness in Beloved (1987) by Toni Morrison through the use of scholar La Marr Jurelle Bruce's mad category, psychosocial madness. I argue that this category can be extended to Black mothers in academia, offering them "mad communities" that can serve as aces of empowerment and mad knowledge-making processes surrounding Black mother scholarship. Several questions guide my analysis: How might literary depictions of mad Black motherhood produce new understandings of how Black motherscholars operate and engage with motherhood? How might madness be used as a tool to create Black mother scholarship?

Keywords Mad Black motherhood · Madness · Psychosocial · Communal · Black women · Black motherhood

Madness and Black Motherhood: Reimagining Scholarship for a Radical Future

The best thing she was, was her children.

—Toni Morrison, *Beloved* (1987).

The epigraph above reflects Sethe's belief, the protagonist of *Beloved*, that her children define her identity and worth as a person. The novel is set after the American Civil War and centered on Sethe, a formerly enslaved woman, and her daughter, Denver. After being assaulted, Sethe flees the plantation that she lives on, Sweet Home, for Cincinnati, Ohio, where her husband's mother, Baby Suggs, lives. After 28 days in Cincinnati, Schoolteacher, Sethe's former master, arrives to take her and her children back to slavery. Instead of complying, Sethe runs to the house shed to kill her children to prevent them from being forced back into slavery. She is known as "the murdering mother" because she kills one of her daughters, Beloved, and attempts to kill her other children, according to scholar, Marta Caminero-Santangelo (1998, p. 164).

J. Green (✉)
University of Illinois Urbana-Champaign, Urbana, IL, USA
e-mail: jgreen41@illinois.edu

C. R. Turner and M. L. Green (eds.), *Black Motherscholarship Within and Beyond the Academy*, https://doi.org/10.1007/978-3-031-99758-7_6

Throughout the novel, the central theme of motherhood is reflected through Sethe's sense of belonging to her children. Therefore, her maternal actions were motivated by her intense love for her children. Sethe's intense love and fierce devotion caused her to commit infanticide in an attempt to save her children from slavery. Her actions have garnered much critical attention, causing her to be labeled as a murderer who is interpreted as a figure representing cultural resistance by killing her child as a form of protection.[1] This interpretation is limiting because it provides a shallow justification for Sethe's behavior and ignores her personhood outside of being a mother.

Therefore, I argue that Sethe's action and her behavior towards her children is grounded in madness, which stems from enslavement. While madness has negative connotations, such as cognitive disability and excess, Sethe's madness invokes radical transformation in her life.[2] Examining the portrayal of Black women characters in literature can be a powerful tool for fostering community and empowering Black women scholars. In particular, the exploration of literary representations of madness and Black motherhood can challenge real-world conventional narratives about—and amplify marginalized voices, specifically those of Black women perceived as mad. Through my analysis, I aim to connect academic discourse with literary narratives to deepen the understanding of the challenges faced by Black mothers and their invaluable contributions to shaping societal narratives and structures.

Mad Studies: Origin and Methodology

Richard A. Ingram is credited with having coined the term "mad studies" in 2008.[3]Ingram defines the term as an "in/discipline" that exists within and outside the academy, focusing on the survivors and patients of psychiatric treatment (Ingram, 2022, p. 93). Currently, Mad Studies is primarily seen as an interdisciplinary field, but it is expanding beyond this scope into mad methodology.[4] Approaching mad studies as a methodology means prioritizing perspectives and methods rooted in the experiences of people labeled "mad." Applying mad methodology to literary studies is useful because literature allows one to explore characters' subjectivity.

In this chapter, I will build on existing studies of madness through a literary examination of madness within the context of Black motherhood, focusing specifically on the behavior of Sethe. Through this analysis, I offer new insights into the complex workings of the institution, and I will explore how madness operates through the mother–child relationships in Toni Morrison's *Beloved* (1987). Specifically, my

[1] See Marta Caminero-Santangelo's The Madwoman Can't Speak: Or Why Insanity is Not Subversive (1998).

[2] See Jane M. Ussher's "The Daughter of Hysteria: Depression as a 'woman's problem'?" (2011) and Theri Pickens's *Black Madness: Mad Blackness* (2019).

[3] See further commentary in "Doing Mad Studies: Making (Non) Sense Together" (2016).

[4] See *How to Go Mad Without Losing Your Mind: Madness and Black Radical Creativity* (2021) and Hayley C. Stefan's *A (Head) Case for a Mad Humanities: Sula's Shadrack and Black Madness* (2018).

analysis will focus on Sethe's relationship with her two daughters, Beloved and Denver. By analyzing the mother–daughter relationship within the text, I extend La Marr Jurelle Bruce's (2021) argument that madness can be a creative and liberating force for Black people, helping them resist societal oppression and reimagine ways of being and existing.

Bruce outlines four mad categories: phenomenal, medicalized, rage, and psychosocial madness. Even though Sethe exhibits some or all of these types of madness, I am particularly invested in psychosocial madness, which Bruce (2021) defined as "a radical deviation from the normal within a given psychosocial milieu" (p. 8). "Normal people" are those connected to the dominant system of power—white, heterosexual, patriarchal society. By observing accepted notions of normality, individuals can question these standards and challenge the dynamics between those who hold power and those who are powerless. Analyzing Black women characters through the lens of psychosocial madness provides examples of how marginalized people assert their agency to resist mainstream cultural narratives to sustain themselves and their families. These Black female characters can inspire real Black women who are labeled "mad" simply for defying patriarchal norms.

Bruce (2021) argues that the scrutiny these "mad" individuals face reveals more about the judges than the judged. Psychosocial madness critiques dominant ideologies, questioning whether those who deviate from societal norms are truly mad or if the self-proclaimed sane individuals are the real mad ones. For example, behavior considered odd or unfavorable, such as certain hairstyles or outfits, are often labeled as "mad" by those who claim to be sane. Yet, individuals who exhibit such behavior may instead intentionally resist and disturb notions of normal, sometimes to expose and challenge societal norms and power structures.

Mad Black Motherhood

In what follows, I argue that Sethe in *Beloved* adopts what I call "mad Black motherhood," which I define as a site where Black women can carve out a necessary space within motherhood that they have traditionally been excluded from. Their historical exclusion from traditional definitions of motherhood has forced them to become outlaws.[5] Mad Black motherhood has not been formally defined in academic spaces until now. My definition aims to expand the field of Mad Studies by providing a literary analysis focusing on the connection between madness and Blackness, specifically in Black motherhood, that can be applicable to Black motherscholars as well. Much of the scholarship on *Beloved* overlooks the possibilities that the mother's seemingly mad actions spark. Many critics pathologize Sethe's infanticide but do not specifically label it as "mad" or analyze it within the context of black motherhood. It is vital to explore madness and black motherhood to show how madness is

[5] See Douglas et al. (2021)'s Mad Mothering: Learning from the Intersections of Madness, Mothering, and Disability.

employed as a survival strategy to raise children within the afterlife of slavery[6] and how it affects subsequent generations. Ultimately, my analysis is guided by the questions: How might depictions of mad black motherhood produce new understandings of how black mothers—past and present, fictional and real—operate and engage with motherhood? To what extent can madness sustain or repair maternal bonds, particularly when systemic conditions continue to oppress black mothers?

Within mad Black motherhood, Black mothers can "mother against patriarchal versions of motherhood" (O'Reilly qtd. in Douglas et al., 2021, p. 46). Male perspectives of motherhood reinforce traditional gender roles where the woman is responsible for taking care of the home and the family. These views often lead to the subordination of women (Douglas et al, 2021, p. 46). Within patriarchal society, women are held to specific standards of normativity. Failure to comply with these standards causes women, including mothers, to be labeled as mad. Consequently, Black mothers who resist the heteronormative standards associated with motherhood are also perceived as mad. This perception, rooted in the institution of slavery, which forced Black mothers to create survival strategies for themselves and their families, has extended to control the bodies and social-psychological aspects of Black womanhood and motherhood.

Also, Toni Morrison's maternal standpoint informs my analysis on Black motherhood, which she mentions is a site of power, as Andrea O'Reilly (2004) highlights when calling Morrison's perspective "motherwork." According to O'Reilly (2004), Morrison asserts that the responsibility of the Black mother today is to "protect, nurture, and pass on customs of African American culture" (p. 29). At the same time, I agree with Morrison's claim that "motherhood is a cultural construction that varies with time and place; [and that] there is no essential or universal experience of motherhood" (29). Therefore, it is vital to define Black motherhood in the context of madness within this chapter.

I argue that by strategically adopting madness as their identity, Black mothers resist and persist in the afterlife of slavery. Mad Black motherhood "brings into light the meaning and dimensions of motherhood under the slavery system that especially erased the identity of the black female by removing maternity from the realm of the human" (Wilt qtd. in Ghasemi, 2010, p. 246). Enslaved Black women, like Sethe, were viewed as breeders to increase the labor market, bearing children without being allowed mother–child relationships with them after birth. The objectification of enslaved Black women reinforces the fact that "slavery sever[ed] the mother-child relationship" (Ghasemi, 2010, p. 246). Enslaved Black women were not regarded as mothers but as breeders, valued primarily for producing offspring to expand the labor force and increase profitability. Within the context of mad Black motherhood, we can arrive at new understandings of how one can understand Sethe's decision to commit infanticide.

Ultimately, I argue that psychosocial madness can be extended to Black mothers in academia, which can cultivate mad communities. These mad communal spaces for Black mother scholars are vital because they serve as spaces of empowerment

[6] See Saidiya Hartman's *Lose Your Mother: A Journey Along the Atlantic Slave Route* (2006).

where madness can contribute to the knowledge-making processes surrounding Black motherhood scholarship.

Exploring Mad Black Mothering in *Beloved* (1987)

To explore madness within Black motherhood, I will begin with my analysis of *Beloved.* Specifically, analyzing Sethe's behavior through the lens of psychosocial madness allows one to reframe her alleged "mad" behavior as a response to the societal trauma inflicted upon Black enslaved mothers, which is passed down to modern-day Black mothers. When Sethe is confronted with the newspaper clipping of her crime, she can't explain why she killed her child highlighting the complexity of her trauma. Her perceived madness becomes a protective mechanism against a reality too painful to confront:

> Sethe knew that the circle she was making around the room, him, the subject, would remain one. That she could never close in, pin it down for anybody who had to ask. If they didn't get it right off— she could never explain. Because the truth was simple, not a long drawn-out record of flowered shifts, tree cages, selfishness, ankle ropes and wells. Simple: she was squatting in the garden and when she saw them coming and recognized schoolteacher's hat, she heard wings. Little hummingbirds stuck their needle beaks right through her headcloth into her hair and beat their wings. And if she thought anything, it was No. No. Nono. Nonono. Simple. She just flew. Collected every bit of life she had made, all the parts of her that were precious and fine and beautiful, and carried, pushed, dragged them through the veil, out, away, over there where no one could hurt them. Over there. Outside this place, where they would be safe. (Morrison, 1987, p. 192)

The repetition of "simple" suggests that Sethe's decision was uncomplicated and necessary. Yet, her words don't accurately describe the situation so that others can understand her crime. It appears to be used as a way to cope with her crime because the situation was not simple but challenging to endure. To protect her children from slavery, she had to make the difficult decision to kill them. Also, the imagery of the hummingbird coupled with the mantra "no" suggests that she has disassociated from the event, which shows the "impact of its very incomprehensibility… [and] the way that its violence has not yet been fully known" (Caruth, 1996, p. 6). This detachment underscores the incomprehensibility and lingering impact of the violence, hinting at the fact that Sethe has unresolved trauma, which is impacting her psyche: "The loss of her child leaves her with an unbounded grief, irresolvable and unconfessable to anybody" (Ghasemi, 2010, p. 243). Sethe's internal language fails to accurately depict the murder, highlighting her failure of sight, which is "a failure to see adequately inside and a failure to see adequately outside" (Caruth, 1996, p. 103). Sethe acts out of a deep-seated fear, unable to grasp the full internal ramifications of killing Beloved to protect her from the horrors of enslavement. Sethe's infanticide can be interpreted as a manifestation of psychosocial madness because her behavior deviates from the conventional norms of motherhood; it also highlights the severe psychological burden of slavery on enslaved mothers.

Psychosocial madness also changes the way Sethe's maternal actions are perceived. Denver is the first person to notice the "fully dressed woman [Beloved, who] walked out of the water... sopping wet and breathing shallow... smiling" (Morrison, 1987, p. 60), who appears at the doorsteps of 124. Sethe has an immediate somatic response when she sees Beloved, the child she murdered: "[T]he moment she got close enough to see the face, Sethe's bladder filled to capacity" (Morrison, 1987, p. 61). Although Sethe is speechless when she sees Beloved, her reaction suggests she feels anxious. Her immediate need to urinate can be labeled as psychosocial madness because it is a "mundane phenomenon, perceived to be odd and undesirable" (Bruce, 2021, p. 8), and it is not behavior that "avowedly sane majorities" would engage in when reconnecting with someone from their pasts.

Obsessive Mothering

Interpreting Sethe's intense need to urinate as psychosocial madness allows readers to recognize that Sethe harbors much guilt for murdering Beloved. Sethe's behavior is triggered by the fight-or-flight response of her sympathetic nervous system. Because Sethe has repressed the guilt and pain associated with Beloved's murder, Beloved's reappearance forces her to face not only those emotions but also the tragic memory that she has always wanted to ignore. To combat her guilt, Sethe devotes most of her attention and resources to Beloved, resulting in her obsessive mothering. Therefore, Sethe "played all the harder with Beloved, who never got enough of anything: lullabies, new stitches, the bottom of the cake bowl, the top of the milk. If the hen had only two eggs, she got both" (Morrison, 1987, p. 282). Sethe's all-consuming behavior towards Beloved reflects her desperate attempt to make amends for her past actions.

Sethe's behavior is actually an expression of her intense desire for redemption. By showering Beloved with excessive affection and attention, Sethe tries not only to escape from the memory of the trauma she inflicted but also attempts to compensate for it: "Sethe wants to become the omnipotent mother who can save her children, even bring one back from the dead despite the cost to herself" (Vickroy, 2002, p. 58). Ultimately, Sethe neglects every aspect of her life that doesn't revolve around Beloved, including her job: "[S]he took to going to work later and later each day until the predictable happened: Sawyer told her not to come back" (Morrison, 1987, p. 282). Her loss of financial stability highlights her inability to maintain balance in her life.

Even though Sethe is no longer employed, she uses "[t]he thirty-eight dollars of life savings ... to feed themselves with fancy food and decorate themselves with the ribbon and dress goods" (Morrison, 1987, p. 282). Sethe's actions reflect her deeply rooted guilt and trauma, as she sacrifices her well-being to try to appease Beloved, whom she sees as the embodiment of her past sins. This desperate attempt to maintain Beloved's happiness illustrates Sethe's unresolved trauma and her ongoing struggle to atone for her past actions. Sethe's behavior can be interpreted as psychosocial madness and also raises the question: How do Black mothers navigate raising their children amid intergenerational traumas and systemic inequities rooted in the legacies of slavery? For Sethe, she operates within mad Black motherhood.

Sethe's obsession with repairing her relationship with Beloved highlights her perceived madness, which causes her to neglect Denver. At first, Denver assumes that her mother exhibits mere madness, a mistake some readers might also make after witnessing Sethe's self-sacrificing behavior to keep Beloved happy. Denver feels "it was as though her mother had lost her mind" (Morrison, 1987, p. 282), so she becomes hypervigilant of Sethe's behavior while showing contempt toward Sethe to get attention. Sethe offers food to Paul D, another former slave, upon his arrival at 124, the address of their home, as a sign of hospitality. Sethe's gesture of hospitality triggers Denver to ask Paul D, "Why don't you spend the night, Mr. Garner? You and Ma'am can talk about Sweet Home all night long" (Morrison, 1987, p. 16). Although it is unclear whether Denver recognizes the immediate chemistry between Sethe and Paul D after reconnecting, Denver's invitation to Paul D is disrespectful because she hadn't consulted her mother before extending the offer. By saying this to Paul D, she is seeking her mother's attention to respond to her because since Paul D has arrived, Sethe seems to be focused on his needs and not Denver's. This interaction does gain the attention of Sethe, who "took two swift steps to the stove, but before she could yank Denver's collar, the girl [Denver] leaned forward and began to cry" (Morrison, 1987, p. 17). Within the context of mad Black motherhood, Sethe's abrupt behavior of grabbing for her daughter's collar can be classified as psychosocial madness because it deviates from what might be considered appropriate in the situation. Recognizing Sethe's behavior as psychosocial madness helps readers understand that while her actions might seem violent, closer analysis reveals that Sethe fails to see Denver's need for attention and instead tries to assert her authority to maintain order in their home.

Recognizing the "Thing"

As the novel progresses, Denver's feelings toward her mother shift from disrespect to fear. In her stream-of-consciousness monologue, Denver attempts to justify her feelings: "I'm afraid the thing that happened that made it all right for my mother to kill my sister could happen again… so I never leave this house and I watch over the yard, so it can't happen again and my mother won't have to kill me too" (Morrison, 1987, p. 242). Denver is unsure of what "the thing" is that caused her mother to kill Beloved; however, she is overly cautious because she doesn't want to trigger Sethe's madness. In this context, "the thing" can be inferred as something that might trigger unresolved feelings that manifest into madness, specifically rage.

Denver's recognition of "the thing" inside her mother helps explain Sethe's rage during slavery. This "thing" compelled Sethe to protect her children from being captured and brought back to slavery. However, Denver still can't understand the necessity of Sethe's madness—the survival of her and her mother. Because of this lack of awareness, Denver feels she must monitor the yard to prevent any harm and warn Beloved to "not love her too much. Don't. Maybe it's still in her the thing that makes it all right to kill her children. I have to tell her. I have to protect her" (Morrison, 1987, p. 243). Denver's attempt to warn Beloved against loving Sethe too much reflects her misguided attempt to protect Beloved from potential harm.

Self-sacrificing as Madness

Towards the novel's end, Denver finally recognizes the origin of Sethe's madness—her traumatic past, which becomes evident as the family faces starvation: "The pain was unbearable when they ran low on food, and Denver watched her mother go without—pick-eating around the edges of the table and stove" (Morrison, 1987, p. 285). Sethe highlights the stereotypical strong Black mother attempting to meet the needs of her family first. She ensures that her children have enough to eat, even if it means she goes hungry herself. Her self-sacrificing behavior is alarming to Denver because she now recognizes that their difficult circumstances are due to Beloved's excessive appetite for everything.

Denver can visibly see how the unresolved trauma has wreaked havoc on Sethe's body: "Listless and sleepy with hunger, Denver saw the flesh between her mother's forefinger and thumb fade. Saw Sethe's eyes bright but dead, alert but vacant" (Morrison, 1987, p. 285). Denver's observation of Sethe's physical deterioration symbolizes Denver's belated recognition of the deep wounds inflicted by slavery and unresolved trauma. Suddenly, Denver feels an emotional burden as she struggles to balance her needs with her concern for Sethe. Therefore, Denver's job of protecting Beloved from Sethe "changed to protecting her mother from Beloved" (Morrison, 1987, p. 286). At this point in the novel, Denver recognizes that Sethe isn't solely to blame for her mad mothering. So, Denver must act to save her mother and herself.

Denver replicates her mother's self-sacrificing behavior by putting her needs aside to help Sethe: "She would have to leave the yard; step off the edge of the world, leave the two behind and go ask somebody for help" (Morrison, 1987, p. 286). Therefore, she asks for work from Lady Jones, her former schoolteacher, who instead offers "rice, four eggs and some tea," (Morrison, 1987, p. 292). Denver's initiative to seek work and provide food for her family demonstrates her maternal instinct because she shows her commitment to care for them; her actions also highlight her attempt to restore the maternal bonds between her and Sethe. While the food does sustain the family temporarily, Denver recognizes that she needs a permanent solution to their problem, so she enlists communal support, which is vital to her and Sethe's sustainment. Denver's decision to seek communal help shows that she no longer blames Sethe for her madness. She recognizes that racist societal conditions have forced Sethe to seek out alternative methods of survival, such as madness. Similarly, modern Black women must seek alternative methods of survival, such as reclaiming narratives of resilience, resistance, and sometimes even embracing forms of perceived madness to navigate the emotional and psychological toll of systemic oppression.

Radical Compassion in Community

Denver's realization that Sethe is not simply mad demonstrates her growing willingness to understand her mother. Because of Denver's insight, readers understand that Sethe's mad mothering is a survival strategy to persist in the afterlife of slavery. This newfound understanding pushes Denver out of her comfort zone beyond the confines of their home to help her mother. Therefore, Denver goes to the residence of Mr. Bodwin, who has helped Baby Suggs and Sethe in the past. Upon arrival at the Bodwin residence, Denver recognizes that "nobody was going to help her unless she told it– told all of it" (Morrison, 1987, p. 298). Denver confesses to Janey, the housekeeper, about Sethe's condition and the danger that Beloved poses to her family. Ultimately, "[t]he news that Janey got hold of spread among the other colored women... It was Ella, [neighbor], more than anyone, who convinced the others that rescue was in order (Morrison, 1987, pp. 300–301).

The Black women within the community recognize that Sethe needs to be saved from Beloved because she is in danger of dying. Therefore, they decide to perform an exorcism to rid Sethe of the evil spirit they know to be Beloved:

> [Sethe and Beloved] saw the rapt faces of thirty neighborhood women. Some had their eyes closed; others looked at the hot, cloudless sky. Sethe opened the door and reached for Beloved's hand. Together they stood in the doorway. For Sethe it was as though the Clearing had come to her with all its heat and simmering leaves, where the voices of women searched for the right combination, the key, the code, the sound that broke the back of words. Building voice upon voice until they found it, and when they did it was a wave of sound wide enough to sound deep water and knock the pods off chestnut trees. It broke over Sethe and she trembled like the baptized in its wash. (Morrison, 1987, p. 308)

Despite the complexities of Sethe and Beloved's relationship and their unresolved traumas, their hand-holding symbolizes a moment of solidarity between mother and daughter. At the same time, the mention of the Clearing, a communal space where Black residents came to fellowship, connects Sethe to her past and the community's collective memory. Moreover, the exorcism highlights the importance of community and shared history in healing and redemption.

The women's voices build upon one another, creating a wave of sound that washes over Sethe. This provides her with the release she needs to confront her past traumatic experiences and find solace in the collective support of her community. This moment is important because Denver and the community's decision to help Sethe highlights the need for radical compassion for mad people. Bruce defines radical compassion as "a will to care for, a commitment to feel with, a striving to learn from, and an openness to be vulnerable before a precarious other, though they may be drastically dissimilar to yourself" (Bruce, 2021, p. 10). Radical compassion is essential for coexistence, as it fosters mutual understanding, particularly among marginalized individuals seeking liberation within a white supremacist society. Although the community doesn't agree with Sethe's infanticide, they recognize that her act is in the past. The community shares the collective pain from slavery and acknowledges that Beloved is a reminder of her past. To move forward in the present, the past must be let go. The exorcism is supposed to help Sethe heal and reintegrate into the community.

However, just as she seems prepared to confront her traumatic past, a wave of rage overwhelms her "when she lowers her eyes to look again at the loving faces before her ... she sees him... He is coming into her yard and he is coming for her best thing" (Morrison, 1987, p. 308). Sethe's traumatic memory is triggered when Mr. Bodwin comes into the yard to pick Denver up for work. This sudden trigger reminds readers that trauma endured from slavery persists and must constantly be confronted for the traumatized person to heal. As a result of the trauma, madness persists as a survival strategy that, too, can be triggered by perceived danger.

Sethe mistakes him for Schoolteacher; therefore, she attempts to attack him: "She flies. The ice pick is not in her hand; it is her hand...Sethe is running away from [Beloved]...running into the faces of the people out there, joining them and leaving Beloved behind. Alone. Again. Then Denver running too" (Morrison, 1987, p. 309). Sethe's behavior exemplifies misplaced rage as she perceives that her family is threatened again, leading her to target Bodwin. Confronted with the past trauma of killing her daughter, she's determined not to repeat the mistake, hence her pursuit of the alleged predator. Denver's decision to run after her mother shows that she will stop her from making another costly mistake. This moment is significant because both Sethe and Denver experience rage through the perceived threat that their family will be torn apart again. Instead of letting madness consume Sethe, Denver's choice to stop her mother shows her attempt to repair their maternal bond and her acceptance of Sethe. At the novel's end, "Beloved is truly gone. Disappeared, some say, exploded right before their eyes" (Morrison, 1987, p. 310). Although Sethe is listless after Beloved disappears, her absence is the catalyst for Sethe to begin to heal from her traumatic past. Denver's restoration of the maternal bond between her and Sethe allows for a renewed connection that empowers both mother and daughter to heal and cultivate a new relationship collectively.

Analyzing Sethe through the lens of mad methodology allows perceptions of Sethe to shift because she no longer has to be perceived as a one-dimensional character who operates as the "murdering mother" but as a mother who, under the conditions of slavery, had to make difficult choices for the survival of her family (Caminero-Santangelo, p. 164). Specifically, the institution of mad Black motherhood allows scholars to reconceptualize Sethe as a mad Black mother, which could offer new interpretations of her personhood and a chance to foster radical compassion for her. Also, Black motherscholars can gain a more expansive understanding of their own actions in mad Black motherhood as they navigate oppressive institutional spaces.

Beloved's Impact on Black Motherscholars in Academia

Reynolds-Dobbs et al. (2008) argue that "[h]istorically, organizations were designed to benefit White males...therefore women are constantly forced to crossover and breakdown barriers to achieve success in the workplace" (p. 133). These organizations include academic institutions where women, specifically Black women, "are forced to contend with many negative racial stereotypes, which can obstruct their professional lives and connections" (Reynolds-Dobbs et al., 2008, p. 130). Therefore, Black women must constantly negotiate their varying identities, including their gender, race, and professional and personal titles within the academy. Black motherscholars can draw from Sethe's experience to understand the historical and emotional burdens that still resonate today. Through Sethe's fierce maternal love, Black mothers can see the resilience and strength required for mothering and apply these characteristics to sustain themselves in the academy.

Although Black women occupy a marginalized status, they offer a unique perspective within the academy: "[a] critique within the various communities by challenging the reification of Blackness around maleness, the reification of gender around Whiteness, and the reification of intellectualism around White maleness," according to scholar, Denise Taliaferro Baszile (2006). Patricia Hill Collins defines this space as the "outsider within status" (qtd in Taliaferro Baszile, 2006). For Black motherscholars, this position within the academy fosters community building among themselves. Throughout *Beloved*, the significance of community is evident. The support and solidarity Sethe and Denver receive from other Black women within the community provide a buffer against the isolating effects of their trauma.

While Black women stereotypes persist, these communal academic spaces allow Black mothers to express "radical black female subjectivity" (Taliaferro Baszile, 2006, p. 206). Baszile metaphorically defines this term as a way to "seek out and develop mutually empowering relationships with other Black female colleagues, who have helped [her] unload, not feel alone, see from another perspective, and continue to challenge [herself] in significant ways" (p. 206). I define these communal spaces as mad because they deviate from traditional academic spaces where Black motherscholars must practice strategic emotionality, which is defined as "the deliberate and conscious thought Black women engage in when considering whether they do or do not, can or cannot theorise their emotions as part of their race research and, the extent and type of emotions they are prepared to reveal," according to sociologist, Nadena Doharty (2019).

Within mad communal spaces, Black women can express their intersectional identities, which might often be perceived as mad, any deviation from the white patriarchal norm. These spaces, in fact, allow for Black mothers to share counterstories as a way to resist and disrupt the racist power structure within the academy, but they also "depict a kind of complexity that is unattainable through traditional academic discourse" (Taliaferro Baszile, 2006, p. 200). Sethe's story is one of resistance against dehumanization and a struggle for identity and autonomy. Black mothers in academia can learn from this depiction of resilience, recognizing their acts of resistance within institutional spaces. Embracing a mad identity for Black mothers within these communal academic spaces allows them to develop a collective vulnerability that can and will inform their scholarship on Black motherhood.

Through these mad communal spaces, Black mother scholars can amplify their own stories to "consciously and critically cultivate [their] wild in the company and comfort of other wild women in academia…[to continue] nurturing the pedagogical promise of Black women" (Taliaferro Baszile, 2006, p. 206). Mad communal spaces can offer Black women navigating motherhood and academia essential areas of rest, peace, wholeness, and joy, providing relief from the exhausting demands they often face. These spaces inform radical futurity where the act of rest, wholeness, and community care becomes a form of resistance and transformative scholarship. By prioritizing wellness alongside the demands of academic life, Black motherhood can be redefined beyond mere survival, fostering a future rooted in empowerment, balance, and radical change. Toni Morrison's *Beloved* inspires the radical futurity of Black motherscholars through Sethe's mad behavior, which serves as a testament to resistance and resilience, both necessary qualities to sustain Black mothers in the academy.

Competing Interests The author has no conflicts of interest to declare that are relevant to the content of this manuscript.

References

Bruce, L. M. J. (2021). Mad is a place. In *How to go mad without losing your mind: Madness and Black radical creativity* (pp. 1–35). Duke University Press.

Caminero-Santangelo, M. (1998). *The madwoman can't speak: Or why insanity is not subversive*. Cornell University Press.

Caruth, C. (1996). *Unclaimed experience: Trauma, narrative and history*. Johns Hopkins University Press.

Doharty, N. (2019). The 'angry Black woman' as intellectual bondage: Being strategically emotional on the academic plantation. *Race Ethnicity and Education, 23*(4), 548–562. https://doi.org/10.1080/13613324.2019.1679751

Douglas, P., Runswick-Cole, K., Ryan, S., & Fogg, P. (2021). Mad mothering: Learning from the intersections of madness, mothering, and disability. *Journal of Literary & Cultural Disability Studies, 15*(1), 39–56. https://doi.org/10.3828/jlcds.2021.3

Ghasemi, P. (2010). Negotiating Black motherhood in Toni Morrison's novels. *CLA Journal, 53*(3), 235–253. College Language Association. https://www.jstor.org/stable/44325640

Ingram, R. A. (2022). A genealogy of the concept of "mad studies". In P. Beresford & J. Russo (Eds.), *The Routledge international handbook of mad studies* (pp. 93–97). Routledge.

Morrison, T. (1987). *Beloved*. Alfred A. Knopf.

O'Reilly, A. (2004). *Toni Morrison and motherhood: A politics of the heart*. State University of New York Press.

Reynolds-Dobbs, W., Thomas, K. M., & Harrison, M. S. (2008). From mammy to superwoman: Images that hinder Black women's career development. *Journal of Career Development, 35*(2), 129–150. https://doi.org/10.1177/0894845308325645

Taliaferro Baszile, D. (2006). In this place where I don't quite belong: Claiming the ontoepistemological in-between. In L. L. Brinkley & J. Lee (Eds.), *From oppression to grace: Women of color and their dilemmas within the academy* (pp. 195–208). Stylus Publishing.

Vickroy, L. (2002). *Trauma and survival in contemporary fiction*. University of Virginia Press.

Javiera Green is a lecturer in the Department of English at the University of Illinois Urbana-Champaign. Dr. Green's research examines madness as a critical lens in twentieth- and twenty-first-century African American novels, exploring how literature engages with questions of sanity, care, and survival. Her work engages in interdisciplinary conversations across Black Studies, Gender and Sexuality Studies, Medical Humanities, and Critical Psychology.

A Duty of Care: Re-envisioning Academia Through the Intersectional Lenses of Gender, Race, Disability, and Black Feminist Praxis

Melissa A. Green

Abstract This chapter critically examines the intersections of race, disability, and academia through the lens of Black feminist praxis. It challenges traditional academic norms by radically reevaluating perceptions of disability and Blackness, advocating for a subversion of dominant, stereotypical views. As a Black motherscholar of autistic children, the author proposes foundational changes to support diverse academic experiences. This work contributes to discourses on inclusive practices and revolutionary mothering, urging a transformative approach to higher education.

Keywords Black feminist praxis · Disability & academia · Revolutionary mothering · Inclusive practices · Autism

Introduction

My grandmother, Nan-nan, often reminded me, "people don't need to see your struggles," a mantra rooted in her survival as a first-generation immigrant from Jamaica and part of the Windrush generation. Alongside my grandfather, 'Grandie,' she imparted lessons meant to shield us from a society that often sought to diminish us. This philosophy, combined with my grandfather's insistence on being better than my white peers, taught me to internalize pain and trauma. As a Black woman grappling with mental health challenges since my teenage years—manifesting as an eating disorder, severe depression, and anxiety—I have lived much of my life masking my struggles. From dropping out of university without telling my grandparents to leaving my teaching career after a mental breakdown, I learned to hide my pain, just as I had been taught.

This ingrained survival strategy shapes how I navigate academia today, a space where the challenges of Black motherscholars often remain unseen. As I write this chapter, I also prepare for an emergency review of my autistic son's specialist school placement. His recent struggles, marked by sensory overload and withdrawal, weigh

M. A. Green (✉)
The Open University, Milton Keynes, UK
e-mail: mel.green@open.ac.uk

C. R. Turner and M. L. Green (eds.), *Black Motherscholarship Within and Beyond the Academy*, https://doi.org/10.1007/978-3-031-99758-7_7

heavily on me, as do the pressures of academic deadlines. During online meetings, my outward composure contrasts sharply with my inner turmoil, as I deflect inquiries about my quietness with a smile: "Oh, gosh. Yes, I'm fine." No one needs to know I'm struggling.

I do not blame my grandparents for their advice. Their guidance reflected the survival strategies necessary for two Black immigrants navigating the UK in the 1960s. Their belief in assimilation enabled me to succeed in education, though it took a toll on my mental health. Similarly, academia often imposes survival strategies on Black motherscholars, who balance professional expectations, caregiving responsibilities, and personal well-being.

The concept of "duty of care," originating in healthcare, reflects the obligation to prioritize the needs of those under one's care. In academia, however, this duty often neglects the compounded pressures faced by Black motherscholars. Reflecting on my grandparents' lessons and my own experiences, I consider how survival strategies intersect with academia's failure to fully embrace a duty of care. In the sections that follow, I examine how this concept is—or isn't—applied to support scholars like me.

A Duty of Care in Academia

The concept of 'duty of care' frequently arises in discussions about how universities support both students and staff. In UK academia, this notion is grounded in the Equality Act 2010, which establishes the moral and legal obligation to ensure the well-being and safety of others (Equality Act, 2010). However, for many, the idea of a university having a duty of care conjures up a problematic image of institutions acting in *loco parentis*, that is, assuming the responsibilities of a parent for adults, a notion that oversimplifies the responsibilities of universities. This institutional interpretation of this duty often conflicts with the lived experiences of students and faculty members like myself—Black, a woman, a carer of a disabled child—who navigate pressures that fall outside the simplistic frameworks institutions rely on.

For staff, the notion that universities offer a meaningful duty of care is often overstated. Institutions are regarded as equitable employers, yet this is not always reflected in practice, particularly for faculty who are Black, women, mothers, and/or carers (Osho & Alormele, 2024). Just as my grandparents' duty of care taught me to hide my struggles and work harder than my white peers, academia's duty of care often demands conformity to institutional norms that disregard lived experiences. The weight of institutional expectations falls unevenly on those who bear the intersectional pressures of race, gender, disability, and caregiving responsibilities.

The last decade has seen an increase in scholarly work within the field of higher education that explores mental health and well-being in relation to both staff and students (Halat et al., 2023; Riva et al., 2024), but much of this work isolates identities rather than addressing their intersections (Collins, 2000; Crenshaw, 1989). For Black women who are also carers of disabled children, the intersectionality of race, gender, and caregiving creates pressures that institutions fail to account for. The standard duty of care frameworks rarely consider how these intersectional pressures require a rethinking of support structures.

Ultimately, universities' duty of care remains superficial when it does not address the challenges faced by those of us who live at the intersection of multiple marginalised identities. Without meaningful support structures that recognise these intersections, the academy perpetuates a form of care that is more performative than practical.

Navigating Academia and Care: My Positionality

I am a mother, carer, daughter, granddaughter, wife, student, and worker. Currently, I am a Lecturer in Education Studies at the UK's largest university by student number, working full-time with flexible, primarily online responsibilities. Alongside this role, I am completing a part-time, fully funded Doctorate in Education, now in its fourth year. My responsibilities extend beyond academia, as I navigate motherhood to two sons: an eight-year-old diagnosed with autism and sensory processing disorder (SPD) and a five-year-old with autistic traits aligned with Pathological Demand Avoidance (PDA) and SPD.

As the granddaughter of Jamaican immigrants, I inherited survival strategies shaped by my grandparents' experiences in the UK during the Windrush era. My upbringing instilled resilience but also internalized the need to mask struggles, a lesson carried into adulthood. Despite battling mental health challenges, including an eating disorder, depression, and anxiety since adolescence, I have learned to navigate life while concealing my struggles—a skill both protective and burdensome.

This positionality statement is not a "pretension" of reflexivity, as Patai (1994) critiques, but a contextual framework for understanding the perspectives offered in this chapter. Rooted in lived experience, it provides the epistemological grounding necessary to appreciate the arguments presented here. I contend that academia's relationship with a 'duty of care' is fundamentally one-sided. While it addresses inequality in theory, it fails to embed care and compassion into its own systems, leaving marginalized individuals, particularly Black motherscholars, unsupported in balancing academic demands with caregiving and intersecting identities.

Drawing on autoethnography (Butz & Besio, 2004; Le Roux, 2016), I examine how Black motherscholars navigate academia's institutional demands while balancing motherhood, caregiving, and other responsibilities. My analysis highlights the structural inequities that perpetuate bias against Black women and caregivers in higher education (HE). As Ahmed (2012) argues, institutional practices often reinforce these inequalities, necessitating systemic change.

This chapter centers two key questions: (1) How do the intersecting roles of race, gender, motherhood, and disability shape Black motherscholars' experiences? and (2) How do they manage the dual demands of academic and personal life? Through personal narratives, I call for academia to recognize and support the complexities of Black motherhood and caregiving. Contributing to work like Rollock (2019), this chapter seeks to advance the conversation on racial inequities in HE and promote inclusive, equitable support systems for motherscholars.

Conceptual Framework: Foundations of Duty and Care in Academia

In my current doctoral research into the intersection of the personal and professional identities of distance educators, I include autoethnographic data alongside ethnographic data from other participants. To gather my autoethnographic data, I revisited photo albums, letters, emails, and journal entries, focusing on six key life stages: early childhood; primary and secondary schooling; university; early teaching experiences in primary education; my initial years in higher education; and my promotion to a central academic role. These reflections were organised into six vignettes through journaling, drawing connections between personal milestones and professional development. Data from eight other distance educators at my institution were collected through participant-created artefacts and online teaching observations, which served as stimuli for stimulated recall interviews. Narratives from my autoethnography and participants' artefacts, observations, and interviews were thematically analysed using my Critically and Culturally Integrated Educators' Identities (CCIEI) framework (Green, unpublished). This framework, informed by Critical Race Theory (Delgado & Stefancic, 2012), Intersectionality (Crenshaw, 1989), Sociocultural theory of identity and agency (Holland et al., 1998), and Cultural Contracts Theory (Jackson, 2002), positions educators' identities as shaped by the convergence of personal and professional experiences within cultural and institutional contexts.

While the CCIEI framework forms a theoretical foundation for my doctoral examination, this chapter draws primarily on intersectionality and the tensional model of disability as the conceptual frameworks that guide my analysis. Intersectionality (Crenshaw, 1989) provides the lens through which I examine how the intersecting social roles of race, gender, motherhood, and caregiving create significant challenges for Black motherscholars. The tensional model of disability, as articulated by Williams (2021), deepens this analysis by allowing me to explore how the physical and emotional tensions of caregiving for a disabled child impact academic responsibility, further complicating the balance between professional and personal life. Together, these frameworks allow me to critically engage with the chapter's central questions: How does the intersectionality of social roles and identities impact Black mothers' scholarship? How do Black mother scholars navigate the responsibilities of academic life alongside homelife and motherhood?

Intersectionality

We should not have to hide our identities as mother-scholar-activists or compromise community connections for academic careers (Hidalgo et al., 2022). For Black motherscholars, navigating academia means balancing professional demands with caregiving responsibilities while confronting structural inequalities. The expectation to excel professionally, manage caregiving, and face racial discrimination creates a triple bind, worsened by academia's lack of institutional support (Rollock, 2019). Intersectionality highlights the need for tailored policies—flexible work, mental health resources, and recognition of additional labor—to genuinely support marginalized academics. Critiques of intersectionality (Nash, 2018) caution against its depoliticization, urging a focus on embodied experiences. Extending this framework, the tensional model of disability (Williams, 2021) emphasizes the material realities of intersecting identities.

Tensional Model of Disability

My reflections draw on Williams' (2021) tensional model of disability, which moves beyond the social model to emphasize the material and embodied realities of disability. While the social model highlights societal barriers, the tensional model recognizes the physical and emotional toll of disability, offering a crucial lens for understanding the experiences of Black motherscholars navigating race, motherhood, and caregiving alongside academic life.

Parenting an autistic child is deeply demanding, with stress levels among these parents higher than those of parents of children with other disabilities (Fletcher-Randle, 2022). The day-to-day challenges—like masking pain after witnessing a child's sensory dysregulation—underscore the material realities of caregiving, compounded by academia's relentless demands. For someone managing anxiety, the pressure to appear able-bodied while continually justifying the need for accommodations highlights the persistent tension between institutional expectations and personal well-being. The tensional model acknowledges how intersecting oppressions—racism, misogynoir, and the challenges of disability—shape the lives of Black motherscholars materially and emotionally. As Allegra (Williams, 2021) notes, embodying multiple marginalized identities inherently involves tension. My experiences as a Black mother-scholar raising an autistic child reveal how these identities interweave, creating compounded struggles and the need for academia to move beyond performative inclusivity by providing tangible, comprehensive support systems.

Methodology

This chapter explores the intersection of race, disability, motherhood, and academia, weaving autobiographical reflections with theoretical analysis. Employing autoethnography, I place my lived experiences at the center of inquiry, using personal narratives to illuminate systemic inequities. This approach, rooted in feminist theories of the personal as political, contests traditional notions of detached scholarship and frames my narrative within broader societal and institutional contexts. Through "showing" and "telling" (Adams, 2006), I offer both an immersive and analytical perspective on the tensions of navigating academia as a Black motherscholar.

Central to this analysis is the tensional model of disability (Williams, 2021), which highlights the material and emotional toll of disability. As noted, unlike the social model, which emphasizes external barriers, the tensional model highlights the physical and psychological demands of caregiving and academia. For Black motherscholars, this tension is compounded by intersecting oppressions, including race and gender, creating a constant negotiation of professional and personal identities.

Motherhood, particularly for Black women, is inherently political (Nash, 2019). My journey into motherhood began with ideals of staying home and homeschooling my children, ideals that quickly collided with societal expectations and institutional pressures. Motherhood became a public experience, shaped by norms that demanded conformity and perpetuated feelings of inadequacy. Navigating these pressures, alongside the challenges of raising an autistic child, deepened my understanding of the complexities of identity and caregiving.

The COVID-19 pandemic further amplified these tensions, coinciding with significant personal and professional transitions, including the pursuit of a doctorate. During this time, I also navigated the health and social care systems to secure an autism diagnosis for my eldest son, a process marked by emotional and logistical challenges. These experiences reshaped my academic focus, leading me to examine how intersecting identities influence both scholarship and personal life.

The duty of care required to mother a disabled child in a society that marginalizes Black and disabled lives is an ongoing struggle. The tensional model of disability acknowledges this conflict, highlighting how societal and institutional barriers create friction against caregiving responsibilities. For Black motherscholars, this tension extends to academia, where expectations often disregard the complexities of intersectional identities.

Motherhood for Black women is a site of resistance, where personal and political struggles converge. Raising disabled children while navigating academic spaces is an act of defiance against systems that devalue both our labor and lives. This chapter calls for academia to move beyond tokenistic diversity initiatives and implement structural changes that address the material and emotional realities of caregiving and intersecting oppressions. By centering the experiences of Black motherscholars, this work advocates for an academic environment that truly supports the complexities of our identities and lived experiences.

Motherhood and Identity: A Critical Perspective

It is strikingly obvious when exploring the lives and circumstances of Black women, that categories such as "womanhood" and "motherhood" lose their universality (Lorde, 1984; Rich, 1986). Motherhood is not a monolithic experience, even without considering Black women, but Black women's unique experiences of living under oppressive systems (Craddock, 2015) means we must consider motherhood to be a cultural construct that varies across societies and historical periods, shaped by both macro structures and daily practices. Despite this complexity, society continues to view motherhood as an essential aspect of a woman's identity, a universal goal imposed upon all women. Psychological models like Bowlby's (1988) attachment theory emphasize the importance of the mother–child bond for a child's emotional and psychological development, placing the mother's role under intense scrutiny. This model highlights a mother's duty to provide security and stability, often without considering the diverse realities faced by different mothers. For mothers of autistic children, this expectation is fraught with additional challenges. Outdated and harmful notions such as the 'refrigerator mother' theory (Bettelheim, 1967), which erroneously blamed a mother's emotional coldness for causing autism, have compounded the burden and guilt these mothers carry.

Bowlby's (1988) attachment theory, while influential in shaping ideas about the mother–child bond, often overlooks the nuances of how mothers, particularly Black mothers and those caring for disabled children, experience this bond. The pressure to provide emotional stability and security becomes even more intense for mothers like me, where the stakes are higher—my child's autism adds layers of complexity to our relationship, yet the expectations placed on me remain unchanged. These models fail to account for the reality of caring for a child who cannot communicate in 'typical' ways, or how society's racialised expectations intersect with the scrutiny I face as both a Black woman and a mother. I have a child that does not say he loves me but shows it in many non-verbal ways.

Motherhood as Unpaid Labor

Motherhood is a form of labor that encompasses both paid and unpaid work, demonstrating the economic value of caregiving and domestic responsibilities traditionally undertaken by mothers. Despite their essential contributions to society, these forms of labor remain largely undervalued and invisible, especially within capitalist and neoliberal frameworks that prioritize paid work. The "good mother" archetype, rooted in white, middle-class, able-bodied ideals, perpetuates narrow and exclusionary norms. This model, which glorifies full-time caregiving and self-sacrifice, fails to reflect the diverse realities of mothers from marginalized backgrounds, such as Black women, disabled mothers, or mothers of disabled children. These mothers, including those like me who allow their children to spin, vocalize in supermarket aisles, or engage in guilt-free screen time, challenge these hegemonic ideals.

Economic dimensions of motherhood further complicate this landscape. The unpaid labor of caregiving, such as serving as a child's speech therapist, learning instructor, or emotional support, is vital yet systematically devalued (Folbre, 2017). This lack of recognition perpetuates economic inequalities, disproportionately affecting women, particularly from marginalized communities. The tension between caregiving and professional work exacerbates these inequities. The societal construct of the "ideal worker," fully dedicated to their professional role without caregiving distractions, excludes mothers from equitable workforce participation. For mothers like me, who often attend mid-day meetings for specialist schools while navigating systemic racism and ableism, the demands of caregiving and academia are an oppressive balancing act.

Black mothers of disabled children experience caregiving as both a deeply personal and inherently political act, confronting significant social, physical, and emotional challenges (Yilmaz & Alemdar, 2020). It is not our children who are burdensome, but the societal expectations and systemic failures that place an overwhelming load on us. Educational systems demand constant advocacy for basic services, and societal biases against non-speaking Black boys frame them as threats rather than individuals to nurture. Preparing my children to navigate a society rife with racism and ableism imposes immense emotional labor. This burden is not a reflection of my children's worth but of the systems that fail to accommodate or value them.

Even as I write, I grapple with institutional failures that have forced me to remove my eldest son from his specialist school due to negligence and staff shortages. Limited schooling options for non-speaking children like my son highlight the systemic neglect that disproportionately affects Black families and children with disabilities. The bureaucratic hurdles, endless paperwork, and the recognition of my son's limited opportunities for self-expression underscore the inequities we face. The system was never designed for families like mine; it fails to see my son's potential or respect his dignity.

This neglect is deeply embedded in broader structures of racism and ableism. The decision between two inadequate schooling options epitomizes the systemic devaluation of Black children and the struggles of Black mothers. It is a reminder that we are continually forced to advocate for our children in systems that marginalize and neglect us. Motherhood, especially for Black women, is not just a role but a resistance against societal norms that seek to confine and devalue our lives and labor.

Motherhood as an Act of Resistance

Motherhood, especially for Black women, is more than nurturing children; it is an act of resistance against societal structures that devalue our humanity. It redefines what it means to mother in a world that often fails to see us. Black feminist theorists such as Collins (2000), hooks (1994), and Lorde (1984) have long argued that Black motherhood is a social and political practice, shaped by both societal and cultural expectations. For Black women like me, these expectations are compounded by the assumption of inherent resilience, creating a framework that places extraordinary demands on our emotional and physical labor.

This framework manifests in everyday experiences. For instance, when I miss appointments due to work, practitioners consistently inquire about my absence in ways they never question my husband. These moments remind me that I am not simply a mother—I am expected to embody strength and perseverance at all times, even when overwhelmed. Motherhood for Black women is thus a daily act of resistance. From navigating healthcare and advocating for my son's education to challenging societal ideals of strength, every decision I make is political. Yet, this resistance is exhausting, forcing me to confront the racialized lens that expects unyielding resilience while I strive to care for my children in a world that often denies their humanity.

Motherhood as Isolation

I struggle with the Black feminist ideal of Black motherhood as communal, collaborative, and collective. While the concept of othermothering—where Black women collectively nurture and raise children (Collins, 2000)—is powerful, it feels distant from my reality. As a mother of autistic children, othermothering demands a deep understanding of disability and unconditional acceptance that I have not found within my extended family. Supporting my children requires nuanced awareness of dysregulation, how to respond, and how to foster regulation—a level of vigilance I cannot entrust to others. This has meant that my husband and I have not left our children with family since my eldest was a baby.

The absence of this communal care leaves me questioning: where is our village? Who are the othermothers I can rely on to nurture and protect my children? The gap is not only physical support but also a deeper misunderstanding of disability within the framework of othermothering. The unconditional love and support required for my children's unique needs feel unattainable within this idealized vision of communal motherhood. My Nan-nan, a spiritual anchor in my life, lives thousands of miles away. Though her words guide me, her physical absence is deeply felt. My mother, just a 10-min drive away, and I share a relationship strained by intergenerational tensions, emotional distance, and unspoken expectations. These dynamics leave little space for the nurturing support I desperately need.

Black feminist thought celebrates communal care as a means of survival (Collins, 2000), but my experience reveals its limitations. Raising children with disabilities in a society that often misunderstands or marginalizes them highlights the gaps in this framework. Without a supportive network, I face burnout, compounded by the demands of academia. I wonder if this isolation will persist and how to create a lasting support system for my children without the help of othermothers.

Navigating Duty and Care in Academia

Navigating the dual roles of motherhood and academia as Black motherscholars requires intentional strategies that center our identities and lived experiences within institutions often designed to marginalize us. Key strategies include integrating personal and professional experiences into research, resisting normative expectations about caregiving, and building support networks that acknowledge the complexities of our intersecting identities. These approaches challenge systemic inequities and affirm our right to academic spaces while aligning our scholarly contributions with our lived realities.

Black Motherscholars' Research Agendas and Identities as Mothers

Hidalgo et al. (2022) argue that academia and motherhood are "crucibles that provide moments of rupture," exposing systemic inequities. As both scholars and caregivers, we bear a responsibility to make visible the racial and ableist inequities in education systems while extending care to those marginalized by these structures. The challenge lies in navigating these identities within spaces that often prioritize the status quo.

When I began my doctorate, I faced persistent questioning about my ability to balance academia and motherhood, with concerns about neglecting my children's formative years. However, as Hidalgo et al. (2022) assert, there is no inherent incompatibility between motherhood and higher education. My lived experience enhances my scholarly work, making my contributions both valuable and necessary. By centering our lives in research, Black motherscholars like me ensure that our perspectives gain recognition and reshape academic discourse.

Collaborating with Dr. Claire Malcolm, a fellow Black mother of autistic children, we developed *Mothering at the Margins: Black Mothers Raising Autistic Children in the UK*. Using collective autoethnography alongside interviews and focus groups, we foregrounded the voices of Black mothers, disrupting dominant narratives that often exclude marginalized communities (Crenshaw, 1991). As Perry and Medina (2011) argue, raising awareness of embodied discourses is crucial. This research not only challenges systemic erasure but also validates the experiences of Black mothers navigating caregiving and academia.

While some Black motherscholars centralize their identities as mothers in their work, others may resist integrating these roles as a form of self-protection. In spaces that fail to champion or support us, this resistance is an equally valid strategy for preserving one's well-being.

Disclosing Disabilities and Resisting Productivity Pressures

Another form of resistance lies in navigating whether to disclose disabilities in academia. Disabled academics often face misunderstanding, undervaluation, and stigma, leading many to conceal their disabilities (Yerbury & Yerbury, 2021). The neoliberalization of higher education amplifies these challenges, enforcing relentless productivity standards that silence marginalized voices (Brown & Ramlackhan, 2021).

For me, sharing my mental health struggles and my children's challenges has created meaningful connections with students who face similar issues, fostering a sense of empowerment. However, disclosing my anxiety to colleagues often leads to condescension or assumptions about my competence. This reinforces harmful stereotypes and highlights the risks of vulnerability in academic spaces.

Disclosing disabilities becomes a powerful act of resistance, challenging hegemonic norms that marginalize disabled academics. Yet, the pressure to prove oneself in an environment that commodifies labor remains daunting. As a Black mother with caregiving responsibilities and mental health struggles, the expectation to continuously produce research often feels overwhelming. This tension between productivity and personal care underscores academia's failure to provide adequate support for scholars like me.

While my university offers flexibility in balancing teaching and research, the internalized pressure to measure up to colleagues in traditional academic settings persists. Impostor syndrome, particularly common among Black women and first-generation graduates, compounds this struggle. It was through the support of Dr. Malcolm that I overcame these pressures and achieved significant milestones, demonstrating the importance of support networks for Black motherscholars.

Embracing Visibility

Another way I resist erasure in academia is by integrating my children into my academic life. Whether it's my son interrupting a meeting or waving during a virtual class, these moments assert my identity as both a mother and a scholar. This visibility challenges the expectation that motherhood must remain hidden or minimized in professional spaces. By embracing this duality, I affirm my full self and disrupt the notion that caregiving and academia are incompatible. This integration forces academia to recognize scholars like me—mothers, caregivers, and academics—whose identities are inseparable.

Navigating Academia Through Storytelling, Collaboration, and Resistance

In examining the intersections of race, motherhood, and disability within academia, it becomes clear that these overlapping identities profoundly shape experiences. The challenges faced are not merely personal but deeply rooted in systemic inequities. Through storytelling, collaboration, and resistance, I navigate these complexities to create a more inclusive and supportive academic environment. These strategies form a foundation for transforming academia for Black motherscholars and individuals with intersecting identities.

Storytelling: Reclaiming My Voice

To tell my story is to resist erasure. My Nan-nan emphasized silence as survival, but within academia, I reclaim my voice through storytelling. Using autoethnographic methods in my doctoral research and other projects has been cathartic and empowering, legitimizing the struggles of other women in academia. Storytelling challenges the disembodiment and invisibility Black women often face in higher education. Perry and Medina (2011) emphasize that raising awareness of the discourses embedded in our bodies is vital. Delgado (1989) describes counterstories as tools of resistance, amplifying marginalized voices. My autoethnography is a form of activism, disrupting traditional and exclusionary academic discourses. It challenges institutional structures that erase the contributions of Black women, asserting our presence and reshaping knowledge production.

Collaboration and Community: Building Support Networks

Collaboration has been essential in navigating academia, particularly in creating bonds through shared experiences. My work with Dr. Malcolm exemplifies this, as we connected over our positionalities as Black mothers raising disabled children. Together, we developed *Mothering at the Margins*, amplifying the voices of Black mothers raising autistic children—a group often overlooked in academic and public discourse. Our collective autoethnography disrupts dominant narratives and provides a space where marginalized mothers can share their experiences.

This partnership fills the gaps left by the absence of traditional othermothering in my personal life. Family dynamics and caregiving challenges make communal caregiving difficult, but academic collaborations have become a substitute for this support. These intentional networks validate our experiences as Black motherscholars and carers of autistic children, fostering solidarity and sustainability in academia.

Resistance: Unlearning, Pedagogy, and Flexibility

Resistance is central to my academic journey. Unlearning the need to people-please and overachieve has been transformative, moving me from the "pet" phase of my career to asserting autonomy, as described by Thomas et al. (2013). This journey from "pet" to "threat" involves reclaiming agency and rejecting unrealistic expectations placed on Black motherscholars. In my pedagogy, resistance takes the form of centering my identity as a Black woman and mother. Inspired by Yao and Boss (2020), I embrace embodiment in online education, using my presence to challenge disembodied academic contexts. By integrating my lived experiences into teaching, I have been able to foster authenticity and connection with students.

Flexibility in academic life is another crucial act of resistance. The ability to work from home and manage my schedule supports both my family and professional well-being. Like Hidalgo et al. (2022), I question academia's sustainability without flexibility, which allows me to integrate personal and professional identities while resisting rigid institutional structures. Through storytelling, collaboration, and resistance, I challenge systemic inequities, striving to create a more inclusive academic landscape for marginalized identities.

Implications and Conclusion

Reflecting on the journey of Black mother scholars like myself, this chapter highlights the need for an academic environment that truly supports the integration of personal identity with professional roles, advocating for systemic changes to enhance inclusivity and equity within academia. The *duty of care* in academia cannot simply be an abstract ideal—it must be a tangible commitment to supporting those who navigate complex identities and responsibilities. Institutions must not only recognize the contributions of Black motherscholars but also provide the structural support needed to sustain both their personal and professional lives.

Our stories, our struggles, and our triumphs must be heard and validated. We know what our elders had to do to survive but now I implore us to thrive. For this, academia must move beyond a deficit model and create space for Black mothers' lived experiences to be fully recognized as valuable and necessary in scholarly work. Rather than positioning us as resilient by necessity or silent for survival, institutions must address the systemic barriers that marginalize us, ensuring that our identities and challenges are reflected in academic structures and practices. This transformation requires a commitment to dismantling the systemic barriers that hinder our progress, from the identity erasure to the rigid productivity expectations of neoliberal higher education to the pervasive stereotypes that marginalize our identities.

For Black mother scholars raising children with disabilities and managing their own mental health challenges, the balance between academic duties and caregiving often feels overwhelming. My autoethnographic reflections illustrate how in an attempt to balance work, home and study requires navigating multiple forms of labor: emotional, intellectual, and physical. We juggle the demands of caregiving, without care being given back, all whilst managing the pressures of academic productivity in environments that are often unforgiving of personal challenges or systemic inequality.

This navigation is made possible through resistance strategies like *storytelling*, which allows us to share our experiences and resist erasure; *collaboration*, which builds networks of support; and *self-advocacy*, in which we demand flexibility and accommodations from our institutions. However, these strategies alone are insufficient without institutional change. The *duty of care* in academia must include policies that provide mental health support, flexible working conditions, and adequate accommodations for caregivers. Without such structures, the burden on Black mother scholars will remain unmanageable.

The intersectionality of race, gender, disability, and mental health distinctively shapes the scholarship of Black motherscholars. My experience reveals that these overlapping identities affect not only how we are perceived within academic spaces but also the kinds of research we are able to pursue. The expectations placed upon us to perform at the same level as our non-disabled, non-caregiving colleagues ignore the additional labor we undertake. Furthermore, the pressures of navigating mental health challenges—whether our own or our children's—often go unacknowledged in academic settings that prioritize productivity over well-being.

These compounded experiences shape our scholarship in ways that make visible the systemic inequities within academia. However, without institutional support, this work often comes at a personal cost. The *duty of care* must therefore encompass not only recognizing these challenges but also providing concrete solutions—such as mental health resources, reduced workloads for caregivers, and genuine flexibility—that allow Black mother scholars to fully engage with their work without compromising their health or caregiving responsibilities. Our duty is to advocate for these changes, ensuring that future generations of Black mother scholars can thrive in an environment that honors their full humanity. Through collective action and institutional commitment, we can pave the way for a more inclusive, equitable, and compassionate academia. We do this because we care.

Competing Interests The author has no conflicts of interest to declare that are relevant to the content of this manuscript.

References

Adams, M. (2006). Hybridizing habitus and reflexivity: Towards an understanding of contemporary Identity? *Sociology, 40*(3), 511–528. https://doi.org/10.1177/003803850663672

Ahmed, S. (2012). *On being included: Racism and diversity in institutional life*. Duke University Press.

Bettelheim, B. (1967). *The empty fortress: Infantile autism and the birth of the self*. Free Press.

Bowlby, J. (1988). *A secure base: Parent-child attachment and healthy human development*. Basic Books.

Brantley, M. (2023). Can't just send our children out: Intensive motherwork and experiences of Black motherhood. *Social Problems, spad047*. https://doi.org/10.1093/socpro/spad047

Brown, N., & Ramlackhan, K. (2021). Exploring experiences of ableism in academia: A constructivist inquiry. *Higher Education, 83*(6), 1225–1239. https://doi.org/10.1007/s10734-021-00739-y

Butz, D., & Besio, K. (2004). The value of autoethnography for field research in transcultural settings. *The Professional Geographer, 56*(3), 350–360.

Collins, P. H. (2000). *Black feminist thought: Knowledge, consciousness, and the politics of empowerment*. Routledge.

Craddock, K. T. (2015). *Black motherhood(s): Contours, contexts, and considerations*. Demeter Press.

Crenshaw, K. (1989). Demarginalizing the intersection of race and sex: A black feminist critique of antidiscrimination doctrine, feminist theory, and antiracist politics. *University of Chicago Legal Forum, 1989*(1), 139–167.

Crenshaw, K. (1991). Mapping the margins: Intersectionality, identity politics, and violence against women of color. *Stanford Law Review, 43*(6), 1241–1299.

Delgado, R. (1989). Storytelling for oppositionists and others: A plea for narrative. *Michigan Law Review, 87*(8), 2411–2441. https://doi.org/10.2307/1289308

Delgado, R., & Stefancic, J. (2012). *Critical race theory: An introduction* (2nd ed.). NYU Press.

Equality Act 2010. (2010). *Legislation.gov.uk*. https://www.legislation.gov.uk/ukpga/2010/15/contents

Fletcher-Randle, J. (2022). Where are all the autistic parents? A thematic analysis of autistic parenting discourse within the narrative of parenting and autism in online media. *Studies in Social Justice, 16*(2), 389–406. https://doi.org/10.26522/ssj.v16i2.2701

Folbre, N. (2017). *The care penalty and gender inequality*. Stone Center on Socio-Economic Inequality, The Graduate Center, City University of New York. https://stonecenter.gc.cuny.edu/files/2022/09/Folbre-care-penalty.pdf

Halat, H. D., Soltani, A., Dalli, R., Alsarraj, L., & Malki, A. (2023). Understanding and fostering mental health and well-being among university faculty: A narrative review. *Journal of Clinical Medicine, 12*(13), 4425. https://doi.org/10.3390/jcm12134425

Hidalgo, L.-A., Vega, C., Cisneros, N. A., & Reyes, J. M. (2022). Fierce mothers: The cords that bind us. *Feminist Formations, 34*(1), 122–146. https://doi.org/10.1353/ff.2022.0005

Holland, D., Lachicotte, W., Skinner, D., & Cain, C. (1998). *Identity and agency in cultural worlds*. Harvard University Press.

hooks, b. (1994). *Teaching to transgress: Education as the practice of freedom*. Routledge.

Jackson, R. L. (2002). Cultural contracts theory: Toward an understanding of identity negotiation. *Communication Quarterly, 50*(3–4), 359–367.

Le Roux, C. S. (2016). Exploring rigour in autoethnographic research. *International Journal of Social Research Methodology, 20*(2), 195–207. https://doi.org/10.1080/13645579.2016.1140965

Lorde, A. (1984). *Sister outsider: Essays and speeches*. Crossing Press.

Nash, J. C. (2018). The political life of black motherhood. *Feminist Studies, 44*(3), 699–712. https://www.jstor.org/stable/10.15767/feministstudies.44.3.0699

Nash, J. C. (2019). *Black feminism reimagined: After intersectionality*. Duke University Press.

Osho, Y. I., & Alormele, N. (2024). Negotiated spaces: Black women academics' experiences in UK universities. *Higher Education*. https://doi.org/10.1007/s10734-024-01279-x

Patai, D. (1994). When method becomes power (response). In A. Gitlin (Ed.), *Power and method* (pp. 61–73). Routledge.

Perry, M., & Medina, C. (2011). Embodiment and performance in pedagogy research: Investigating the body in curriculum experience. *Journal of Curriculum Theorizing, 27*(3), 62–75.

Rich, A. (1986). *Of woman born: Motherhood as experience and institution.* W.W. Norton & Company.

Riva, E., Lister, K., & Jeglinska, W. (2024). Student and staff mental well-being in European higher education institutions. *NESET Report*. Publications Office of the European Union. https://doi.org/10.2766/14628

Rollock, N. (2019). *Staying power: The career experiences and strategies of UK black female professors.* University and College Union.

Thomas, K. M., Johnson-Bailey, J., Phelps, R. E., Tran, N. M., & Johnson, L. N. (2013). Women of colour at midcareer: Going from pet to threat. In L. Comas-Díaz & B. Greene (Eds.), *Psychological health of women of color: Intersections, challenges, and opportunities* (Chapter 14). https://doi.org/10.5040/9798216002536.ch-01

Williams, T. (2021). Materialising tension: The laborious, woven documentation of a black, queer, crip body mind in Indira Allegra's documented disability. *CLA Journal, 64*(1), 82–99.

Yao, C. W., & Boss, G. J. (2020). "A hard space to manage": The experiences of women of color faculty teaching online. *Journal of Women and Gender in Higher Education, 13*(1), 1–15. https://doi.org/10.1080/19407882.2019.1639197

Yerbury, J., & Yerbury, R. (2021). Disabled in academia: To be or not to be, that is the question. *Trends in Neurosciences, 44*(7), 507–509. https://doi.org/10.1016/j.tins.2021.04.004

Yilmaz, G., & Alemdar, D. K. (2020). Evaluation of care burden among mothers of children with a disability: Correlation between physical activity, quality of life, and sleep quality; a cross-sectional study. *Perspectives in Psychiatric Care, 57*(2), 770–778. https://doi.org/10.1111/ppc.12534

Black While Mothering: Retaining Motherhood, Scholarship, and Presence

Eghosa Obaizamomwan-Hamilton

Abstract This chapter explores the multiple challenges faced by Black motherscholars in academia and motherhood. Grounded in BlackCrit, endarkened feminist epistemology, and intersectionality, it examines how Black motherscholars navigate oppressive systems while nurturing intellectual and maternal identities. By reframing Black motherscholars' experiences as acts of refusal, this work challenges dominant narratives and elevates the voices of Black motherscholars through autoethnography. Ultimately, this chapter works to define/redefine Black motherscholars as producers, illuminating our multifaceted contributions to scholarship and society while aiming to cultivate a more inclusive academic environment.

Keywords Black motherscholar · Intersectionality · Blackgirl autoethnography · Black women

Introduction

What does it mean to survive an institution never designed to make space for your existence? What does it mean to give birth in a nation whose gross negligence continues to impact Black women disproportionately? Both questions are marked by my standpoint and rooted in the way my world is animated as a Black woman, first-generation Nigerian, secondary educator, and first-time mother. I entered motherhood and the academy without my mother and brought grief and ancestral strength with me. As a Black motherscholar, making room for all parts of myself within the educational apparatus is a constant struggle; and it is easy to get swallowed up by the carcinogenic nature of society and the academy. As an educator and a doctoral student, my drive to prove my worth left little room for me to be. Giving birth to my daughter at 38 years old in 2022... world stop! In many ways, she forced me to limit who and what had access to me. I had to confront what it meant to be a present mother and lean into my desire to replicate and improve on the loving relationship I

E. Obaizamomwan-Hamilton (✉)
Stanford University, Stanford, CA, USA
e-mail: eghosa@stanford.edu

C. R. Turner and M. L. Green (eds.), *Black Motherscholarship Within and Beyond the Academy*, https://doi.org/10.1007/978-3-031-99758-7_8

had with my mother (Gumbs, 2010; 2006). To be Black, and Mother and Scholar is a beautiful amalgamation of our prowess.

The memories of my mother and the present presence of my daughter powered this new and divine engine inside of me. For the first time in my life, I saw myself as beautiful and worthy because I could see myself in my daughter. The delicate balance of recognizing myself as a worthy scholar whose thoughts, concepts, and understandings of the world have value and as a worthy mother whose ability to love and nurture is now infinite is just one of the tight rope walks that many Black motherscholars face. In the context of racial violence in Rio de Janeiro, Rocha (2014) argues that Black mothering is essentially about creating, nurturing, resisting, and restoring the depleted parts of ourselves. The same is true of Black motherscholars who work to create (Walker, 1994) in stifling academic spaces, nurture the self and our children, resist hegemonic ways of knowing, and are constantly en route toward restorative acts. This chapter highlights the radical possibilities of Black mothers and Black motherscholars' ability to produce in a world often too small for our presence.

Problem Statement

I was enmeshed in power and pain at the start of graduate school in 2020. In the midst of finding my scholarly voice at the University of San Francisco, I was dealing with the wound of being told that my husband and I should make *no attempt* at having children. Quite callously, a doctor (an older white woman) told me that getting pregnant would be a risk to my life and/or the life of our unborn child. She concluded that becoming a mother was not a viable option for me. But who was she to determine such a thing, especially with the mothering of society that Black women have *been* doing? As an educator, I was already doing a level of othermothering (Case, 1997), particularly as it pertained to my Black girl students. According to Beauboeuf-Lafontant (2002),

> African-American women did not rely on the school's appropriation of the maternal to circumscribe their own desire to relate to students in a familiar, maternal way. In fact, these teachers saw their maternal qualities and the mother-child relationship as central to their resistance to domination, both patriarchal and racial. (p. 76)

After some processing, I knew better than to rely on this doctor to find my path toward motherhood. My deep-seated need to nurture and protect was spiritually bound, and I would eventually be able to share that with my daughter.

I recognized the need to take better care of myself, and that first meant making additional space to deal with the rooted grief I had been carrying since I was twenty-two. Losing my mother at that formative age left an abiding wound. It was also that same year that I adopted a coping mechanism that would prove difficult to shed. I learned early on from my dad that high performance in academics and athletics would yield great results regardless of the sacrifices. It made sense for me to focus on performing at a high level; I buried myself in work, multiple projects, and chasing various streams of income to avoid confronting the pain that felt insurmountable.

This relentless work allowed me to compartmentalize my grief, keeping thoughts of my mother and all I lost with her, somewhere in the realm of my never-ending to-do list. I did not have time to focus on her absence from my dating life, my marriage, my graduation, or my entry into motherhood. When I did pause, I felt deep sorrow because of the love missing, the friend missing, the nonjudgmental ear missing, the unconditional support missing—just missing my mom. So, I continued to work and keep myself distracted.

Giving birth to my daughter in 2022 put that coping mechanism to the test. As a Black motherscholar, there were no systems of support in place for the unique experience of entering motherhood as a scholar. For me, maintaining my full-time job as a secondary educator, beginning the process of my dissertation, running a non-profit organization, maintaining my presence as a co-founding editor to an academic journal, saying yes to every consulting gig, losing four liters of blood and having an emergency myomectomy while bringing life into this world was just the type of juggling I'd become accustomed to. But, finding myself and my balance came through my entry into motherhood.

Theoretical Framing

Black gaze (Campt, 2021) situates my theoretical framing in that it centers on the "creativity, ingenuity, cunning, and courage that allow [Black women] to acknowledge the forces that would define us, and yet not succumb to that definition" (p. 40). This paper is grounded in BlackCrit, endarkened feminist epistemology, and intersectionality as all are rooted in foregrounding the Black experience, with a specific focus on Black women.

BlackCrit

Critical Race Theory (CRT) describes the parasitic relationship between the social construction of race and the oppression of racial groups (Bell, 1995; Ladson-Billings, 2021). BlackCrit is built upon CRT but investigates the Black experience in a way that CRT does not. Dumas and Ross (2016) argued that anti-Blackness goes beyond racism against Black people as it "refers to a broader antagonistic relationship between blackness and (the possibility of) humanity" (p. 416). As a Black motherscholar, BlackCrit makes space for me to interrogate the relationship between race, scholarship, and motherhood.

Endarkened Feminist Epistemology

Cynthia Dillard's (2000) endarkened feminist epistemology places Black women's experiences at the forefront and rejects the white gaze. Dillard argued that endarkening epistemological spaces was a way to embrace, highlight, and examine Black women's knowledge and deeper knowings. She stated that Black women's knowledge is essential for understanding the world and challenging oppressive systems. Dillard's work helps situate my understanding of Black motherscholars as an important and intersectional identity that needs to be centered in academic spaces.

Intersectionality

In addition to endarkened feminist epistemology and BlackCrit, the seminal work on intersectionality (Crenshaw, 1989; Lorde, 1984) informs my work because it underscores and acknowledges how multiple standpoints affect how Black women experience the world. Crenshaw conceptualized intersectionality and articulated the point that race and gender cannot be mutually exclusive (Crenshaw, 1991). Intersectionality clarifies identity and its relationship to power, but more so the relationship to structural oppression. By using BlackCrit, endarkened feminist epistemology, and intersectionality, I can frame my Black motherhood and scholarhood as refusal and cast an additional perspective on the experiences of Black motherscholars through my narrative.

Methods

(Re)membering

To (re)member in the context of Black mothering means to understand the power that I have and have always had as a Black woman. It is being confident in the inherent restoration that happens when Black women remember who we are. Cynthia Dillard (2021) marshals the prefix "(*re-*) in parenthesis [as a] way of (re)minding all of us that Black [women] have inherently and always existed as brilliant holders of knowledge, culture, and humanity" (p. xv). (Re)membering is rooted in embracing all parts of our lineage and accessing the most authentic parts of our being to reveal how we put ourselves back together in a society built on ripping us apart. Dillard (2021) posits that there is power for Black women's identities in (re)membering as it impacts all aspects of our lives and is an avenue toward freedom because when we (re)member, "everything is possible" (p. 25). (Re)membering is beyond temporal reach. Ultimately, when we, as Black motherscholars, understand ourselves by understanding the experiences of our past, our inner Black girl, our wounds, we too can begin healing.

Critical Blackgirl Autoethnography

To examine my experiences as a Black motherscholar, I leaned on critical autoethnography, as a form of qualitative research that examines interpersonal and cultural experiences of identity (Boylorn, 2016). It creates space to connect personal experiences of culture, race, gender, and other aspects of oppression to the broader context of society. More specifically, I utilized Blackgirl autoethnography to disrupt the singular representations of Black women presented in research (Boylorn, 2016). Boylorn (2016) argued, "Blackgirl autoethnography is blackened in that it centers and makes claims about particular, but shared, experiences of women of color; but it also troubles traditional ways of knowing and being in the world by embracing the tenets of autoethnography" (p. 50). Both (re)membering and critical Blackgirl autoethnography underscore the importance of the knowledge that grows within our bodies as Black motherscholars and is rooted in our lived experiences.

Black Women Produce

> Those of us who nurture the lives of those children who are not supposed to exist, who are not supposed to grow up, who are revolutionary in their very beings are doing some of the most subversive work in the world. If we don't know it, the establishment does.
>
> —Alexis Pauline Gumbs

When I think of a producer, I initially connect it to music. I've always loved music as it was a Black haven of sonic possibilities. Outside of recording songs from the radio onto my cassette tapes, the first legit album (CD) I ever bought was Whitney Houston's 1998 *My Love is Your Love.* I was the eldest of three siblings at 14 years old and over two decades away from becoming a mother. The title of that album is fitting because when I think of my relationship with my mother and my relationship with my daughter, I understand the permanence of this type of love. Our lives are wrapped up in this foundational love that shapes our sense of self and influences the way we give and receive love throughout life. The love from Black Mother to Black Daughter is an inherently embodied and subversive love produced in revolution (Gumbs et al., 2016). It is embodied as we begin this relationship in our mother's womb. It is not only trauma that is passed from generation to generation, but an embodied connection and bond that begins with our mothers and our mother's mothers and stays with us as we begin the physical and emotional journey of carrying our own children (Ocasio-Stoutenburg & Boveda, 2024). This continues when they arrive here on earth as our voice soothes, our milk nourishes, and there is safety in our touch. As Black Mothers, we defy the anti-Blackness of society as we find ways to love and care for another in a world that does not love and care for us; Gumbs articulates this by stating, "Love is possible even in a world that teaches us to hate ourselves and the selves we see waiting in each other... [the] world that says that we should not be born, and that says "no" to our very beings everyday, I still wake up wanting you with a "yes" on my heart" (Gumbs, 2023, Para 2). We, as Black motherscholars, boldly push back against the societal conditions that threaten the well-being of our spirits and our children, making Black Motherhood a pathway to freedom.

To produce is to create and will a way to something beautiful. As Black motherscholars, we are often producing in ways that redirect and refine arrangements and concepts society attempts to make us beholden to by ensuring the final "product" we present (ourselves and our children) is reflective of our foremothers. To produce in a world set on stifling our existence and to still create life and culture, be experts in pedagogy and praxis, be innovative in leadership and sur-thrival—the "reclaiming of the Black American spirit; a means of reconditioning so that we may navigate the world with a strong sense of our Black selves" (Jenkins, 2024)—is a feat. And quite simply, *produce* is what Black motherscholars do.

As Black motherscholars, we produce our beautiful babies, we produce scholarship, and we produce liberatory pedagogies. By positioning Black motherscholars as producers, this chapter explores the balancing act of being Black, Mother, and Scholar and has implications regarding the significant role of Black women in shaping the lives of our children and future scholarship, with both working to push back against dominant narratives. In producing, we make the academy a space where we can access, acknowledge, and share assets rooted in being Black motherscholars.

Slow Down Momma

Free to be
Overjoyed with gratitude
Leading with my heart
And walking in my Mother's garden
Scorching the earth with love and purpose
Adapting to the world around me
Daring to be
Eternally free

Rocha (2014) asserts that Black mothering is a creative, nurturing, recuperating, and resisting act against genocidal practices. Although she is speaking about the violence Black mothers experience in Rio de Janeiro's poorest areas, Black Mothers are fighting against constant, deliberate, and systematic destruction in everything from schools (Powell & Coles, 2021), to hospitals (Blackstock, 2024), the criminal system (Mitchell & Davis, 2019), and more (Das et al., 2022; Leath et al., 2022). My pathway to motherhood was a fight, and I had to navigate several systems to get to my blessing, my healing.

In 2019, I had 17 fibroids removed to prepare my womb to create life and house a tiny human. That also meant I would eventually need to have a planned C-section to give birth. In 2022, when I was a few weeks from my due date, I had a meeting with my dissertation committee chair and told her that my planned C-section on August 16th was three days before the first day of the fall semester. In my mind, at the time, I could still attend class because it was on Zoom. Despite having a beautiful and spiritually connected pregnancy, I was still thinking about being productive and could not fathom missing any classes to start the semester. Thankfully, my Black motherscholar chair made clear that she was not feeling that at all! She articulated that attending class would not be acceptable, and I needed to be okay with missing class for the first two weeks. I made a compromise and missed the first week, but when my daughter arrived, when I saw her face and held her tiny body against my skin, everything changed. It was clear that I had to begin mothering myself to begin mothering this beautiful being. I saw beauty and possibility in myself because I saw myself in her. My daughter's name is Folasade, which means crown and glory; and my name, Eghosa, means God's time is the best. The two Nigerian names converged in real life because God's timing asked that I slow down to bask in the glory that is my daughter and motherhood.

I was able to be home full-time for just under four months with my baby girl before returning to work. In part, I returned to work 60% of the school year because if I did not, I would not qualify for the annual raise the following year. In fact, for my school district, they offered six weeks for maternity leave, but those weeks were taken from my sick days. It is ironic that education, which is dominated by women who are in community with so many children, gives so little respect and time to grow our own families. I knew when I stepped back into the classroom as a mother, things were different. I loved my students, but unlike before, when the school day ended, so did much of my time and devotion to that place. Unlike before, I created boundaries. After losing my mom in 2007, much of my life had been like climbing a mountain but never finding a spot to pitch my tent for rest. The distorted armor I had used to move through the world needed to be reshaped so that I could take care of myself in a way I had not before.

Gumbs et al. (2016) argues that we can learn to mother ourselves even in a world bent on constraining our growth and sense of self. Whether it is the high mortality rate for pregnant Black mothers (Smith et al., 2018) or the exclusion we face in academic spaces (Ferguson et al., 2021), Black motherhood allows us to be righteously born again. It makes space for us to nurture ourselves while we nurture a new being. For me, surviving the birth of my daughter and surviving the permanence of anti-Black ideological lynching (Garrett-Walker, 2021) in the academy required that I begin mothering myself. It required a complete shift in what had become my way of being and coping mechanism—staying busy and skipping rest. By *rest*, I mean the type of rest Tricia Hersey (2022) advocates for; the type of rest that is inherently bound to disrupt dominant systems and break the internalized productivity rooted in capitalism, synthetic white supremacy, patriarchy, and anti-Blackness.

In many ways, Folasade (meaning: crown and glory) Efosa (*my mother's name*; meaning: God's Blessing) Abeni (meaning: we prayed for her and she arrived) Hamilton, saved me from myself and made space for me to find pockets of unbridled joy. Instead of thinking of my future plans, research projects, curriculum development, or potential conferences, I was following the path of being present. Each month, I documented her growth, her gurgles, her giggles, and her gaze, retaining those moments while retaining and meshing my identity as a Black woman scholar.

Retaining All the Things

> The radical potential of the word "mother" comes after the 'm'. It is the space that "other" takes in our mouths when we say it. We are something else. We know it from how fearfully institutions wield social norms and try to shut us down. We know it from how we are transforming the planet with our every messy step toward making life possible.
>
> —Alexis Pauline Gumbs

As Black motherscholars, what we create, how we create, and why we create is also represented in our little human creations. They learn through us how to be conduits of creativity in their own right. Together, we find creative pathways to freedom, healing, and liberation. Walker (1994) highlights the power and creativity of Black women, even when we are not always aware. She beautifully articulates how Black women, even under the heavy force of structural oppression, create. We create life in so many different ways; we do so with the radical edge that society works hard to obfuscate.

With a growing number of Black women attaining advanced degrees, there has also been an increase of Black women in faculty positions working to create as teachers and researchers (Baldwin & Griffin, 2015; Gregory, 1999; Huston, 2006). Unfortunately, even with that growth, there are fewer opportunities for Black women with regard to "three key areas of academia: (a) type of institutions, (b) the rank and tenure process, and (c) salary" (Huston, 2006, p. 594). This marks the already hegemonic space of the academy as more contentious for Black women, as race and gender extend barriers. Black mothers are often rendered disposable within structures of anti-Blackness, synthetic white supremacy, capitalism, and patriarchy (Dillard, 2021; Lawson, 2000). When I went on the job market in 2024, I happily accepted the job offer that I believed was best for my family. Thirty days after I accepted a verbal offer, and twenty days after being told a written contract was still processing, Northeastern University decided not to run the program and did not honor their offer to me and my family. I could not help but wonder if I were a white male, would they have had such disregard for me? Would I have been as disposable? Often, this is what it means to be a Black motherscholar. It is a confusing amalgamation of uncertainties that are not reflective of our prowess.

In addition, mothering as an academic comes with "a triple shift in which [mothers] must navigate domestic tasks, work, and childcare" (Donoso et al., 2023, p. 2). This makes upward mobility challenging for mothers as academic spaces do not align with motherhood due to "a triple shift of triple expectations: work excellence at the university, excellence in mothering, and excellence in domestic tasks and chores" (Donoso et al., 2023, p. 3). This form of marginalization for mothers is threefold for Black women experiencing anti-Black and gendered racism. The strong Black woman trope insists that Black women have the physical and emotional strength to withstand the oppressive onslaught of society, even when embarking on the all-embodying journey of motherhood.

How does a Black woman navigate *all the things* while retaining motherhood, scholarship, and presence? I am not sure if this question can be answered generally, but for me, presence in both motherhood and scholarhood was key. As a Black mother, my definition of presence is: to be present in spirit, emotion, mind, and body. To be present means to embrace balance, healing, and joy even as they struggle to coexist alongside the destruction that often comes with being a Black motherscholar. Presence is loving and raising a Black child while navigating the specific challenges faced by Black women in the academy. It is amplifying my voice as both Black Mother and Scholar while bringing that unique, embodied, ancestral, and powerful perspective to an academic space built on keeping Black women out (Sims, 2011). Being present means manifesting our mothers, their mothers, and their mothers, effectively creating an ancestral chain that is linked to our sense of self and can be passed down to our children. Infusing them with the ability to navigate the world BIG. TALL. *SURE.* AND **BLACK**.

Conclusion

> *And I will lead you down that road if you lose your way*
> *Born to be your protector*
> *Even though I know someday you're gonna shine on your own*
> *I will be your projector....*
> *There's a long line of hands carryin' your name, ooh*
> *Liftin' you up so you will be raised*
> —Beyoncé & Rumi Carter, PROTECTOR

I grew up believing that much of my worth was reflected in what I could produce and often had intrinsic motivation to perform well to prove my worth, especially when it came to my dad. That often meant getting all A's, making the honor roll, and playing well on the basketball court. It is ironic because when it came to my most important producer role by way of having my daughter, no one could tell me nothing. My worth needed no external validation. In my daughter's eyes, I was a worthy sight as is:

> You've seen those eyes of those children. They don't want to hear it. They want to know, what are you going to do now, today? And somehow, all of the baggage that I had accumulated as a person about what was valuable, so much of that just fell away. And I could not only

> be me, whatever that was, somebody actually needed me to be that. (Morrison & Moyers, 1990, 19:13)

To see myself in my daughter is to see a beauty and a softness I never saw in myself before. That is why Black mothering is rooted in resistance and a pathway to "radically recovering humanness and joy" (Ocasio-Stoutenburg & Boveda, 2024, p. 2). The radical possibilities embedded in being a Black motherscholar are endless. In my twenty-three months into motherhood, I understand the most critical A's of my lifetime (access, acknowledge, assets):

1. In producing our babies, we make Black Motherhood and the academy a space where we can **Access** care, love, joy, knowledge, freedom, and possibility as "the practice of mothering [is] an alternative building practice of valuing ourselves and each other and creating the world we deserve" (Gumbs et al. 2016, p. 31).
2. In **Acknowledging** the realities of being a Black motherscholar, we are better able to weave the impact of this identity into our scholarship and our sense of self.
3. Through access and acknowledgment, we nourish and build on the **Assets** rooted in Black Mother/Scholar-hood; confident and guided in what we specifically bring. We assert the value of our intersecting identities as Black/women/mother/scholars.

These pivotal A's position Black motherhood as a critical and epistemological asset to the academy. We insist on being. We insist on creating. We insist on. Toni Morrison reminds us that listening to our children allows us to free ourselves from baggage. She reminds us that even though we think we did not ask to be born, we did:

> That is why we are here. We are here, and we have to do something nurturing that we respect before we go... it is more interesting, more complicated, more intellectually demanding, and more morally demanding to love somebody, to take care of somebody, to make one other person feel good. (Morrison & Moyers, 1990, 5:43)

Ultimately, Black motherscholars are revolutionary, and we know why we are here—to be connected and complicated beings that put love into the ether through the embodiment of transformative motherhood and scholarhood. As a Black motherscholar, I walk through the world with my baby girl next to me, my mother guiding above me, and behind the lineage of Black motherscholars before me. I am healing my inner Blackgirlchild as I find presence and purpose in a new light. My daughter reminds me of my power, my love, my worth, my influence, and my ability to embody my lineage by giving her what my mother gave me and more: freedom through love.

Competing Interests

The author has no conflicts of interest to declare that are relevant to the content of this manuscript.

References

Baldwin, C. P., & Griffin, M. D. (2015). Challenges of race and gender for Black women in the academy. In *Disrupting the culture of silence* (pp. 55–66). Routledge.

Beauboeuf-Lafontant, T. (2002). A womanist experience of caring: Understanding the pedagogy of exemplary Black women teachers. *The Urban Review, 34*(1), 71–86.

Bell, D. A. (1995). Who's afraid of critical race theory. *University of Lllinois Law Review, 4*(3), 823–846.

Blackstock, U. (2024). *Legacy: A Black physician reckons with racism in medicine.* Penguin Publishing Group.

Boylorn, R. M. (2016). On being at home with myself: Blackgirl autoethnography as research praxis. *International Review of Qualitative Research, 9*(1), 44–58. https://doi.org/10.1525/irqr.2016.9.1.44

Campt, T. (2021). *A Black gaze: Artists changing how we see.* The MIT Press.

Case, K. I. (1997). African American othermothering in the urban elementary school. *The Urban Review, 29*(1), 25–39.

Crenshaw, K. (1989). Demarginalizing the intersection of race and sex: A Black feminist critique of antidiscrimination doctrine, feminist theory and antiracist politics. *University of Chicago Legal Forum, 1.*

Crenshaw, K. (1991). Mapping the margins: Intersectionality, identity politics, and violence against women of color. *Stanford Law Review, 43*(6), 1241–1299. https://doi.org/10.2307/1229039

Das, S., Pitts, J., Arevalo, K., Cox, B., Blood, T., Hughes, D., …, & Way, N. (2022). Lessons of resistance from Black mothers to their Black sons. *Journal of Research on Adolescence, 32*(3), 981–998.

Dillard, C. B. (2000). The substance of things hoped for, the evidence of things not seen: Examining an endarkened feminist epistemology in educational research and leadership. *International Journal of Qualitative Studies in Education, 13*(6), 661–681.

Dillard, C. B. (2021). *The spirit of our work: Black women teachers (re)member.* Beacon Press.

Donoso, G. R., LaBrenz, C. A., & Valderrama, C. G. (2023). Tensions, challenges, and resistance among academic mothers during the COVID-19 pandemic. In *Psychosocial, educational, and economic impacts of COVID-19.* IntechOpen.

Dumas, M. J., & Ross, K. M. (2016). "Be real black for me" imagining BlackCrit in education. *Urban Education, 51*(4), 415–442.

Ferguson, T. L., Berry, R. R., & Collins, J. D. (2021). "Where is our space within this ivory tower?" The teaching experiences of Black women faculty in education programs. *Journal of Research on Leadership Education, 16*(2), 140–157.

Garrett-Walker, W. L. (2021). *Replanting a wild seed: Black women school leaders subverting ideological lynching* (Doctoral dissertation). University of San Francisco.

Gregory, S. T. (1999). *Black women in the academy: The secrets to success and achievement.* University Press of America.

Gumbs, A. P. (2010). *We can learn to mother ourselves: The queer survival of Black feminism* (Doctoral dissertation).

Gumbs, A. P. (2023, October 22). Mothering not motherhood. *Parapraxis.* https://www.parapraxismagazine.com/articles/mothering

Gumbs, A. P., Martens, C., & Williams, M. (Eds.). (2016). *Revolutionary mothering: Love on the front lines.* PM Press.

Hersey, T. (2022). *Rest is resistance: A manifesto.* Hachette UK.

Huston, T. A. (2006). Race and gender bias in higher education: Could faculty course evaluations impede further progress toward parity? *Seattle Journal for Social Justice, 4*(2), 34.

Jenkins, T. G. (2024). *For the love of Black children: Towards Black liberatory educational subversion* (Doctoral dissertation). https://repository.usfca.edu/diss/695

Ladson-Billings, G. (2021). Critical race theory—What it is not! In M. Lynn & A. D. Dixson (Eds.), *Handbook of critical race theory in education* (pp. 32–43). Routledge.

Lawson, E. (2000). Black women's mothering in a historical and contemporary perspective: Understanding the past, forging the future. *Journal of the Motherhood Initiative for Research and Community Involvement*.

Leath, S., Butler-Barnes, S., & Haynes-Thoby, L. (2022). "They just keep coming": A study of how anti-Black racial violence informs racial grief and resistance among Black mothers. *Journal of Child and Family Studies, 31*(12), 3450–3467.

Lorde, A. (1984). An Open Letter to Mary Daly (pp. 66–71). Na.

Mitchell, M. B., & Davis, J. B. (2019). Formerly incarcerated Black mothers matter too: Resisting social constructions of motherhood. *The Prison Journal, 99*(4), 420–436.

Morrison, T., & Moyers, B. (1990). Toni Morrison: A writers work. *Manufacturing Intellect*. https://www.youtube.com/watch?v=53F0lFMSwpc

Obaizamomwan-Hamilton, E. (2025). (Re)storative (Re)membering: Exploring Black womanhood, Black hair, and the power of collective (Re)membering. In C. Southwell, D. Lewis, & C. A. Olatunji (Eds.), *Blessed positionality*.

Ocasio-Stoutenburg, L., & Boveda, M. (2024). "Who raised you?": Black women's indispensable conceptualizations of mothering for theorizing and researching DisCrit. *International Journal of Qualitative Studies in Education, 1–19.*

Powell, T., & Coles, J. A. (2021). "We still here": Black mothers' personal narratives of sense making and resisting antiblackness and the suspensions of their Black children. *Race Ethnicity and Education, 24*(1), 76–95.

Rocha, L. (2014). *Outraged mothering: Black women, racial violence, and the power of emotions in Rio de Janeiro's African diaspora* (Doctoral dissertation). University of Texas.

Sims, D. J. (2011). A muted voice on holy ground: Reflections on the dialectics experienced as an African American female professor in a Christian university. In M. N. Niles & N. S. Gordon (Eds.), *Still searching for our mothers' gardens: Experiences of new, tenure-track women of color at "majority" institutions* (pp. 21–40). University Press of America.

Smith, I. Z., Bentley-Edwards, K. L., El-Amin, S., & Darity, W. Jr. (2018). *Fighting at birth: Eradicating the Black-White infant mortality gap*. Duke University Press.

Walker, A. (1994). In search of our mother's gardens. In A. Mitchell (Ed.), *Within the circle: An anthology of African American literary criticism from the Harlem Renaissance to the present* (pp. 401–409). Duke University Press.

Black Motherhood, Adoption and Academia: One Black Motherscholar's Journey Building Family

Atiya Kai Stokes-Brown

Abstract Women in academia are often told it is difficult to achieve tenure because their childrearing years coincide with pre-tenure years. This chapter explores how Black motherscholars navigate the responsibilities of academic life with motherhood, focusing specifically on the experience of a Black mother who adopted a baby pre-tenure and three young children post-tenure. This chapter centers the development of my mothering, which has been influenced by a unique journey of resistance against norms embedded in the foster care system designed to destroy family bonds; resistance against the 'ideal worker' norm embedded in academia; and support from other Black motherscholars and Black women scholars.

Keyword Black motherscholars · Adoption · Foster care system

Introduction

As of September 2022, the number of children awaiting adoption in the public foster care system was 368,530, with Black children accounting for 23% of the total percentage of children (U.S. Department of Health & Human Services, 2024). The concept of adoption informal and formal (i.e. the termination of parental rights) is quite common for African-American families (Gillum, 2011, p. 324). Yet, while extant scholarship has highlighted the perspectives of Black adoptive families (e.g. Gillum, 2011; Prater & King, 1988), few studies have explored the experiences of Black women adoptive motherscholars. A major challenge women scholars face is caregiving for children (Hochschild, 2011). Yet, we know little about the unique caregiving challenges facing Black women adoptive motherscholars.

Regardless of their motivations for adopting, Black women adoptive motherscholars who formally adopt children become part of a larger governmental system that disproportionately shatters maternal bonds between Black children and mothers

A. K. Stokes-Brown (✉)
Coastal Carolina University, Conway, SC, USA
e-mail: astokesb@coastal.edu

C. R. Turner and M. L. Green (eds.), *Black Motherscholarship Within and Beyond the Academy*, https://doi.org/10.1007/978-3-031-99758-7_9

(Hall, 2021). Black children are only fourteen percent of the U.S. population, yet they account for twenty-three percent of the children in foster care (Roberts, 2002). Black mothers are more likely than women from other races to be reported to the child welfare system, lose custody of their children as a result, and are less likely to be reunited with their children (Harp & Butting, 2020, p. 258). Being a Black woman scholar is to not only be aware of gross inequities deeply ingrained in governmental systems, but to actively advocate for reforms that deconstruct and dismantle those systems. Yet, there is no escaping the reality that the decision to build my family via formal adoption and the joy that comes with building that family was facilitated by a system that disrupts Black families and communities.

Acknowledging this gap in the literature, this chapter seeks to answer the following research questions: (1) How do adoptive Black families navigate and experience the adoption process? and (2) How does the adoption process impact Black mother-scholars and influence their mothering? To investigate these research questions, I offer my unique perspective of the experience for adoptive Black families as a motherscholar. My journey into mothering and my connection to my children has been characterized by two distinct internal conflicts: first, the struggle to reject both the demonization of my children's biological mother and notions of heroism encouraged by the foster care system; and second, the struggle to provide the care my children need as a result of past trauma in an environment where Black women's navigation of academic spaces has been compared to navigating a rival gang's territory (Baszile, 2006; Turner & Allen, 2022). Instead of weapons, Black women scholars navigate racism, sexism, revisionist history, differential racialization, interest convergence, and white fragility in an environment that tolerates few interruptions to professional life (Berry, 2018). It is this reality that draws me to reflect often on what it means to reorganize myself to "meet the common needs in this historical moment, including the capacity to raise and nurture whole, resilient individuals, as well as autonomous communities of resistance" (Oka, 2016, p. 53). As I struggle to nurture, teach, love, protect, and empower my children in a world resistant to our intersecting identities rooted in our shared Blackness, this chapter also highlights how my relationships with other Black motherscholars and Black women scholars have nurtured, empowered, challenged, and sustained me.

Theoretical Framing

Critical race theory (CRT) and critical race feminism (CRF) are used in this chapter to explore nuances between and the intersectional nature of racialized and gendered experiences, offering a roadmap to better understand the challenges faced by Black women adoptive motherscholars. Examining the legacy and lasting impact of race and racism in the U.S., CRT provides scholars a critical avenue to centralize the voice of marginalized racial identity groups, creating opportunities to explore how lived experiences of racism and sexism might affect women of color (Tate, 1997). Elevating the narratives of people, CRT highlights the unique positions and challenges experienced by those who "exist at an intersection of recognized sites of oppression" (Delgado & Stefancic, 2001, p. 51; Nixon, 2013, p. 45). CRT holds that race and racism (conscious and unconscious) are endemic, permanent, and a fundamental part of defining and explaining how U.S. society functions (Bell, 1992; Russell, 1992). CRT also recognizes the experiential knowledge of people of color as legitimate and appropriate, thus highlighting the importance of qualitative research methods as storytelling, biographies, and narratives (Bell, 1992; Delgado, 1989). Critical race feminism (CRF) is a branch of CRT. Whereas CRT has been criticized for omitting the perspectives of women of color, CRF explicitly highlights the interconnectedness of race, gender and class, centering the intersectional identity and broad experiences of these women (Ngwainmbi, 2004; Wing, 2003).

The tenets of CRF highlight the uniqueness of women of color. The first tenet asserts that the experiences that shape the lived realities and perspectives of women of color are different from those that impact men of color, white women, and white men (Wing, 2003). Secondly, CRF focuses on the ways in which various forms of oppression are connected and manifest in the lives of women of color as a result of their intersectional identities (Wing, 2003; hooks, 1984). Third, CRF rejects essentialism, noting that no one has a single, easily stated, unitary identity. Women of color have multiple political identities, and their experiences cannot be assumed to be similar to those of white women or Black men (Wing, 2003). The last two tenets of CRT call for a multidisciplinary approach that draws meaning and value from various fields of study and theories; and the development of theories and approaches that critique and dismantle all forms of oppression (Wing, 2003). This theory rests firmly on Crenshaw's (1991) foundational research on intersectionality which highlighted how multiple forms of oppression are experienced when various social identities intersect. These frameworks have been particularly useful when examining the underrepresentation, isolation, and marginalization of Black women in academia (Collins, 2000).

As theoretical frameworks, CRT and CRF allow for a nuanced discussion of how my identity as a Black woman intersects with other social identities: adoptive mother, teacher-scholar, wife, daughter, friend, and more. CRF places women like me at the center, rather than the margins, of research and reflections about topics like adoption, mothering, sisterhood, and work-life 'balance' in academia. Thus, CRF provides an appropriate framework for examining the experiences of Black mother-scholars, giving voice to perspectives and experiences that are otherwise marginalized or ignored.

Methodology

To offer my unique perspective of the experience for adoptive Black families as a motherscholar, I engaged in an autoethnographic study, making meaning of and interpreting my own experience. Autoethnography is an approach to research and writing that seeks to describe and systematically analyze personal experiences in order to understand cultural experience (Ellis et al., 2010). Combining autobiography and ethnography, the methodological approach used in this chapter affords the opportunity to connect self-exploration and self-awareness with cultural description, with the goal of better understanding myself and others (Bhattacharya, 2017; Chang, 2008). This form of academic writing is commonly used to explore racialized and gendered experiences (e.g. Bochner, 1997; Ellis, 1995; Goodall, 2006; hooks, 1994), offering new insights into personal experiences that can fill gaps in knowledge (Goodall, 2001).

Data Collection

The themes that emerge from this chapter were generated from personal journals and recollections of detailed conversations with Black motherscholars and Black women scholars. My initial review of the journal entries refreshed my memory and began the process of exploring how my reflections address the research questions. Specifically, I reviewed the entries with a focus on how the entries spoke to (1) navigating the adoptive process and (2) how the adoption experience impacted me as a Black motherscholar. After several readings, themes were identified using a deductive coding process to identify codes in the entries. Entries that reflect the themes are woven into this chapter.

The choice to use personal journal reflections and recollections of detailed conversations with Black motherscholars and Black women scholars as the primary autoethnographic method for this study was based on espoused value of counter-stories to expose and critique dominant perspectives and ideologies which perpetuates various stereotypes (e.g. DeCuir & Dixson, 2004; Delgado Bernal & Villalpando, 2002). From a very young age, I have used journaling as a tool for remembrance, critical reflection, and self-discovery. Thus, it felt natural to write about this transformative experience, using the journal as a safe space to describe, question, and interrogate my approach to and understanding of mothering and its impact on myself and my children. I wrote in my journal, on average, twice a week, with the goal of documenting my observations, feelings (positive and negative), and lingering questions.

Spending time with other Black women scholars and Black motherscholars and reflecting on those conversations also proved essential in making meaning of my experience. These sister talks, otherwise defined as genial conversations between Black women in which they share narratives, jokes, and life lessons, were vital, life-affirming spaces (Few, et al., 2003; Majors, 2001; Turner & Allen, 2022). For several years, we gathered in each other's homes to share food, drinks, laughter and tears. These small group conversations focused on a multitude of discussion topics including: navigating negative socio-emotional behaviors, navigating academia as Black women scholars and Black motherscholars, work-life 'balance', family reactions to and understandings of adoption, the bond of motherhood, caregiving, and societal views of motherhood and adoption. The resulting narrative draws on years of participant observation, specifically journal entries about those conversations, with the aim of advancing the research on Black motherscholars in higher education, spotlighting my distinctive, layered, and intersectional journey of resistance, joy, and mothering.

The Journey to Motherhood—A Private Adoption

> A child born to another woman calls me mom. The magnitude of that tragedy and the depth of that privilege are not lost on me.—Jody Landers

In her article, "Losing Black Mothers, Finding Revolutionary Mothering", K. Melchor Quick Hall tells of her adoption journey, noting that her daughter's "life has been disrupted by government authorities who have separated her from her mother" (2021, p. 770). When my husband and I decided to adopt, the realities of this shattered bond were far from our understanding about the adoption process. In all honesty, we were pretty clueless about all aspects of adoption, including how to start the process. It was only by God's divine intervention that we just happened to be members at a church where we knew of a couple who had also adopted. We asked them out to lunch one Sunday to hear their experiences and learn more. We knew that the husband, who worked as a lobbyist for private adoption agencies in the state, was himself adopted and, with his wife, had adopted several children. But otherwise, we had no idea what to expect, as I had fully intended on giving birth to children. When it became clear that we would not be able to create a child without costly interventions, we prayed, talked, and found that we both were open to adoption. Despite our faults, we believed that we could provide a child with a positive family experience, thus making a real difference in a child's life (Tyebee, 2003). Adopting a Black child aligned with our espoused social justice values, demonstrating our "commitment to the survival of Black people" (Hollingsworth, 2000, p. 128).

We met the church member/lobbyist for lunch later that week. I recall thinking that the timing was serendipitous, as we had recently finished planning our schedule for a week of community engagement in honor of Rev. Dr. Martin Luther King's sacrifice and service. Our new friend spoke lovingly about his personal experience; how he was adopted as a baby and how adoption had positively changed his life for the better. He shared stories about how he and his wife came to adopt their children and the great joy they experience raising their family. By the end of the meal, we were essentially sold; and we were eager to work with an agency and start the process. Little did we know that when we arrived for lunch, two weeks later we would have a baby in our home. A beautiful two month old Black baby boy whose mother had given him up at birth with the expressed hope of a new life. Seventeen and with no support from her family, our son's birth mother worked with an agency to have him placed at birth. For approximately two months, he lived with his first adoptive mother, a white single woman, who unexpectedly contracted a serious illness and was hospitalized. As she was no longer able to care for him, the baby was placed with a short-term foster family and had been living with that family for about a week when we asked for the meeting to learn more about adoption. So, in three short weeks, we were interviewed twice, had our backgrounds checked, and approved to drive across the state to pick up our child at the agency.

Given the uniqueness of our adoption process, we met our son's birth mother one week after bringing him home. It is clear from my journal entries that I was extremely apprehensive about the meeting. I couldn't help but wonder if our son's birth mother would, for some reason, disapprove of us raising her son. At that moment, I felt desperate to have her approval, despite the reality that it was the agency, through its monthly visits and reviews, that would determine whether we were fit to adopt and parent the baby, not her.

> Tomorrow we meet [baby's birth mom]. A two-hour drive and we will be standing in front of the woman who made me a mama and [my husband] a papa. I've told some people that I am nervous about the meeting but if I'm completely honest, what I really feel is fear – soul-sucking fear. I am terrified that she will take one look at me and conclude that I am the worst mother ever and will fight the adoption. [The case manager] assures us that this scenario won't happen, but I can't get the possibility out of my mind. Let's be real – one week ago I had never changed a diaper before in my life, babysat maybe once or twice, and now I am now this precious sweet boy's mama. His mama. Mama.
>
> This child has my whole heart. I know it's only been one week, but I can't bear the thought of being without him. Is she going to look at me and see how woefully unprepared I feel? Will she decide that we are undeserving of this precious gift? Even if she can't stop the process, I truly want her to walk away believing that her baby is in good hands. We adore [baby's name] and he is fiercely loved. We will do everything in our power to give him all the love and support he could ever need. We are forever indebted to her. For her sacrifice. Her sacrifice. Ok, so I know this song is not about adoption but whenever I think about her that Elton John song pops in my mind –
>
> *And it's no sacrifice*
> *Just a simple word*
> *It's two hearts living*
> *In two separate worlds*
> *But it's no sacrifice*
> *No sacrifice*
> *It's no sacrifice at all*
>
> Sacrifice. [The case manager]uses that word often and says that for [baby's birth mom], this adoption is truly a selfless act of love. That kind of love demands that this [baby] have the best. What if she doesn't think we are the best? That I am the best mama for him? God, please help me be the best.

While we were not told much about our son's birth mother before the meeting, the language used by the case manager to describe her and her choice to give her child up for adoption was extremely positive—words like *selfless, wise*, and *thoughtful* were commonly used. The narrative was clear; by giving up her child, she was doing what was best for the baby and giving us a gift that we would otherwise never have. And we, in turn, were to be applauded for saving this child by providing a better life. I remember thinking that our son's birth mother was so brave to recognize that this was the 'best' decision. After all, she was a seventeen-year-old Black girl with no family support. Our son was her second unexpected pregnancy and when her family learned that she was pregnant again, they refused to support her and the new baby. She was forced out of her home and for months lived in a maternity home for expectant teenage mothers.

When we finally met, she was just as she had been described. A beautiful young girl, extremely tall, with wide brown eyes shook our hands and bluntly told us that she was in no position to raise a child and could not give him what he needed. With very little emotion, she told us that she felt little to no connection with the baby and believed that she would be able to move forward with her life if she knew that he was placed with a family that would love and care for him. I recall thanking her for the gift of raising her son and offering to send pictures and written updates beyond that which was required by the agency. She politely declined and asked us to simply love him as our own. Approximately 30 minutes later, the meeting ended, and we left the building, taking a child who she has not seen since.

A Mother's Sacrifice?

I left that meeting feeling an overwhelming sense of gratitude for the opportunity to be a mother because of her sacrifice. I still feel it despite the fact that I have very little evidence, other than the case manager's words, to prove that our son's birth mother truly viewed the adoption as a sacrifice. Yet, that is the word that immediately comes to mind when I try to understand her decision. Despite her claim of feeling little to no connection with our son, I have a difficult time imagining that the maternal bond between mother and child ever fully dissipates. Perhaps I hold romanticized notions of this bond because I have never given birth, have always wanted children and, given my positionality, lack a deep understanding of the complexities of teenage pregnancy decision-making (e.g. Mantovani & Thomas, 2014). I do know that when given the option to terminate her pregnancy, our son's mother did not. For nine months she gave up her body and emotional autonomy to ensure that she would deliver a healthy baby boy. I believe that her decision to have him and give him away was motivated in some large part by a specific, deep unspoken love that only a birth mother can feel for a child. But I do not know for sure. I regret not taking more time to learn more about her interpersonal relationships and her interpretation about how those relationships affected the decision-making process of her unexpected pregnancy. I cannot help but wonder if a part of her grieves because of all of the things she did not get to experience with her biological child; all the things that we have experienced and have brought us so much happiness.

Indeed, holding our baby boy and watching him grow into a young man has been, without a doubt, one of the greatest joys of my life. Our son was the most beautiful, inquisitive and huggable baby and is now, in what seems like the snap of my fingers, the most handsome, intelligent, and empathetic young man. Our son knows he is adopted and throughout his life, we have spoken about his birth mother. When he was young, I instinctually gravitated to the 'birth mom as saint' framework in our conversations in large part because of his age and because, frankly, I believed it. I needed to believe it because our joy is the result of a broken bond. The 'birth mom as saint' narrative gave me permission to ignore my role in breaking that bond and the possibilities of collective mothering. Only years later, when my son was much older and we began the adoption process again, did I pause to consider what it might have looked like to support and nurture our son's birth mother as part of our family so that their connection, their bond would not be broken. His mother was young, isolated, and unable to raise him in the context of a social and community network (Hall, 2021, p.771). When she gave him to us, I never once took time to think critically about bringing our son's mother into *our* social and community network so that we could mother him *together*. Might it have been complicated? Stressful? Probably, but it also might have been fulfilling and restorative for us all. We will never know. Fueled by my desire and comforted by the frame of the sacrificial birth mom, I did not, for a very long time, question how we could have reimagined the adoptive process in such a way that would have given us both the gift of mothering by providing support that extends beyond biological ties (Roberts, 2002, p. vii).

Adoption the Second Time Around—Engaging the Foster Care System

Seven years later when we made the decision to expand our family, we intentionally chose to foster a child in a pre-adoptive home. By this time, we'd left our racially diverse community in a state in the southern portion of the U.S. and were living in an overwhelmingly white community in a state in the northern portion of the U.S where Blacks made up less than three percent of the town's population and six percent of the population in the county. Still, Black children made up fifteen percent of the children in foster care. I had recently been awarded tenure and promotion at the private university where I taught, and we were living in a large home with an empty bedroom—perfect for another child. Our son was about seven and loved the idea of having a sibling. So, once again we opened ourselves up to adoption, hopeful that the foster care experience via public child welfare agencies would give us the opportunity to build a relationship with the child's family and keep the child connected to their biological family. We were also aware that there was a good chance that our foster child would experience unique social and emotional challenges (e.g. Gillum, 2011; Harden, 2004).

After a substantially longer application and review process, we were matched with a nine-year-old Black boy who had recently been placed in foster care. His mother was just eighteen years old when he was born; and for much of his life, he experienced housing insecurity, moving frequently to live with various members of his biological family. At some point, his mother came back into his life and lived with him until she married. She then gave birth to additional children and moved to a different county in the state and left her son with her mother. Eventually, our son's birth mother left her husband and the other children, took her boy from her mother, and moved with the boy to an apartment in the county where we lived. His mother had been living with a serious mental illness and struggled for years to find the right treatment and support to parent with her mental health condition. Without treatment, she neglected the boy and when members of his biological family declined to take him in, he was placed in foster care. We met our son forty-eight hours after we agreed to foster him.

Almost immediately, we begin to hear negative stories about our son's birth mother, painting her as evil, unfit, and undeserving of her child. It is true that our son was not thriving when we met him. He was malnourished and wearing the only clothes and shoes he owned, all way too big. When we put him to bed that first night, he couldn't believe that he had a bed with a mattress to sleep on, as he was accustomed to sleeping on the floor. And when we met with his teacher, we learned that as a second grader he was reading and writing at a kindergartner level. Records showed that he was moved from school to school (based on where he was living at the time), started school a year late, and missed school often. His social worker was not shy with her opinions, making it clear that she faulted his birth mother for his condition. In her experience with the adoption process, Hall (2021, p. 771) mentions the demonization of biological mothers—the idea that "the government system trains pre-adoptive families to have tunnel vision that judges Black mothers harshly and unfairly". Without any deep knowledge or understanding of her life nor any discussion about the services and supports available and offered to her, we were immediately encouraged and expected to despise her, advocate against reunification, and push for our legal rights to the child.

This intensified when, approximately two months later, we were asked to take in additional children from the same mother. We were aware that our son had two siblings in the foster care system in an adjacent county. His half-sisters, ages three and five at the time, had been living with a white pre-adoptive family for more than a year. In an effort to maintain a bond between the three siblings, the social workers took the children once a month to a playground or indoor activity center to spend time together. One Thursday morning, we received a call from the girls' social worker notifying us that their foster family decided not to move forward with adoption and they needed to be moved to a new home. We were given twenty-four hours to decide whether they would move in with us or be sent to a new foster family. We discussed the situation with both boys later that evening and agreed to foster all three children. Early Monday morning, the girls arrived with their social worker and moved in with us.

Our adoption experiences were drastically different in almost every way. Our first adoption was quick and easy, with no resistance. Approximately three months after meeting our first son, the adoption was finalized. Our second experience was sluggish and emotionally difficult, filled with family meetings and phone calls (with the goal of reunification), court dates in different counties, and counseling sessions for the children individually, collectively, and for the entire family. After about four months, we started the adoption process. Knowing that Black families are less likely to be offered services than white families (e.g. Roberts, 2002), we advocated for their mother and the children, exhausting all possible solutions before making the decision to adopt. When we started the process, the children's birth fathers immediately gave up their parental rights and their birth mother fought against the termination of rights. Despite the circumstances, we tried to maintain bonds between the children and their birth mother and to cultivate a relationship, again with the hope of reimagining the adoptive process in such a way that would give us both the gift of mothering. Those efforts were consistently rejected; and the relationship was tenuous at best, and at times, outright hostile. Our children's birth mother despised us—to her, we were simply pawns in a system designed to vilify her and take her children. There was no way to build a relationship where our children's birth mother could become an extended part of the children's new family so we could in essence mother them together.

I vividly remember meeting our second son and our girls for the first time and instantly falling in love with them. It was as if parts of my heart that I never knew were missing had returned and healed my soul. Regardless of whether we legally adopted them, I knew these children would forever be part of my family and us part of their community. Our four children are our greatest joy; yet as a Black woman adoptive motherscholar, I live with the knowledge and understanding that our joy comes from a system rooted in the destruction of Black familial bonds, particularly maternal bonds. This is true, regardless of the frame used to define Black birth mothers (saint or villain). This has truly been one of the more disturbing aspects of adoption.

The foster care system often judges Black mothers harshly and unfairly. Yet, even the mothers who are not poorly treated in the adoption system (e.g. Gordon, 1985; Kunzel, 1993; Solinger, 1994) ultimately experience the same degree of isolation and marginalization as they are praised for essentially giving their children away. It is a strange thing to know that our happiness, our joy is rooted in shattered bonds, grief and pain. My journey into mothering has been characterized by this conflict and a second conflict rooted in my identity as a Black adoptive motherscholar working in academia—a space that was never created for women like me.

Resistance Against the Academic 'Ideal Worker' Norm

> A lot of these effects really are very much due to a cultural bias against mothers…The best hope we have for getting rid of these effects is policy that conveys that people have the right to coordinate work and family.—Professor Shelley Correll, Sociologist on the Motherhood Penalty

In their book *Do Babies Matter? Gender and Family in the Ivory Tower*, authors Mason et al. (2013) found that having children negatively affects women's academic careers. For example, following graduate school, women with young children are more likely than other women or men to opt for contingent or non-academic positions than to pursue tenure track positions. This is consistent with additional research which finds that having children slightly increases fathers' likelihood of being in tenure-track positions compared to their childless peers but does not benefit mothers (Cheng, 2020; Mairesse et al., 2020). For women, having children is a career killer; yet this is not the case for men. Men who become fathers within five years of earning their Ph.D. are far more likely than women who become mothers within the same time span to get tenure-track academic jobs (Mason et al., 2013). Despite changes to the culture and structure of academia in the form of family-friendly policies, and changing marriage and family attitudes in American society, women are presumed to be the primary caregiver for children and are less likely to fit the 'ideal worker' stereotype.

During my second year of my Ph.D. program at a large public research university, a white female student a few years ahead of me in the program that I'll call Jenny became pregnant. Jenny and her husband were excited to start a family and when she shared the news with her dissertation advisor, he blatantly told her that getting pregnant was a mistake and she should abort her child to save her promising career. Eventually the faculty member was reprimanded, and Jenny was assigned to another advisor; but none of the faculty or departmental leadership created space to discuss with the students what had occurred. Everyone just moved on, without any critical discourse about how his comments and behavior, while expressly condemned by the administration, was indeed the unspoken norm in the profession. That student's experience was fresh in my mind when we adopted our first child.

Studies show that women academics face some form of bias at almost every step of their career (e.g. Chenoweth et al., 2016). Parenthood can cause many changes to careers and even the most sympathetic employers and male colleagues often have a difficult time relating to the experience of women academics. I was in the second year of my first tenure track job at a large public research university when our adoption journey started. Initially, that institution felt like a great place to start my career; but quickly, it began to feel less and less welcoming. Some of my colleagues were truly kind and inclusive; yet at the end of my first year, I recall meeting with the department chair and being told that some of my colleagues would always be less than welcoming because they viewed me as the 'diversity hire' (because of my race and my area of study) and questioned my scholarly potential. At the time, I was the only Black faculty member and the only Black woman in the department. Already feeling unsupported and isolated, I became a mother almost overnight just a few weeks after the start of the new semester. Immediately, I felt the conflicting pressures of the tenure clock that leaves little room for absence and the pressure to bond with our new baby.

The university leave policy offered six months paid parental leave for birth/adoption with the stipulation that the leave commenced within six months of the event. I met with the department chair to discuss my situation. I was asked whether I really needed to take a leave and to consider waiting until the end of the semester if I insisted upon using leave time. There was doubt as to whether a replacement could be hired so quickly to teach that semester. There was also concern about me taking a leave before my upcoming third year review. How might that leave be viewed by the department review committee? Would this 'extra time' change my scholarship expectations? It might not have been explicitly expressed, but it was clear to me that if I took time to be with my child I would be penalized—penalized for not putting the department and its needs first and/or penalized for having 'extra' time away from teaching and service commitments. When I prioritized my child, choosing to take the leave rather than teach that semester, I couldn't help but feel that I would pay a motherhood penalty and my choice would be used as evidence that I was not to be taken seriously as a scholar (e.g. Ward & Wolf-Wendel, 2012). I have never regretted taking that time to bond with my son; but I am keenly aware that my decision further marginalized me within that academic community.

I would eventually leave that position and take a job at a private liberal arts university where I was one of two Black faculty members and the only Black woman in the department. The family-friendly culture in the department was a breath of fresh air. Several colleagues had wives who were working mothers and understood their spouse's struggle to balance work and family. Other colleagues knew of or were friends with someone like Jenny, the pregnant graduate student I referenced earlier. The department was committed to fostering a supportive work environment and created policies and processes that recognized my identity as an academic and a mother. Requests to coordinate my teaching schedule and service commitments with my son's daycare schedule were treated as legitimate and met with understanding and empathy. The department meetings were intentionally held during the day as opposed to late afternoons or evenings to maximize faculty participation. I truly felt seen and valued as I juggled caring for our young son with the demands of the assistant professorship. While no community is without its problems, I can honestly say that the department policies and norms designed to recognize scholars' multiple identities and obligations created an enjoyable community where I had permission and the ability to devote time and energy to both motherhood and professorship.

Years later, when we began the adoptive process through the state, it became clear that university level policies were hostile toward adoptive parents. Children in the foster care system usually experience some form of maltreatment, which can lead to problems in emotional and social development (Harden, 2004). A great deal of our time as pre-adoptive parents was filled with medical appointments, meetings with social workers, teachers, tutors, and counselors, and eventually court dates. Per university policy, the amount of leave offered to adoptive parents (six weeks paid or unpaid) was much less than that offered to biological parents (one semester paid). One journal entry highlights my deep frustration with this policy and its dismissive stance toward adoptive parents. My frustration was compounded when my efforts to learn the reasoning behind the policy from Human Resources were ignored and efforts to change the policy were dismissed.

> Are you kidding me? Seriously?! Seriously?! I am so angry right now I can't see straight. How any organization can write and support policy like this in this day and age is beyond maddening to me. Six weeks? Six weeks for adoptive parents and one semester for biological parents? Why would you offer adoptive parents less time than biological parents? Whoever wrote this has clearly never spoken with an adoptive parent 'cause six weeks simply doesn't cut it. Look here, just because I didn't give birth to these children and they aren't babies

> doesn't mean that they require less care or time to acclimate to this new environment. **Everything** is new. New home, new school, new roles, norms and expectations. And between doctor's appointments, counseling appointments, tutoring appointments, and court proceedings in two different counties, none of us know if we are coming or going. There isn't a day I'm not going mach 5 with my hair on fire trying to keep all of this straight and everyone sane!
>
> I can't count how many times I've been told [by white peers at the predominately white institution] that I can come off as overbearing when I am passionate about something, so I am trying to suppress my personal feelings and experience and frame my inquiries with leadership as rational and legitimate policy questions about the implementation of equitable practices. Clearly, it's not working because I still can't get a serious response from [faculty] committee or HR despite the institution's 'commitment to DEI'. S[haking] M[y] H[ead] – so much for promoting a culture of shared responsibility, inclusion and equity. At this point, all I can do is be thankful for God's perfect timing – if it weren't for this sabbatical, I have no clue how'd we would manage all of this.

It just so happened that our adoption process aligned with my year-long post-tenure sabbatical, so my plans to research and write a significant portion of my next book were replaced with writing two book chapters and an exorbitant number of child-related appointments, hearings, and meetings. I count myself fortunate that the timing worked out and I was able to prioritize my children and their needs and still tend to my sabbatical responsibilities (publications). Yet, it is not lost on me that the institutional expectation was that my sabbatical would produce a book. A few years later when I put forth my file for promotion for full professor, I couldn't help but wonder if I would pay an adoptive mother penalty. I was promoted, but some negative comments from a few colleagues in the review process about my lack of commitment to academia and drive to create meaningful new scholarship (translation, a book) made it clear that I did pay a price.

Who Cares for the Caregiver?

> Hear me as a woman./Have me as your sister./On purpled battlefield breaking day,/So I might say our victory is just beginning,/See me as change,/Say I am movement,/That I am the year,/ and I am the era/of the women.—Amanda Gorman

In her book, *Black Feminist Thought: Knowledge, Consciousness, and the Politics of Empowerment*, Patricia Hill Collins (2000) highlights the importance of Black sisterhood, arguing that Black women understand each other and their experiences best. This is especially true for Black women in academia who often have to "bend" and "shift" to navigate their predominantly white environments and rely on coping mechanisms to navigate professional environments not created for them (Harris-Perry, 2011).

My relationships with Black motherscholars and Black women scholars initially developed in response to the institutional environment. In every place of employment, I was the first and only Black woman and had no one like me to share my experiences. I did not stay long enough at my first institution (a large public research university) to develop these relationships. When I moved to take a job at a private liberal arts university, I intentionally sought out other women scholars and was enthusiastically welcomed in a small, supportive women scholars of color community.

I became especially close with two Black women, with whom I began to meet regularly. Our small, intimate gatherings came about organically, as we had all experienced being the only or one of a few Black women scholars in our respective departments and wanted to create a space where we could openly and freely discuss our professional challenges as Black women. As our friendships grew and trust deepened, we met more often and our conversations turned to personal topics and issues, including motherhood and mothering.

While neither of them fully understood my experience as a Black woman adoptive motherscholar, their experiences with mothering greatly influenced my thinking. The first woman was just a few years older than me and a single mother of two preteen biracial boys. She was raised in a large, close-knit family and traveled regularly to her home state so she and the boys could spend time with them. Her approach to mothering focused on racial identity and an awareness of the ways race and racism would impact her children's lives. This intensive motherwork was a constant form of racialized parenting stress that placed a significant burden on her (Brantley, 2023).

The second woman, about twenty years older than me, was the designated elder of the group. Not only was she the oldest in age but she had been at the institution the longest and knew most of the faculty, staff, and administration. She was the first Black woman to receive tenure at the university and often joked that she knew where the bodies were buried. She was adopted as a child and made the decision to be child-free. As the self-proclaimed 'auntie' of the group, she took a deep interest in our children, helping out in small and large ways. She was also very open and shared her adoption story in detail.

We would intentionally take turns meeting at each other's homes, reserving a few hours for us to eat and fellowship. These meetings provided a safe space and a sense of community and belonging. These meetings were also spaces where honest and critical feedback was given and received with love. As my family moved through the highs and lows of the adoption experience, these women gave me the space to sit with my emotions, lending an empathetic ear. They also held the mirror up to my face and forced me to ask difficult questions about myself and my mothering in light of the challenges.

Regardless of the topic, our time together felt like a rare opportunity to be authentic and gather our whole selves (Turner & Allen, 2022). It has been written that "[m]othering is *worked* by chosen and accidental mentors who agree to support the growing unpredictable thing called future" (Gumbs, 2016, p. 24). I felt mothered by these women and their friendship which nurtured, empowered, challenged, and sustained me.

Conclusion

Motherhood and adoption are common in American society; but there is little research on Black families who formally adopt Black children (but see Gillum, 2011). Even fewer studies explore the experiences of Black motherscholars who build their families through adoption. In this chapter, I explore how one Black motherscholar has come to understand her journey, as well as the impact of the journey on her mothering. Through analyzing personal journals, I conclude that my journey into mothering has been characterized by two distinct conflicts and made easier by my relationships with other Black motherscholars and Black women scholars.

The uniqueness of my experience does not go unnoticed. Few Black women, and even fewer Black women scholars find themselves in a position of adopting not one but four children over the course of their lives. However unique it might be, my experience illuminates the belief that while the idea of traditional adoption as a method of family planning is not widely embraced within the Black community (e.g. Johnson, 2023), there are Black women adopting Black children through private agencies and the foster care system to build families. These adoptive experiences reveal the troubling frameworks often used to characterize Black birth mothers and show how there is little to space for birth mothers, adoptive mothers, and their children to think creatively about how to build dynamic familial bonds.

My experiences also demonstrate that while often promoting inclusivity and work-life balance, institutions of higher learning have far more work to do to live up to their espoused values. As a Black woman adoptive motherscholar who has spent her life in academic spaces as a graduate student, tenure track professor, full professor and administrator, I strongly believe that as institutions of higher learning seriously consider how policies create workplace barriers for working women and people of color, they must also be aware of the unique barriers for Black women adoptive motherscholars. Thus, it is my hope that this scholarship makes visible Black women adoptive motherscholars, informs the broader conversation about adoption, mothering, the motherhood penalty, and reframes social and institutional understandings of family-friendly workplace policies.

Competing Interests

The author has no conflicts of interest to declare that are relevant to the content of this manuscript.

References

Baszile, D. T. (2006). In this place where I don't quite belong: Claiming the onto-epistemological in-between. In T. Berry (Ed.), *From oppression to grace: Women of color dealing with issues in academia* (pp. 195–208). Stylus.

Bell, D. (1992). *Faces at the bottom of the well: The permanence of racism*. Basic Books.

Berry, T. R. (2018). *States of grace: Counterstories of a Black woman in the academy*. Peter Lang.

Bhattacharya, K. (2017). *Fundamentals of qualitative research: A practical guide*. Routledge.

Bochner, A. P. (1997). It's about time: Narrative and the divided self. *Qualitative Inquiry, 3*(4), 418–438.

Brantley, M. (2023). Can't just send our children out: Intensive motherwork and experiences of Black motherhood. *Social Problems*. https://doi.org/10.1093/socpro/spad047

Chang, H. (2008). *Autoethnography as method*. Left Coast Press.

Cheng, S. D. (2020). Careers versus children: How childcare affects the academic tenure-track gender gap. *Working paper*. https://scholar.harvard.edu/files/sdcheng/files/sdcheng_jmp.pdf

Chenoweth, E., Fortna, P., Mitchell, S., Savun, B., Weeks, J., & Cunningham, K. (2016, April). How to get tenure (if you're a woman). *Foreign Policy*. https://foreignpolicy.com/2016/04/19/how-to-get-tenure-if-youre-a-woman-academia-stephen-walt/

Collins, P. H. (2000). *Black feminist thought: Knowledge, consciousness, and the politics of empowerment* (2nd ed.). Routledge.

Crenshaw, K. W. (1991). Mapping the margins: Intersectionality, identity politics, and violence against women of color. *Stanford Law Review, 43*, 1241–1299.

DeCuir, J., & Dixson, A. (2004). So, when it comes out, they aren't that surprised that it is there: Using critical race theory as a tool of analysis of race and racism in education. *Educational Researcher, 33*(5), 26–31.

Delgado, R. (1989). Storytelling for oppositionists and others: A plea for narrative. *Michigan Law Review, 87*(8), 2411–2441.

Delgado, R., & Stefancic, J. (2001). *Critical race theory: An introduction*. New York University Press.

Delgado Bernal, D., & Villalpando, O. (2002). An apartheid of knowledge in academia: The struggle over the "legitimate" knowledge of faculty of color. *Equity & Excellence in Education, 35*(2), 169–180.

Ellis, C. (1995). *Final negotiations: A story of love, loss, and chronic illness*. Temple University Press.

Ellis, C., Adams, T. E., & Bochner, A. P. (2010). Autoethnography: An overview. *Forum Qualitative Sozialforschung/Forum: Qualitative Social Research, 12*(1).

Few, A. L., Stephens, D. P., & Rouse-Arnett, M. (2003). Sister-to-sister talk: Transcending boundaries and challenges in qualitative research with Black women. *Family Relations: An Interdisciplinary Journal of Applied Family Studies, 52*(3), 205–215. https://doi.org/10.1111/j.1741-3729.2003.00205.x

Gillum, N. L. (2011). Review of research on Black families who formally adopted Black children. *Families in Society, 92*(3), 324–328.

Goodall, B. H. L. (2001). *Writing the new ethnography*. Alta Mira.

Goodall, B. H. L. (2006). *A need to know: The clandestine history of a CIA family*. Left Coast Press.

Gordon, L. (1985). Single mothers and child neglect, 1880–1940. *American Quarterly, 37*, 173–192.

Gumbs, A. P. (2016). M/othering ourselves: A Black queer feminist genealogy for radical mothering. In A. P. Gumbs, C. Martens, & M. Williams (Eds.), *Revolutionary mothering: Love on the front lines* (pp. 84–96). Between the Lines.

Hall, K. M. Q. (2021). Losing Black mothers, finding revolutionary mothering. *Hypatia, 36*(4), 764–780.

Harden, B. J. (2004). Safety and stability for foster children: A developmental perspective. *The Future of Children, 14*(1), 31–47.

Harp, K. L. H., & Bunting, A. M. (2020). The racialized nature of child welfare policies and the social control of Black bodies. *Social Politics, 27*(2), 258–281.
Harris-Perry, M. V. (2011). *Sister citizen: Shame, stereotypes, and Black women in America.* Yale University Press.
Hochschild, A. R. (2011). Inside the clockwork of male careers. In A. I. Garey & K. V. Hansen (Eds.), *At the heart of work and family: Engaging the ideas of Arlie Hochschild* (pp. 17–29). Rutgers University Press.
Hollingsworth, L. D. (2000). Africentric theory as a predictor of adoption among African Americans: An exploratory study. *Journal of Ethnic and Cultural Diversity in Social Work, 9*(1/2), 119–133.
hooks, b. (1984). *Feminist theory: From margin to center.* South End Press.
hooks, b. (1994). *Teaching to transgress: Education as the practice of freedom.* Routledge.
Johnson, B. N. (2023, November). Black children are overrepresented in the foster care system. Why aren't we adopting them? *Essence.* https://www.essence.com/lifestyle/adoption-stories/
Kunzel, R. G. (1993). *Fallen women, problem girls: Unmarried mothers and the professionalization of social work 1890–1945.* Yale University Press.
Mairesse, J., Pezzoni, M., & Visentin, F. (2020). Does gender matter for promotion in science? Evidence from physicists in France. *NBER Working Paper Series* (No. 27789). https://doi.org/10.3386/w27789
Majors, Y. J. (2001). Passing mirrors: Subjectivity in a Midwestern hair salon. *Anthropology & Education Quarterly, 32*(1), 116–130.
Mantovani, N., & Thomas, H. (2014). Stigma, intersectionality and motherhood: Exploring the relations of stigma in the accounts of Black teenage mothers "looked after" by the state. *Social Theory & Health, 12*(1), 45–62. https://doi.org/10.1057/sth.2013.19
Mason, M. A., Wolfinger, N. H., & Goulden, M. (2013). *Do babies matter? Gender and family in the ivory tower.* Rutgers University Press.
Ngwainmbi, J. M. (2004). Feminism, feminist scholarship, and social integration of women: The struggle for African-American women. *Journal of International Women's Studies, 5*(5), 93–104.
Nixon, M. L. (2013). Women of color chief diversity officers: Their positionality and agency in higher education institutions (Order No. 3588822). *ProQuest Dissertations & Theses Global.*
Oka, C. D. (2016). Mothering as revolutionary praxis. In A. P. Gumbs, C. Martens, & M. Williams (Eds.), *Revolutionary mothering: Love on the front lines* (pp. 157–169). Between the Lines.
Prater, G., & King, L. T. (1988). Experiences of Black families as adoptive parents. *Social Work, 33*(6), 543–545.
Roberts, D. (2002). *Shattered bonds: The color of child welfare.* Basic Civitas Books.
Russell, M. (1992). Entering great America: Reflections on race and the convergence of progressive legal theory and practice. *Hastings Law Journal, 43*(4), 749–767.
Solinger, R. (1994). Race and value: Black and white illegitimate babies, 1945–1965. In E. N. Glenn, G. Chang, & L. Forcey (Eds.), *Mothering: Ideology, experience, and agency* (pp. 275–295). Routledge.
Tate, W. F. (1997). Critical race theory and education: History, theory, and implications. *Review of Research in Education, 22*(1), 195–247.
Turner, C. R., & Allen, K. R. (2022). "She's a friend of my mind": A reflection of Black sisterhood in academia. *Race Ethnicity and Education, 25*(6), 1–18. https://doi.org/10.1080/13613324.2022.2105981
Tyebee, T. (2003). Attitude, interest, and motivation for adoption and foster care. *Child Welfare, 82*(6), 685–706.
Ward, K., & Wolf-Wendel, L. (2012). *Academic motherhood: How faculty manage work and family.* Rutgers University Press.
Wing, A. K. (Ed.). (2003). *Critical race feminism: A reader* (2nd ed.). New York University Press.

Critical Counternarratives

Ivory Towers, Bassinets and Wheelchairs, Oh My!

Brandy D. James

Abstract Poetry and storytelling can be a way to heal broken pieces of ourselves. The author hopes to use poetry to share her voice as a Black woman scholar, and mother to a Black daughter with disabilities to address the dichotomies in disability and motherhood spaces. The use of poetry in this submission will unlock some of the guarded spaces in Black disability educational studies and Black motherhood disability discourse. The author's lived experiences of knowing and being a Black mother to a disabled Black child and Black academic can be a way of healing and resistance in an ableist society.

Keywords Disability · Pregnancy · Higher education

Ivory Towers, Bassinets and Wheelchairs, Oh My!

The double pink lines

They give you a glimpse into the future

The future of a new life

The future of a new being

The future where you would give your life for another

The first appointment

The first sonogram

The first sound of life

The heartbeat

B. D. James (✉)
Ball State University, Muncie, IN, USA
e-mail: Bdj913@gmail.com

C. R. Turner and M. L. Green (eds.), *Black Motherscholarship Within and Beyond the Academy*, https://doi.org/10.1007/978-3-031-99758-7_10

Then the look of fear and pause the doctor gave
There's something wrong

Then the questioning begins
It's a girl
At the third, fourth and fifth appointments
The look of fear sets in, your stomach drops
You grip his hand; he tries to be brave
For his girls, he tries to be brave
Her measurements off
More specialists
No answers
Blank stares
There's something wrong

They try to explain it, a syndrome
You try to hold back your tears,
You grip his hand; he tries to be brave
For his girls, he tries to be brave
No answers, more specialists, more waiting rooms
Dopplers, monitors, waiting rooms, blank stares
There's something wrong

Back to work
You need to take a break
However, will you finish your degree?
There's no way a Black family can…
You can't manage a childbirth like this
You can't manage a child and…
The blank stares
Ivory Towers, Oh My!

A missing letter from a specialist

Bed Rest

Grading

You need to take a break

However, will you finish your degree?

There's no way a Black family can…

You can't manage a childbirth like this

You can't manage a child and…

An emergency helicopter flight

Ivory Towers, and Bassinets, Oh My!

You grip his hand; he tries to be brave

For his girls, he tries to be brave

She's here!

Cold, sterile, and alone

The NICU

More specialists

No answers

Blank stares

There's something wrong

The NICU

Day 5

No answers

Blank stares

There's no way a Black family can…

Can you manage a child like this?

You can't manage a child and…

She's going to need more care

There's something wrong

The NICU

Day 11

No answers

Blank stares

There's no way a Black family can…

Can you manage a child like this?

The maternal instincts kick in

I record all whispers from the specialists

I will be her ADVOCATE

The NICU

Day 12

No answers

Blank stares

There's no way a Black family can…

Can you manage a child like this?

We graduate from the NICU

I will be her ADVOCATE

Specialty Unit

Day 1

I will find answers

I begin to question the "experts"

Can you manage a child like this?

A Black mother can

We pass the car seat test

Makenna earns her first 'A'

Specialty Unit

Day 2

I search for answers

Can you manage a child like this?

A Black mother can

We pass the breastfeeding test

We earn our second 'A'

Specialty Unit

Day 3

I search for answers

Can you manage a child like this?

A Black mother can

We fail the hearing test

We learn how to pivot

I will be her ADVOCATE

Specialty Unit

Day 4

We graduate to home

You grip his hand; he tries to be brave

For his girls, he tries to be brave

Ivory Towers, and Bassinets, Oh My!

The Happy One

She changes our dynamic

The family of three settle in

Back to work

Back to graduate school

There's no way a Black family can…

Can you manage a child like this?

A Black mother can

The electrical storm begins

Epilepsy

We learn how to pivot

Ivory Towers, and Bassinets, Oh My!

I search for more answers

More specialists

More early interventionists

Blank stares

We start to learn a new language

ASL

The electrical storm continues

Epilepsy

I began to feel helpless

I sign "I love you"

I sign "I AM HERE"

I search for answers

A diagnosis begins to emerge

Catastrophe strikes

The electrical storm continues

Epilepsy

Water on the brain

I record all the whispers from the specialists

Cold, sterile, and alone

The PICU

I sign "I love you"

I sign "I AM HERE"

I sign "I WON'T GIVE UP"

New specialists

New hospital

New family dynamic

The three must become a two

You grip his hand; he tries to be brave

For his girls, he tries to be brave

He goes back to work

I sign "Daddy loves you."

I sign "I WON'T GIVE UP"

I continue to search for answers

I continue to pursue academia

Back to graduate school

Can you manage a child like this?

A Black mother can

Ivory Towers, and Bassinets, Oh My!

Shuffle, repeat

Catastrophe strikes

The electrical storm continues

Epilepsy

Water on the brain

Shunts, Shunts, Shunts

The PICU

The diagnosis

I sign "I love you"

I sign "I AM HERE"

I sign "I WON'T GIVE UP"

Surgery 10

The Happy One

Greats us all with a giggle and a grin

She turns 2

I sign "I love you Makenna"

We dance to the music, and she claps her hands

Could it be?

We retake our hearing test

She earns her third 'A'

I sign "I love you"

I sign "I AM HERE"

I sign "I WON'T GIVE UP"

We learn to pivot

New wheels

More surgeries

The electrical storm continues

Epilepsy

Water on the brain

Shunts, Shunts, Shunts

Feeding tube

Custom wheelchair

The PICU

Ivory Towers, Bassinets, and Wheelchairs Oh My!

We have a pause from surgeries

Preschool here we come

New friends

New school bus

Makenna gives a giggle and a grin

She claps her hands

We sang happy birthday

We dance around the room

She turns 3

I sign "I love you"

I sign "I AM HERE"

She signs, "Mommy"

I sign "I love you"

I sign "I AM HERE"

I sign "School Bus"

She signs, "Ready Go!"

Shuffle, repeat

Catastrophe strikes

The electrical storm continues

Epilepsy

Water on the brain

Shunts, Shunts, Shunts

Stroke

Surgery 13

I sign "Brave Girl"

I am scared

I know a Black Mother can

I pray for peace

Hospice Nurses

I sign "I need more time"

She signs "Mommy"

We dance and I cry

There's nothing more we can do

No more surgeries

Ivory Towers, Bassinets, and Wheelchairs Oh My!

The Happy One

She turns 4

We dance, we sing

I cry

I know this will be the last party

My borrowed baby

She signs "Mommy"

I sign "I AM HERE"

We hug and I cry

There's nothing more we can do

No more surgeries

I sign "Goodnight my angel until we meet again"

Ivory Towers, Bassinets, and Wheelchairs Oh My!

I grieve

I move forward

I return to work

I try to return to graduate school

Attempt denied

Ivory Towers

I grieve

I move forward

A Black mother can

I start over

PhD

I grieve

I move forward

I say "I AM HERE"

I gain new mentors

A Black mother did

I graduate

I ADVOCATE

For the Happy One

I move forward

I use my voice

I sign, "I WON'T GIVE UP"

Ivory Towers, Bassinets, and Wheelchairs Oh My!

Because

A Black Mother Can

A Black Mother Did

Competing Interests The author has no conflicts of interest to declare that are relevant to the content of this manuscript.

Brandy D. James , Ph.D., is an Assistant Teaching Professor of Early Childhood, Youth, and Family Studies at Ball State University. Her research interests include Early Intervention with a specific interest in children with special healthcare needs, Black father engagement, and educator collaboration. She holds her Ph.D. in Elementary Education from Ball State University. She is an angel mom to a daughter diagnosed with a rare syndrome called Macrocephaly Capillary Malformation (M-CM). She is the author of a children's book titled *Makenna the Mighty*, a book highlighting the impact of childhood illness, hope, grief, and loss, based on her own experiences raising a medically fragile child.

Backing Our Babies: The Praxis of Three Black Muslim Mothers at Home and in the Academy

Lakya Goss, Yetunde Alabede, and Tasleem Firdausee

Abstract Drawing on Black feminist theories, three doctoral students engage in kitchen table talks to situate their lived experiences of being Black Muslim mothers in academia. By interweaving everyday talk with theoretical considerations, we examine: (1) How is the motherhood and scholarship praxis of Black Muslim mothers (in)formed in graduate school? and (2) How do Black Muslim mothers navigate their roles as mothers and graduate students at predominantly white institutions? We found that our praxis is (in)formed, in part, through resistance and characterized by hope. This collaborative auto-ethnographic study expands discourse around mothering, Black feminist theories, and spirituality in academia.

Keywords Collaborative autoethnography · Mothering discourse · Black Muslim mothers

> "Her heartbeat echoes freedom, her grandmothers now only dream in soil buried, waiting to rupture again in the wind, her feet heavy, burdened, but brilliant, resilient headwraps hold hymns, ancient coded, giving instructions for resistance" (Firdausee, 2023, p. 50).

Introduction

Wrapped in long pieces of cloth, its ends securely tied across the mother's chest, backing, or carrying babies on the back, is a traditional practice across the African diaspora that predates colonialism and the Transatlantic Slave Trade. With babies literally and/or metaphorically strapped to their backs, mothers do what they must to

L. Goss (✉) · Y. Alabede
Michigan State University, East Lansing, MI, USA
e-mail: gosslaky@msu.edu

T. Firdausee
Western Michigan University, Kalamazoo, MI, USA

C. R. Turner and M. L. Green (eds.), *Black Motherscholarship Within and Beyond the Academy*, https://doi.org/10.1007/978-3-031-99758-7_11

sustain themselves, families, and communities. As three Black spiritually led graduate students at predominantly white institutions (PWIs) who share interests in critical research that centers the African diaspora, we too, do what we must as we labor, nurture, teach, and mother. Black Muslim women as mothers and scholars are worthy of scholarly examination as the experiences of Black Muslim women are understudied in mainstream qualitative research. In this chapter, our intention is to examine our praxis as Muslims, Black women, mothers, and doctoral students. Through analysis of two kitchen table talks, we seek to gain insight on the following: (1) How is the motherhood and scholarship praxis of Black Muslim mothers (in)formed in graduate school? and (2) How do Black Muslim mothers navigate their roles as mothers and graduate students at PWIs?

Framework

Black Feminist Thought (BFT) is a framework that centers the lived experiences of Black women within their intersecting identities (Collins, 1999). Black feminisms linked to BFT examine the positioning of Black women against oppressive structures like gendered racism and racial capitalism. This work, formed and informed by our social, cultural, economic, and political positioning within a global matrix of dominance, is inspired by BFT. A theoretical framework that recognizes Black women's work inside and outside of the home, BFT helps to explicate the diverse paradigm of their activism and scholarship (Coleman-King et al., 2023; Collins, 1990). Examinations of *motherwork*, labor performed inside and outside the home for the survival of children and communities, are crucial for gaining more insight into the racialized and gendered experiences and perspectives of Black women (Collins, 2016). BFT and one of its offshoots, endarkened feminist epistemology (EFE), offer critical analytical lenses in which to examine how motherhood and scholarship overlap and interact to generate collective knowledge about ourselves and our work. EFE as put forth by Dillard (2000) is a framework that foregrounds the spiritual pursuits, ways of knowing, and responsibilities of Black women in qualitative research. Black women who engage in EFE remember and draw on their experiences. They employ practices and research methods that challenge dominant structures out of necessity and for their survival (Porter et al., 2022). Dillard's framework, which assumes that knowledge is not solely intellectual, resonates with Chan-Malik's (2018) insistence that for Black Muslim women in America, spiritual practices are tools of and a form of resistance. In her work, she outlines the role and influence of Black feminisms in the narration of American Islam in the twentieth and twenty-first centuries. Also, the concept of intersectionality helps us situate our experiences and perspectives at the intersection of our racial, gender, and religious identities (Crenshaw, 1995). Together, these frameworks offer a multidimensional lens in which to examine our experiences and perspectives as multi-faceted Black Muslim motherscholars.

Mothering in the Academy

Black mothers in academia, at their multiple intersections, are met with institutional barriers such as gendered racism. Fulton (2023) demonstrates how a seventeenth-century slave code, *partus sequitur ventrem* (the child follows the mother), ensured the reproduction of enslavement by assigning enslaved status to any child born to an enslaved mother. She argues this system, through "plantation politics" prevalent on college campuses, continues to exploit Black women by ignoring Black mothers' ontologies, epistemologies, and needs (Fulton, 2023, p. 261). For example, disregarding, undermining, and appropriating are some of the ways in which institutions of higher education, through policies and practices, reproduce structures of oppression that reproduce gendered racism.

What it means to *mother* has been researched by motherscholars who examine the praxis of simultaneous mothering and scholarship (Lapayese, 2012; Matias, 2022). For mothers in academia, existing research has shown that the influence of motherhood on professional work, and vice versa, is overlapping. For example, Cioè-Peña (2020) explains how her research interests and commitments to Black Latin(x) communities were birthed out of her experiences as a bilingual person and mother of a child with special needs. Mothering—within families, communities, and educational settings—includes teaching, healing, mentoring, and activism while maintaining an ethics of care that considers people's holistic needs (Bernard et al., 2012; Evans-Winters, 2019). According to Hill-Brisbane (2005), Black women educators embrace ethics of care by employing various pedagogies that include community upliftment and justice-seeking. In educational spaces across contexts, Black women play multiple roles, simultaneously acting as nurturer, teacher, and othermother (Samuels et al., 2021). This is evident in Coleman-King et al. (2023)'s collaborative autoethnography that explicates the social-historical context of Black motherscholars as they provide a nurturing home-place for students through their praxis.

Community Mothers

In *All About Love*, bell hooks draws on Peck's (1978) definition of love as "the will to extend one's self for the purpose of nurturing one's own or another's spiritual growth" (hooks, 2001, p. 4). Despite Black women in the United States and across the African diaspora, living under what hooks calls "white supremacist capitalist patriarchy" (hooks, 1984, p. 51), they curate educational spaces, orientated with an ethics of care, and engage in acts of mothering by extending themselves to the spiritual growth of their children and communities.

One example is Sister Clara Muhammad (1899–1972)—visionary educator, community leader, and mother—who was instrumental in the establishment of dozens of schools. Refusing to send her children to public schools, she co-founded and became the first teacher at the University of Islam. Started in her Detroit home in the 1930s, her schools continue to operate across the U.S. as The Clara Muhammad Schools (Rashid & Muhammad, 1992). Under the principles of knowing, loving, and doing for self, they laid critical foundations for subsequent independent Black schools, including several African centered schools (Ross, 2003). Before her son, Warith Deen Muhammad, transitioned from the Nation of Islam (NOI) to Sunni Islam in the 1970s, she helped to establish the Muslim Girls Training schools which provided education in aspects of motherhood, behavior, and etiquette based on the NOI's teachings. While critiqued by some for perpetuating societal gender norms, classes were meant to affirm the identities of Black Muslim girls and women who sought alternatives to white mainstream notions of womanhood (West, 2023). Exercising educational autonomy as a mother by resisting public schools and creating her own, Clara Muhammad helped revitalize the educational opportunities for children by attending to their academic, socio-emotional, and spiritual needs. As primary caretaker of her own children and co-leader of a national organization, Muhammad engaged in community mothering, educational activism, and spiritual nurturing (Muhammad, 2006).

A century before Clara Muhammad, Nana Asma'u, born in 1793 was a teacher, poet, and mother of six sons. Asma'u, whose grandmother and great-grandmother were also educators, was the daughter of West African scholar, Usman Dan Fodio, who advocated for women's rights to education (Azuonye, 2006). Asam'u engaged in community mothering by imparting spiritual knowledge, disseminating Islamic scholarship, and training other women to go to rural areas of northern Nigeria to teach. Described as a pearl on a string of women's Islamic scholarship, grounded in the Holy Qur'an and other religious sources, her work was transnational and transracial (Mack & Boyd, 2013). Muhammad's and Asma'u's legacies endure as Clara Muhammad Schools continue to operate and impact the realities of Black American Muslims while Asma'u continues to serve as a model in teaching and scholarship in northern Nigeria.

Positioning Ourselves

We each enter this work committed to our families and communities as Black Muslim women shaped, in part, by our lived experiences. We come from different backgrounds and hold diverse perspectives as multifaceted Black women, yet we share interests in and commitment to work that is critical and rooted in care.

Lakya: I am a Black Muslim woman from Detroit and mother of three. I enter this work committed to researching the traditions and futurity of Black people globally. The factors shaping my approaches to this work are rooted in my experiences as a Black American Muslim woman. My goal as an educational researcher in my final year of doctoral study was to better understand community-based education through a spiritually led critical research praxis.

Yetunde: When I moved to the U.S. Midwest as a first-time mom, first generation, international student, I became aware that I would be universally identified as Black.

As a Muslim born in Nigeria, it did not occur to me that my religion would mark me as a minority in most spaces. As a heterosexual, married, and formally educated woman, I have a level of privilege in Nigeria. My academic journey in the U.S. while raising a second-generation Black Muslim (im)migrant child in a predominantly white environment has prompted me to evolve my thinking around motherhood. My research interests, focused on the language/parenting practices of Black African (im)migrant families, have been shaped by my experiences in Nigeria and the U.S.

Tasleem: As a Black Muslim motherscholar from the southside of Chicago, I center my lived experiences of motherhood, spirituality, and community care in my academic and professional practice(s), drawing from my bloodline and spiritual mothers. My approach to education and holistic health is deeply rooted in Islamic and Black diasporic spiritual principles, guiding how I nurture my biological children, my students, and the broader community. This stance empowers me to personify and exemplify the concept of mothering as a healing and empowering process, breaking through conventional limits to foster nurturing and transformative environments.

Kitchen Table Talk

From the standpoint of EFE, Black women's talk generates specialized bodies of knowledge which helps to reveal epistemological perspectives of Black women in higher education (Dillard, 2000). As a methodological tool, kitchen table talks interweave theories presented across literature and the positionality of researchers through everyday talk (Kohl & McCutcheon, 2015). We found kitchen table talks to be fitting because they encourage dialogue and facilitate transformation and healing spaces through critical reflexivity and interrogation of systems (McCutcheon & Kohl, 2019). In the summer of 2024, we conducted two kitchen table talks virtually which lasted over three and a half hours total. A virtual medium provided flexibility and convenience as the three of us lived in different cities. The content of our talks was rooted in existing research and theories and the experiences we brought to our talks as we conceived this chapter. Our talks included presentations and discussions of artifacts including emails, letters, and poems we had written about our racialized and gendered interactions; this is a practice that has been adopted in kitchen table talks in multiple contexts (Lyiscott et al., 2021; McNeill et al., 2021). In our discussions, guided by auto-theoretical approaches, we interlinked exisiting theories presented across literature and our own experiences as Black Muslim mothers pursuing doctoral degrees at PWIs in the Midwest.

Overall, our data collection and analysis tools were critical in that they trouble the separation of academic and everyday discourse (Souto-Manning, 2014). Analysis of our kitchen table talks illustrate how we navigated our experiences as students, scholars, mothers, and spiritually led people. Through two recorded virtual kitchen table talks, we participated in collective knowledge generation from a Black feminist perspective by identifying factors that (in)form our praxis as we navigate our home and professional roles. Following our talks, we transcribed each of them using transcription software. We then analyzed the content by independently reading the transcripts, pulling out key words and phrases, then indexing them into themes through a process of open coding using qualitative data analysis software (Strauss & Corbin, 1990). We first independently engaged in open coding by assigning a word or short phrases to parts of our data (Saldana, 2021). For example, when discussing decisions we have made regarding our children's education, ideas related to resistance emerged. Our goal during analysis was to look for patterns within our racialized and gendered experiences. We conducted a second round of independent coding while considering theoretical frameworks BFT and EFE in our analysis. After two rounds of independent coding, we cross-checked our codes among the three of us to identify patterns in the transcripts and came to consensus on the following themes: resistance and hope.

Findings

While historical messaging of PWIs across contexts has been that motherhood is not in alignment with pursuing professional goals, mothering may be fuel for motivation and a source of complex knowledge(s) in institutional spaces as motherhood and scholarship (in)form the other (Hinton-Johnson, 2011). In conversation with existing literature, our analysis uncovered some of the ways in which we, as Black Muslim women navigated our roles as we carried out our mother work, professional work, and spirit work. We found that we did not necessarily isolate our identities as motherscholars; our motherhood and scholarship formed and informed each other.

Analysis of our kitchen table talks revealed that, as Black Muslim mothers in graduate programs at PWIs, our praxis is (in)formed, in part, through resistance. Through a mutually interdependent process, one (in)forming the other, our praxis is one that is hopeful. Mothering as an act of resistance and hope is a pertinent framing of mothering because of our positioning within a global matrix of oppression (Collins, 1990). We support our findings by including brief excerpts from our kitchen table talks that illuminate examples of resistance and hope. In the tradition of similar discourse such as sister talks, we include excerpts from our talks to intertwine our experiences through collaborative storytelling, recall, and reflection with broader social contexts and discourse (Turner & Allen, 2022).

Resistance Through Criticality

Criticality, or "the ability and practice of naming, researching, understanding, interrogating, and ultimately disrupting oppression" (Muhammad, 2023, p. 12), is an essential component of our resistance as Black women in the academy. As we gain deeper understandings of the constructions and conditions our children are met with, we become more critical in *what* and *how* we teach. The following excerpt is from one of our kitchen table talks that offers an example of our resistance in the critical decisions we make as mothers as it pertains to our children's school experiences.

> **Tasleem**: I'm always involved in my daughter's schooling. From an early age, I'd bring in books to her classes that offered multiple perspectives, books about Ramadan or Indigenous populations during Thanksgiving. I stayed active in her high school years too, making sure she joined extracurriculars like the junior NAACP and poetry clubs. At one point, I decided to homeschool her for a year because of my dissatisfaction with the school's practices and policies. I continued this kind of involvement with my youngest daughter. I presented about Islam in Africa to her sixth-grade class because the curriculum only mentioned Muslims from the Middle East. It's crucial for me to step in when the curriculum falls short, so my daughter and her classmates know that Black Muslims are everywhere.
>
> **Yetunde**: The way I think about it is from somebody who is navigating the U.S. as an international student, and it's stressful. We are still learning how to navigate these white spaces. I've really been intentional about telling my four-year-old daughter that she doesn't have to look like other people she sees around here. More than outward expressions, I want her to embody Islam in her character. So, I keep teaching her all it entails while affirming her Black Muslim female identity, especially because I know that when she goes to school, there's very few Black children and maybe a handful of Black teachers in the building.

Criticality, at the intersection of race and gender, troubles, disrupts, and challenges dominant ways of thinking and speaks back to a universal voice of whiteness. The autonomy of Black women has been substantially undervalued and left out of educational decision-making processes when it comes to their children (Coleman-King et al., 2022). Therefore, it is crucial that we advocate for our own children and children in our communities. Diverse in our expressions, our praxis includes criticality that we model for our children, students, and communities within and beyond academia.

Being Our Whole Selves

Refusing to be a political tool synonymous with struggle, brokenness, or in need of intervention, mothering can be political on its own terms (Nash, 2021). The following excerpts are examples of how we have resist by bringing our whole selves to our work. This wholeness, developed through our ways of knowing (Turner & Allen, 2022), means resisting dominant epistemologies and defining for ourselves our ontological positionings as Black women who do not cut off parts of ourselves for the sake of the institution.

> **Tasleem**: I'm an artist, playwright, and poet, mainly. My writings come from God. I don't have to think about things that I write usually, but I keep notes for when ideas come to me. When I first attended college in Chicago, that's when I really got into poetry and film; all my art and poetry was about knowing who I am as an advocate and as a God-conscious person. It was just in everything. My experiences as an artist made me who I am today, and it was because of my environment. I was in the hip hop scene, studying, learning from Islamic scholars, and on college campuses. After hearing people like Dr. Ruth Nicole Brown, who talked about Black girlhood studies, I was inspired to go to grad school. My daughter

was a baby then, and I would take her to events on campus. On one occasion, I went to a dissertation defense and was like, "Wow, there is a need for what I want to study: our people, the African diaspora." Then I was interviewed for a couple of research studies, and I was thinking, "Alright, if these people are studying me, I want to put my voice in there from my perspective," because some of what I read would be from a distant perspective, in a way. I saw a need for artist, scholarship, and activism. So that's why I'm in grad school. I see a need for all of us here.

Lakya: I think we need to talk about our mental health and how it's neglected. There are Black women in academia who are not well. They're under a lot of stress, and it's killing them. Also, Black women have to be extra careful in academia, because anything we say, anything we do, could limit our opportunities, especially if we're vocal. I've found comfort in being around people who have a critical approach to their work. It's been inspiring to be around grad students and faculty who are like, "Nah, this is how I'm showing up, this is what I care about, this is what I'm researching." We have to be intentional about not letting the institution kill us or make us sick, you know, because they try to kill that revolutionary spirit in academia. Just having conversations like this are motivating because our energy is similar when it comes to our families and our work. We're Muslim, we're unapologetically Black women, and this is what we're about.

hooks (1984) asserts that Black women have historically viewed their motherhood not as a hindrance to their work, rather as a way to humanize their labor and a way to display love and care. We, too, are committed to being our full, loving, caring selves wherever we are. In the tradition of BFT which positions self-valuation as resistance (Collins, 1990), we draw on our multiplicity within and beyond the academy.

Hope in Community

As Black graduate students at PWIs, we have racialized and gendered experiences; and as Muslims, we carry the added layer of being part of a religious minority in the U.S. The emotional and mental backing due to the tensions of navigating white-centered, male-dominated spaces in higher education, has caused us to feel stretched and overwhelmed at times. Grounded in spirituality, one way we seek to navigate our experiences is through hope *in* and *for* our communities. An excerpt from one of our kitchen table talks reveals that through our praxis, we seek to transmit hope for our children and communities.

Yetunde: I was a visiting scholar teaching with a Nigerian professor at a Historically Black College/University (HBCU). It was my first time living and teaching in the U.S., so I didn't know much about the higher education system here. I needed community and noticed that some of my students were also in need. Although some of them were parents themselves, I felt like I needed to be like a mother to them. So beyond teaching them Yorùbá language, I supported them throughout their program and while they were applying for grad school. Even though I was a visiting scholar and didn't have firsthand experience with structural racism in the United States, I felt they needed some care and guidance. I would invite them to my house and tell them, "Let's cook. Let's do this. Let's be in community". You know, these small acts of community-building gave me hope that I could plant some roots here. I hope that it did the same for them as well.

> **Lakya**: I decided to homeschool my son this year. I'm going to do what I have to do: write the dissertation, work my assistantship, and homeschool him because they spirit murder Black boys. It already started a couple years ago in [suburban district], and when he went to [private Islamic school], my children faced anti-Blackness. So, I want to homeschool him while I can because I don't know if I'll have the same flexibility once I finish the program. What my children really could benefit from is community.

Pan African at its roots, BFT assumes that mothering can be enacted by aunties, grandmothers, sista-friends, teachers, God mothers, and othermothers (Collins, 1990; Waters, 2016). By stretching the concept of mothering beyond a biological mother-child dynamic to community mothering, we challenge stereotypes and expectations of motherhood rooted in dominant narratives (Story, 2014). Removing children from anti-Black school environments to homeschool them is one example of resistance. Furthermore, being hopeful in community in the face of anti-Blackness and spirit murder demonstrates resistance.

A Spirit of Hope

From the perspective of an EFE, spirit work is necessary in the centering of Black women's spiritual selves and how they make sense of the work they do (Dillard, 2000, 2021). Attending to our spiritual self-care is a form of resistance. An excerpt from one of our kitchen table talks is an example of how sustaining our spiritual practices such as prayer and remembrance of God help us to maintain a spirit of hope in our work.

> **Lakya**: I've been sleeping with the Qur'an playing for years, and it just helps me sleep better. Sometimes I get up and check on my children in the middle of the night, and they're playing Qur'an on their phones. I never really got good sleep, but when I started playing Qur'an, my dreams were more peaceful. Qur'an and *thikr* (remembering God) helps to ground me as I raise my vibrations. I listen to music too, but I try to keep it at a high frequency. In general, I'm careful about what I consume so that I'm well in all aspects of my life. When I'm spiritually well, I show up better for my children and in my work. That gives me hope.
>
> **Tasleem:** The first year of my PhD program, I was like that [too], where I didn't take time for myself. But then it got to the point where I was like, "Okay, I teach holistic wellness, so I need to practice it." I prayed and asked Allah to put *baraka* (blessings) in my time, and He answered my prayers. I told myself, "I'm not going to make myself sick by working all the time." So, I make sure I have balance. Sometimes I go to Detroit, to be around the *jamaat* (community), just to be in the space where other people are worshiping and remembering God. I went to *umrah* (Islamic pilgrimage), and at first, I was worried about my work. Finally, I said, "You know what, I'm not about to be in Makkah thinking about work." Once I returned, I caught up and everything worked out. As I think about it, balancing my spirit, mother, and academic work can be stressful, but I wouldn't take any of it back, and I'm hopeful for the future.

Overall, our resistance and hope are rooted in spirituality and, as Black women, we labor with spiritual intuition. Drawing on aspects of our spirituality such as prayer, remembrance, and other acts of worship helps to ground us and maintain a spirit of hope in our work.

Conclusion

In traditions across cultural and religious identities, our families are not always marked by a biological relationship. In the families that we construct for ourselves, whether due to need or desire, mothers and othermothers play a pivotal role in both the resistance they model and the hope they bear and pass on. In Islam, the status of mothers is an elevated one as illuminated in the following hadith:

> "A man came to Allah's Messenger (peace be upon him), and said, 'O Allah's Messenger (peace be upon him), who is more entitled to be treated with the best companionship by me?' The Prophet (peace be upon him) said, 'Your mother.' The man said, 'Who is next?' The Prophet (peace be upon him) said, 'Your mother.' The man further said, 'Who is next?' The Prophet (peace be upon him) said, 'Your mother'" (Ṣaḥīḥ al-Bukhārī, p. 17).

Also, the Yorùbá sayings, *Ìyá ni wúrà iyebíye* (the mother is priceless gold) and *ọj'ọtí ìyá bá kú ni wúrà ọlá bàj'ẹ* (the day a mother dies is the day, wealth is destroyed) shed light on the regard in which mothers are held in diasporic traditions. The wealth referred to in these sayings is, of course, not of monetary value but refers to the love, care, and nurturance that is carried, birthed, and passed on through mothering. Through our lived experiences as Black women in Ph.D. programs at PWIs, we have given and taken lessons from motherhood and made connections within our work as graduate students and vice versa. These connections can be life-giving and pull on philosophies that center collectiveness such as *ubuntu* (I am because we are), and in Yorùbá culture, *omọlúwàbí* (living in community and being collective-centered). By drawing on the perspectives of Black Muslim women, this chapter contributes to broader discourse on mothering, Black feminist theories, and spirituality in academia. Our kitchen table talks, which we found to be therapeutic, centered our racialized and gendered experiences while challenging stereotypes and misconceptions about gender and religion through sister-sharing and critical reflexivity. As Black Muslims who carry out our roles in motherhood and scholarship simultaneously, we do not detach our identities. Rather, we seek to situate ourselves wholly as mothers and scholars as we mother, teach, resist, and hope while honoring those who labored for us.

Competing Interests The authors have no conflicts of interest to declare that are relevant to the content of this chapter.

References

Azuonye, C. (2006). Feminist or simply feminine? Reflections on the works of Nana Asmā'u, a nineteenth-century West African woman poet, intellectual, and social activist. *Meridians, 6*(2), 54–77.

Bernard, W. T., Issari, S., Moriah, J., Njiwaji, M., Obgan, P., & Tolliver, A. (2012). Othermothering in the academy: Using maternal advocacy for institutional change. *Journal of the Motherhood Initiative for Research and Community Involvement, 3*(2), 103–120.

Chan-Malik, S. (2018). *Being Muslim: A cultural history of women of color in American Islam.* NYU Press.

Cioè-Peña, M. (2020). Wanting to leave; needing to stay: Issues for undocumented mothers of children with disabilities. *Multiple Voices: Disability, Race and Language Intersections in Special Education, 20*(2), 6–23.

Coleman-King, C., Brown, T. T. C., Haynes-Thoby, L., & Dowie-Chin, T. (2023). Reclaiming our time: Black mothers cultivating the homeplace during times of crisis. *Journal of Social Issues, 79*(3), 1022–1034.

Collins, P. H. (1990). *Black feminist thought: Knowledge, consciousness, and the politics of empowerment.* Hyman.

Collins, P. H. (1999). What's going on? Black feminist thought and the politics of postmodernism. In E. St. Pierre & W. Pillow (Eds.), *Working the ruins* (pp. 47–79). Routledge.

Collins, P. H. (2016). Shifting the center: Race, class, and feminist theorizing about motherhood. In E. N. Gleen, G. Chang, & L. R. Forcey (Eds.), *Mothering* (pp. 45–65). Routledge.

Crenshaw, K. W. (1995). Mapping the margins: Intersectionality, identity politics, and violence against women of color. In K. Crenshaw, N. Gotanda, G. Peller, & K. Thomas (Eds.), *Critical race theory: The key writings that formed the movement* (pp. 357–383). The New Press.

Dillard, C. B. (2000). The substance of things hoped for, the evidence of things not seen: Examining an endarkened feminist epistemology in educational research and leadership. *International Journal of Qualitative Studies in Education, 13*(6), 661–681.

Dillard, C. B. (2021). *The spirit of our work: Black women teachers (re)member.* Beacon Press.

Evans-Winters, V. E. (2019). *Black feminism in qualitative inquiry: A mosaic for writing our daughter's body.* Routledge.

Firdausee, T. (2023). *From Mississippi clay to African skies in search of sacred presence.* My Soul Speaks.

Fulton, L. N. (2023). The uses of 'partus sequitur ventrem': Black mothers in higher education. *Journal of Women and Gender in Higher Education, 16*(4), 261–274.

Hill-Brisbane, D. (2005). Black women teacher educators, race uplift, and the academic othermother identity. *Advancing Women in Leadership Journal, 19.*

Hinton-Johnson, K. (2011). Choosing my best thing: Black motherhood and academia. In T. R. Berry & N. Mizelle (Eds.), *From oppression to grace* (pp. 155–167). Routledge.

hooks, b. (1984). *Feminist theory: From margin to center.* Pluto Press.

hooks, b. (2001). *All about love: New visions.* William Morrow Paperbacks.

Kohl, E., & McCutcheon, P. (2015). Kitchen table reflexivity: Negotiating positionality through everyday talk. *Gender, Place & Culture, 22*(6), 747–763.

Lapayese, Y. V. (2012). Mother-scholar: Women who we intellectualize and women who mother. In Y. V. Lapayese (Ed.), *Mother-scholar* (pp. 1–10). Brill.

Lyiscott, J., Green, K. L., Ohito, E. O., & Coles, J. A. (2021). Call us by our names: A kitchen table dialogue on doin'it for the culture. *Equity & Excellence in Education, 54*(1), 1–18.

Mack, B., & Boyd, J. (2013). *Educating muslim women: The West African legacy of Nana Asma'u 1793–1864.* Kube Publishing Ltd.

Matias, C. E. (2022). Birthing the motherscholar and motherscholarship. *Peabody Journal of Education, 97*(2), 246–250.

McCutcheon, P., & Kohl, E. (2019). You're not welcome at my table: Racial discourse, conflict and healing at the kitchen table. *Gender, Place & Culture, 26*(2), 173–180.

McNeill, O., Love, B. L., Patel, L., & Stovall, D. O. (2021). "No trifling matter": A kitchen table talk on abolition and fugitivity. *Equity & Excellence in Education, 54*(2), 112–120.

Muhammad, G. (2023). Illuminating the call: On criticality. *Voices from the Middle, 30*(4), 12–14.

Muhammad, Z. (2006). Faith and courage to educate our own: Reflections on Islamic schools in the African American community. In Z. Muhammad (Ed.), *Black education* (pp. 291–310). Routledge.

Nash, J. C. (2021). *Birthing black mothers.* Duke University Press.

Peck, M. S. (1978). *The road less traveled: New psychology of love, traditional values and spiritual growth.* Simon & Schuster.
Porter, C. J., Sulé, V. T., & Croom, N. N. (2022). Applying black feminist epistemologies, research, and Praxis: An introduction. In C. J. Porter, V. T. Sulé, & N. N. Croom (Eds.), *Black feminist epistemology, research, and praxis* (pp. 1–11). Routledge.
Rashid, H. M., & Muhammad, Z. (1992). The Sister Clara Muhammad schools: Pioneers in the development of Islamic education in America. *The Journal of Negro Education, 61*(2), 178–185.
Ross, R. (2003). Clara Muhammad: Supporting movement ideas outside its mainstream. In R. E. Ross (Ed.), *Witnessing and testifying: Black women, religion, and civil rights* (pp. 141–158). Fortress Press.
Ṣaḥīḥ al-Bukhārī. (Vol. 8, Book 78. No. 2). Darussalam.
Saldana, J. (2021). *The coding manual for qualitative researchers.* SAGE Publications Limited.
Samuels, S. S., Wilkerson, A., & Dacres, S. S. (2021). Why they struggle to stay: Black women educators reflect on the state of teachers. *The Clearing House: A Journal of Educational Strategies, Issues and Ideas, 94*(3), 137–150.
Souto-Manning, M. (2014). Critical narrative analysis: The interplay of critical discourse and narrative analyses. *International Journal of Qualitative Studies in Education, 27*(2), 159–180.
Story, K. A. (2014). *Patricia Hill Collins: Reconceiving motherhood.* Demeter Press.
Strauss, A., & Corbin, J. (1990). *Basics of qualitative research.* Sage.
Turner, C. R., & Allen, K. R. (2022). "She's a friend of my mind": A reflection of Black sisterhood in academia. *Race Ethnicity and Education*, 1–18.
Waters, B. S. (2016). *We can speak for ourselves: Parent involvement and ideologies of Black mothers in Chicago.* Brill.
West, C. (2023). *Nation women negotiating Islam: Moving beyond boundaries in the twentieth century.* Rowman & Littlefield.

Lakya Goss received her Ph.D. from Michigan State University. She is committed to work that centers the holistic well-being of her communities. Before entering academia, she was an elementary school teacher and post-secondary instructor in Detroit, United Arab Emirates, and Saudi Arabia. Rooted in spirituality, within Black feminist and decolonial frameworks, she seeks to understand resistance in education across the African diaspora.

Yetunde Alabede is a daughter, wife, mother, friend, educator and a teacher-educator. She is a Yorùbá liberal muslim from Nigeria but a doctoral student in the curriculum, Instruction and Teacher Education at Michigan State University.

Tasleem Firdausee is a Ph.D. candidate at Western Michigan University, whose research focuses on Black women, Sufism, healing, Islam, and the African diaspora. She is an acclaimed published poet, professor, workshop facilitator, and holistic wellness therapist. Additionally, Firdausee is a registered and certified yoga teacher, reiki energy healer, and sound therapist, having led workshops and taught at various venues nationwide and globally, spanning from college campuses and K-12 schools to community centers and retreats. Her reach extends internationally, encompassing countries such as Senegal, Ghana, Canada, England, South Africa, and Malaysia.

Self-Efficacy in the Brilliant Black Girl: Exploring the Impact of Exceptionalism on Academic and Professional Success

LoRen Modisa

Abstract This essay explores the implications of exceptionalism on the lives of Black women. More specifically, it seeks to uncover how being labeled exceptional or brilliant, if not done with intention, can have harrowing effects on the academic and professional lives of Black women. Guided by parent racial socialization and academic identity development theories, Black women who were labeled exceptional in earlier years often have a commonality of experiences and mental models: excellence being synonymous with perseverance, intelligence being synonymous with work ethic, and feelings of invisibility. Black women collegiate students (and Black girls, generally) who struggle through navigating their academic identity are likely to become Black women scholars who are navigating the same. This work will shed light on the complexities of the burden associated with being a brilliant Black woman.

Keywords Exceptionalism · Academic identity · Invisibility · Burden of Brilliance

Introduction

For most of my childhood, school was the safest place in the world for me. Not only did I feel physically safe, which is something I do not take for granted, I also felt psychologically safe. Of course, elementary, middle and high school came with their own host of crisis points—navigating friend groups, crushes and relationships, desires to shave my legs or wear makeup or the peer pressure to begin "adult" things. However, school was where I went to learn; and I adored learning. My mother always tells the story of me being 3 or 4 years old, sitting on the kitchen floor with a telephone book (aging myself here) as I flipped through the pages, searching for a school to attend. She would often recall to me that I was so eager to go to a place where learning happens all day. Some of the fondest memories that I have with my mother

L. Modisa (✉)
University of South Alabama, Mobile, AL, USA
e-mail: lmodisa@southalabama.edu

C. R. Turner and M. L. Green (eds.), *Black Motherscholarship Within and Beyond the Academy*, https://doi.org/10.1007/978-3-031-99758-7_12

are connected to my love of learning: Saturdays spent at either Barnes and Noble or our public library and my first day of pre-kindergarten. On that day that I started school, I was probably the happiest girl in the world. As we approached the door of my class, my mother hugged me, kissed my forehead, prayed over me, and gifted me with my very first Bible. It was small and pink and had more illustrations than words. It was perfect.

All of these early moments and memories shaped how I viewed learning and myself as it relates to learning. I soon became a straight "A" student. I began to acquire all the related accolades: perfect attendance award, model student award, honor roll, special privileges in the library, and added classroom responsibilities. And, with those accolades also came invitations to participate in gifted programs and special, accelerated activities at different schools. Elementary school was a dream. It felt good to be recognized for my deep love of learning. I felt affirmed, seen, and validated. It felt as if I had been given unlimited permission to be, wholly and completely, a smart, well-behaved girl. But, what else was I?

Middle school was different from elementary school in many ways. For one, the learning experience became less joyful (and, ultimately, began to feel a little less safe). My parents enrolled me in a magnet middle school with an accelerated, college preparatory curriculum with an emphasis on math and science. The atmosphere was incredibly competitive; and the perfect grades that came easily to me in elementary school now required blood, sweat, and tears. Anxiety and stress visited me for the first time as a middle schooler; and they never left. This time in my life also felt different than earlier years because the pressure to *perform* my knowledge had increased substantially. For the first time, it did not seem like it was enough to simply love learning—I had to prove my love of learning. Deciphering what it took to prove my love of learning (in accordance with curricular standards) in a highly rigorous, highly competitive environment was a jolting and unsettling experience.

Simultaneously, my family, who had been accustomed to the ways by which my love of learning manifested itself in academic settings, was unprepared to support me through the challenges of middle school. In fact, much of the stress and anxiety I felt during this time came from my family's expectation of me to academically perform at the highest level, no matter what. While I struggled with new body image issues, puberty, and run-of-the-mill middle school drama, I also was struggling with the changing relationship that was unfolding with an institution that once felt like the safest place in the world for me. Although I still excelled, my academic identity was evolving right before my eyes.

Developing Academic Identity

Academic identity (Butler-Barnes et al., 2017), also known as academic self-concept, refers to the intellectual and scholarly elements of a person's identity. It also involves how one sees themselves as it relates to their school/learning environment. Being Black in America means grappling with, to some extent, the stereotypes that involve the academic ability and achievement of people of color (Miller & Wang, 2019; Rodriguez et al., 2004; Sellers et al., 1998). Stereotypes that suggest a lack of ability and intellect are born out of generations of racist ideology. One component of the racial identity development process concerns itself with accepting or challenging stereotypes and tropes about one's race group (Miller & Wang, 2019). To accept a negative stereotype about one's group often means to internalize it, to incorporate it into one's identity, to live in a way that affirms it, and to have a view of self that is dictated by said stereotype. To challenge a negative stereotype often involves a refusal to accept the stereotype and a personal commitment to dismantle and redefine the stereotype for oneself and one's identity group.

This is also true of academic-related stereotypes for people of color (Butler-Barnes et al., 2017). Black adolescents, in particular, undergo a rigorous process to find a place of reconciliation between their racial identity and their academic one. Often done unconsciously, both Black children and caregivers alike, who are striving to renegotiate negative academic stereotypes, find themselves enacting forms of rebellion against systemic oppression within academic spaces. For children, this rebellion is often manifested through their performance. For the parent or caregiver, the rebellion is often manifested through the expectations placed on the child. Either way, rebellion can be exhausting for all parties involved.

Parental Racial and Academic Socialization

In many respects, Black parenthood is rebellion. Raising Black children in a racialized society often has very specific implications for the parents of these children, who desire to combat negative societal messaging and protect their children's self-concept. Parents of Black children, specifically, consider the racial socialization of their children as a vital component of their parenting responsibilities (Lloyd, 2022). The process of parent racial socialization involves the installation of proactive and protective messaging meant to help children and adolescents develop their racial identity while providing means of protection from negative, racialized, or discriminatory acts (Turner, 2020). When parents incorporate ethnic/racial socialization into their parenting regime, they aid in the development of their children's ethnic/racial identity. Studies show (Aldana & Byrd, 2015; Huguley et al., 2019; Rodriguez et al., 2004) that positive or strong ethnic/racial identity in children and adolescents leads to positive outcomes socially, mentally, and academically. More specifically, when an individual develops a healthy racial identity, they are more likely to have higher self-esteem, higher professional and academic self-efficacy, greater degrees of adjustment in college or other post-secondary paths, and diminished likelihood of depressive symptoms throughout their lifespan (Benner & Wang, 2017; Sheikh et al., 2023). Even once children reach late adolescence or early adulthood, the impact of parent racial socialization cannot be refuted.

Parents posit several reasons for their commitment to socializing their children. Often, one of the primary reasons is a desire to protect their children from adopting negative stereotypes about their identity (Lloyd, 2022). The second most common reason for parental commitment to socializing their children is to improve their children's self-esteem. Lastly, parents often commit to these practices to prepare children for the world around them, a world that has historically not been a friendly, safe, or nurturing environment for people of color to flourish into whole, autonomous, confident versions of themselves (Huguley et al., 2019; Ulerio & Mena, 2020).

Conceptual/Theoretical Grounding

This work is rooted in the interplay of parental racial socialization and the implications of this socialization on academic identity development. A child's parent or caregiver is the first person to socialize them and to help give the pieces of their identity meaning. Through socialization, parents and caregivers are tasked with preparing their children for the world around them (Aldana & Byrd, 2015). Unfortunately, for children of color, this preparation often involves preparation for bias, mistreatment, and discrimination (Huguley et al., 2019). Parent socialization can have many manifestations. Some of which include affirming a child of their beauty or intellect, instilling racial pride, and promoting community, and/or preparing a child for responding to discrimination when it occurs. For parents, the socialization process can be both proactive and reactive. By simultaneously preparing children for the world around them and instilling messaging that resists negative tropes or stereotypes, parents play a vital role in the identity development, and particularly the academic identity development of their children.

Self-Efficacy, Socialization, and the Brilliant Black Girl

For the Black caregiver, affirming their child of their intellect and ability is part of a healthy racial socialization process. Within many Black families, proactive messages about their child/ren's ability and intelligence begin being communicated to a child soon after birth. As mentioned before, this is a tool in the arsenal of our collective Black rebellion against the messages our children will inevitably receive from the world around us. However, as positive and necessary as it may be, if not done with balance, nuance, and intention, the socializing activities and practices Black caregivers employ with their children may have negative effects on the child's self-concept. This is particularly true as it relates to parental socialization done in the area of academic identity. It was certainly true for me.

High school came and went for me; and on the surface, everything was as it should have been: invitations to honor societies, scholarships to every college that I applied to, national merit scholar recognition, and, of course, participation in an array of social, civic, and leadership activities. However, at a deeper level, I no longer loved school. I was simply performing my love of school. I knew all of the right steps to take and academic moves to make. I knew how to participate in the call-and-response of academic settings. I graduated high school at the top of my class and went off to college already set to pursue a career in an area that everyone in my family and close circle was advising me to pursue: STEM (science, technology, engineering and math). Because, of course, smart girls that made good grades needed to major in STEM, right?

Had you asked me nearly 14 years ago—while I was wrapping up my freshman year of college—if I thought that the academic struggle I was experiencing would teach me something later in life, I would have sobbed in your face. Now, I feel peace when I reflect on that time because I know how good that season in my life was for my personal growth and development. I needed it more than anything I've ever needed in life. I needed to feel true academic struggle. I needed to know what it felt like when my performance of learning was not sufficient to "get the grade", when I could not simply "fake it until I made it". I needed to know what it felt like to have everything I thought I knew about myself (which was largely wrapped within my academic identity) turned upside down.

If I had to summarize what that season in life taught me (and continues to teach me), it would be this: Brilliant people struggle, too. As simplistic and reasonable as that may sound, this was completely counter to what I was socialized by my family to believe. While enthusiastically affirming my intelligence and encouraging my love of learning all those years, my family, particularly my parents, were unconsciously setting me up for struggle. Studies show that when parents indiscriminately tell their children that they are smart or that they can do anything (without appropriately contextualizing these comments), it can lead to the possession of a fixed mindset (Huguley et al., 2019). Simply put, positive affirmation without nuance and balance can lead to negative self-concept. It is the difference between communicating "You are smart. You should be able to figure this out" and "You are smart. Yet, struggling is okay; and it doesn't make you any less smart. What is this struggle communicating to you?".

I often think back to my younger self. With the purest of intentions, I received implicit and explicit messaging from my family that communicated that, because I was brilliant, I should and would be expected to excel at the highest level, in all the areas. There was no mention of different types of intelligences, or the necessary nuance required when we talk about cognitive ability that clarifies skill and aptitude can be built and nurtured, that being good at something does not always mean that it will come easily or naturally. I was socialized to believe that I should not academically struggle and, if I did, something was wrong with me.

So, when academic struggle and hardship darkened my doorstep early in college, they sent my self-confidence, self-efficacy, and overall self-concept spiraling. They were unfamiliar to me; and I was unprepared for them. Well, this is not completely true. I had experienced this type of struggle earlier on. This time around, however, I could not study or work the struggle away. It required a deeper exploration of the ways by which my identity was wrapped into warped concepts of productivity, performance, and value alignment; and I was neither prepared nor had the skills to do that inner work. And so, too, goes the story of far too many brilliant Black girls.

Far too many of us are expected to hold the world on our shoulders without adequate support (Hooks, 1993). Then, something falls off our shoulders (we struggle, fail, or face an obstacle) and, instead of knowing how to look around us and assess the support we needed but did not receive, we turn inwardly and judge, critique, and tear down.

Implications

In my profession, I see myself mirrored in the faces of Black women college students almost daily. As a Black woman, self-proclaimed scholar, and lifelong learner, I have always been called "exceptional" or "bright." For most of my life, those labels constituted the foundation (and totality) of my self-identity. However, it was not until my late twenties and early thirties (my current age) that I began to realize that I was worth so much more than my academic ability. It took a lot of intentional unlearning and commitment to self-discovery to fully actualize a healthier and more complete self-concept. I am still on this journey (as are many other Black motherscholars).

It brings me joy to do for Black college women what I had wished had been done for me: urge them to step into a fuller identity, one that does not require them to be overworked, overwhelmed, or feeling chained to an identity that is incomplete or limiting. When I have a young Black woman in my office, I find myself needing to tell them that smart or exceptional people *do* experience adversity and challenges. For many of the young Black women with whom I work, I am the first person to tell them this, to give them permission to not be perfect. So many of the young women that I work with have been conditioned to be "all of the things, all at once." Or, they have been socialized to believe that their ability to carry, cope, and handle multiple responsibilities while carrying everything without error or fault was the epitome of excellence. It is such an exhausting perspective to have; and it absolutely shows up in how they experience college. For those of us that have not done the healing work, these perspectives are showing up far beyond the manifestations of our college days.

On a surface level, collegiate and professional Black women have been breaking barriers, destroying stereotypes, and experiencing high levels of academic success for decades. However, the deeper story to tell is that for many of us, while enacting rebellion against our outside world through our intellect and brilliance, there is an inner self in need of release from the pressure (Jacobs, 2016). To add more layers to the complexity, our academic and professional identities are often intertwined with "strong Black woman" schema (Jacobs, 2016), community and familial expectations, and trauma related to societal stereotypes (Barr & Neville, 2014). As brilliant Black women and girls, what would it mean if we shifted our view of self-efficacy from "I can do everything" to "I am not meant to do everything"? Imagine how much collective healing can be found, as a whole, by arriving at that revelation.

Even further, what does it mean to get to a place of understanding where you can acknowledge the things you needed in your childhood (for many of us, freedom to be imperfect and still be considered "good" and "worthy") while also having gratitude for the immense sacrifices your caregivers endured? This is a rhetorical question for us all (myself included). All in all, as scholars, mothers, and educators, we must interrogate and challenge what it means to be exceptional (Also read as: productive, brilliant, hard-working, etc.) and, then hopefully, re-define that meaning guided by self-love and self-agency. Then, we can do the same for the brilliant Black children and future scholars within our reach.

Competing Interests The author has no conflicts of interest to declare that are relevant to the content of this manuscript.

References

Aldana, A., & Byrd, C. M. (2015). School ethnic–racial socialization: Learning about race and ethnicity among African American students. *The Urban Review, 47*(3), 563–576. https://doi.org/10.1007/s11256-014-0319-0

Barr, S. C., & Neville, H. A. (2014). Racial socialization, color-blind racial ideology, and mental health among Black college students: An examination of an ecological model. *Journal of Black Psychology, 40*(2), 138–165. https://doi.org/10.1177/0095798412475084

Benner, A. D., & Wang, Y. (2017). Racial/ethnic discrimination and adolescents' well-being: The role of cross-ethnic friendships and friends' experiences of discrimination. *Child Development, 88*(2), 493–504. https://doi.org/10.1111/cdev.12606

Butler-Barnes, S. T., Varner, F., Williams, A., & Sellers, R. (2017). Academic identity: A longitudinal investigation of African American adolescents' academic persistence. *Journal of Black Psychology, 43*(7), 714–739. https://doi.org/10.1177/0095798416683170

Hooks, B. (1993) Sisters of the Yam: Black women and self-recovery. South End Press.

Huguley, J. P., Wang, M. T., Vasquez, A. C., & Guo, J. (2019). Parental ethnic-racial socialization practices and the construction of children of color's ethnic-racial identity: A research synthesis and meta-analysis. *Psychological Bulletin, 145*(5), 437–458. https://doi.org/10.1037/bul0000187

Jacobs, C. (2016). Developing the "oppositional gaze": Using critical media pedagogy and black feminist thought to promote black girls' identity development. *The Journal of Negro Education, 85*(3), 225. https://doi.org/10.7709/jnegroeducation.85.3.0225

Lloyd, D. D. (2022). African American mothers' racial socialization practices with preschoolers: A mixed methods study. *Family Relations, 71*(5), 1859–1877. https://doi.org/10.1111/fare.12639

Miller, R. S., & Wang, M.-T. (2019). Cultivating adolescents' academic identity: Ascertaining the mediating effects of motivational beliefs between classroom practices and mathematics Identity. *Journal of Youth and Adolescence, 48*(10), 2038–2050. https://doi.org/10.1007/s10964-019-01115-x

Rodriguez, J. L., Jones, E. B., Pang, V. O., & Park, C. (2004). Promoting academic achievement and identity development among diverse high school students. *The High School Journal, 87*(3), 44–53. https://doi.org/10.1353/hsj.2004.0002

Sellers, R. M., Smith, M. A., Shelton, J. N., Rowley, S. A. J., & Chavous, T. M. (1998). Multidimensional model of racial identity: A reconceptualization of African American racial identity. *Personality and Social Psychology Review, 2*(1), 18–39. https://doi.org/10.1207/s15327957pspr0201_2

Sheikh, I. S., Lanni, D., Mekawi, Y., Powers, A., Michopoulos, V., & Carter, S. (2023). What is the power of identity? Examining the moderating role of racial-identity latent profiles on the relationship between race-related stress and trauma symptoms among black american women. *Clinical Psychological Science*, 216770262311610. https://doi.org/10.1177/21677026231161064

Turner, J. L. (2020). Black mothering in action: The racial-class socialization practices of low-income black single mothers. *Sociology of Race and Ethnicity, 6*(2), 242–253. https://doi.org/10.1177/2332649219899683

Ulerio, G., & Mena, J. A. (2020). Parental cultural socialization practices among underrepresented ethnoracial groups in a predominantly white rural college community. *Journal of Child and Family Studies, 29*(10), 2697–2709. https://doi.org/10.1007/s10826-020-01778-2

LoRen Modisa currently serves as the Director of the Office of Health Advancement within the University of South Alabama Whiddon College of Medicine. With over 10 years of experience in educational advocacy and program development, LoRen has learned to see all opportunities through the lens of accessibility, equity, and inclusion. Most of her professional career has been dedicated to community development and social impact work. She has worked with the United States Peace Corps, Clinton Foundation, and Big Brothers Big Sisters of America. Currently, her research focuses on the racial socialization of historically marginalized students on higher education campuses. Socially, LoRen is an investor with the Society of Clotilda Giving Circle, founding investor with the Black Girl Scholarship Fund, member of Alpha Kappa Alpha Sorority, Incorporated, Board Member of Prism United, and a Young Professionals Board Member of the Alabama Humanities Alliance.

Academic Mothering for Black Women in the Caribbean: A Matricentric Caribbean Feminist Approach

Talia R. Esnard

Abstract Negotiating work and children can compromise the wellbeing (Gatrell et al., 2017) and academic trajectory of mothers (Guarino and Borden, 2017). In the context of the academy, academic mothers are often challenged by the lack of institutionalized systems of support to cushion the effects of competing tasks, efforts, and agendas across work-family domains. With heightened levels of gender inequalities for women academics, the "systematic failure to recognize the ways that motherhood can alter a female academic's career in profound ways" remains an area *of* contention and *for* intervention (Castenada and Isgro, 2013, p. 9). Yet, there is little empirical literature that seeks to both locate and trouble the structural and situational forms of precarity for academic mothers within the Caribbean, the subjectivities that are formed through these experiences, and the implications of these for promoting issues of equity and diversity. The paper uses matricentric Caribbean Feminist approach and narrative inquiry to draw on the stories, challenges, and strategies for navigating academic mothering. Through this examination this chapter assesses the status and scope of scholarship on academic mothers in the Caribbean and connects this to global scholarship to demonstrate the need for contextualized understandings of and interventions.

Keywords Academic mothers · Matricentric feminism · Caribbean

Introduction

Within the academy, mothers are often challenged by the lack of supportive institutional mechanisms to cushion the effects of competing demands, tasks, and agendas across work-family domains (Mason & Goulden, 2002). Key points of tension for academic mothers are the unbounded nature of work and family domains as well as for the contending discourses of the selfless mother and the ideal worker (Connelly & Ghodsee, 2011; Swanson & Johnston, 2003) that penalize women who attempt to

T. R. Esnard (✉)
The University of the West Indies, St. Augustine, Trinidad and Tobago
e-mail: Talia.Esnard@sta.uwi.edu

C. R. Turner and M. L. Green (eds.), *Black Motherscholarship Within and Beyond the Academy*, https://doi.org/10.1007/978-3-031-99758-7_13

bridge these two worlds (Raddon, 2002). While these challenges and the struggles that follow differ based on the stages of motherhood, the rank/status within an institution, available systems of support, and that of family dynamics (Castaneda & Isgro, 2013; Pinela & Muñoz, 2005), a consensus is for the persistent pressures and vulnerabilities that academic mothers face within their personal and professional journeys (Gatrell et al., 2017; Guarino & Borden, 2017; Ward-Wolf-Wendel, 2017). Researchers note that this level of vulnerability is amplified for single mothers, mothers of color (Schlehofer, 2012) and for pregnant mothers who often struggle through their professional journeys (Yoo, 2020). Thun (2020) contends that such level of susceptibility is particularly the case where there is the presence of institutionalized gender blindness that dismisses or renders invisible the contradictions between the cultural expectations of motherhood and those of working within the academy.

A central problem, however, is that despite the advancement of the scholarship on academic mothers, there are many unfinished agendas related to persistent and new structures and relations of power within and beyond the academy that differently impact constituent groups of mothers (Ward & Wolf-Wendel, 2008, 2017). Of note is what Castenada and Isgro (2013, p. 9) describe as a "systematic failure" of academic institutions to recognize and to address the negative impacts of contending discourses and expectations around institutionalized forms of labor and those related to mothering. Other scholars center the compounding effects and weight of neoliberal shifts within higher education, including those related to increased infiltration of new public management, (with a growing emphasis on productivity with accountability), but without substantive changes in the ideal worker norms, which celebrate adaptability and availability within the workplace (Miller & Riley, 2022). The effects of the COVID-19 pandemic on academic mothers reiterated this level of precarity and the need for better support systems that cushion the blow of such crises (Fulweiler et al., 2021).

These accounts call for more contemporary and expanded interrogations of the realities for academic mothers that unpack the assumptions and intricacies of mothering while professing (O'Brien Hallstein & O'Reilly, 2012; Smith-Carrier et al., 2021; Thun, 2020). These trepidations also warrant deeper examinations of the challenges experienced by academic mothers within specific contextual (cultural and social) considerations. This type of contextual framing is certainly instructive for the Caribbean where, despite the growing presence of mothers within higher education, mothers continue to bear the weight of care and nurturing within the family. This is certainly evident in the rich scholarship within the region that speak to the strong disparities within the social responsibilities, expectations, and status for women and mothers (Bailey, 2003; Mohammed & Perkins, 1999), which negatively impact their experiences and progression within the academy (Esnard & Cobb-Roberts, 2018; Gregory, 2006). For Gregory (2006) this is particularly concerning for Black women in the Caribbean where the cultural constructions of race, gender and class impact their negotiation of competing tasks across work-and-family domains. These concerns also emerge within more generalized examinations of the women's educational and professional experiences with noted findings on the prevalence of pervasive gender norms, that are complicated by the socio-economic challenges for mothers, including lower levels of education and income (see Pinella and Muñoz, 2005).

At a general level however, research on academic mothers within the Caribbean and on the intersections of race and gender within the work-family integration dynamics remain substantively absent (Esnard & Cobb-Roberts, 2018; Gregory, 2006). This type of scholarship, however, is particularly important to capture how gendered and raced constructions have been historically rooted in dysfunctional, deficit notions of the Black matriarchal household (Esnard, 2019). This type of research is useful to show how such perceptions of matriarchal households have impacted the framing of the thinking and practices around formal employment and mother work (Mohammed & Perkins, 1999; Rowley, 2011). To some extent, researchers have attempted to link broader racialized and colonized histories to the maternal thinking, stereotypes and practices on child rearing and caring of Black women within the region (Carty, 1988; Reynolds, 2005). However, this type of scholarship has been limited, with a relative absence of research that locates and situates the experiences and challenges for Black mothers within the context of the academy. By centering the voices and experiences of Black academic Caribbean mothers, the chapter attempts to bridge the empirical gap by:

(i) advancing knowledge on work life-integration for academic mothers
(ii) problematizing the weight of color and ethnicity to social stratification in the Caribbean and the historical gaze and neglect that have resulted for Black mothers in the region.

Using a matricentric feminist Caribbean perspective and narrative inquiry, this chapter advances a critical engagement of work-life integration for academic mothers that is situated within more muddled contextual factors that centers their everyday lived realities.

Positioning Matricentric Feminism as a Caribbean Perspective

Existing theorizations of academic mothers are generally located within the United States [US] and Canada, with few extensions or explorations of these issues beyond these borders. Within this body of literature, researchers generally contend that the integration of academic work with that of mothering unfolds as a source of work-family conflict with growing strains for mothers who desire to sustain their scholarship (Ward & Wolf-Wendel, 2008, 2017). A consensus within the field is for the tendency of academic mothers in the US to sacrifice their academic trajectory or pathways with the prioritization of maternal responsibilities, albeit with varying degrees and strategies over time. However, there is noticeable ambivalence for mothers within that nexus (Hinton-Johnson, 2011) and with others who opt for reduced opportunities for leisure and professional gain (Fothergill & Feltey, 2003). However, the core concern within these studies is for the weight of gender-based norms that surround the biological and tenure clock (O'Brien Hallstein & O'Reilly, 2012). Related apprehensions are for the extent to which these gender norms are nested within patriarchal discourses and structures—a reality, which disproportionately impacts the career progression for academic mothers (Swanson & Johnston, 2003; Williams & Ceci, 2012).

Clear gaps emerge within this overall body of work. As a case in point, the racialized aspects of these experiences and the extent to which these intersect with gender to impact the experiences of Black women are not substantively visible. Even where authors have examined the experiences of Black women, these have been historically framed within the broader use or application of Black feminist and womanist perspectives, but without needed extensions and theorizations of academic mothers within scholarship focused on mothering and across social geographies. An opportunity exists however for advancing the field with the use of matricentric feminism, but with the problematization of Eurocentric framing of Black mothers and interrogations of the patriarchal and colonial processes that have influence their thinking and practices (Esnard, 2019). This type of examination is positioned as uniquely valuable given the lack of research that seeks to redress the historical mis-representation of Black mothers who have worked outside of normalized family structures and institutionalized work- family dynamics (Barrow, 1996a; Esnard, 2019).

As an emerging perspective, matricentric feminism allows scholars to focus on mothering (as a practice) and motherhood (as an institution). Often referred to as the unfinished business of feminist scholarship, this perspective advances a theory and a politic *on* and *for* mothers that centers the experiences, thinking and concerns as the starting point of that process (O'Reilly, 2016, 2019). This type of theorization extends feminist scholarship with needed distinctions between motherhood as institution, experience, and practice. The framework illuminates the context, cultures, and structures of mothering and motherhood, counters the patriarchal and oppressive systems that underpin this formulation, and makes recommendations for interventions that empower these women (O'Reilly, 2016). Related mandates or governing principles within this matricentric feminist perspective are for analyses that (1) address mothers, motherhood and mothering as the basis for theorization and scholarship, (2) speak to the framing of mothering as experience and work, (3) contest those oppressive aspects of motherhood, (4) push back against the child-centered nature of motherhood, and (5) commit to social change and justice *for* mothers but empowerment *of* mothers (O'Reilly, 2016, 2019).

To advance these ideas within the context of the Caribbean, this chapter situates the academy and the family, both as sites of power and struggle, but through the lenses and experiences for Black academic mothers. This framing is particularly important given the "racialized discourses" of African mothers that stem from our colonial history (Bush, 2010, p. 71). The framing also makes visible related "pathologization of matrifocality [focused on Black single mothers] that imposes functional, heteronormative and Eurocentric notions of the family" (Esnard, 2019, p. 260) and that has shaped social re-engineering agendas. What is clear is that the negative constructions of Black matriarchal families in the Caribbean have influenced a contextual complexity "within identity politics [that] materialize through …issues related to sexuality, conjugality, as well as the respectability of Afro-Caribbean women" (Esnard, 2019, p. 263). Despite this reality, there is little understanding and theorization of how these constructions have shaped more contemporary realities for Black mothers within the region. Without sustained and critical analyses that capture the experiences of Black mothers, the insights that we hold and the attempt to address the challenges remain limited.

This application of matricentric feminism to academic mothers represents a political stance and point of resistance, and an attempt to bridge the gaps in the theorizations of mothers for Black academic mothers in the Caribbean. The perspective represents an attempt to make visible the ways in which oppressive structures and cultures can be reproduced and resisted within the comparative sites and institutions. A central goal of this work is for the resituating of academic mothers in the Caribbean to counter the patriarchal and sacrificial underpinnings of motherhood, the ways in which these have been silenced within academic settings, and the consequences for their lived realities and practices. This type of analytical lens allows for the advancement of a scholarship and advocacy that is capable of transgressing some of the societal, political, and institutional failings, which continue to impact the subjectivities and potentialities for academic mothers within the region.

Method

While there are a few studies on gender disparities within Caribbean institutions of higher education (Chip-Johnson & Vanderpool, 2003; Hamilton, 1999), these are generally limited to analyses that underscore issues of representation and engagement across educational levels, programs, and disciplines. There is a lack of in-depth qualitative explorations that provide needed insights into the experiences of academic mothers across ethnicities, classes, and institutional types and ranks (Carty, 1988; Gregory, 2006). These points of investigation are specifically needed to capture or to story the diverse experiences of women (Clandinin & Rosiek, 2007) with attention to those who are single mothers, who do or do not benefit from the support of families, or who resists the narratives that are being imposed. The promise therefore is for the application of more deliberate explorations that situate the voices, experiences, and standpoints of academic mothers within the region.

Endarkened Narrative Inquiry

The chapter draws on the use of the endarkened narrative inquiry that is grounded in Black woman-centric onto-epistemologies (Dillard, 2000; McClish-Boyd & Bhattacharya, 2024) and centers the lives and stories of Black academic mothers within specific contexts. As a Black academic mother with three children, this issue for me is both real and experienced, but rarely discussed, studied or contested within the

Caribbean. While as a scholar, I have worked to illuminate the realities for women scholars within the region, in my previous work, I also call out the pathologization of Black mothers within the Caribbean (Esnard, 2019) and the invisibility *of* and inequity *for* academic mothers (Esnard & Cobb-Roberts, 2018). To disrupt these silences and deficit perspectives, I commit through this work the storying of these realities and the use of endarkened narrative inquiry to make visible the many lived realities, experiences and stories of academic mothers, but within the context of the Caribbean. This application of the endarkened narrative inquiry represents an extension of narrative inquiry but with the focus on the stories *of* and *for* Black women. This approach is consistent with the work of qualitative researchers who push for scientific inquiry that is epistemology grounded in lived experience, while understanding the social interactions, places and space that define experience with a given phenomenon (see Connelly & Clandinin, 2006; Clandinin & Connelly, 2000). Presented in this way as an endarkened narrative composed experience, the objective is to center the perceptions and positionality of Black academic mothers but also to underscore their representation and engagement of the matter under investigation.

Data Collection

To do this, I engaged in the execution of twelve narrative semi-structured interviews with academic mothers from diverse disciplines, ranks, and with a varied number of children. This initial work is intended to provide exploratory understanding of the realities for Black mothers and to inform more sustained research in this area. These women were recruited through the use of purposive sampling and snowballing, with the initial dissemination, (via institutional emails), of an invitational flyer to Black women mothers across Caribbean higher education institutions. The flyer solicited the participation and referral of Black academic mothers as part of this research project, which lasted for 3 three months. Seven Black academic mothers across Caribbean based higher education institutions responded to this call. Three of these women provided referrals, which resulted in the further inclusion of five participants. Collectively, twelve Black academic mothers participated in this research. Table 13.1 reflects the personal and professional background of the interviewees, with attention to their academic rank, discipline and number of children.

Though the number of interviews remain limited to the experiences of twelve (12) academic mothers, these represent an explorative take on the phenomenon, with in-depth engagement of their stories and experiences that are used to capture the many layers of narratives explored within the inquiry space (Clandinin & Connelly, 2000). These interviews, posed as a conversation with Black academic mothers, allowed for engagement of key issues and experiences of working within the academy. Interview questions therefore addressed their experiences, challenges, points of struggle, agentic expressions, and reflections on what is needed to improve their experiences as academic mothers. Some of these questions included: (i) where were you in your career when you had your first child, and how would you describe the experiences

Table 13.1 Personal and professional background of interviewees

Name (Pseudonym)	Academic rank	Number of children	Discipline
Maria	Senior Lecturer	2	Economics
Jennifer	Professor	2	Sociology
Sancha	Professor	2	Medicine
Justine	Instructor	2	Psychology
Cheryl	Senior Lecturer	1	Education
Mellisa	Senior Lecturer	1	Management Studies
Merium	Lecturer	1	Criminology
Shania	Lecturer	1	Agriculture
Chandra	Senior Lecturer	2	Medicine
Samantha	Assistant Lecturer	1	Marketing
Sherry	Lecturer	1	Engineer
Judith	Lecturer	1	Geography

around this, (ii) how did you manage the integration of work and childcare, (iii) how did what were some of the institutional accommodations, if any, during this time, (iv) if you had to reimagine the university, to better support mothers who are taking this journey, what would that be like? These questions were part of a list of semi-structured questions, which allowed for probing based on the responses of participants. These interviews ranged from 1 to 2 hours; and were conducted with academic mothers who were hired as instructors, lecturers, senior lecturers, and professors.

Data Analysis

Interviews were recorded, transcribed, and coded using emergent codes, to inform the broader themes for the study. Field texts were coded with reference to the events, experiences, perceptions, and points of tension. These transcriptions were reviewed with member checking to ensure the accuracy of the stories and the interpretations that followed. Using Braun and Clarke, (2020) reflexive thematic analysis, the interviews were reduced to significant codes to create a cohesive story from mothers as a necessary aspect of narrative inquiry methodology (see Wells, 2011). The transcripts were also theoretically and epistemologically reviewed to ensure attention to cultural standpoints of Black academic mothers and the significance of race and gender within their experiences and negotiations of the work-family interface. The challenges of managing reproduction with production, of managing the impact on one's career, and the strategies for negotiating work-family tensions emerge as key themes that are discussed in the subsection that follows.

Managing Reproduction, Representation and Production

A central aspect of the lived experience for Black academic mothers was that of addressing the constructions related to the social representations and expectations related to reproduction and production. In most cases, a reported challenge was around the lack of attention to the needs of expectant and nursing academic mothers, which participants linked to the constructions of and expectations for Black women within the professional space.

Maria located the struggles within broader normative expectations of mothering as sacrificial, with a requirement for nursing mothers to stay home with young children. Where academic mothers chose to return to work within three months, they also spoke to the high levels of social scrutiny. Maria, for instance, reflected on the experiences of being asked to "extend the nursing of her infant" where possible, but also, to "make the necessary adjustments at home, [not at work], to ensure that this happens". While as an academic mother, she lamented on the need to return to work in the shortest possible time, she also spoke of the absence of a middle ground position that makes possible the ability for mothers to "breastfeed their children while at work..." and, the introduction of institutional policy that negate the "frowning of expectant or nursing mothers while at work". Justine connected these realities to the historical construction and denigration of the Black single mother. She noted that this type of institutional intervention is particularly needed to address the not so silent scrutiny of her pregnancy as a single Black woman and the general lack of concern or care as it relates to her wellbeing. For Justine, the invisibility and lack of attention to the representations and expectations of Black mothers remained a "thinking within the broader society that is not often discussed but that becomes visible in how persons respond to Black mothers who are single".

The non-negotiable aspects of the maternal and professional job dynamic remained a burning issue for mothers. In such cases, Black academic mothers remained troubled by the lack of sensitivity among academic leaders of the precarity for Black mothers. Maria storied her experience of working with another Black academic chair who denied her of an adjusted workload or location of classes and who "blamed [her] for not making the adjustments that were needed as an academic".

While Justine stressed on her inability to negotiate "workload" or to demonstrate "job flexibility" within the workplace, she also underscored the "increasing number of antenatal views, especially among those who occupy positions of leadership within the university." She also noted the tendency for academic colleagues to ignore differentiated responsibilities, particularly for Black mothers with young children. She speculated that this dismissal reflected a "kind of distancing from the realities for Black women, particularly for those who work as single mothers, and a buy into the expectations for one to balance their academic and family responsibilities".

Sancha pointed to the cold nature of academia, which does not "make it easy for those with children...especially when you are single mother" or "for those who have children before exploring opportunities for growth within the university". For Sancha, this extended into the lack of accommodation for Black single mothers with adopted children, who were not able to obtain maternal leave, and who are not seen as legitimately entitled to time or flexibility to stay with their newborn. Justine suggested therefore that this lack of support from institutional colleagues represented systemic issues that are associated with negative representations of Black academic mothers, but that are reproduced by other academic peers. She suggested within her conversation that this tendency emerges from a general sentiment that "having children [outside of normalized bounds of the nuclear family]" is a disadvantage" for those who desire to "move up within the academy".

Navigating Self, Others, and Institution

To address these challenges, participants spoke of the importance of critical consciousness, social awareness, and professional restoration. All participants consciously recognized the weight of motherhood within their social landscapes and spoke critically of how this influenced their personal and professional journeys.

In some cases, academic mothers opted to pause their career advancements and to prioritize the raising of their children. Sancha shared her own observations of the academy, with the normalization of the Eurocentric family (married with children), with an internalization of this ideal from Black and other non-Black academic colleagues (across genders). She also spoke of a lack of support to circumvent institutional barriers that are complicated by these social constructions of Black women. Sherry noted in her conversation that these pressures were reinforced by 'friends, family, and academic colleagues who remind you of the need to put your responsibility as a mother first". Where there was no support, Cheryl, Judith and Sherry all spoke of the curtailing of their traveling and scholarly engagements or exchanges as necessary points of intervention for the benefit of their young children. This resulted in "shortened visits or research exchanges" for Cheryl, to "adjustment in the academic schedule" and a decision by Maria "to discontinue all travels at least for the first two years post-delivery".

In other cases, participants shared their motivations for pushing across both work-family domains. As a professor, Jennifer reflected on her need in the early stages of her career to seek psychological support through her association of other Black academic colleagues outside of her country. She stressed on the "broader openness of Black colleagues in the US who also experienced gendered racism to challenge their own experiences within these institutions and to write on these". She spoke of her engagement with these women as "motivating and sustaining, with useful mentoring that helped with how [she] addressed some of the subtle forms of discrimination that exists within the academy".

While she emphasized the "silence around these issues within the Caribbean", Jennifer also shared her own attempts to "adjust how she negotiated the university space and how she understood the actions of others". Similarly, Chandra identified with the silences around the experiences of Black academic women and more importantly, of the need to work around these representations and constructions of Black women that exist within the wider society. In speaking to her own experiences, she reminisced on her encounters with other Black women in the academy and of one person who "told [her] that Black women would only survive in the university, if they did not have children and worked their way to professional success". She cited in her recall, her decision to "prove others wrong after [her] conversation with another colleague which pointed to a continuous stereotype around single Black mothers who attempted to move their careers forward".

Other mothers suggested that the situation was further problematized by the increasing pressures for academic workers at a broad level to demonstrate the impact of their research, teaching and service functions, without attention to how disadvantaged groups (including mothers and early career academics) may be situated to respond. Merium hinted that while there is a "lack of support for mothers in the university, there is also increased pressure to perform." For her, this becomes "gamble or juggle with work-life balance, or, to ensure that things with the family and work do not falter". Mellisa saw these discursive parameters as a reflection of "emerging trends within the university" that force mothers to "straddle their commitments to the children and to work" as a "statement by these mothers of their ability to manage work and family responsibilities." Samantha noted however the need to recognize how these increasing demands create "more challenges for mothers within the university and makes them feel somehow that they are not capable of meeting these targets". Where these considerations and goal posts are often depersonalized, Samantha spoke to the importance of teaching her daughter "independence, self-worth, and self-reliance" as an important part of creating room for personal and professional growth that does not reproduce how young girls and women are framed within this Caribbean context. For Shania, this level of consciousness and types of decision, required that Black women recognize where and how they are positioned and "wise up, until they come to a place where they know that they are enough".

Yet, others called for institutional responsibility and responsivity. All participants spoke to the need for institutional day care centers as a way to disrupt notions of care that are still centered with the home. Shania remarked that "the university continues to do a real disservice to Black mothers as long as they do not have a daycare facility on site". Jennifer supported this position with the statement that "each campus should have a childcare facility, with a reduced cost, where children can have the pre-primary care and education, where mothers can pay a nominal fee, not a market rate and where they can breastfeed if needed". Similarly, Shania called on the need to recognize institutional responsibility and empathy, where there "is a designated area for breastfeeding and for storage of the breast milk, if people don't have a safe space and support system to do so." Others suggested the need for training of leaders to ensure inclusive leadership practices that ensure sensitivity to the matters of diversity and inclusion and that allow for flexible schedules, support networks, mentoring opportunities and for the creation of safe spaces. Sancha also pointed to the significance of finding allies and mentors (both within and outside of the university) who can provide professional and psychological support and who can offer some critical points of intervention along the way.

Discussion

While motherhood is historically and culturally positioned as privilege or as a mark of respectability for Caribbean women (Boucher, 2003; Green, 2006), the realities around these experiences for diverse mothers is less than understood. Related points of interrogation within these writings, therefore, include cultural constructions of gender and the implications for how issues of responsibility (as it relates to childbearing and caring), matrifocality (with the discussion on the growing nature of female headed households) and respectability (related to status that comes with adherence to the expectations of a mother) are represented and internalized to shape identity, positionality, and action. What emerges within the broader scholarship within the region is the pathologization of Black mothers (Reynolds, 2005), with racialized constructions that are locked within classed constructions of "respectable mothers", who prioritize care, child and upbringing over work or career advancement.

While the Black mothers interviewed did not explicitly mention class structures within their stories, the findings demonstrate a persistence of intensive mothering as a Eurocentric ideal of middle-class motherhood (Hays, 1996), with the expectations for mothers to work within nuclear family structures and with the prioritization of their maternal responsibilities albeit with a lack of institutional support to do otherwise. The findings serve as a reinforcement of the weight of these cultural or normative discourses on motherhood, with the expectation for this to be a priority for mothers and with a demonstration of how these can be further institutionalized within the academy to reproduce inherent structural inequities and adverse forms of marginalization for academic mothers.

The prevalence of this material ideology can be explained by the fact that there is little disruption of the colonized narratives that have located women within the domestic sphere (Barrow, 1988), and that have seeped into institutionalized spaces (Carty, 1988; Reynolds, 2005). These discourses continue to shape the experiences of Black mothers who work outside of heteronormative relationships, familial structures, and normalized patriarchal relations. Yet, the findings also suggest the need to move beyond gendered analyses to also address the importance of race and class within discussions for mothering. This type of sensitivity to racialized and classed subjectivities is particularly necessary given the historical representations of and functionalist framings of Black lower-class family structures and relations within early anthropological research on the Caribbean family (see Barrow, 1988, 1996b). While there is little research on how these have translated into the experiences for Black mothers within the contemporary period, the findings suggest that these remain significant to how Black single mothers are scrutinized, invisibilized, and marginalized within the academic space.

These realities call for greater scrutiny of institutional structures and cultures that impact Black academic mothers (Esnard & Cobb-Roberts, 2018; Gregory, 2006; Leo-Rhynie, 2005) with the need to decolonize institutional knowledge and practices to differently position the realities and prospects for Black women (Stewart, 2019). An important starting point is that of advancing research on the epistemic forms of violence and systemic injustices (related to motherhood and institutional employment) that are experienced by Black women and academic mothers. This type of scholarship represents a critical step in changing the historical canons of knowledge that create deficit notions of Black women and mothers.

Yet, the concerns for mothers on the changing cultures of measurement and assessment within the university also echo increasing findings on the differential impacts of these trends for different types of academics (Guarini et al., 2020) and the need for more explorations that advance understandings around these. This is particularly important given the findings of the study which show that while Black academic mothers are actively working to reform institutional spaces and relations of engagement, they are subject to the decisions of academic colleagues and leaders who carry out these mandates and who are not consciously working to address the inequities that exists within the academy. The findings call for more theorization and research to interrogate the impact of changing educational landscapes and cultures and to situate how these become muddled within structural and cultural realities that are linked to race, gender, and class.

Addressing institutional invisibility presents another critical point of intervention. This is particularly important given the persistence of institutional silences and the absence of institutional policies to address the challenges for academic mothers (Esnard & Cobb-Roberts, 2018). The lack of a maternal policy that protects mothers during, within, and after the birth of their children remains a critical point for change. While The University of the West Indies, as one of the leading institutions in the region has made some headway with this, (with the introduction of a gender justice and sexual harassment policy), the findings suggest that more is needed to produce structural changes particularly in relation to policy, strategic initiatives, and interventions that consider the realities for academic mothers in the region. This discovery is the same for other institutions within the region where the default is to national labor policies that provide defined periods of leave, neonatal and financial support. While academic mothers' have benefitted from legislative allowances with maternity leave and grants to support the initial stages within the birth of a child or children with disabilities, there is a lack of understanding of the extent to which these protect or cover the challenges that women face within the academy. These require that other institutional policies, legislation, and health related guidelines be assessed to better understand the wider parameters for which academic mothers work within these contexts.

However, what is also clear is that there is a lack of institutional regulations and mechanisms that further cushion the weight of these material and custodial care as a cultural reality for mothers in the region and the impact this has on academic mothers. The findings also point to needed sensitizations that reduce the tendency for cultural reproduction of the dominant narratives and masculinized representations of successful academics and leaders. These discourses must be further explored in connection to the leaky pipeline for women and mothers who often struggle within the academy. Moving beyond these limitations also requires a broader assessment of how institutions protect pregnant mothers, recent mothers, mothers with young children, and the extent to which these institutional structures and dynamics impact how they are being evaluated within the assessment and promotion criteria. Such analyses must also be contextualized to capture the historical structures and relations of power that have unfolded to make vulnerable specific groups of mothers, including Black academic mothers, as demonstrated through this paper.

More is needed by way of institutional change. Hamilton (1999) suggested that institutions set reasonable targets for the promotion of qualified female staff, of creating institutionalize mechanisms to support their progression within the academy, with allocation of resources, childcare, and policies that address sexual harassment. Esnard (2016) points to the need for social and institutional transformations that center notions of responsibility, vulnerability, and productivity for academic mothers. Other regional scholars have pushed for more institutionalized or formalized opportunities for mentoring and networking, with needed support for women and mothers (Esnard, 2016; Esnard & Cobb-Roberts, 2018; Hamilton, 1999). Outside of the region is a push for creating alternative tenure routes (Williams & Ceci, 2012) with accommodations for childcare and professional development opportunities that support and empower mothers (Smith-Carrier et al., 2021; Wilton et al., 2017). These standpoints all reinforce the need and call to action.

Conclusion

The thinking, experiences, and practices of mothers is deserving of "serious and sustained scholarly inquiry" (O'Reilly, 2019, p. 18). This study speaks to the need for more critical engagement of academic mothers who continue to struggle but whose inability to progress within institutions of higher education has not been positioned as an institutional failure but as an individualized one. This work calls for an advancement of matricentric feminism within the region but for considerations of the cultural and political underpinnings of gender and race as central systems of power that continue to impact Black academic mothers within the region. While the scholarship remains substantively absent, there is an opportunity to advance this perspective with a focus on mothers across diverse social groups and within institutions of higher education. This work, therefore, offers a starting point with the promise of matricentric feminism, but with a more situated level and degree of theorization that deals with the fluid yet complex realities of academic mothers in the Caribbean. The potential within this proposed body of scholarship is for a more insightful understanding of academic mothers within the region, with a possibility for more evidenced based, targeted interventions that systemically address the challenges that they encounter within the academy. This type of theorization, once advanced, can also add to the span and scope of global scholarship that signals the need for more contextual treatments that locate and enhance the identities, subjectivities, and trajectories of academic women. Quinn and Litzler (2009) suggest that if these concerns are ignored, then the risk is for the increased numbers of mothers, and I would add, Black mothers, who turn away from academic careers.

Declarations

Competing Interests The author has no conflicts of interest to declare that are relevant to the content of this manuscript.

References

Bailey, B. (2003). The search for gender equality and empowerment of Caribbean women: The role of education. In G. Tang Nain & B. Bailey (Eds.), *Gender equality in the Caribbean: Reality or illusion* (pp. 108–145). Ian Randle.

Barrow, C. (1996). *Family in the Caribbean: Themes and perspectives*. Ian Randle Publishers.

Barrow, C. (1996b). Living in sin: Church and common law union in Barbados. *The Journal of Caribbean History, 29*(2), 47–70.

Barrow, C. (1988). Anthropology, the family, and women in the Caribbean. In P. Mohammed & C. Shepherd (Eds.), *Gender in Caribbean development* (pp. 145–164). The University of the West Indies.

Boucher, L. (2003). Respectability and reputation: A balancing act. *TOTEM: The UWO Journal of Anthropology, 2*, 85–87.

Braun, V., & Clarke, V. (2020). One size fits all? What counts as quality practice in (reflexive) thematic analysis? *Qualitative Research in Psychology*. https://doi.org/10.1080/14780887.2020.1769238

Bush, B. (2010). African Caribbean slave mothers and children: Traumas of dislocation and enslavement across the Atlantic world. *Caribbean Quarterly, 56*(1–2), 69–94. https://doi.org/10.1080/00086495.2010.11672362

Carty, L. (1988). *The political economy of gender inequality at the University of the West Indies* (Unpublished doctoral dissertation). University of Toronto.

Castenada, M., & Isgro, K. (2013). *Mothers in academia*. Columbia University Press.

Chip-Johnson, R., & Vanderpool, J. (2003). *Higher Education Attainment by gender, enrolment, and employment in the Anglophone Caribbean*. IESALC/UNESCO.

Clandinin, D. J., & Connelly, F. M. (2000). *Narrative inquiry*. Jossey-Bass.

Clandinin, D. J., & Rosiek, J. (2007). Mapping a landscape of narrative inquiry: Borderland spaces and tensions. In D. J. Clandinin (Ed.), *Handbook of narrative inquiry: Mapping a methodology* (pp. 35–75). Sage.

Connelly, F. M., & Clandinin, D. J. (2006). Narrative inquiry: A methodology for studying lived experience. *Research Studies in Music Education, 27*(1), 44–54. https://doi.org/10.1177/1321103X060270010301

Connelly, R., & Ghodsee, K. (2011). *Professor Mommy: Finding work-family balance in academia*. Rowman and Littlefield Publishers Inc.

Dillard, C. B. (2000). The substance of things hoped for, the evidence of things not seen: Examining an endarkened feminist epistemology in educational research and leadership. *International Journal of Qualitative Studies in Education, 13*(6), 661–681. https://doi.org/10.1080/09518390050211565

Esnard, T. (2016). (Re)Turning to motherhood and academe: An autoethnographic account. *Journal of the Motherhood Initiative for Research and Community Involvement, 6*(2), 109–124.

Esnard, T. (2019). Towards matricentric feminism in the Caribbean: Inroads and opportunities. *Journal of the Motherhood Initiative, 10*(1/2), 257–272.

Esnard, T., & Cobb-Roberts, D. (2018). *Black women, academe, and the tenure process in the United States and the Caribbean*. Palgrave Macmillan.

Fothergill, K., & Feltey, A. (2003). I've worked very hard and slept very little: Mothers on the tenure track in academia. *Journal of the Association for Research on Mothering, 5*(2), 7–19.

Fulweiler, R., Davies, S., Biddle, J., Cooperdock, E., Hanley, T., Kenkel, C., Maracarelli, A., Matassa, C., Mayo, T., Santiago-Vasquez, L., Traylor-Knowles, N., & Ziegler, M. (2021). Rebuild the academy: Supporting academic mothers during COVID-19 and beyond. *PLoS Biology, 19*(3), e3001100. https://doi.org/10.1371/journals.pbio.3001100

Gatrell, C., Cooper, C. L., & Kossek, E. E. (2017). Maternal bodies as taboo at work: New perspectives on the marginalizing of senior-level women in organizations. *Academy of Management Perspectives, 31*(3), 239–252.

Green, C. (2006). Between respectability and self-respect: Framing Afro-Caribbean women's labour history. *Social and Economic Studies, 55*(3), 1–31.

Gregory, S. T. (2006). The cultural constructs of race, gender, and class: A study of how Afro-Caribbean women academics negotiate their careers. *International Journal of Qualitative Studies in Education, 19*(3), 347–366. https://doi.org/10.1080/09518390600696877

Guarini, E., Magli, F., & Francesconi, A. (2020). Academic logics in changing performance measurement systems: An exploration in a university setting. *Qualitative Research in Accounting & Management, 17*(1), 109–142.

Guarino, C. M., & Borden, V. M. (2017). Faculty service loads and gender: Are women taking care of the academic family? *Research in Higher Education, 58*(6), 672–694.

Hays, S. (1996). *The cultural contradictions of motherhood*. Yale University Press.

Hamilton, M. (1999). Women and higher education in the Commonwealth Caribbean: UWI, a progressive institution for women? *Caribbean Review of Gender Studies, 9*, 245–286.

Hinton-Johnson, K. (2011). Choosing my best thing: Black motherhood and academia. In T. R. Berry & N. Mizelle (Eds.), *From oppression to grace: Women of color and their dilemmas within the academy* (pp. 155–167). Stylus Publishing.

Leo-Rhynie, E. (2005). A woman's academic career: Seasons of change and development. *IDEAZ, 4*(1–2), 38–49.

Mason, M. A., & Goulden, M. (2002). Do babies matter? The effect of family formation on the lifelong careers of academic men and women. *Academe, 88*(6), 21–27.

McClish-Boyd, K., & Bhattacharya, K. (2024). Methodological considerations for endarkened narrative inquiry. *Qualitative Inquiry, 30*(7), 584–594. https://doi.org/10.1177/10778004231186565

Miller, K., & Riley, J. (2022). Changed landscape, unchanged norms: Work-family conflict and the persistence of the academic mother ideal. *Innovative Higher Education, 47*, 471–492. https://doi.org/10.1007/s10755-021-09586-2

Mohammed, P., & Perkins, A. (1999). *Caribbean women at the crossroads: The paradox of motherhood among women of Barbados*. Canoe Press.

O'Brien-Hallstein, O., & O'Reilly, A. (2012). Academic motherhood in a post-second wave context: Framing the conversation. In L. O'Brien-Hallstein & A. O'Reilly (Eds.), *Academic motherhood in a post-second wave context: Challenges, strategies and possibilities* (pp. 1–46). Demeter Press.

O'Reilly, A. (2016). *Matricentric feminism: Theory, activism, and practice*. Demeter Press.

O'Reilly, A. (2019). Matricentric feminism: A feminism for mothers. *Journal of the Motherhood Initiative for Research and Community Involvement, 10*(1/2). Retrieved from https://jarm.journals.yorku.ca/index.php/jarm/article/view/40551

Pinnela, B., & Muñoz, S. (2005). Educational opportunities and academic performance: A case study of university student mothers in Venezuela. *Higher Education, 50*(2), 299–322.

Quinn, K., & Litzler, E. (2009). Turning away from academic careers: What does the work-family have to do with it? *NASPA Journal about Women in Higher Education, 2*(1), 68–92.

Raddon, A. (2002). Mothers in the academy: Positioned and positioning within discourses of the 'successful academic' and the 'good mother.' *Studies in Higher Education, 27*(4), 387–403. https://doi.org/10.1080/0307507022000011516

Reddock, R., & Bobb-Smith, Y. (2008). Reconciling work and family: Issues and policies in Trinidad and Tobago. *Conditions of Work and Employment, 18*. International Labor Organization.

Reynolds, T. (2005). *Caribbean mothers: Identity and experience in the UK*. The Tuffnell Press.

Rowley, M. (2011). *Feminist advocacy and gender equality in the Anglophone Caribbean.* Routledge.
Schlehofer, M. (2012). Practicing what we teach? An autobiographical reflection on navigating academia as a single mother. *Journal of Community Psychology, 40*(1), 112–128. https://doi.org/10.1002/jcop.20490
Smith-Carrier, B., Benbow, S., Lawlor, A., & O'Reilly, A. (2021). "My only solution is to work later and sleep less": Exploring the perspectives of parenting in academia in Ontario, Canada. *Equality, Diversity and Inclusion: An International Journal, 40*(8), 930–946. https://doi.org/10.1108/EDI-12-2020-0357
Stewart, S. (2019). Navigating the academy in the post-diaspora: #Afro-Caribbean feminism and the intellectual and emotional labour needed to transgress. *Caribbean Review of Gender Studies, 13*, 147–172.
Swanson, H. D., & Johnston, D. D. (2003). Mothering in the ivy tower: Interviews with academic mothers. *Journal of the Association for Research on Mothering, 5*(2), 1–10.
Thun, C. (2020). Excellent and gender equal? Academic motherhood and 'gender blindness' in Norwegian academia. *Gender, Work, and Organization, 27*(2), 166–180. https://doi.org/10.1111/gwao.12368
Ward, K., & Wolf-Wendel, L. (2008). Choice and discourse in faculty careers: Feminist perspectives on work and family. In J. Glazer-Raymo (Ed.), *Unfinished agendas: New and continuing gender challenges in higher education* (pp. 253–272). The John Hopkins University Press.
Ward, K., & Wolf-Wendel, L. (2017). Academic motherhood: Mid-career perspectives and the ideal worker norm. In L. Wolf-Wendel, K. Ward, & A. M. Kulp (Eds.), *How ideal worker norms shape work-life for different constituent groups in higher education* (pp. 11–24). Jossey-Bass.
Wells, K. (2011). *Narrative inquiry*. Oxford University Press.
Williams, S. J., & Ceci, S. J. (2012). When scientists choose motherhood: A single factor goes a long way in explaining the dearth of women in math-intensive fields. *American Scientist, 100*(2), 138–145. https://doi.org/10.1511/2012.95.138
Wilton, S., & Ross, L. (2017). Flexibility, sacrifice and insecurity: A Canadian study assessing the challenges of balancing work and family in academia. *Journal of Feminist Family Therapy, 29*(1–2), 66–87. https://doi.org/10.1080/08952833.2016.1272663
Yoo, J. (2020). An autoethnography of mothering in the academy. *Qualitative Report, 25*(8), COV19–3184. https://doi.org/10.46743/2160-3715/2020.4582

Talia Esnard Ph.D. is a Senior Lecturer and sociologist in the Department of Behavioral Sciences. She has published within education and gender specific journals, with coauthored, coedited, and sole authored books in the areas of diversity, inclusion, mothering, leadership, entrepreneurship, and the tenure process. She also serves as a co-editor, associate editor, and reviewer on educational and sociological related editorial boards within and beyond the Caribbean.

I Have My Sister's Back: Cultivating Counterspaces in the Academy to Keep Black Motherscholars Safe

Dionne L. Davis and Ann Marie Mobley

Abstract Mothering or motherhood has been presented as a labor-intensive duty for women in which the child is centered, and the woman is rendered invisible and relegated to the margins to assume the duties associated with motherhood (e.g. nurturing and cultivating the child) (Delgado-Herrera et al. PLoS ONE https://doi.org/10.1371/journal.pone.0298750, 2024). Black women striving for success in academia face insurmountable challenges linked to their race and gender and rely on friendship, kinship, and sisterhood to aid in overcoming obstacles and led to the achievement of our academic goals. This chapter focuses on the personal and academic experiences that led to the creation of a counterspace that resulted in a formidable sisterhood between two Black motherscholars navigating the dissertation process. Black feminist thought coupled with Intersectionality informed our focus on the necessity of counterspaces in academia to offset the gendered, racialized threats to the emotional, personal, and professional identities of Black motherscholars. We employed collaborative autoethnography as a methodological tool to capture our individual and collective experiences. The findings provide insight into how Black women fulfilling the role of mother and scholar in the halls of the academy may benefit from a multilayered system of support.

Keywords Black women · Motherhood · Academia · Counterspaces · Collaborative autoethnography

As Black women, mothers, and scholars, our perceptions of motherhood are deeply rooted in the love and admiration we hold for our mothers and the othermothers who nurtured us through various stages of our development (Collins, 1987, 1995, 2013; Foster, 1993). When we think of our mothers and othermothers, the word that

D. L. Davis (✉)
Texas State University, San Marcos, TX, USA
e-mail: qfd7@txstate.edu

A. M. Mobley
University of South Florida, Tampa, FL, USA
e-mail: annmarierita@gmail.com

C. R. Turner and M. L. Green (eds.), *Black Motherscholarship Within and Beyond the Academy*, https://doi.org/10.1007/978-3-031-99758-7_14

most readily comes to mind is *powerful*. They embodied the perseverance required to navigate adversity, doing so with grace and compassion. We attribute our intellectual confidence, emotional resilience, and academic achievements to the values they instilled in us that Collins (1987) identifies as "essential to survival as African American women" (p. 112).

We believe motherhood is a gift for all women who are *able* and *choose* to bear children. We agree that *our* children are gifts from God and relish in the blessings of the mother–child bond we have with them. We share our stories to highlight the complexities incurred with motherhood as we continue to become "all that we can be" (Christian, 1985, p. 212). We hope our audience will "see" and "hear" us as we share how we navigated our personal and academic responsibilities. The depth, reciprocity, and vulnerability woven throughout our narratives are meant to dispel the fear of the ghosts of 'invincible Black mothers past' and normalize the power of negotiating the world as intelligent, flawed Black mothers *and* scholars.

Mothering or motherhood has been presented as a labor-intensive duty for women (e.g. nurturing and cultivating the child) wherein the child is centered, and the woman is rendered invisible and relegated to the margins (Delgado-Herrera et al., 2024). Perceptions about Black motherhood are complex, interwoven, varied (Collins, 1987), and rooted in dominant narratives depicting Black women as mammies or invincible matriarchs (Amanova & Rajabboyeva, 2024).

These deficit attitudes stem from narratives dating back to the 1800s through the late 1900s which depicted the mammy as a submissive, docile, faithful caretaker of white children by day, who transformed into an invincible matriarch upon returning to her own home in the evenings as she silently shed her cloak of docility at her doorstep. Afrocentric perspectives on motherhood (Adebayo, 2023), aid in diminishing these limiting beliefs by removing racist boundaries and centering the cultural and religious aspects of motherhood that Black women within the African American community experience. McClain (2019) best captures this idea as she recalls her mother's words to her when she was seven years old—"We don't live for I. We live for the we." (p. 15).

Scholarly Significance

Black mothers are often regarded as the backbone of their families, a role accompanied by a unique pressure to maintain their families by any means necessary. As a result, many Black working mothers, who pursue higher education to uplift themselves and their families face the overwhelming challenges of balancing familial responsibilities, academic demands, and the quest for a sustainable work-life balance (Craddock, 2013; Haskins et al., 2016). The significance of this collaborative autoethnographic reflection is to contribute to the research about the experiences of Black mothers in doctoral programs (Rogers et al., 2019) and illuminate the positive outcomes forged in counterspaces created by Black motherscholars in academia. By being transparent and vulnerable, we hope to deconstruct the myths of "superstrong"

Black mothers (Collins, 2000, p. 188; Rogers et al., 2019) capable of wielding unlimited amounts of cognitive and physical energy to achieve success while traversing racialized, gendered oppressions (Griffith & Ford, 2022).

Theoretical Influence: Black Feminist Thought and Intersectionality

Collins' (2000) Black feminist thought (BFT) and Crenshaw's (1989) theory of intersectionality offer a critical lens for examining the intersecting demands of academia and Black motherhood. BFT informs how we use our voices to center personal narratives that shape our understandings of motherhood and academic success. Integrating BFT into our critical framework deepens our awareness of the multiple oppressions we face as Black women and provides clarity and validation for our experiences as doctoral students (Alinia, 2015; Newcomb & Niemeyer, 2015). Self-actualization, individualism, and shared experience are the aspects of Black Feminist Thought that underscore the importance of counterspaces where transformation and liberation from injustice can take root. The implementation of these components yielded outcomes that (a) illuminated the multifaceted nature of our lived experiences, (b) affirmed our identities, enabling us to replace damaging representations with authentic portrayals, and (c) fostered a unique collective consciousness through which we recognized ourselves in one another. Intersectionality (Crenshaw, 1989), a multidimensional and reflexive framework, provides a critical lens for examining how social and systemic factors impact personal and academic experiences. This approach allowed us to engage in an unrestrained exploration of the elements that either supported or hindered our success.

Positioning Ourselves as Black Mothers and Scholars

Our positionalities as Black motherscholars navigating personal and academic responsibilities in a doctoral program at a Hispanic-serving institution in the southeastern region of the United States guide this collaborative autoethnography. We hope to illuminate how we maintained our focus on earning a Ph.D. amidst various existential occurrences (e.g. loss, grief, birth, relocation) while navigating the nuanced performativity of the dual socio-political identities within the halls of the academy.

Dionne: I am a first-generation college student and graduate. I acquired my bachelor's, master's, and doctoral degrees from predominantly white institutions (PWIs) in the southeastern region of the United States. As a descendant of sharecroppers, I carry forward a legacy grounded in resilience and perseverance. Earning multiple college degrees and securing a role in academia are achievements I believe would make both my ancestors and my two sons proud. My siblings and I were raised by a single mother who had high standards related to academic achievement. My mother acquired an associate's degree from the local community college and had dreams of becoming a nurse. She was not shy about sharing the barriers caused by being a single mother raising three children and encouraged us to get an education to solidify a better future than she'd been able to provide. Fortuitously, I always loved school and knew it represented something more than academic accomplishments. School was my safe space and lifeline out of poverty.

> As I reflect on my journey through academia, from student to
> full-time faculty, the highs and lows of motherhood are included.
> For me, academia and motherhood go hand in hand. I understand
> what it means to be a full-time student while working full-time,
> caring for two Black boys in America, and managing a household.
> I often say that God made me out of titanium because navigating those responsibilities simultaneously was extremely difficult. The halls of
> the academy can be dark and isolating without support, and I am
> grateful for all the women who saw me, shaped me, and encouraged
> me, as I negotiated motherhood and academia. As early career faculty,
> I choose to decolonize teaching by centering an ethic of care for all
> students, especially mothers, single or otherwise, seeking to enhance
> their lives by pursuing a master's and/or doctoral degree.

AnnMarie: I am a Black Millennial woman from the southeastern United States, shaped by a family deeply committed to education and faith. My upbringing in a nuclear family was grounded in values that emphasized the importance of personal development and academic achievement. My father earned a doctorate in pharmacy; and my mother, with a master's in education, dedicated 38 years to teaching in the public school system before retiring. They instilled in me a strong belief that education is both a privilege and a responsibility. Growing up in the 1950s, my parents deeply valued education, seeing it as a gateway to opportunities they hadn't always been afforded. They instilled in me a strong sense of personal responsibility for learning, teaching her that education was not only self-directed but also a powerful tool for bettering oneself and creating a legacy for future generations. Their unwavering support and high expectations taught me to strive for excellence, not only in academics but also in personal growth. My journey continued when I enrolled in a doctoral program in 2016 as a part-time doctoral student while assuming the role of a first-year teacher. It was during this period that I met my now-husband, and life took a profound turn. Marriage and motherhood brought some unexpected challenges as well as profound joy. The arrival of my first child, in May of 2022, dramatically shifted my focus, intertwining my personal and academic trajectories in ways I had not anticipated.

Cultivating a Safe Space Through Sisterhood

Throughout history, Black girls and women have learned how to adapt, survive, and function within society based on the development of communal relationships. Forming bonds and kinship was essential for survival during slavery. These sisterhoods facilitated the transmission of educational and cultural knowledge, strengthening their ability to be resilient (Mawhinney, 2011). As such, we created a counterspace that spanned the halls of academia and our realities to form an unbreakable bond that allowed us to offset the psychological, emotional, and intellectual warfare we experienced throughout our doctoral journeys (Aguilar et al., 2024; Case & Hunter, 2012; West, 2024). As we engaged in a "realm of safe discourse" and cultivated our sisterhood (Collins, 2002, p. 111), the recollections of the loneliness we felt emerged as a shared occurrence.

> AnnMarie: When I met you, I was really struggling because I had just lost my brother. I was so moved by your concern for me and the care you extended to me. You don't know how much it meant to me to have you bring me food to class on days when I was not capable of picking up something for myself. I was just trying to make it from point A to point B.
>
> Dionne: I had just changed programs and was very skeptical of meeting new people, as the people in my previous program were not trustworthy. I was also accustomed to being the only Black woman in my classes. I was so happy to see you when I walked into my first leadership course.

Case and Hunter (2012) describe three processes through which counterspaces thwart marginalizing ideologies entrenched in various contexts, (a) narrative identity work, (b) acts of resistance, and (c) direct relational transactions. Though we did not enact these processes in a particular order, we discovered the necessity of all three processes as we advanced in our program and recognized the insidious, oppressive, racist nature of the academy. We endured biased pedagogical strategies implemented by a seasoned professor and racist comments made by students, about professors who looked like us. As a result, we engaged in subversive acts of resistance to ensure we were seen and heard in academia to avoid "hiding self-defined standpoints from the eyes of dominant groups" (Collins, 2000, p. 107). The relational transactions (e.g. bringing each other food) that seemed innocuous when we first met became direct and intentional to thwart emotional reactions elicited by class discussions laden with deficit ideologies or narratives. These events enriched the authenticity of our narratives that led to this study.

Methodology and Methods

Our pre-existing relationship served as the impetus for unpacking the tenets of our experiences as Black Motherscholars. We deem collaborative autoethnography (CAE) as an introspective, vulnerable, and transparent method that allows us to oscillate between individual (autobiographical) narratives and our sociocultural (ethnographic) experiences in academia. The authentic dialogical exchanges resulted in the integration of "rich texture to our collective work" (Chang et al., 2016, p. 24). As participants in our own qualitative study, we interrogated our individual life stories through the lens of one another. Through CAE, we engaged with each other to co-construct our research, identifying both common and differing experiences (Chang, 2013). We were able to explore motherhood using a sequential process, resulting in authentic dialogical exchanges that aided in the integration of our individual experiences.

Story Collection

As we sought a deeper understanding of how we navigated the responsibilities of academic life alongside motherhood and home life, the co-construction process and continuous interactions produced a richer perspective, enabling us to share riveting stories about our experiences. This exchange stirred our memories, prompted further questions, and helped us identify similarities while challenging each other's assumptions. We both were wrong about the ways we believed we were managing the responsibilities of our doctoral program. Annmarie thought I had it "all together" by the way I dressed and carried myself in class and articulated my academic thoughts amongst our white peers. I was assured that she had no problems since she lived at home, had "no bills", and seemed blissfully happy in her long-term relationship. We laughed as we both shared similar struggles related to managing our familial obligations, doctoral studies, full-time jobs, and our almost extinct social lives. These revelations aligned with the research of Hernandez et al. (2017) about auto ethnographers as participant-researchers, as we navigated our collaborative research process while holding each other accountable in meaningful ways.

Stage One

In stage one of our data collection, we each wrote our initial stories and drafted questions related to these narratives to elicit in-depth responses from each other. For example, Annmarie asked questions related to my upbringing as she noticed I did not include personal information about my childhood. I was able to explain that my hesitation was rooted in shame because I had not grown up with both parents as she had. I wanted to avoid judgment from someone who may not understand the inner workings of single-parent households. I wanted to know more about how she and her significant other met and how he supported her during the pursuit of her Ph.D. Upon completion of this phase, we read each other's stories, created more questions, and posed them to one another to create an organic conversation centered around the topic of motherhood. This dialogue covered issues related to motherhood, academia, sisterhood, support, fear, and stories related to familial and communal influences. We prioritized our research by meeting several times per week to gain greater insight into each other's lives and effectively live in the work. This approach increased the reliability of our work.

Stage Two

Next, we selected topics from the answers given to questions that emerged during our dialectical exchanges. This was an iterative process and aided in narrowing down areas for further exploration, which created a pathway to reveal our themes. During this dialogic exchange, we listened intently to the details and emotions expressed during our conversations and took copious notes. For example, Annmarie was struck by the story I shared related to being chastised by my mentor and the program coordinator of the doctoral program I was enrolled in before transferring to her program. I mentioned the mannerisms of the white women, such as them banging on the desk, and raising their voices. She paused to console me as she heard my voice crack during our conversation. Our actions allowed us to be organized which made data collection and analysis easier. Subsequently, we wrote responses to these questions separately, filling any gaps that might have emerged. We repeated this process until we had gathered enough data, ultimately identifying four themes that encapsulated our research.

Analyzing Our Stories

We engaged in secondary analysis via the informal sharing of our narrative stories (Heaton, 2008) to specifically examine how we were able to balance the demands of the doctoral program with homelife/motherhood. The depths of our relationship surprised us in ways we had not anticipated. We truly believed we had answered the call by bell hooks (1986) to "learn the true meaning and value of sisterhood" (p. 127). Our stories and existential realities as Black women, mothers, and scholars reinforced our bond, and we gained an understanding of the power of a unified front. The relationship we established in the counterspace we created while pursuing our doctoral degrees would forever be the measure of a sisterhood. It helped us thrive rather than survive.

Findings

A thematic analysis of our narratives and the interactive conversations had within and beyond the counterspace (s) we created, led to a renewed understanding of the adage, "It takes a village to raise a child". We discovered four themes informed by the integration of Black feminist thought (Collins, 2000) and intersectionality (Crenshaw, 1989): (1) Welcome to the Academy, (2) Race and Gender matter, (3) Broken hearts, and (4) Life happens. While we relied on various forms of external support, such as our families, friends, and significant others, the bond we cultivated as Black motherscholars navigating the academy transformed our relationship. It propelled us into new, enduring roles in each other's lives. The village we once knew before meeting and conducting this study, no longer exists in the same way. The familiar adage is no longer a passing phrase; it has become a lived reality. We are now a part of each other's villages, embodying that truth every day. A more in-depth description of the themes and the intricacies of our sisterhood is provided in the following sections.

Welcome to the Academy: The (Re)Socialization Process

As intellectuals with university experience, we thought we were prepared for the demands of our doctoral program, but attending an R1 university exposed us to new and foreign experiences. The pressure to complete our studies successfully was a consistent, glaring reality. The challenges related to navigating the campus, working with unfamiliar software, and tackling challenging coursework caused us both to struggle; and it was through our struggles that we found each other. We were fully aware of the statistics related to Black women earning a Ph.D. and knew we had to finish by any means necessary. As our bond grew, so did our involvement in each other's lives. We became deeply invested in one another's worlds, providing support beyond academics and truly engaging in each other's relationships, interests, and hobbies. This friendship transcended academic success, encompassing overall life success. Our mutual goal was to see each other thrive not only in our studies but also in life. The goal shifted from "I am going to finish" to "we are going to finish." We quickly became more than accountability partners. We became sisters who reminded each other when assignments were due, listened to each other's ideas, and stayed up all night to ensure the completion of all work.

> Ann Marie: Entering a predominantly white institution [PWI] for the first time was very difficult. I was a proud HBCU graduate who had the backing of classmates and professors who held a collective ideology of "we must excel". However, at this new University, I was alone. It was not until my third year, that I met Dionne and other Black women who pulled me out of isolation. I finally felt like I belonged, and that I was in the right place. With them, I started to enjoy class and make connections as to why I was doing this. I felt that old sense of community and support again. The sisterhood that formed was instrumental in helping me navigate the challenges of being in a PWI.

Dionne: Being a single mom and a doctoral candidate is HARD. I just remember trying to survive working full-time, shuttling my youngest back and forth to school, and attempting to complete multiple assignments. AnnMarie lived about 40 minutes from me but would come to my house during the week to complete assignments with me. She finished her qualifying exam before me but sat with me at my dining table until 4 AM to ensure I finished before the deadline. When I was at my wit's end trying to get my son to his magnet school after the boundaries in the district changed, she and her new husband volunteered to take him to school and pick him up on the days I had meetings or needed to be away at a conference. Every single mom needs an AnnMarie on their team. She is a true "ride or die" friend/sister. I will never forget her commitment to my success. Just thinking about it makes me emotional.

Our shared commitment to each other's personal and academic success sustained us through the challenges of the doctoral program. This mutual support not only helped us endure but also underscored the vital role of solidarity in overcoming adversity.

Race and Gender Matter

We were struck by the literature by Haskins et al., 2016, Nzinga-Johnson, 2013, and Torres et al., 2024 describing the gendered, racialized consequences experienced by Black mothers in academia related to the constant pressure of seeking acceptance in contexts rife with stereotypes related to the angry Black woman and "colonizing images", such as the mammy (Collins, 1995). We both recalled the emotional and performance fatigue, that we now understand as racial battle fatigue (Corbin et al., 2018; Quaye et al., 2020, 2024). We persevered through the overt, intentional discriminatory attacks because we know education is vital to honoring the legacy of our ancestors and creating a better future for ourselves and our children.

Dionne: I describe the acts endured in the program I was enrolled in before meeting AnnMarie as psychological warfare. I did not anticipate having to defend my integrity or pedagogical prowess against the perceptions and attitudes of white pre-service teachers. After the students complained about the enactment of the course requirements, such as attending seminars and submitting assignments on time, the program coordinator and my assigned mentor reminded me that they paid my tuition, and I should be grateful for the opportunity to supervise the interns. I was floored and left their office in tears. I was going to quit the program that day. God intervened and I saw a Black woman from the AnnMarie's program who encouraged me to reconsider. I am so happy I did but will never forget how those women made me feel.

Ann Marie: I have never been a person to try to prove my intelligence, however, it was a constant challenge and battle to prove to some of my classmates that I was in the program because of my own merits. In one instance I commented on an article and another student (a white woman) said "I just don't understand what you're saying". In the same span of time another student, a white man, said the same thing and she was like "OOOHHH I get it". At that moment I recognized that they believed I needed a white translation of what I was trying to convey. I did not need a translator. I spoke English. It was so insulting and belittling but did not even matter. I later learned that she dropped out of the program. I will admit it gave me a bit of satisfaction, and I earned my degree despite her efforts to make me feel small.

As evidenced by the descriptions above, our experiences align with the sentiments of Jean-Marie et al. (2009) and Walkington (2017) who affirm that the discrimination against Black women existing as 'double outsider[s] in the academy can be attributed to: (1) being both Black and female persons, (2) controlling images of the mammy that spur expectations related to giving deference to white students, (3) perceptions about [in]capabilities of doing graduate level work, and (4) being viewed as recipients of affirmative action. Black women's experiences in academia generally, and Black motherscholars specifically may be enhanced by the acknowledgement of the existence of racialized events by institutions and the implementation of strategies to combat injustices.

Broken Hearts: Managing Personal Loss

Balancing the demands of our doctoral studies with the complexities of personal and social relationships proved to be a significant challenge. The dynamic nature of these relationships elicited a spectrum of emotional responses, ranging from joy to stress. Allocating emotional, psychological, and physical resources to ensure we were viewed as successful mothers, significant others, and friends was exhausting. We both experienced profound and traumatic losses, causing us to view the world through a lens of mourning and grief. Unbeknownst to us, "major life events are unexpected yet common during graduate school." (Sooso & Wise, 2022, p. 326). We persevered and our sisterhood evolved into something much deeper—a true familial bond.

> Dionne: I started dating this guy (RIH) in 2021, my last year of coursework in the doctoral program. It was so beautiful and exciting! I hosted a party for all my friends to meet him. AnnMarie said, "There's something about him I can't put my finger on". The next month, things started to get rocky and toxic. I cried A LOT. I was angry A LOT. I was not focusing on my studies at all. AnnMarie assumed the role of mother, big sister, and everything in between. She coached me and gave me so many words of wisdom. The twenty years between us did not matter, as I was in crisis. Eventually, the relationship ended, and I was in shambles. My sister, my friend, came to my house almost every single day to ensure I ate and wrote at least one paragraph to strengthen my dissertation proposal. Because of this, I will move mountains to support her in any way I can.

> AnnMarie: My brother passed away unexpectedly during Christmas break in 2018 due to a heart attack. Saying that my world fell apart would be an understatement. In an instant, I lost everything, and yet the world kept spinning. As a result, I started to spiral down, not caring about my work, my classes, or anything at all. During that spring semester, Dionne's kindness was a lifeline for me, though she had no idea of the gravity of her actions. She stood by me, providing dinners, reminding me of important dates, and checking up on me regularly. Her insistence that I finish the semester gave me the strength to push through. I honestly didn't have it in me to keep going, but I didn't have to bear the burden of schoolwork alone. I had her to lean on when I was weak, and that support made all the difference.

Sharing our trauma and grief with one another was powerful and yielded an understanding that we were not alone and that care, "a relational set of discourses and practices between people…", per Hobart and Kneese (2020), was essential to our survival as Black women in all our personal and professional glory (p.2). We were intentional about ensuring the other felt seen and heard. We showed up and created opportunities to silence the busyness of the world around us, even if it meant sitting still (in person or on the phone) and embracing the sound of falling tears. We learned to name our emotions, express the related reactions or responses, and establish some semblance of self-care routine(s). Amid the darkness, we did not view our actions as revolutionary, but as we expanded our exploration of relevant literature, we embraced the radical nature of our collective care and self-love without guilt as we came to know it as an act of "self-preservation" rather than "self-indulgence" as written by Audre Lorde in *A Burst of Light* (p. 130). Lorde's critique of racialized international events on the sociopolitical climate in America as she battled cancer made plain the "link between self-care and revolution" (Nicol & Yee, 2017, p. 134). Our pact to each other to complete our degrees together served as a guiding light. We were each other's constant reminder that quitting was not an option.

Life Happens: Moving Beyond the Academy

As we progressed through the doctoral program. Life happened and we had to adjust to our new realities. A wedding, interview, job talk, the birth of a beautiful baby boy, and a cross-country move challenged us in ways we had not imagined. We had to get creative and chart new pathways to maintain the closeness we'd become accustomed to having. We agreed to continue our daily phone conversations, make plans to visit each other and chat via Zoom when we felt inundated with the demands of our new lives.

> Ann Marie: In 2021, I became pregnant with my son. It was a joyous moment, but it also brought significant stress. Being a mother and a graduate student was incredibly challenging. I had always feared that having children while pursuing my education would diminish my opportunities. I truly believed I would graduate before returning to work from maternity leave, but that did not happen. Motherhood proved to be far more difficult than I had ever imagined. Balancing the demands of being a student and a new mom was full of challenges. In the beginning, I often felt like a failure because I did not bond with my son in the way I imagined most mothers would. My writing schedule left me with little time to hold him, and I was unable to breastfeed as I had initially intended. The best I could do was pump and give him breast milk, but I still felt inadequate. However, it was through my sisterhood with Dionne and others that I learned to be gentle with myself and understand that I was not alone in this experience. My support system provided the encouragement and understanding I needed to navigate the complexities of being both a mother and a student.
>
> Dionne: I am from North Carolina and all my circle lives there. When I moved to Florida, I was of the mindset that I did not need any new friends. I fellowshipped with the women from my church and when I needed my girls, I hopped on a plane or made the ten-hour drive to NC. I had no idea how much I needed a new friend until I met AnnMarie in my doctoral program. She is amazingly funny, has an old soul, and is extremely stubborn…just like me. I am so grateful that she has been a part of the major life events I have experienced in the second act of my life. I am looking forward to all the years of friendship to come.

Navigating our personal lives, inclusive of motherhood, alongside the demands of doctoral study, brought unexpected challenges as well as profound joy. These shared experiences highlighted the evolution of a sisterhood that became essential to our journey. What began as a collegial relationship rooted in mutual academic goals gradually transformed into a lasting bond. As we faced pivotal moments in our lives, the supportive sisterhood we developed enriched and strengthened us, evolving beyond a professional alliance into a lifelong connection.

Discussion

Sisterhood stood at the forefront of our journey, providing the resilience and strength needed to carry us through the intersecting challenges of motherhood, scholarship, and systemic marginalization. Drawing on Black feminist thought (BFT), which foregrounds the experience of Black women and the pervasive layers of oppression they face, we recognize how race, gender, and societal expectations placed us in an ongoing struggle to prove our value in spaces often shaped by exclusionary norms (Jones et al., 2023). These expectations to be mature, beautiful, intelligent, composed, and calm can feel suffocating, almost impossible to bear alone. Yet, through a shared counterspace, we found a profound bond that helped us withstand the weight of these demands (Aguilar et al., 2024; Case & Hunter, 2012; West, 2024). This counterspace, both within academia and in our personal lives, became a sanctuary that offset the psychological, emotional, and intellectual warfare we experienced along our doctoral journeys.

Motherhood intensified these pressures, transforming them into a multi-layered burden that called for unique cognitive and physical energy (Griffith & Ford, 2022). Navigating the demands of academia alongside motherhood required us not only to juggle but also to draw on untapped reserves of resilience. As intersectionality highlights, the interplay of social systemic variables and our identities as Black women, mothers, and scholars created a set of expectations rooted in racialized, gendered marginalizations that demanded we constantly perform and excel despite these compounded challenges. This intersectionality influenced our experience with work-life balance, a struggle primarily framed as a gendered issue affecting women, particularly those with children, which often limits academic aspirations for women generally, and Black women specifically (Craddock, 2013; Haskins et al., 2016).

The fear of failure in our studies was intense, magnified by the sense that our academic success was inseparable from our success as mothers. Falling short as scholars felt as though it would mean failing our children. But through this pressure, sisterhood was our lifeline—both grounding us and driving us forward. It was the shared commitment to each other, the collective understanding of our struggles, that helped us balance the question, "Is this best for my child?" with the reassurance, "I am doing this for my child's future." Together, we forged ahead, building resilience in one another and reminding ourselves that our education would provide greater opportunities for our families.

As life unfolded unpredictably, with all its highs and lows, our sisterhood was unwavering. When one of us stumbled, the other lifted her. When one was uncertain, the other was there to offer encouragement. This shared experience transformed our bond into something deeply rooted in understanding and mutual support. As mothers in academia, this sisterhood became essential more than a support network, it became the anchor that allowed each of us to flourish.

Implications

Our narratives compel us to beseech the Black community to support Black women as they explore and embrace their multifaceted identities. We hope to inspire a unified effort to name and address the societal, institutional, and systemic barriers that Black women face due to intersecting racial and gender identities. Black girls must be socialized to understand that they can pursue any path they choose, including motherhood and scholarship.

Research (Ali & Burrell, 2023) outlines the institutional barriers Black women face such as "lack of support… contending with negative stereotypes about Black women, …experiencing microaggressions, being both invisible and hyper-visible, and the lack of flexible workplace policies" (p. 576). The assumptions about the innate strength of Black women also serve as a barrier to understanding their need for support as they engage in mental, spiritual, and sometimes physical warfare when attempting to "overcome barriers, while advocating for social change" (Curtis, 2017; Johnson & Scott, 2023; Vital et al., 2023). Institutions have a responsibility to provide support for Black motherscholars to diminish the impact of the barriers noted above on their emotional, mental, and physical health and academic outcomes. The creation and implementation of strategies by program coordinators and other influential personnel that encourage well-being practices, provide networking opportunities, and enhance the work-life balance could positively impact the personal and professional outcomes for Black motherscholars.

Institutional Support

Institutions should adopt a holistic approach to student success that prioritizes as foundational to academic achievement. By acknowledging and addressing these barriers, institutions can provide essential support systems—such as collaborative discussion groups, counseling services, and time management resources—that empower students to balance their diverse responsibilities.

Well-Being and Networking

The needs of Black women in higher education differ markedly from those of their white counterparts, and Black men (Hirshfield & Joseph, 2012). The dual roles of motherhood and scholarship accentuate the need for extensive institutional support tailored to Black Motherscholars. The profound effect of personal loss on academic performance highlights the need for robust emotional and mental health resources within academic settings (Nicol & Yee, 2017; Vital et al., 2023). Programs that provide counseling, peer support, and flexible academic schedules are vital to allow Black Motherscholars to navigate personal challenges without jeopardizing their academic pursuits (Wilkins-Yel, et al., 2022).

Opportunities for connection with others who understand the cumulative toll of racialized, gendered microaggressions are crucial for the well-being and academic success of Black women (Jones et al., 2023; McCLure, 2019; Patterson-Stephens et al., 2017). Dedicated spaces on campus, targeted resources, and support for travel to academic conferences are necessary for Black Motherscholars to see themselves reflected among students and faculty within and beyond their institutions (Rogers et al., 2019).

Familial Relations

Graduate students often have complex lives outside academia, including child-rearing, jobs, caregiving for older parents, and other significant responsibilities (Jones & Matthews, 2023; Patterson-Stephens et al., 2017) Academic institutions should promote a culture of self-compassion, where students are taught to manage their expectations and understand that setbacks are part of the learning process. This could include flexible deadlines, on-campus childcare, and parental leave policies that accommodate the unique needs of student-parents, ensuring they do not have to choose between their education and their family responsibilities.

Conclusion

In the past decade, scholarship on the experiences of Black women doctoral students has grown (Briscoe & Steele, 2024; Jones et al., 2023; Pope & Edwards, 2016; Shavers & Moore, 2014). However, few works (e.g., Craddock, 2013; Haskins et al., 2016; Rogers et al., 2019) capture the distinct challenges faced by Black women with children pursuing terminal degrees. The literature clearly shows that Black women pursuing doctoral degrees face complex layers of racial and gendered microaggressions—a reality that demands acknowledgment rather than dismissal. This collaborative autoethnography captures the intricate journey of Black women with children through the doctoral process, illuminating: (1) the (re)socialization process, (2) the intersections of race and gender, (3) coping with personal loss, and (4) adapting to life beyond the academy. By centering the lived experiences of Black Motherscholars, we highlight the essential role of counterspaces as protective mechanisms, fostering mutual success and resilience within and beyond academia.

Declarations

Competing Interests The authors have no conflicts of interest to declare that are relevant to the content of this manuscript.

References

Alinia, M. (2015). On Black feminist thought: Thinking oppression and resistance through intersectional paradigm. *Ethnic and Racial Studies, 38*(13), 2334–2340. https://doi.org/10.1080/01419870.2015.1058492

Amanova, M. X., & Rajabboyeva, S. O. (2024). Analysis of motherhood in African American literature: Exploring sociocultural and gender representations. *Mental Enlightenment Scientific Methodological Journal, 5*, 8–13.

Collins, P. H. (1987). The meaning of motherhood in Black culture and Black mother/daughter relationships. *SAGE: A Scholarly Journal on Black Women, 4*(2), 3–10.

Collins, P. H. (1995). Black women and motherhood [1991]. In *Justice and Care* (pp. 117–136). Routledge.

Collins, P. H. (2002). *Black Feminist Thought: Knowledge, Consciousness, and the Politics of Empowerment.*

Collins, P. H. (2013). The meaning of motherhood in Black culture and Black mother/daughter relationships. In *Toward a New Psychology of Gender* (pp. 325–340). Routledge.

Corbin, N. A., Smith, W. A., & Garcia, J. R. (2018). Trapped between justified anger and being the strong Black woman: Black college women coping with racial battle fatigue at historically and predominantly White institutions. *International Journal of Qualitative Studies in Education, 31*(7), 626–643.

Craddock, K. T. (2013). Mothering and mentoring: Exploring relational dynamics among Black women in the academy. *Journal of the Motherhood Initiative for Research and Community Involvement.*

Crenshaw, K. (1989). Demarginalizing the intersection of race and sex: A Black feminist critique of antidiscrimination doctrine, feminist theory, and antiracist politics. *University of Chicago Legal Forum, 1989*(1), 139–167. https://doi.org/10.2139/ssrn.1234567

Curtis, S. (2017). Black women's intersectional complexities: The impact on leadership. *Management in Education*, 31(2), 94–102.

Delgado-Herrera, M., Aceves-Gómez, A. C., & Reyes-Aguilar, A. (2024). Relationship between gender roles, motherhood beliefs, and mental health. *PLoS ONE*. https://doi.org/10.1371/journal.pone.0298750

Foster, F. S. (1993). *Written by Herself: Literary Production by African American Women*, 1746–1892. Indiana University Press.

Griffith, T. O., & Ford, J. R. (2022). Say her name: The socialization of Black women in graduate school. *Journal of Student Affairs Research and Practice, 60*(3), 279–292. https://doi.org/10.1080/19496591.2022.2042006

Haskins, N. H., Ziomek-Daigle, J., Sewell, C., Crumb, L., Appling, B., & Trepal, H. (2016). The intersectionality of African American mothers in counselor education: A phenomenological examination. *Counselor Education and Supervision, 55*(1), 60–75.

Heaton, J. (2008). Secondary analysis of qualitative data: An overview. *Historical Social Research/Historische Sozialforschung*, 33–45.

Hernandez, K. A. C., Chang, H., & Ngunjiri, F. W. (2017). Collaborative autoethnography as multivocal, relational, and democratic research: Opportunities, challenges, and aspirations. *a/b: Auto/Biography Studies, 32*(2), 251–254.
Hirshfield, L. E., & Joseph, T. D. (2012). 'We need a woman, we need a Black woman': Gender, race, and identity taxation in the academy. *Gender and Education, 24*(2), 213–227.
Hobart, H. I. J. K., & Kneese, T. (2020). Radical care: Survival strategies for uncertain times. *Social Text, 38*(1), 1–16.
Jean-Marie, G., Williams, V. A., & Sherman, S. L. (2009). Black women's leadership experiences: Examining the intersectionality of race and gender. *Advances in Developing Human Resources,* 11(5), 562–581.
Johnson, J. M., & Scott, S. (2023). Nuanced navigation: Narratives of the experiences of Black 'All but Dissertation' (ABD) women in the academy. *International Journal of Qualitative Studies in Education, 36*(4), 612–626.
Jones, T. B., Brewster, B., & Matthews, D. Y. (2023). Shining the light: Black women thriving in graduate school. *New Directions for Student Services, 2023*(182), 57–68.
McClure, C. L. (2019). Where are all my sista's@?! Exploring the graduate school experiences of Black women and implications on faculty career choice. *Journal of Underrepresented & Minority Progress, 3*(1), 51–66.
Newcomb, W. S., & Niemeyer, A. (2015). African American women principals: Heeding the call to serve as conduits for transforming urban school communities. *International Journal of Qualitative Studies in Education, 28*(7), 786–799. https://doi.org/10.1080/09518398.2015.1036948
Nicol, D. J., & Yee, J. A. (2017). "Reclaiming our time": Women of color faculty and radical self-care in the academy. *Feminist Teacher, 27*(2–3), 133–156.
Nzinga-Johnson, S. (2013). *Laboring positions: Black women, mothering, and the academy.* Demeter Press.
Patterson-Stephens, S. M., Lane, T. B., & Vital, L. M. (2017). Black doctoral women: Exploring barriers and facilitators of success in graduate education. *Higher Education Politics & Economics, 3*(1), 5.
Pope, E. C., & Edwards, K. T. (2016). Curriculum homeplacing as complicated conversation:(Re) narrating the mentoring of Black women doctoral students. *Gender and Education*, 28(6), 769–785.
Quaye, S. J., Karikari, S. N., Carter, K. D., Okello, W. K., & Allen, C. (2020). Why can't I just chill?": The visceral nature of racial battle fatigue. *Journal of College Student Development, 61*(5), 609–623.
Quaye, S. J., Satterwhite-David, E. M., Carter, K. D., & Karikari, S. N. (2024). "Who looks out for us?": Black women student affairs educators working to heal from gendered racial battle fatigue. *Journal of Diversity in Higher Education.*
Rogers, J., McLean, A., & Mentor, M. (2019). A seat at the table: Womanist narratives of Black mothers in doctoral programs. *Taboo: The Journal of Culture and Education, 18*(1), 7.
Sosoo, E. E., & Wise, E. H. (2022). When the expected happens: Facing a major life event in graduate school. *Training and Education in Professional Psychology, 16*(4), 325.
Torres, A. J. C., Barbosa-Silva, L., Oliveira-Silva, L. C., Miziara, O. P. P., Guahy, U. C. R., Fisher, A. N., & Ryan, M. K. (2024). The impact of motherhood on women's career progression: A scoping review of evidence-based interventions. *Behavioral Sciences, 14*(4), 275.
Vital, L. M., Lane, T. B., Perez, E., & Patterson-Stephens, S. (2023). Professors behaving badly: Exploring sabotaging behaviors that impact Black women doctoral student persistence. *Journal of Diversity in Higher Education.*
Walkington, L. (2017). How far have we really come? Black women faculty and graduate students' experiences in higher education. *Humboldt Journal of Social Relations, 39*, 51–65.
Wilkins-Yel, K. G., Arnold, A., Bekki, J., Natarajan, M., Bernstein, B., & Randall, A. K. (2022). "I can't push off my own mental health": Chilly STEM climates, mental health, and STEM persistence among Black, Latina, and White graduate women. *Sex Roles, 86*(3), 208–232.

Dionne L. Davis, Ph.D. is an Assistant Professor in the Educational and Community Leadership, Program at Texas State University. Her research interests include: (1) how discourses in policies constrain and facilitate educational successes amongst historically marginalized groups at the intersections of race and language and (2) the leadership experiences of Black women in PK-12 educational contexts.

Ann Marie Mobley, Ph.D. is a recent graduate of the Educational Leadership and Policy Studies Program at the University of South Florida in Tampa. She earned her Ph.D. in May 2024. She currently serves 7th grade students as a Civics Teacher and Subject Area Leader in the School District of Hillsborough County. Her research interests include examining the experiences of Black women serving as educational leaders in PK-12 contexts.

Centering Our Children's Voices

The Unrelenting Duality of Black Motherhood: A Dialogical Examination of the Role of the Radical Black Motherscholar

Jendayi Mbalia

Abstract The Black motherscholar is responsible for both the rearing and radical educating of her children. Thus, she often toggles between preparing her children for an unjust world and encouraging them to radically and critically dream of a liberated futurity. This chapter will examine this duality of Black Motherhood by highlighting the role of the radical Black motherscholar. Written in dialogue, this work will reveal the lived experiences of a radical (single) Black motherscholar and her son. This chapter concludes with an homage to all Black mothers and an intentional call to honor the role of the radical Black motherscholar.

Keywords Radical Black motherscholar · Radical futurity · Resistive joy · Black Mother–Son dynamic · Dialogical analysis

> Well, son, I'll tell you: Life for me ain't been no crystal stair. It's had tacks in it, And splinters, And boards torn up, And places with no carpet on the floor—Bare. But all the time I'se been a-climbin' on, And reachin' landin's, And turnin' corners, And sometimes goin' in the dark Where there ain't been no light. So boy, don't you turn back. Don't you set down on the steps.'Cause you finds it's kinder hard. Don't you fall now—For I'se still goin', honey, I'se still climbin', And life for me ain't been no crystal stair. (Hughes, 1922).

Langston Hughes's (1922) poem *Mother to Son* details an intimate conversation between a Black mother and her son. The mother shares the hardships she's endured while challenging her son to resist the urge to cease struggling amidst difficulty. The mother's words are laced with both radical truth and critical hope (Duncan, 2009). Though life has been laborious for her, her advice for her son rests on the back of a radical futurity.

The hardships mentioned in Hughes's (1922) work and experienced by Black mothers dates back to enslavement when Black mothers watched their children being ripped from their arms, endured sexual abuse from the enslaver, and were often forced to nourish the bodies of children not born to them (Freeman, 2018). During the war on

J. Mbalia (✉)
University of Wisconsin-Milwaukee, Milwaukee, WI, USA
e-mail: mbalia@uwm.edu

C. R. Turner and M. L. Green (eds.), *Black Motherscholarship Within and Beyond the Academy*, https://doi.org/10.1007/978-3-031-99758-7_15

welfare era, Black mothers were forced to 'prove' their need for support while being mislabeled as *Welfare Queens* (Cammett, 2016). Currently, Black mothers continue to carry loads too heavy to bear and are described as *super women* strategically negating their need for help (Kendall, 2021; Nelson et al., 2016). Though originally stated in 1922, life still ain't no crystal stair for the Black mother in the 21st century.

Still, amidst the storms, Black mothers often continue to nurture, educate, and protect their children. The Black mother is forced to prepare her children for an unjust world; their lives, often perceived as less valuable than whites' by those in places and spaces of wealth and power, literally depend on Black mothers' forewarnings. All the while, Black mothers postulate critical hope in efforts of prophesying a more radical future. The Black mother juxtaposes the imminent threat of physical, mental, spiritual, and emotional death with *life*.

Too often, the aforementioned duality is overlooked. Informed by intersectionality (Crenshaw, 1989), this work will examine the experiences of a single, Black mother and her Black son via narrative inquiry. This work will apprise readers of the duality experienced by radical Black motherscholars by advancing the understanding of their lived realities. This chapter concludes with a charge to intentionally value the *life-changing* role of the radical Black motherscholar.

Researcher Positionality

When defining the term motherscholar, Matias (2022) states that, "the motherscholar is both a mother that draws from her practice of mothering to inform her research and pedagogy inasmuch as she is a scholar who draws from her activism to inform her practice of mothering" (p. 247). I deeply resonate with her conceptualization of motherscholar. As the single mother of a Black child, my work and teaching heavily center on the importance of anti-racist and anti-oppressive learning experiences for Black and Brown children. I actualize this work both at the university and elementary school level. While I am professionally connected to these two institutions, I agree with Yu et al. (2022) in that my *scholarship* is not defined by the systems that pay me. My scholarship is informed by my "mother-knowledge" (p. 3). This re-defining of scholarship is furthered when the authors engage in a critical examination and discussion of the term 'scholar.'

> I think for me, being a mother is being a scholar. I don't need the institution to validate my mother-knowledge. I'm not a scholar because of what they pay me to do. I'm a scholar because I'm a mother and I have all of this ancestral knowledge that has been passed on to me, and that I call on, in that role. Maybe we could rethink that. We're not a scholar because some institution calls us scholars. I love the idea of lifting up mother-knowledge as scholarly knowledge. This feels different than lifting up mothers who are professors producing knowledge for a scholarly community (Yu et al., 2022, p. 3).

This is a critical point to make explicit as this work hinges greatly upon my role and teachings as a *mother*scholar. I emphasize mother in the aforementioned term as I seek to amplify the voices of mothers who may not be deemed as 'traditional scholars' due to their lack of collegiate affiliation. Mothers are, however, specialists in a particular branch of study. Black mothers specifically must negotiate parenting in unique and critical ways. As a result, my unique form of mother-knowledge rests at the intersection of my radicalness, Blackness, and motherhood. Thus, I seek to further the concept of motherscholar by naming the unique ways in which I, and others, must enact a particular form of motherscholaring as a result of the racist policies and practices that continue to exist and threaten the lives of our offspring.

The Radical Black Motherscholar

Black mothers parent at the intersection of radical rearing and critical hope; they must balance radical rearing and critical hope in ways that both prepare their children for systemic racism and consequential outcomes, as well as ensure that their children have a sense of critical hope (Duncan-Andrade, 2009) necessary in overturning said systems. Thus, she embodies what I refer to as radical Black motherscholaring.

Radical Black motherscolar*ing* is the act of existing at the intersection of revolutionary struggle and radical futurity. The radical Black motherscholar experiences life in a dual realm; due to her lived experiences and mother-knowledge, she feels compelled to teach, raise, and nurture in a way that prepares her child for life in an inherently racist and oppressive society. Yet and still, she leans into a radical futurity that mandates critical hope. This work explores this duality via a dialogical analysis of an intimate conversation on survival, sustainment, and resistive joy between a Black mother and her son. It is unique in that it hinges heavily upon the narrative of my son, Muhammad. Few scholars have explored the Black mother and son dynamic through *his* lens (see Hawkins, 2023); thus, this work is revelatory in its aim to explore and introduce an understanding of my role and identity as a radical Black motherscholar through the eyes of my son.

Literature Review

Black motherhood in the United States began in a most horrific and dehumanizing way; women were ripped from their homes in Africa, often separated from their children and families, and forced to travel deadly waters only to arrive on stolen land and expected to give all of themselves (physically, mentally, spiritually, and emotionally) in the name of capitalism. This expectation was also extended to childbirth. Black mothers experienced sexual assault at the hands of the enslaver often resulting in pregnancy (Cooper, 2015; King, 2014). Beyond those egregious and horrific acts of sexual violence, children of Black mothers were considered property of the enslaver (Owens & Fett, 2019). Thus, enslavers became hyper focused on the use of Black mothers' children for continued exploitation and profit. As a result, Black mothers in this country feared for themselves and for their offspring.

Black Mothers' Sons: Teaching Survival and Sustainment

Motherhood during enslavement also introduced a balancing act necessary in ensuring both the physical and spiritual safety of the Black child. This is still true today (Coleman-King et al., 2022). When analyzing the state of the world, little has shifted for the Black mother in terms of the need to teach both the ways in which this world targets the Black body (Elliot & Reid, 2016; Lawson-Bush, 2004) *and* the active fight for and towards a more radical, liberated future (Das et al., 2022; Dormire et al., 2021).

Survival

One of the most crucial factors for Black mothers when discussing the raising of their sons is their safety (Dormire et al., 2021; Hawkins, 2023; Joe et al., 2019; Turner, 2020). Black mothers often feel an obligation to teach their sons how to survive (Harris & Amutah-Onukagha, 2019; Johnson, 2013). Hawkins (2023) examined the teaching of Black mothers via interviews with mothers and their sons. They name these teachings *endangerment conversations.* These conversations centered on survival and highlighted an emphasis on white fear, the need for suspicion, management of anger, and intergenerational strength and trauma.

Relatedly, Joe et al. (2019) detail similar sentiments around intergenerational trauma shared by Black mothers. They state that:

> African American mothers live with daily fear for their sons of all ages. This fear exists despite most of the participants reporting that their sons had not been directly involved in or exposed to violence. These mothers constantly relive psychological trauma because of media exposure of incidents of community and state violence involving African American boys and young men (p. 75).

Although the sons in the aforementioned study had not directly experienced violence, there is a preparation that often occurs by Black mothers (and, more generally, by Black families). This is done as a direct result of their lived experience in effort to protect their sons. Das et al. (2022) refer to this practice as *preparation for bias.* In discussing this preparation amongst Black families, they found that while both parents implemented this practice, "Black mothers provided preparation for bias at a much higher frequency" (p. 983).

While scholars have shed light on the role of Black mothers in preparing, teaching, and conversing with their sons about the dangers associated with being Black and male in this society, there is also room for the discussion of their consequential hope. We must acknowledge how Black mothers also make space for faith, hope, and liberation in their rearing practices. In fact, Das et al. (2022) discuss how some of those same practices, such as *preparation for bias,* simultaneously serve as catalysts for resistance.

Sustainment: Faith, Hope, and Liberation

Das et al. (2022) further examined the practices of Black mothers and found several examples of resistance. Namely, they discuss *resistance for liberation strategies.* They state that:

> Of the mothers in our sample, five transmitted messages of self-advocacy or equipping sons with skills that encourage them to use their voice and agency in the face of discrimination and bias, challenging the status quo and anti-Black racial oppression. Self advocacy emerged as a resistance for liberation strategy by equipping sons, Black boys, with skills and techniques that allow them to use their voice and agency in the face of discrimination and bias, challenging the status quo and anti-Black racial oppression (p. 989).

Dormire et al. (2021) expand on the translation of fear into faith when examining the child rearing beliefs of Black mothers. They state that, "although women in this study described the profound fear of sons being killed, they at the same time described how they stay strong and hopeful as mothers, regardless of circumstance" (p. 4494). Meaning, Black mothers' teachings and warnings about the racism that permeates our society are often laced with feelings and messages of critical hope. In his note to educators, Duncan-Andrade (2009) shares that critical hope is the resistance of hopelessness paired with an active struggle against inequality and injustice. Therefore, the Black mother must balance the lived realities and experiences of her Black child, and consequential emotional toll, with a sense of radical futurity.

Theoretical Framework

While Black feminist scholars have discussed the unique oppression experienced by Black women (Collins, 1986; Combahee Collective, 1978; Cooper, 1892; Davis, 1981; hooks, 1981, Lorde, 1979; Truth, 1851), Kimberle Crenshaw coined the term intersectionality. In an article written to explain the need for a new theoretical lens to view the issues faced by Black women, she stated the following:

> Black women's experiences are much broader than the general categories that discrimination discourse provides. Yet the continued insistence that Black women's demands and needs be filtered through categorical analyses that completely obscure their experiences guarantees that their needs will seldom be addressed (p. 150).

Crenshaw (1989) posited that the issues faced by Black women could not be limited to an anti-racist or feminist lens. Finding that there were multiple ways in which Black women could be discriminated against, Crenshaw asserted that the intersection of multiple identities called for its own theory. Crenshaw (1991) states "because of their intersectional identity as both women and people of color within discourses that are shaped to respond to one or the other, the interests and experiences of women of color are frequently marginalized within both" (p. 1). Crenshaw (1989) explains that the basic tenet of intersectionality is that the unique experiences of Black women cannot and should not be limited to a "single axis theory" since their discrimination is situated in both racist and sexist practices. She states that "because the intersectional experience is greater than the sum of racism or sexism, any analysis that does not take intersectionality into account cannot sufficiently address the particular manner in which Black women are subordinated" (p. 140).

The use of an intersectional lens is also most relevant when exploring the unrelenting duality experienced by the radical Black motherscholar. This dual reality, the balancing of radical rearing and critical hope, is best viewed through a lens designed to see how and why this intersection exists, and why its existence is imperative for the rearing of the Black child. Exploring the lived experience of the radical Black motherscholar also mandates an examination of the child's experience. Consequently, this work highlights the unique perspective of my son. Intersectionality is crucial in framing his inextricably linked lived experience as both Black and cis male. While the gender he identifies with is often associated with greater privilege in a patriarchal society, his Blackness is what is often seen *and* negatively responded to first (Howard & Reynolds, 2013). Our identities are complicated by the society that socially constructed race to begin with. Therefore, at the crux of this work is the use of, and emphasis on, intersectionality.

Methodology

Narrative inquiry is a qualitative research method often used for the exploration of a single lived experience or the experiences of a small group of people. It makes space for storytelling, healing, and authenticity of voice (Wang & Geale, 2015). For Black women especially, the personal telling of one's own narrative is critical in resisting hegemonic approaches to producing *traditional* research too often "controlled by the majority" (Laye, 2023, p. 29). In addition, when examining stories centered on youth, the voices of marginalized children are too often silenced and neglected (Bostic, 2022). While the erasure of marginalized youths' voices has been explored primarily within children's literature (Mohamed, 2016), few opportunities exist for those voices to be heard, or authentically represented, in *scholarly works*, too. To combat the silencing of Black women and marginalized youth, this work is rooted in narrative inquiry. Narrative inquiry amplifies the voices of those storytellers traditionally placed at the margins (Esposito & Evans-Winters, 2022) and makes way for truth telling. Thus, this qualitative method is best suited for this work as its intent is to explore the lived experience of a radical Black motherscholar through a personal and interpersonal lens.

Data Collection

Growing up, my parents ensured that my siblings and I gathered around the kitchen table on Sundays to share our thoughts on the previous week and our goals for the week ahead. This cultural tradition of fellowship and intimate conversation at the kitchen table is one many Black families engage in; thus, Black scholars have used the term *kitchen-table talks* to refer to conversations surrounding issues of prevalence to Black families and communities (Bolding et al., 2022; Haddix et al., 2016). With the goal of this work being the illumination of the role of the radical Black motherscholar, specifically through the lens of my son, this intimate form of information gathering and dialogical exchange solely between Muhammad and I felt most appropriate.

Prior to beginning our conversation, Muhammad had an opportunity to review the questions I developed. Then, he and I discussed the potential risks and benefits associated with our work. I recorded our hour-long conversation to ensure that our true sentiments were captured.

Data Analysis

Our audio recorded *kitchen-table talk* was transcribed using transcription software. After reading the transcript, I engaged in the coding cycle process by first conducting line-by-line coding and following that process with a deeper analysis and chunking of previously determined codes (Esposito & Evans-Winters, 2022). Throughout the coding process, I wrote memos to myself to connect with the data more deeply (Esposito & Evans-Winters, 2022). These memos allowed me to *sit* with the codes I had discovered making space for mental processing. Next, I engaged in the thematic analysis process, moving from single-worded codes to phrases. This process helps to ensure that the argument developed from the codes is effectively portrayed in writing (Esposito & Evans-Winters, 2022; Saldaña, 2016). Finally, I shared all the documents with Muhammad. This included the transcript, memos, and initial write-up of findings. This form of member-checking allowed him to see how readers might interpret his lived experience (McKim, 2023; Wang & Geale, 2015) ensuring that his truth was carefully conveyed.

Through careful analysis of a conversation between a mother and son, this work reveals the lived reality of the radical Black motherscholar by a) discussing the role of the radical Black motherscholar, b) unveiling the impact of the duality on the child of the radical Black motherscholar, c) stressing the importance of resistive joy to offset the inevitable emotional and mental stress, and d) putting forth suggestions for policy, practice, and promise.

Findings

I define radical rearing as the act of teaching and preparing a child for their lived reality. It is the intentional and political raising of a child or children in ways that prepare them for societal ills and inequities. It is a series of calculated actions made by a parent, from knowledge of conception through death. To radically raise a child involves an illumination of historical events and connection to/preparation for present day inequities.

The Role of the Radical Black Motherscholar

Muhammad and I talked about how, if at all, the radical Black motherscholar engages in radical rearing. He shared that she does and defined it as "the steps that an African[1] parent has to [take when] raising a child in order for them to make sure that their child is living the best possible life that they can live." He further elaborated by adding that radical rearing is providing the child with information necessary to their survival. He named its importance when saying the following:

> Because of the fact that we are African people in a very systemically racist world…and it's gonna be very difficult for us to literally wake up and walk outside. So I feel like there's gonna be certain situations that the parents are gonna have to prepare us for.
>
> They're gonna have to give us specific instructions on how to avoid or get out of certain situations.

For Muhammad, the act of radical rearing makes it possible for the Black son to exist in this world. It serves as the teachings and 'rules' necessary in keeping him alive.

The Impact of Radical Black Motherscholars' Dual Rearing Practices on Their Children

Radical rearing is often inextricably tied to critical hope. This balancing act, or dual reality, means that the radical Black motherscholar must share life-saving knowledge with a sense of faith, hope, and liberation. Muhammad and I discussed how critical hope differs from the general definition of hope: a feeling or desire for something to happen. Critical hope seeks to combat feelings of hopelessness via resistive, intentional action necessary in changing the lived reality for those too often marginalized and oppressed (Duncan-Andrade, 2009). When asked about his thoughts on critical hope as it relates to the radical Black motherscholar, he shared that "it's something that she gives to the child to help them in knowing that everything will be alright." The teaching, or *giving* as Muhammad said, of critical hope is imperative to pair with radical rearing. Without it, Muhammad shared that he or others might succumb to feelings of despair. He stated that "it's important because it's something to hold onto.

If they don't have critical hope, they will give up and give in to this systematically racist world." Critical hope operates as a sustaining measure. It serves as a means to radical dreaming, planning, and, ultimately, change.

Resistive Joy as a Protective Factor

While Muhammad named radical rearing and critical hope as necessary pieces in the effective rearing of Black sons by radical Black motherscholars, he also shared that it does not come without ramification. Muhammad shared that these practices can lead to "stress, worry, and hopelessness" due to the intersecting pressures of existing as a Black male, surviving in a world that is inherently racist, and seeking to create actionable change. Preparations for such pressures, however, may have adverse effects (Hawkins, 2023). Muhammad expanded on this thought when stating that these survival strategies or forwarnings may "cause mental trauma to the child [and] maybe lead them to depression." Caughy et al. (2006) expand on this belief when sharing the following:

> messages related to prejudice and racism may be anxiety provoking, especially among young children. This anxiety could be expressed through higher rates of externalizing behavior such as aggression or higher rates of internalizing behavior such as depression or heightened anxiousness. (p. 1221)

After learning of the negative impact radical Black motherscholaring had on Muhammad, I criticized myself for not making space for joy. I thought that what I lacked as a radical Black motherscholar was the provision of a light-hearted and fun upbringing. Muhammad quickly corrected me. He named that joy did exist; he specified by sharing that the joy that exists in our relationship, and the type of joy that must accompany radical rearing and critical hope, produces a feeling of worth, value, and ability. It is *resistive joy*. This joy, as Muhammad shared, is essential "in ensuring that there is no loss of happiness."

According to Muhammad, resistive joy is different from other forms of joy in that it involves a level of seriousness and internal illumination not usually associated with joy as it is most commonly defined and understood. Muhammad deepened my understanding of this type of joy by highlighting the fact that "it's a more stern or straightforward type of joy." I asked him to further explain so that we could define this joy needed to combat hopelessness. Muhammad thought it important to share how it could be actualized. He shared that:

> Speaking upon the child's talents or the child's pros can bring joy…because it's like you're saying to the child, oh yes, this might happen, [but] you already do this. So I know that this won't be difficult for you to follow or understand. You get what I'm saying?

I did understand and attempted to restate his explanation by synthesizing it in the following way:

> So, we balance radical rearing: making sure you're aware of the racism that exists in the world, with critical hope, which means "yes, racism exists, but you can make a change". Further, I know you can do it because of the *greatness* that's inside of you. So, highlighting those characteristics that make it possible for you to maintain a sense of critical hope is what you think inspires joy?

Muhammad responded excitedly with, "yes!" He illuminated the fact that this form of joy combats feelings of hopelessness by reaffirming what Black children innately possess. I wondered if this would be enough to sustain the Black child. Muhammad reassured me that it did when sharing the following:

> I do feel like that's enough…I feel like especially as an African African male, and I'm speaking generally, many relationships don't have that kind of uplift[ment] or words of affirmation that are that are given. So, I feel like that'll bring much joy to that conversation. 'Cause it's telling [me] that although I have to look out for this and that, my parent thinks, and my parents see in me, that I already have [it]. I'm already good at ***this***, so I don't have to worry about ***that***.

Resistive joy illuminates the strengths and truths inside of the Black child. It will not only sustain them, but help them in resisting feelings of stress, hopelessness, and worry. It reassures them of their abilities and value. *Resistive joy* makes life worth living, especially so for the Black son.

Discussion

After completing the interview, I thought it important to ask Muhammad his thoughts on moving forward. Where should radical Black motherscholars and their children go from here? It was initially quite difficult for Muhammad to make suggestions on ways to move systems forward. He felt 'stuck.' He shared that while there were ways in which things might be temporarily 'fixed,' he felt that he had no real suggestions for moving forward. I inserted my thoughts by sharing that I agreed with him, but that his observation in and of itself was a suggestion—there are no quick or temporary fixes. The entire system must be rebuilt. It must be built on a foundation that is *not* rooted in racism, capitalism, and exploitation. Muhammad listened and wholeheartedly agreed. He noted that realization as the reason for him feeling stuck. He agreed that there is no temporary improvement to the structure that can sustain its fractured state; there is only room for intentional, careful, and culturally intricate rebuilding. There was silence before Muhammad ended by stating, "I'ma leave it there."

"Dear Mama"

Muhammad had twofold advice for the radical Black motherscholar that highlighted the need for his suggested resistive joy. He stated that radical Black motherscholars should, "try to find the joy in the conversation…continue to be a loving parent and continue to uplift your African child in this very systemically racist world." One could then conclude that love and upliftment are tenets of resistive joy; those actions must be present in order to help sustain the child and keep them believing in, and working towards, a radical futurity.

For the Culture

While I asked Muhammad about systemic suggestions, suggestions for the radical Black motherscholar, and suggestions for the child of the radical Black motherscholar, I neglected to ask him about suggestions for Black people as a whole. He did not let that stop him from sharing. He encouraged us all to "take pride in who you are; take pride in your skin color, take pride in your culture, [and] take pride in your family."

All of Muhammad's suggestions on ways to move forward included the very topics we had been discussing: radicalness, critical hope, and resistive joy. It is imperative to name this as it provides insight into the role and lasting impact of the radical Black motherscholar; it illuminates the reality that her teachings exist *in*, and are continued *through*, her son. I concluded the interview in tears and thanked Muhammad for his contribution to scholarship via his exploration of the dual reality of the radical Black motherscholar and his consequential experiences as a Black son.

From the review of literature to Muhammad's interview, the role of the radical Black motherscholar is inherent to the effective navigation of life for her Black son. Her practices, carefully inclusive of both radical rearing and critical hope, have existed since her beginnings in this country (Cooper, 2015; King, 2014; Owens & Fett, 2019). The ways in which she balances the two exemplifies her ability to vehemently juxtapose death with life. Nestled within this dual reality is her cultivation of resistive joy.

Resistive joy builds upon other understandings of Black joy (Alexis et al., 2020; Scott, 2022) by elucidating the internal, life-sustaining qualities possessed by the Black child. Thus, this is a call for others to explore the radical Black motherscholars' instinctive tendency to produce and cultivate *resistive joy*. This exploration could be imperative in naming the ways in which she calls out the best in her child; not for mere recognition and honor, but to speak *and* save life. It is also critical in understanding how the Black child; namely, the Black son, not only survives, but thrives in this world (Love, 2019).

Study Significance

The purpose of this work was to highlight the role and impact of the radical Black motherscholar through the eyes of her Black son. As a result, this work also shed light on the ways by which *all* Black mothers deserve to be regarded as scholars in their own right. Whether at the university or not, their teachings are imperative to the sustainment, safety, and spirit saving of their children—reinforcing their standing as scholars. This work also adds to the dearth of literature on Black mothers' rearing of their sons *and* the perspective of the Black son in relation to these experiences. The findings of radical rearing as survival, critical hope as sustainment, and healing through resistive joy reinforce the importance of her role, teachings, and mother-knowledge.

Concluding Thoughts

While I agree with Muhammad in that this society must be rebuilt to effectively and equitably address the neglected needs and identities of people placed at the margins, I also know that until such time comes, the radical Black motherscholar must continue to rear her child in ways that offer protection, provide hope, and inspire the promise of a better tomorrow—the lives of her children depend on it. Nevertheless, I understand firsthand the difficulty and mental stress the balancing act can bring (Coleman-King et al., 2022). Therefore, I find it imperative to leave you, radical Black motherscholar, with the following sentiment: "*Don't you fall now—For I'se still goin', honey, I'se still climbin', And life for me ain't been no crystal stair*" (Hughes, 1922).

Declarations

Competing Interests The author has no conflicts of interest to declare that are relevant to the content of this manuscript.

References

Alexis, N., Mayes, J., Coleman, S., Stoltzfus, R., & Pierson, A. (2020). I will rejoice: Reflections on Black Joy. *Vision: A Journal for Church and Theology, 21*(2), 52–60.

Bolding, A., Glover, K., Mouton, A., & Routt, J. (2022). Spades, dominoes, and hot combs the kitchen-table talk that is necessary to redesign our PK-12 schools. *International Journal of Leadership in Education*, 1–17.

Bostic, Q. (2022). *When they see us in the pages: The representation of Black and Brown males in children's literature.* [Doctoral Dissertation, Georgia State University]. Early Childhood and Elementary Education Dissertations.

Bumpers, T. (2022). *The impact of implicit education debt on the lives of African American Mothers in PhD programs: A phenomenological research study.* (Publication No. 1519 [Doctoral Dissertation, Illinois State University]. ISU ReD: Research and eData.

Cammett, A. (2014). Deadbeat dads and welfare queens: How metaphor shapes Poverty Law. *Boston College Journal of Law & Social Justice, 34*(2), 233–265.

Caughy, M., Nettles, S., O'Campo, P., & Lohrfink, K. (2006). Neighborhood matters: Racial socialization of African American children. *Child Development, 77*(5), 1220–1236.

Crenshaw, K. (1989). Demarginalizing the intersection of race and sex: A Black feminist critique of antidiscrimination doctrine, feminist theory and antiracist politics. *The University of Chicago Legal Forum, 140*, 139–167.

Crenshaw, K. (1991). Mapping the margins: intersectionality, identity politics, and violence against women of color. *Stanford Law Review, 43*(6), 1241–1299.

Creswell, J. (2009). *Research design: Qualitative, quantitative, and mixed approaches* (3rd ed.). Sage Publications.

Coleman-King, C., Brown, T., Haynes-Thoby, L., & Dowie-Chin, T. (2022). Reclaiming our time: Black mothers cultivating the homeplace during times of crisis. *Journal of Social Issues, 79*(3), 1022–1034.

Combahee River Collective. (1978). *The Combahee River Collective Statement.* Retrieved from https://americanstudies.yale.edu/sites/default/files/files/Keyword%20Coalition_Readings

Cooper, I. (2015). Commodification of the Black Body, sexual objectification and social hierarchies during slavery. *The Earlham Historical Journal: An Undergraduate Journal of Historical Inquiry, VII*(II), 21–43.

Cooper, A. J. (1892). *A voice from the South. Xenia, Ohio, The Aldine printing house.* [Web.] Retrieved from the Library of Congress, https://lccn.loc.gov/12002877

Das, S., Arevalo, K., Keryc, C., Way, N., Pitts, J., Cox, B., Blood, T., Hughes, D., Coulanges, V., & Rogers, O. (2022). "Good Trouble, Necessary Trouble": Dismantling oppression through resistance and activism. *Journal of Research on Adolescence, 32*(3), 981–998.

Davis, A. Y. (1981). *Women, race & class.* Random House.

Dormire, S., Gary, J., Norman, J., & Harvey, I. (2021). Insights into fear: A phenomenological study of Black mothers. *Journal of Advanced Nursing, 77*, 4490–4499.

Duncan-Andrade, J. (2009). Note to educators: Hope required when growing roses in concrete. *Harvard Educational Review, 79*(2), 181–194.

Elliot, S., & Reid, M. (2016). The superstrong Black Mother. *American Sociological Association, 15*(1), 48–53.

Esposito, J., & Evans-Winters, V. (2022). *Introduction to intersectional qualitative research.* Sage.

Freeman, A. (2018). Unmothering Black Women: Formula feeding as an incident of slavery. *Hastings Law Journal, 69*(6), 1545–1606.

Gondré-Lewis, M., Abijo, T., & Gondré-Lewis, T. (2022). The opioid epidemic: A crisis disproportionately impacting Black Americans and urban communities. *Journal of Racial and Ethnic Health Disparities, 10*, 2039–2053.

Haddix, M., McArthur, S., Muhammad, G., Price-Dennis, D., & Sealey-Ruiz, Y. (2016). Provocateur pieces: At the kitchen table: Black women English educators speaking our truths. *English Education, 48*(4), 380–395.

Harris, A., & Amutah-Onukagha, N. (2019). Under the radar: Strategies used by Black Mothers to prepare their sons for potential police interactions. *Journal of Black Psychology, 45*(6–7), 439–453.

Hawkins, H. (2023). Maternal love in the warzone: Exploring how mothers socialize Black Sons to manage racism. *Clinical Social Work Journal, 51*, 283–293.

Hill-Collins, P. (1986). Learning from the outsider within: The sociological significance of Black feminist thought. *Social Problems, 33*(6), S14–S32.

hooks, B. (1981). *Ain't I a woman Black Women and feminism.* South End Press.

Howard, T., & Reynolds, R. (2013). Examining Black Male identity through a raced, classed, and gendered lens: Critical race theory and the intersectionality of the Black Male experience. In M. Lynn & A. Dixson (Eds.), *Handbook of critical race theory in education* (pp. 232–247). Routledge.

Hughes, L., 1902–1967. (1994). *The collected Poems of Langston Hughes.* Random House.

Hughes, L. (1922). Mother to son. In *The Collected Poems of Langston Hughes* (p. 25). Knopf Doubleday Publishing Group

Joe, J., Shillingford-Butler, A., & Oh, S. (2019). The experiences of African American mothers raising sons in the context of #BlackLivesMatter. *The Professional Counselor, 9*(1), 67–79.

Johnson, J. (2013). *The long term effects of racial socialization of African American sons through communication patterns from their mothers sons through communication patterns from their mothers* [Unpublished Master's Thesis]. Smith College.
Kendall, N. (2021). *Hood feminism: Notes from the women that a movement forgot.* Penguin Books.
King, W. (2014). "Prematurely knowing of evil things": The sexual abuse of African American girls and young women in slavery and freedom. *The Journal of African American History, 99*(3), 173–196.
Lawson Bush, V. (2004). How Black Mothers participate in the development of manhood and masculinity: What do we know about Black Mothers and their Sons? [Special focus: Parenting, Family, and Youth]. *The Journal of Negro Education, 73*(4), 381–391.
Laye, C. (2023). *Her story told her way: A narrative inquiry into Black Women's perception of the strong Black Woman* [Unpublished Dissertation]. University of Arkansas.
Lorde, Audre. (1979). *The Master's tools will never dismantle the Master's house.* Sister Outsider: Essays and Speeches. Ed. Crossing Press.
Love, B. (2019). *We want to do more than survive: Abolitionist teaching and the pursuit of educational freedom.* Beacon Press.
Matias, C. E. (2022). Birthing the motherscholar and motherscholarship. *Peabody Journal of Education, 97*(2), 246–250.
McKim, C. (2023). Meaningful member-checking: A structured approach to member-checking. *American Journal of Qualitative Research, 7*(2), 41–52.
McMichael, I. (2019). The lived experiences of single Black mothers in higher education leadership. *All Theses And Dissertations.* 231. https://dune.une.edu/theses/231.
Mohamed, A. (2016). Voicing the voiceless: Including stories of marginalized children in classroom literature. *Language Arts Journal of Michigan, 32*(1), 32–42.
Nelson, T., Cardemil, E. V., & Adeoye, C. T. (2016). Rethinking strength: Black women's perceptions of the "Strong Black Woman" role. *Psychology of Women Quarterly, 40*(4), 551–563. https://doi.org/10.1177/0361684316646716
Owens, D., & Fett, S. (2019). Black maternal and infant health: Historical legacies of slavery. *American Journal of Public Health, 109*(10), 1342–1345.
Saldaña, J. (2016). *The coding manual for qualitative researchers* (3rd ed.). SAGE.
Scott, A. (2022). *Black Joy as an act of resistance and a means of refusal.* [Master's thesis, University of New York at Buffalo]. Proquest Dissertations Publishing.
Showunmi, V. (2023). Visible, invisible: Black women in higher education. *Frontiers in Sociology, 8*, 1–14.
Truth, S. (1851). *Ain't I a woman?* Akron.
Turner, J. (2020). Black mothering in action: The racial-class socialization practices of low-income single Black Mothers. *Sociology of Race and Ethnicity, 6*(2), 242–253.
Wang, C. C., & Geale, S. K. (2015). The power of story: Narrative inquiry as a methodology in nursing research. *International Journal of Nursing Sciences, 2*, 195–198. https://doi.org/10.1016/j.ijnss.2015.04.014
Yu, M., Edwards, E. B., Gonzales, S. M., Robert, S. A., & DeNicolo, C. P. (2022). Remember. (re)member. re-member: Theorizing the process of healing, sustaining, and transforming as MotherScholars. *Peabody Journal of Education, 97*(2), 199–211.

Jendayi Mbalia is an intersectionalist by training; she uses intersectionality to inform her work as a mother, lecturer, literacy coach, qualitative researcher, and community activist. Currently, she serves as a lecturer with The Department of Educational Policy and Community Studies at The University of Wisconsin-Milwaukee. In this role, she teaches courses on the impact of racism on education and the need for anti-racist pedagogical practices in education. Her use of intersectionality also informs the work she does in the community as a Black girlhood advocate. At the crux of her work is her role as a Radical Black Mother-Scholar.

"On My Mama!": A Duoethnography of Black Motherscholars' Contributions Towards Liberatory Education for Black Children

Eboni N. Bango and Salandra Grice-Johnson

Abstract Stories of Black women in education expose their gendered and racially diverse experiences. When possessing dual identities as academics and mothers, this intersection compliments their often emancipatory and activist approaches in academia and the education of Black children. In predominantly white institutions, Black motherscholars need support maintaining such activist stances. Utilizing duoethnography through the lens of Black Gaze, two Black motherscholars seek to use their experiences to encourage other Black motherscholars to continue taking up space and interjecting their liberatory approaches towards true educational equity for Black children.

Keywords Black motherscholars · Black Gaze Theory · Duoethnography

Black mothers have always been the bedrock of social, emotional, political, and educational strength and prowess in the Black community (Cooper, 1988; Harris, 2021; James-Gallaway & Turner & Allen, 2022). Since pre-emancipation, Black mothers have exuded character traits such as resilience, resistance, and persistence in oppression and fighting for justice for their families and communities (Biesecker-Mast, 2022; Lorde & Sarriugarte, 1979). Their resilience and fortitude have been the cornerstone of family and community life, providing unwavering support and guidance in the face of systemic challenges and discrimination (Garry, 2017). Socially, they have fostered unity and solidarity, nurturing networks of care and mutual aid (Minnett et al., 2019). Emotionally, Black mothers have been the source of strength and comfort, instilling confidence and resilience in their children (hooks2003; Morris & Matute-Chavarria, 2022).

E. N. Bango (✉)
Texas A&M University, College Station, TX, USA
e-mail: eboni20@tamu.edu

S. Grice-Johnson
Sam Houston State University, Huntsville, TX, USA

C. R. Turner and M. L. Green (eds.), *Black Motherscholarship Within and Beyond the Academy*, https://doi.org/10.1007/978-3-031-99758-7_16

Politically, Black mothers have been at the forefront of activism and advocacy, fighting for civil rights, justice, and equality (Ali, 2024; Combahee River Collective, 1983; Lorde, 1984, 2012). Educationally, Black mothers have emphasized the importance of learning and personal growth, ensuring their children have the tools and opportunities to succeed (Johnson, 2000; Loder-Jackson et al., 2016). Their enduring legacy continues to shape and empower the Black community, embodying a profound commitment to progress and transformation in the lives of Black people in the U.S. and abroad. In other words, within the Black community, Black mothers are the epitome of authoritative, moral, social, and familial uprightness, and to put something 'on my mama' is the ultimate gesture signifying legitimacy and seriousness of the context/situation/person in which the term is referring. Black mothers 'don't play;' and to put something 'on my mama' means I ain't playin' wit chu either! Within this state of gravity, Black motherscholars are serious about not only the pursuit of their higher educational goals but also the justice-oriented education and socialization of their children even more.

In this chapter, we expound upon the legitimacy of Black motherhood. We focus on Black mothers who hold identities that intersect with womanhood, motherhood, and academia, as they have been the cornerstone of emancipatory educational opportunities for Black children over centuries (Cooper, 1998; Delpit, 2006; Johnson et al., 2014; Ladson-Billings, 2022). This chapter highlights the diverse experiences and challenges faced by Black motherscholars, emphasizing the valuable insights their lived experiences offer about the state of education for Black children. By advancing the underutilized lens of Black Gaze theory (Howell et al., 2019) and embedding vulnerability into our storied experiences, we hope to add to the visibility of the versatility of experiences of Black motherscholars as we touch on themes of motherhood, racism, sexism, and navigating respectability politics often reinforced by PWIs (Higginbotham, 1994; Jefferson, 2023).

Defining Black Motherscholars

We define Black motherscholars as Black women, mothers, and academics whose social roles and responsibilities place them at the cruxes of multiple epistemological vantage points and oppressions due to their racialized, gendered, and educational identities. Black motherscholars are racialized due to their existence in a society that places predominance on whiteness while devaluing Blackness (Dumas, 2016). We are gendered as a result of the dominance of patriarchal ideologies within the U.S. (Crenshaw, 1991; Davis, 1983; James, 1999; Smith, 2024). Educationally, we experience oppression, resistance, and erasure of our authentic selves and contributions due to the white patriarchal spaces we often learn and work within (Matias, 2016). As a result of this triangulation of life experiences and contexts, Black motherscholars often possess cultural and pedagogical skills that reflect an inherently culturally relevant, culturally competent, and socio-politically aware stance regarding the education of Black children, which works in favor of their academic, social, and emotional success

(Ladson-Billings, 2014; Yosso & Burciaga, 2016). In completing this chapter, we hope to encourage both ourselves and others to move towards embracing authentic versions of themselves, unapologetically embracing their Blackness, womanhood, motherhood, and scholarly pursuits in ways that satisfy our cultural, familial, and academic needs. We hope this chapter celebrates not only the revolutionary mothering (Gumbs et al., 2016) of Black women but also sheds light on their unique position as mothers and scholars as they contribute to academia and the successful education of Black children.

Duoethnography as Visibility

Within this piece, we utilized a duoethnographic approach to satisfy our need for not only a healing space within our research pursuit but also a means of visibility. Black women and our perspectives often remain peripheral to discourses in educational reform (Turner & Allen, 2022). We aim to make them front and center. Duoethnography assists in this pursuit as this qualitative research method imagines dialogic practices that promote critical tensions, are multi-voiced, and assist in "understanding our lived experiences as life curriculum" or "currere" (Bakhtin, 1981; Norris & Sawyer, 2012, p. 12). We chose this approach for its ability to examine how our life stories influence the interpretations we make of those events through the use of numerous voices in conversation. We admire its polyvocal/dialogic style, its study of life history, how a conversation can focus on learning and change rather than proclamation, and the significance of education within such conversations (Sawyer & Norris, 2013). Relational in nature, we want to reflexively examine and complicate our identities as Black motherscholars to produce new meanings, bring visibility, and inform even more transformative approaches to our personal and collective contexts towards liberatory expressions of educational pursuits for our Black children.

Seeing Through the Black Gaze

This study employs the conceptual tool of Black Gaze Theory (BGT) (Howell et al., 2019) to emphasize the strengths and perspectives of Black people and presents a counter-narrative to dominant/Eurocentric educational models that overlook the contributions of Black women scholars. Howell et al. (2019) posit that BGT "is an analytical tool that focuses on Black strength and problematizes structures that promote dominant ideologies" (p. 27); however, dominant ideologies are what prove harmful to Black learners. BGT emerged as a response to the need for an analytical tool highlighting Black students' cultural wealth (Yosso, 2016). The theory also supports teaching practices affirming Black students' identities and experiences. A distinct advantage of using BGT is that this theory recognizes and values Black peoples' behaviors, language, and dispositions as cultural assets. This is in contrast to the white gaze, a set of practices that reflect and reinforce whiteness (Rabelo et al., 2021). In this chapter, BGT will establish the kinds of support, influences, and dispositions Black motherscholars embody and must maintain to continue to be the educational revolutionary advocates they have historically been (James-Gallaway & Harris, 2021; Whittington, 2023).

Within this lens, we seek to help higher education stakeholders create practices that are sensitive to the needs of Black motherscholars and support the full inclusion of their strengths, which ultimately supports Black children and the redress of long-standing educational malpractice. As such, we lead our inquiry with the following research questions:

1. How do Black motherscholars interpret their experiences in navigating the responsibilities of academia with motherhood/homelife?
2. How do Black motherscholars transcribe their experiences so that their children can be prepared for their realities while also advocating for radical change?

Our Positionality

This duoethnography exposes the dialogic experiences of two Black motherscholars in higher educational settings, which rest within white patriarchal norms and practices. Giving voice to our shared yet individual experiences within this context supports our much-needed goal of healing and visibility within our scholarly pursuits. Given that duoethnography persists in posing challenging questions about ourselves for which there are not always satisfactory solutions, it is the most direct pathway toward the future we aspire to see. Although we know we won't finish the voyage, the journey within continues to be a source of inspiration and joy.

Eboni

As a Black woman raised in the U.S. South, my identity and experiences have shaped my perspectives and commitment to equity in early childhood education. As a child, I was keenly aware of the importance of political involvement, having worked on local political campaigns since my pre-teen years. This early political engagement taught me the value of civic participation. It instilled a duty to advocate for marginalized communities, ensuring our voices are heard and our needs are addressed in educational policies and practices. My identity was continually affirmed by the supportive educators I encountered throughout my educational matriculation. I endeavor to instill the attributes of critical thinking and civic engagement in my children and to be an educator who creates space for students to be their authentic selves.

Salandra

As a Black mother, educator, and scholar, my lived experiences deeply shape my perspectives and approaches to teaching and learning. In my roles as an educator/scholar, I strive to disrupt inequitable practices and structures within the educational system and work towards cultivating a more just and inclusive environment. My position as a Black mother and scholar compels me to challenge stereotypes, address bias, and support the holistic development of all students (particularly Black), ensuring they have the opportunity to thrive academically, socially, and emotionally. Recognizing the intersectionality of my identity, I remain conscious of the multiple layers of privilege and oppression that exist within our society and within my position as a Black woman in the ivory tower. This awareness drives me to continually reflect on my practices, engage in lifelong learning, and collaborate with colleagues, families, and communities to dismantle barriers and build bridges toward educational equity, excellence, and emancipation for Black children in education.

Data Collection and Analysis

The data for this duoethnography was collected through a one-hour discussion of our guiding research questions conducted over Zoom. Our discussion was recorded to ensure that we captured our narratives accurately. Following the conclusion of our discussion, a transcript was produced using Descript, a third-party transcribing service. We independently reviewed the full transcript to identify themes that emerged from the data and then met to compare and discuss the themes identified. Collaborating in this way was an important part of duoethnography because we brought our unique perspectives to the discussion. We view our life as a course study in shedding light on our experiences while navigating a white-dominated, patriarchal society. Through our conversation we remember and reexamine our experiences, with our dialogue serving as a way to encourage our development of higher forms of consciousness (Norris & Sawyer, 2012). We engaged in dialogue to identify similarities and differences in the themes we each identified, which challenged us to reflect on our interpretations and to co-construct meanings. After we were sure that a holistic understanding of the data was represented, we agreed upon the themes. A presentation of our shared themes is discussed below.

Findings

The findings reveal interconnected themes that shed light on our experiences as Black motherscholars, including the delicate balance of navigating motherhood and academia, the commitment to radical activism, and the role of spiritual capital in sustaining our work and resilience. These findings highlight the complex balance we navigate as we juggle the demands of motherhood and academic responsibilities, often in spaces that were not designed with our realities in mind. Our response to such contexts reveals a strong commitment to our children to help them navigate such spaces and radical activism emerges as both a response to systemic inequities and a means of creating transformative change within and beyond educational spaces. Our spiritual capital also plays a significant role, serving as a source of strength, resilience, and guidance in our personal and professional lives. Together, these themes provide a deeper understanding of how we, as Black motherscholars, navigate, resist, and thrive in academic spaces while remaining deeply connected to our identities, our children, and our communities.

Navigating Academia and Motherhood

The guilt of being stretched between academic obligations and the longing to be present for our children is compounded by a celebrated belief in the Black community that mothers should live a life of sacrifice (Haddix & Sawyer, 2013). Traversing these expectations makes it difficult for us to defend the time spent on academic endeavors. Therefore, to cope with the demands of our dual identities, Black motherscholars often develop creative strategies to manage our responsibilities. The perpetual need to create solutions to manage time effectively is a testament to the resilience and resourcefulness of Black motherscholars.

> **Salandra:** Being at home with kids on summer vacation and still having to grade or conduct class, write papers, and do analysis can be, I know for me, stressful at times to always be juggling multiple things. That's something that I'm still struggling with—balancing.
>
> **Eboni:** That's one of the areas where I struggle too, you know, I still want to have dinner with my kids. That's something we've always done. But I feel guilty when it has to be pizza. [...] I've tried to do things to kind of lighten my load, like I, I order my groceries now. I've even done meal preps.
>
> **Salandra:** So, I'm still working on that (laughing). I think the guilt part of that is always there.[...]And in the back of my mind, I'm doing all this stuff so that I can support my family, help support it, and create, you know, especially within the school system, better school systems for them.
>
> **Eboni:** [...]We carry the guilt of trying to do this good work; but we're losing time with our own kids. Even when I was a teacher in the classroom, it was kind of that same guilt [...] when do we learn how to not feel that guilt?
>
> **Salandra:** Yeah, it's not conducive. The classroom, PhD programs at PWIs are not conducive to family life. And I understand it's a sacrifice. I understand, you know, we're in the one percent and all that kind of stuff and everybody can't do it and ain't able and all that. But again, it's like, for what? In this four-year academic hazing journey that you have me on, is for what?

These revelations reveal how predominantly white institutions (PWIs) present challenges for Black motherscholars that are related to our existence at the intersection of race and gender, and we often find ourselves underrepresented and isolated among faculty, staff, and students (Crenshaw, 2013). Demands and expectations that are placed on Black women in academia often exceed the performance expectations of male counterparts (Domingo et al., 2022). Black motherscholars face pressure to perform exceptionally well while navigating racially-gendered microaggressions, the subtle and everyday verbal, behavioral, and environmental expressions of oppression based on the intersection of one's race and gender (Lewis et al., 2013). Nevertheless, we persist in navigating such landscapes with fortitude and engage in academic activism.

Realities and Radical Change Through Activism

The need for support systems to sustain Black motherscholars as we navigate our activist stance and professional endeavors while fulfilling the role of mother is important as well. Activism is a part of the identity of many Black motherscholars, and our work often centers the devaluation and resistance of Black women and girls (Crenshaw, 1989). Both of us emphasize the importance of instilling a positive self-identity and resilience in our children, preparing them for the realities of a world that often undervalues Black lives. The pervasiveness of negative media images of Black girls and women, such as the "Mammy" (asexual), "Jezebel" (hypersexualized), and "Sapphire" (emasculating) archetypes, and adultification result in the perception that Black girls need less nurturing, less support, and know more about adult topics than other girl groups (Epstein et al., 2017). Our dialogue highlights not only these perceptions but also our focus on empowering our children to think critically and engage in the political process to counter injustices. The commitment to activism we demonstrate extends to our professional lives, where we strive to dismantle oppressive systems in education.

Salandra: With my son, we've already had instances where the teachers, they just let him fall by the wayside. They literally were satisfied with letting him fail. Through my understanding of how the school system continuously fails our Black boys, I had him moved out of that classroom and put with two teachers who he said he wanted to be with because they had a positive relationship with him.

Eboni: So, for me, it's not one conversation that started at a certain point. [...] There are lessons that you have to start teaching at very young ages. [...]And you've got to periodically revisit those lessons in order to protect them from the harm that could possibly come.

Reflecting on this conversation caused us to focus on the complexities of preparing our children for a world where their innocence is not assumed and likely to be misconstrued (Goff et al., 2014). This aspect of parenting is not just about protecting our children, but also equipping them with the skills to recognize, understand, assess and protest racial stigmatization.

Eboni: I want to teach my kids, we don't need society to keep being like it is now. And so, for you to be able to know how to change that, you've got to be able to think about things deeply and critically look at everything. That's a really important lesson that I teach my children so that they know, hey, America is going to do what America is going to do. You've got to be prepared for it.

Teaching our children active civic engagement as an act of resistance against entrenched power structures that privilege whiteness and wealth is critical. Structural racism is a pervasive force in America that permeates all sectors of society and is woven into policies and laws (Godinez-Puig et al., 2024). The long history of Jim Crow laws, redling, and ongoing voter suppression demonstrate how Black communities have been intentionally marginalized from the civic process.

Spiritual Capital

Historically, adherence to the church and otherwise spiritual practices have guided and protected Black communities since pre-emancipation (Balkin et al., 2024; Young, 2005), providing a source of resilience and agency for Black women. We use spirituality, our spiritual capital, as a form of internal guidance and strength to nurture critical thinking and activism in our children. Turner (2024) posits that spiritual capital enables Black women to navigate life's challenges by drawing on ancestral wisdom and a connection to a higher power. These socialization strategies assist us as Black mothers in playing a pivotal role in nurturing critical thinking and activism in our children. Instilling values of resilience, justice, and spirituality, we encourage our children to question hegemony and recognize their agency in creating radical change.

Salandra: Yeah, I've had those same conversations. I have to be the change. I can't just go along with things because this is the way it is[...] Yes, I know those things are difficult, but you know, radical change is radical. You have to do things that go against the grain, and I'm fine with that.[...] I'm trying to build children's resilience in them that can help them stand firm. So spiritually, I'm trying to grow them, too. I want them to know God is on your side. He's gonna help you. I'm not gonna have the answer to everything. And when I don't have answers, you know, I gotta pray about it because I don't always know what to do.

Salandra: I want strong, resilient children because the different things that people go through can break us down differently than they do for other people. And so whatever they go through, whatever their challenges are, I just, I want them to be prepared and be strong minded.

Eboni: Yeah, spirituality is important too, especially when it comes to activating their faith in knowing that things can be different. That's something that, you know, it's important in our house too.

Our approach to carry out positive racial socialization practices amongst our children are evident. Similar to many Black mothers, the conversations we engaged in with our children were meant to prepare and protect them from the racist realities of not only the world we live in but the schools they attend (Grills et al., 2016; Lloyd, 2022; Turner, 2024). In the same way, our emphasis on their spiritual socialization compliments this approach (Gutierrez et al., 2014; Taylor & Chatters, 2010). Ensuring that our children are equipped with critical thinking skills provides a counterbalance to the trend of fast, reactionary thinking, and encourages deep inquiry and thoughtful analysis.

Our Revelations

The purpose of this duo-autoethnography was to give voice to Black motherscholars and our experiences and challenges in advocating for liberatory educational outcomes for our Black children. Our dialogic encounter provides insight into the complex and multifaceted familial and academic conditions Black motherscholars contend with. Black gaze theory is essential in interpreting Black motherscholars' experiences in advocating for Black children (Howell et al., 2019) as it centers our perspectives and acknowledges the profound insights we bring to the fight for educational equity and social justice. This theoretical framework challenges dominant narratives that often marginalize or misrepresent Black experiences, allowing for a more authentic and holistic understanding of the systemic barriers faced by Black children (Legette et al., 2021). By incorporating the Black gaze, we recognize the agency, resilience, and expertise of Black mothers as we navigate and resist these obstacles. This approach not only highlights the critical role Black mothers play in championing the rights and potential of Black children but also calls for a more inclusive and equitable approach to advocacy, policy-making, and educational practice (Morris & Matute-Chavarria, 2022). Embracing Black gaze theory thus amplifies the voices of those most intimately connected to the struggle for justice, ensuring that our lived experiences inform and shape the path toward meaningful and lasting change.

Within our revelations, we discovered varied yet compatible struggles we faced in carrying out our commitments as mothers and our duties as scholars. Within this duoethnography, our dialogues allowed us the opportunity to make visible our experiences and orient our hoped-for futures—even if we didn't have all the answers on how to actualize them. In answering our research questions, we found a way to relationally understand our cultural lives, our conflicts with our familial and academic lives, and still, even with unanswered questions, come to conclusions that confirm our commitments to continue in our pursuits.

Engaging in duoethnography through the lens of Black gaze theory gives us permission to continue speaking up and making noise in spaces that seek to silence our children and us. This Black noise shows up in our advocacy for our children, ourselves, and our communities. Backed by positive affirmations of Black brilliance and beauty, our dialogues are an insight into the integral language, thoughts, vulnerabilities, and cautions Black motherscholars simultaneously contend with while also keeping food on the table and ensuring equitable opportunities and treatment of their children is present within schools. These dialogues provide much-needed insight for educational institutions on the needs and concerns of Black motherscholars within their familial, social, and academic roles. Our experiences underscore the need for administrators to adopt a systems-centered approach to implementing meaningful change to understand how intersectionality influences entire systems (Choo & Ferreee, 2010; Logwood et al., 2023).

Conclusion

This chapter promotes the acceptance and inclusion of the positive perceptions of Black children and Black motherscholars who embody them within academia. While Black motherscholars continue to produce groundbreaking scholarship, their critical viewpoints are made hypervisible or invisible according to how well they fit within institutional goals (Haynes & Stewart, 2024; Jordan-Zachary, 2013; Pitt et al., 2015). By providing a voice to the transformative contributions of Black motherscholars, their struggles, and concerns, this chapter highlights the unique vantage points Black motherscholars possess and their contributions to advance authentic pedagogical dispositions that support the liberatory educational goals of Black academics and Black children.

As Black cultural beings in white hegemonic spaces, embracing pedagogy that liberates us and our communities from such spaces puts us en route to dismantling the centuries of harm suffered as a result. As mothers and scholars, it is our duty to speak up for our children. Our voices, our perspectives, and our experiences matter. The legitimacy of our voices are confirmed within these experiences; and 'on my mama,' we will continue advocating for ourselves and our children.

Competing Interests

The authors have no conflicts of interest to declare that are relevant to the content of this manuscript.

References

Ali, K. (2024). *The conscious cultural worker: Counter-narratives of Black women artivists as radical educators*. Lexington Books.

Balkin, R. S., Keith, S. N., Stewart, K. D., & Hendricks, L. (2024). Associations between forgiveness, spirituality, and justice among Black Americans. *Counseling and Values, 69*(1), 92–116.

Bakhtin, M. M. (1981). The dialogic imagination. In M. Holquist, C. Emerson & M. Holquist, (Ed., Trans.). University of Texas Press.

Biesecker-Mast, A. (2022). Narratives of the Black mother in the US: Exploring the Black maternalist framework in Black activism. *Honors Theses, 346*. https://ecommons.udayton.edu/uhp_theses/346

Choo, H. Y., & Ferree, M. M. (2010). Practicing intersectionality in sociological research: A critical analysis of inclusions, interactions, and institutions in the study of inequalities. *Sociological Theory, 28*(2), 129–150. https://doi.org/10.1111/j.1467-9558.2010.01370.x

Combahee River Collective. (1983). The Combahee River collective statement. In B. Smith (Ed.), Home Girls: A Black feminist anthology. Kitchen Table. (Original work published 1977).

Cooper, A. J. (1988). *A voice from the south.* Oxford University Press.

Cooper, A. J. (1998). *The voice of Anna Julia Cooper: including a voice from the South and other important essays, papers, and letters.* Rowman & Littlefield.

Crenshaw, K. W. (1989). Demarginalizing the intersection of race and sex: A black feminist critique of antidiscrimination doctrine (pp. 139–168). *University of Chicago legal forum.*

Crenshaw, K. (1991). Mapping the margins: Intersectionality, identity politics, and violence against women of color. *Stanford Law Review, 43*(6), 1241–1279.

Crenshaw, K. W. (2013). Mapping the margins: Intersectionality, identity politics, and violence against women of color. In *The public nature of private violence* (pp. 93–118). Routledge.

Davis, A. Y. (1983). *Women, race, and class.* Vintage.

Delpit, L. (2006). *Other people's children: Cultural conflict in the classroom.* The New Press.

Domingo, C. R., Gerber, N. C., Harris, D., Mamo, L., Pasion, S. G., Rebanal, R. D., & Rosser, S. V. (2022). More service or more advancement: Institutional barriers to academic success for women and women of color faculty at a large public comprehensive minority-serving state university. *Journal of Diversity in Higher Education, 15*(3), 365.

Dumas, M. J. (2016). Against the dark: Anti-blackness in education policy and discourse. *Theory into Practice, 55*(1), 11–19.

Epstein, R., Blake, J., & González, T. (2017). Girlhood interrupted: The erasure of Black girls' childhood. SSRN 3000695.

Garry, V. (2017). What preservice teachers can learn from one Jim Crow community engagement program. *American Educational History Journal, 44*(2), 19–28.

Goff, P. A., Jackson, M. C., Di Leone, B. A. L., Culotta, C. M., & DiTomasso, N. A. (2014). The essence of innocence: Consequences of dehumanizing Black children. *Journal of Personality and Social Psychology, 106*(4), 526.

Godinez-Puig, L., Cusella, C., & Balu, R. (2024). *Lessons learned from studying structural racism in national policies.* Urban Institute. https://www.urban.org/research/publication/lessons-learned-studying-structural-racism-national-policies

Grills, C., Cooke, D., Douglas, J., Subica, A., Villanueva, S., & Hudson, B. (2016). Culture, racial socialization, and positive African American youth development. *Journal of Black Psychology, 42*(4), 343–373.

Gumbs, A. P., Martens, C., & Williams, M. (Eds.). (2016). *Revolutionary mothering: Love on the frontlines.* Pm Press.

Gutierrez, I. A., Goodwin, L. J., Kirkinis, K., & Mattis, J. S. (2014). Religious socialization in African American families: The relative influence of parents, grandparents, and siblings. *Journal of Family Psychology, 28*(6), 779.

Haddix, M., & Sawyer, L. L. (2013). I am my child's first teacher: Black motherhood and homeschooling as activism. *Laboring positions: Black women, mothering, and the academy* (pp. 75–90).

Harris, T. W. (2021). *The sisters are alright: Changing the broken narrative of Black women in America.* Berrett-Koehler Publishers.

Haynes, C., & Stewart, S. (2024). Chronicling the intersectional lives of Blackwomen academics and MAMAscholars. *Zeitschrift für erziehungswissenschaftliche Migrationsforschung (ZeM), 2*(2), 126–139.

Higginbotham, E. B. (1994). *Righteous discontent: The women's movement in the Black Baptist church, 1880–1920.* Harvard University Press.

Hooks, B. (2003). *Teaching community: A pedagogy of hope.* Routledge.

Howell, D., Norris, A., & Williams, K. L. (2019). Towards Black gaze theory: How Black female teachers make Black students visible. *Urban Education Research & Policy Annuals, 6*(1).

James, J. (1999). *Shadowboxing: Representations of Black feminist politics*. Martin's Press.
James-Gallaway, A. D., & Harris, T. (2021). We been relevant: Culturally relevant pedagogy and Black women teachers in segregated schools. *Educational Studies, 57*(2), 124–141.
Jefferson, H. (2023). The politics of respectability and black Americans' punitive attitudes. *American Political Science Review,117*(4), 1448–1464. https://doi.org/10.1017/S0003055422001289
Johnson, K. A. (2000). *Uplifting the women and the race: The lives and educational philosophies and social activism of Anna Julia Cooper and Nannie Helen Burroughs*. Routledge.
Johnson, K. A., Pitre, A., & Johnson, K. L. (2014). *African American women educators: A critical examination of their pedagogies, educational ideas, and activism from the nineteenth to the mid-twentieth century*. Roman & Littlefield.
Jordan-Zachery, J. (2013). Now you see me now you don't: My political fight against the invisibility/erasure of Black women in intersectionality research. *Politics Groups and Identities, 1*(1), 101–109. https://doi.org/10.1080/21565503.2012.760314
Ladson-Billings, G. (2014). Culturally relevant pedagogy 2.0: A.K.A. the remix. *Harvard Educational Review, 84*(1), 75.
Ladson-Billings, G. (2022). *The Dreamkeepers: Successful teachers of African American children*. Wiley.
Legette, K. B., Halberstadt, A. G., & Majors, A. T. (2021). Teachers' understanding of racial inequity predicts their perceptions of students' behaviors. *Contemporary Educational Psychology, 67*, Article 102014.
Lewis, J. A., Mendenhall, R., Harwood, S. A., & Browne Huntt, M. (2013). Coping with gendered racial microaggressions among Black women college students. *Journal of African American Studies, 17*, 51–73.
Loder-Jackson, T. L., Christensen, L. M., & Kelly, H. (2016). Unearthing and bequeathing Black feminist legacies of Brown to a new generation of women and girls. *The Journal of Negro Education, 85*(3), 199–211.
Logwood, D., Ali, S., & Barragan, C. (2023). Tired of always grinding: Black Womxn faculty's experiences during COVID-19. *Journal of African American Women and Girls in Education, 3*(1), 58–75.
Lorde, A. (2012/1984). *Sister outsider: Essays and speeches*. Crossing Press.
Lorde, A., & Sarriugarte, D. (1979). *Audre Lorde*. New Letters.
Lloyd, D. D. (2022). African American mothers' racial socialization practices with preschoolers: A mixed methods study. *Family Relations, 71*(5), 1859–1877.
Matias, C. E. (2016). *Feeling white: Whiteness, emotionality, and education*. Sense.
Minnett, J. L., James-Gallaway, A. D., & Owens, D. R. (2019). Help a sista out: Black women doctoral students' use of peer mentorship as an act of resistance. *Mid-Western Educational Researcher, 31*(2), 210–238.
Morris, P., & Matute-Chavarria, M. (2022). Black mother scholars matter: Navigating anti-Black educational spaces for our Black boys. *Journal of Multicultural Affairs, 7*(2), 5.
Norris, J., & Sawyer, R. D. (2012). Toward a dialogic methodology. In J. Norris, R. D. Sawyer, & D. Lund (Eds.), *Duoethnography: Dialogic methods for social, health, and educational research* (pp. 9–39). Left Coast Press.
Pitt, J. S., Vaughn, M., Shamburger-Rousseau, A., Harris, L. L., Martin, J., & Milner, H. (2015). Black women in academia: The invisible life. *Racial battle fatigue: Insights from the front lines of social justice advocacy* (pp. 209–223).
Rabelo, V. C., Robotham, K. J., & McCluney, C. L. (2021). "Against a sharp white background": How Black women experience the white gaze at work. *Gender, Work & Organization, 28*(5), 1840–1858.
Sawyer, R. D., & Norris, J. (2013). *Duoethnography: Understanding qualitative research*. Oxford University Press.
Smith, B. (Ed.). (2024). *Home girls: A black feminist anthology*. Rutgers University Press.

Taylor, R. J., & Chatters, L. M. (2010). Importance of religion and spirituality in the lives of African Americans, Caribbean Blacks, and non-Hispanic Whites. *Journal of Negro Education, 79*(3), 280–294.

Turner, C. (2024). *"God, It's in Your Hands": The spiritual capital of black women family childcare providers*. Authorea Preprints.

Turner, C. R., & Allen, K. R. (2022). "She's a friend of my mind": A reflection of Black sisterhood in academia. *Race, Ethnicity & Education,* 1–18. https://doi.org/10.1080/13613324.2022.2088724

Whittington, E. Y. (2023). 3 Re-imagining queer black motherhood. *Refiguring Motherhood Beyond Biology,* 42.

Yosso, T. J., & Burciaga, R. (2016). Reclaiming our histories, recovering community cultural wealth. *Center for Critical Race Studies at UCLA Research Brief, 5*, 1–4.

Young, J. R. (2005). Spirituality and socialization in the slave community. *A companion to African American history* (pp. 176–198).

Motherscholar Identity Formation

“Torn Between Ways”: Exploring (Non)Dualities Through Visual Duo-Nkwaethnography as Black MotherScholars

Laura Krystal Porterfield and Lynnette Mawhinney

Abstract Taking up the Black critical feminist perspective that the personal is political and that me-search is research (Dillard & Bell, 2011), we explore the everyday ways that our lives are shaped by the interlocking effects of race, gender, class, and our positions as Black motherscholars in higher education. Through photovoice and video diaries, we documented *how* we live and do our work as Black motherscholars. This chapter outlines the guiding prompt: What does it mean to be a motherscholar? Our visual duo-nkwaethnography (Allen-Handy, 2021) project responds to this question, naming and visually articulating the inherent dualities in our work as Black motherscholars and our positions in the academy. We use the concept of the *borderlands* (Anzaldúa, 1987), along with theorizations of *figured worlds* (Hines-Datiri & Carter Andrews, 2020) to tease out the tensions, liminalities, and affordances of being Black motherscholars amidst rampant anti-Blackness and the ableist, neoliberal patriarchy upheld by institutions of higher education in this particular historical and political moment.

Keyword Visual methodologies · Duo-nkwaethnography · Borderlands theory · Black feminist theory

There has been a growing body of literature exploring the daily lived experiences, physical and psychological effects, administrative and political challenges, and career-related impacts of being a motherscholar in the US and beyond (see Matias (2022) for a comprehensive overview of motherscholarship). Motherscholarship contributes to our understanding of the unique ways women, femme, and nonbinary caregivers navigate the demands of the academy and the home, often shedding light on the ways that their obligations exceed their capacity and or time (Cohen-Miller, 2018; Johnson, 2022; Young, 2015). For example, Johnson (2022) states that

L. K. Porterfield (✉) · L. Mawhinney
Rutgers University-Newark, Newark, NJ, USA
e-mail: laura.k.porterfield@rutgers.edu

L. Mawhinney
e-mail: lynnette.mawhinney@rutgers.edu

C. R. Turner and M. L. Green (eds.), *Black Motherscholarship Within and Beyond the Academy*, https://doi.org/10.1007/978-3-031-99758-7_17

many motherscholars were either erroneously or consciously denied earned maternity/leave time, forcing them to return to work early after childbirth/adoption—if they were able to take leave at all. These situations often unfairly require motherscholars to choose between their families and their careers, substantially impacting their overall wellbeing (e.g. higher levels of toxic stress, weight loss/gain, burnout, and other stress-related health issues). Notably, this body of literature has grown substantially over the last four years, particularly with the rise of alternative/at-home work arrangements made simultaneously possible and necessary by the COVID-19 pandemic (Schnackenberg, 2023; Spradley et al., 2020).

Racial trauma, battle fatigue, and diversity double-duty are just some of the battles that motherscholars of Color face navigating their positions inside and outside of the academy (Castro, 2023, 2017; Gumbs et al., 2016; Hemans et al., 2020; Lapayese, 2012; Turner & Allen, 2022; Williams & Gore, 2019). As Lorde (1984), Hooks (1984), Hill Collins (2000), Crenshaw (1989), and others have noted, our personal experiences shape and are shaped by larger power structures, systems, and institutions and cannot be understood or addressed in isolation from one another. As such, better understanding the perspectives and experiences of Black motherscholars *in particular* can help us illuminate the fissures in our academic systems and begin to address those fissures systematically toward better outcomes for all.

Researcher Positionalities: How and Where We Enter

In the preface to the second edition of her groundbreaking work *When and Where I Enter*, Paula Giddings (1984) poses several unanswered questions that are profoundly useful starting points for fleshing out our own positionalities: "we might ask then, who are we as ourselves? […] Who are we when no one yearns for us…? Who are we when we are not someone's mother, or daughter, or sister, or aunt, or church elder, or first black woman to be this or that?" (p. 9). Taking up the Black critical feminist perspective that the personal is political and that me-search is research (Dillard & Bell, 2011), we explore the everyday ways that our lives are shaped by the interlocking effects of race, gender, class, and our positions as Black motherscholars in higher education. In what follows, we attempt to battle with the question of who we are, and how we arrived at the present moment as Black motherscholars in this particular time and space.

Laura's Entry

I am a cisgender, queer, Black woman from the Southwest United States. As a Black person growing up amongst a mostly Latinx population, and as a working-class girl growing up in a solidly middle-class neighborhood, I have often occupied a position on/in the *borderlands*. Since leaving the Southwest, I have worked in multiple educational spaces and capacities over the past two decades in the Northeast and Midwest US: as a faculty member working in teacher education, an informal educator and mentor, a high school Speech and Debate and Track and Field coach, and as a Freedom School teacher.

I became a mother in the fall of 2021, the same time I started a new position at my current institution, a Minority-Serving Institution (MSI) with an incredibly diverse student body. This was a vast change from my previous position teaching at a predominately white institution (PWI) in the Midwest US, where I was the only faculty member of Color in my department. I entered my Urban Education PhD program in 2006, effectively entering the world of academia at that time. As such, I have spent more time cultivating my identity as an academic than I have as a mother. Though I did not intend to pursue a career as an academic after graduate school (my plan was to center my work in the classroom), I was encouraged to pursue this path by mentors who saw more in me than I saw in myself. This is a critical point, as I often found myself—and indeed still do—consumed by the imposter syndrome so many working-class and women of Color face in higher educational spaces (Fields & Cunningham-Williams, 2021).

As a motherscholar, I often find myself working to undo the conditioning that has led me to believe that I do not belong in academia; concurrently, my work in the higher education classroom has centered on undoing the harmful conditioning that contours the educational experiences many of my students encounter as well. This is especially true in teacher education, as the field is predominately white and female (US Department of Education, 2016). As the mother to a Black child, my sense of urgency in preparing the next generation of teachers has unsurprisingly increased tenfold over the past three years. In particular, my work as a motherscholar has centered on uncovering the spirit murdering so enmeshed in the carceral logics of our schools, while at the same time highlighting the need for spiritual revival (Love, 2019) and other liberatory educational practices that have the power to counter them.

Lynnette's Entry

I am a cisgender, biracial (Black/white) woman who identifies (and who the world sees in a US context) as a Black woman. I was a high school urban English teacher who received her Ph.D. in Urban Education. After completing my degree, my intention was to go back into the high school classroom. Yet, during graduate school, I was a "teaching assistant" (read as faculty member and instructor of record without the same pay as an actual faculty member) and quickly realized I had the same students (literally) in my classroom as the high school classroom sans school administration down my back. So, I stayed in higher education.

As a graduate student, I was given a two course teaching load per semester with courses that were so intense that faculty members were literally not allowed to have two sections of the course due to the workload—but not me. This quickly led to my hair falling out from stress, along with developing the nasty habit of being a workhorse.

Many years later as a tenured professor and department chair, I was at my third institution during my higher education career, and the most toxic work environment I have before or since encountered. While at this new institution, I immediately became pregnant in 2018 two months after my wedding. But March 2019, I had contractions during my 2nd trimester while in my office during my 14th hour of the work day. About two hours later, I gave birth in a hospital, but my daughter only lived a few minutes. The only solution doctors could surmise for the early birth was the stress of my job. If I wanted to be a mother, I had to get out of this university and learn to do my job differently.

By Fall 2020, I landed a new job, but I started the academic year at the age of 41 and two-weeks postpartum. I was wrongly and illegally informed by the interim dean that hired me that I was not allowed maternity leave. I moved across the country in a pandemic with a two-week old child. Clearly, I, once again, was not starting my motherscholar journey off well. Between 2020 and having my third child in 2022, I have been working on the both/and as a motherscholar. For me to live in the borderlands, this comes with unlearning the lesson that I am *not* my job, my job does not define me, and the institution does not love me back.

Conceptual Frameworks: Borderlands and Figured Worlds

Given the existing multiple oppressions Black women face as mothers and academics, we seek to unpack the pedagogical and liberatory possibilities of being "torn between ways" (Anzaldúa, 1987), while constructing our own distinctly Black feminist-centered *figured world* as motherscholars. We use the concept of the *borderlands* (Anzaldúa, 1987), along with theorization of *figured worlds* (Hines-Datiri & Carter Andrews, 2020; Holland, 1998) to tease out the tensions, liminalities, and affordances of being Black motherscholars amidst rampant anti-Blackness and the ableist, neoliberal patriarchy upheld by institutions of higher education in this particular historical and political moment.

On Borderlands and Being "Torn Between Ways"

Gloria Anzaldúa's (1987) conceptualization of the *borderlands* provides us with an excellent heuristic through which to examine the metaphysical space of the motherscholar. The borderlands do not simply represent the physical strip of land that separates the United States-Texas-Southwest from Mexico, but they also represent the psychological, sexual, spiritual, and cultural politics of place for *la mestiza*, as "the Borderlands are physically present wherever two or more cultures edge each other" (p. 1). Anzaldúa clarifies that the borderlands are generative spaces, creating and sustaining a borderland/mestiza subjectivity: a *nepantilism* (an Aztec word), which loosely translates to "torn between ways." What makes this theoretical analytic rich and deeply profound is that it does not simply reject binaries or dichotomies—it engages them. She writes:

> The mestiza's dual or multiple personality is plagued by psychic restlessness. In a constant state of mental nepantilism...la mestiza is a product of the transfer of the cultural and spiritual values of one group to another. [...] in a state of perpetual transition, the mestiza faces the dilemma of the mixed breed: which collectivity does the daughter of a darkskinned mother listen to? (Anzaldúa, 1987, p. 78)

In Anzaldúa's formulations, the *borderlands* produces a mestiza consciousness, one that highlights and magnifies the phenomenological and epistemological realities for post-colonial bodies, persons, and groups. Black motherscholars operate in a liminal borderland of contradictions, navigating new, confusing, and at times hostile terrains that shape the form and content of their labor as they navigate their new identities. These contradictions create competing demands—over time, energies, commitments—that give way to the Black motherscholar being in a state of "torn between ways." But as Anzaldúa suggests, "the new mestiza copes by developing a tolerance for contradictions, a tolerance for ambiguity. [...] She learns to juggle cultures" (p. 79). What does it mean to take up such a posture, a mestiza consciousness, in the context of the Black motherscholar? How does such a tolerance for ambiguity develop? And what can we learn from this developmental process that can help us better understand and support Black motherscholars? Considering how this new consciousness fits into her world may provide additional clarity.

On Shifting Identities and (Re)Figured Worlds

Drawing on the work of sociocultural developmental psychologist Lev Vygtosky, Holland (1998) contend that figured worlds "rest upon people's abilities to form and be formed in collectively realized 'as if' realms" (p. 49). They argue that *figured worlds* are collectively co-produced sociocultural spaces in which identities are dialectically produced and negotiated. As such, the identities produced in such 'as if' realms rest upon our continued investment in their production, and the continual development of the competence we gain in engaging in these 'as if' realms we develop as children. Figured worlds live on through cultural practices and activities, such as mother/homemaker, community member, scholar, and the like. Within figured worlds, actors assign and are assigned roles—and value —based on their participation in these activities and practices. Holland et al. state, "by 'figured world,' then, we mean a socially and culturally constructed realm of interpretation in which particular characters and actors are recognized, significance is assigned to certain acts, and particular outcomes are valued over others" (p. 52).

Within the context of the motherscholar, our identities as actors who straddle multiple, often overlapping worlds, are enacted through value-based filters, behaviors, and spaces that we assign value and significance to. Enmeshed in a world figured by systems of privileges and power, our performances as mothers, scholars, and individual cultural actors are assigned value by other actors within the realm in which they are produced (e.g. our performances as mothers are assessed by our families, our performances as scholars are assigned value by other scholars, etc.). Rather than viewing this as fixed, we are constantly negotiating, shifting, and altering our performances and identities through the process of figuring our worlds.

Methodology: Black MotherScholars Figuring the Borderlands

The borderlands, then, become a generative figured world for us to negotiate our budding identities as both mothers and scholars. We used visual duo-nkwaethnography—our own combination of visual and duoethnography with the African and healing-centered methodology of *nkwaethnography* (Allen-Dillard & Bell, 2011; Handy, 2021)—to respond to the larger inquiries regarding what it means to be Black motherscholars in the borderlands of these newly formed, yet generative, figured worlds. Our visual duo-nkwaethnography included a combination of video diaries, semi-monthly photovoice prompts, photoelicitative duoethnographic interviews, as well as critical reflections on our care practices, as we documented how we live and do our work as Black motherscholars and visual researchers. Drawing on Dillard and Bell (2011)'s call to reject the "auto" in auto-ethnography from an endarkened feminist framework, we employed Allen-Handy's (2021) definition of nkwaethnography: "an African-centered ethnographic research approach that affords African ascendant individuals a way by which to engage in a deeply introspective and sacred self-research process at the myriad intersections of their identities" (p. 71). We chose to do this work together to learn about our (new) selves as women of Color academics and mothers and to combat the isolation we, and so many other Black women and motherscholars of Color, face navigating our multiple positions.

Data Collection

Applying a nkwaethnographic/healing approach to our me-search as motherscholars, we embarked on an introspective study to explore what it means to be a motherscholar and the self-care practices needed to support this identity (e.g., work/life balance). This study included weekly video diaries completed over one academic year (2023–2024) coupled with a photovoice component. For photovoice, we met semi-monthly responding to the following four guiding prompts over the course of the year: (1) What does it mean to be a motherscholar?; (2) What does rest and/or rejuvenation mean/look like as a motherscholar?; (3) What are the challenges to being a motherscholar?;

and (4) What lessons have you learned this academic year about your identity as motherscholar?

To hold each other accountable for taking care of ourselves and each other, we made time for periodic self-care activities. These activities included joint family gatherings, going to see a play, manicures/pedicures, and a writing retreat. We took photos of our care practices to add to the photovoice collection, captions, and weekly vlogs. All data was collected and stored in individual cloud-based folders, which we then referenced during data analysis.

Data Analysis

We used photoelicitation (Choo, 2023; McKenzie, 2022) as a guiding framework for our semi-structured discussions to analyze our photovoice responses. The photoelicitation interviews were audiorecorded and later transcribed for further analysis. The photoelicitation interview was part data collection, part data analysis. Each interview was structured around one of the aforementioned four guiding photovoice prompts and included analysis and discussion of the photos and captions we each uploaded to our respective cloud-folders. We used the SHOWED photo-elicitation method (Gant et al., 2009) (adapted for this project) to discuss and co-analyze our photo responses and captions. Questions asked for the SHOWED method include:

S what do you **s**ee?
H what **h**appened or is **h**appening in the picture?
O how does this relate to (y)**o**ur life as a Black motherscholar?
W **w**hy and **w**hen does this happen?
E how could this image **e**ducate others about the experiences of Black motherscholars?
D what can we **d**o with this image?

Using the SHOWED method during our photo elicitation conversations surfaced findings and themes in vivo that we further analyzed using thematic narrative analysis, grounded theory, and purposeful storytelling. We placed these themes and our narratives *in context* (Charmaz, 2006) with our almost two decades of friendship, our knowledge of each others' gremlins, strengths, dreams, and heartbreaks as a means to

> join in harmony with other Black women who have, who are, and who will navigate academic life... across all levels- undergraduate, graduate, doctoral, tenure track, non-tenure track, mid-career, full, distinguished, as well as across transnational boundaries. In this space, [we] strive to illuminate how [our] experiences and the interplay of [our] intersectional identities make room for our collective endeavors, our collective strength. (Allen-Handy, p. 71) (emphasis added)

In this chapter, we reflect on the generative themes that surfaced as a result of our analyses of Laura's first video diary, three photovoice images and prompt responses, and an excerpt from the authors' first photoelicitative duo-nkwaethnographic interview. To make sense of our conversations, photos, and vlogs, we conducted a textual analysis of our data (*elicited texts*) (Charmaz) guided by the following question: how can/are we re-figure(ing) our worlds—free of the either/or—and embrace(ing) the borderlands of our new motherscholar identities?

Theme One: On the Borderlands: The Hard Balance

Here we specifically explore our responses to the first photovoice prompt: *what does it mean to be a motherscholar?* Our visual duo-nkwaethnography (Allen-Handy, 2021) responds to this question, naming and visually articulating our search for balance and the inherent dualities in our work as Black motherscholars and our positions in the academy.

Figures 1a, b and 2 below provide a snapshot of Lynnette and Laura's photographic responses to the guiding question and first prompt. In Fig. 1a and b—two sides of the same coin—Lynnette illustrates the micro-level choices and consequences of our decisions navigating the borderlands of being both mother and scholar.

a b

Fig. 1 *Missed Joy // Choices to First Steps.* **a** Ice cream for dinner = complete happiness and joy! Unfortunately, this is joy I missed, as I was away for work–again. Sigh! Photo by Robert Gachoki. **b** The importance of saying, enough is enough. I said enough work, and because of that, I got to witness my son taking his first steps. Photo by Lynnette

Fig. 2 *Hotel Breakfast, AERA 2023.* I took this photo from the upstairs balcony of my conference hotel. It took a concerted effort for me to attend my first post-baby conference this year. Specifically, my partner and little one had to come with me, or I wouldn't have felt comfortable going. On this particular morning, I left breakfast to go get changed for the conference that day and snapped this on the way back to our room. Photo by Laura

In an excerpt from our first photovoice conversation, Lynnette further explained:

> Lynnette: This one [Fig. 1a] you've seen but just the idea at the end of the day this is joy. This is coming from another late night of me being here. September has been nuts, but they've [the children] come home, they go to the playground, the ice cream truck – all the neighbor kids were there. I finished up [work] the same time as her eating ice cream, *but I missed it.* I missed that joyful moment.
>
> And this is one [Fig. 1b] I think I told you about. This is in Kenya. And this is the day Enoch first walked. And because I chose to come home early from the conference... So this is like the two together: when I don't come home, the moments I miss. And those moments where I say screw it and I'll just go home, and I get those moments though. *That's the hard balance.* (emphasis added) (Photoelicitation Interview 1, Laura and Lynnette, September 18, 2023).

The images and narratives Lynnette shares provide us with a backstage view (Goffman, 1959) of the everyday privileges and struggles motherscholars face in their worlds. *Missed Joy* [Fig. 1b] is the story many motherscholars and working parents know all too well: the everyday moments we miss when we choose (or are required) to stay well beyond traditional working hours to finish the job of the day. As Black motherscholars in particular, this choice/requirement is often a prerequisite to simply exist in our positions, as we live out the adage that we must "work twice as hard to get half as far." As a matter of balance, however, *Choices to First Steps* [Fig. 1a] shows us the afterglow of asserting our right to choose differently, to step beyond the veil of our multiple positions and into the borderlands of a new space altogether.

Laura presents a birds-eye view of her choices, a snapshot of the new space that those choices have created in Fig. 2: *Hotel Breakfast, AERA 2023*.

Laura provides additional detail on why *Hotel Breakfast* (Fig. 18.2) visualizes her feelings on what it means to be a motherscholar mid-COVID 19 pandemic, in the wake of having her first child, and the mental health struggles that have surfaced as a result. In our first photovoice meeting, Laura said:

> Laura: I left breakfast to go get dressed and I snapped this. I felt like the only way I made it to AERA was if they [my husband and my baby] came with me. It was like…I can't leave them. I'm just not at that place in my journey yet. My postpartum anxiety is too high. I just — but I also felt before, I was like I *wanted* to be at AERA. I want to be back on the scene. And so I was like how do we make this work? You know? And again, having… you know the flexibility of like my job could feed us for breakfast in the morning, and I could leave for the day but still have them to come home to at the hotel.

I didn't feel as torn at this particular time because I felt like I did what I needed to do to take care of us and myself for us to be together and for me to really engage in this [the conference]—I didn't do the full conference like I would have if I was solo or prior to being a mother—but I did it the best I could and I was really proud to like fight to get there.

> Lynnette: Hmm.
>
> Laura: I was like…I need to like reengage. I need to step back into this space and I'm different and it's going to be something new and it's still going to be awkward and that's fine. Like but this is the way that we're going to have to do this (Photoelicitation Interview 1, Laura and Lynnette, September 18, 2023).

In keeping with the backstage view, Laura detailed the inner workings of her "fight" to return to academic conferences postpartum. Rather than returning solo—as some colleagues suggested she do to get "back on the bandwagon"—she re-figured her world to merge mothering and academia. Her narrative underscores one of the privileges of academic life, the flexibility and financial support to travel (which can in some cases extend to family members), along with the emotional battles motherscholars face as they are in the midst of a life-changing identity transformation.

Figures 1a, b and 2 illustrate the often-impossible choices Black motherscholars are required to make, especially as we bear primary financial responsibilities for our families while attempting to maintain our scholarly endeavors, to be present spiritually and intellectually in two places at once. Anzaldúa (1987) refers to this phenomenon as *un choque*, a cultural collision. Noting the warring factions taking up space in our minds and hearts at the intersection of our multiple identities, she said, "like others having or living in more than one culture, we get multiple, often opposing messages. The coming together of two self-consistent but habitually incompatible frames of reference causes *un choque*, a cultural collision" (p. 78). As a creative and liberatory exercise, Figs. 1a, b, and 2 call us to (re)imagine what existing in these meta-physical borderlands might teach us, our families, and others, about the ever-present requirement to *choose* and the new balance that may surface as a result.

Theme Two: Figuring the Both/And

A secondary and related theme that surfaced as a result of our inquiry was that of *dualities*. We found that, for both of us, creating a motherscholar identity required us to face the tearing that happens at the juncture of creating something new. Like the tearing required to build new muscles in the body, our consciousnesses were hard at work figuring how we could be both the mother *and* the scholar, not either/or. As Anzaldúa (1987) notes, "the work of mestiza consciousness is to break down the subject-object duality that keeps her a prisoner and to show in the flesh and through the images in her work how duality is transcended" (p. 80) (Fig. 3).

Laura's video diary transcript is an extended commentary on how she is beginning the process of breaking down the subject-object duality of being a mother and scholar toward a new motherscholar mestiza consciousness and identity. She offered the following:

> So I'm recording what my thoughts are right now on what being a motherscholar means. I do feel like the quote "torn between ways" is really helpful for me to have some language that I think gives shape and color to my experiences. I often feel like I'm never present fully in one space or another because I'm worrying about my child or worrying about my job, and finding ways to prioritize either when I'm in [the] other space makes me feel really in-betwixt, in between, all the time. I feel like I am...being a motherscholar means being torn between ways. That is 100% how I feel. And I'm trying to wrestle with whether or not to place a value judgment on that. Like, is that good? Is that bad? Is that just the way it is? I'm not sure. But I do know that I feel hopeful that the tearing will subside and it'll be more like...harmony. It would be more of a harmonious balance instead of feeling torn in one direction or the other. So that's how I feel right now. I'm hoping that over the course of this year, as I get farther along in my motherhood journey and farther along in my career, I will have a different and perhaps more nuanced answer to the question (Laura, vlog transcript, September 18, 2023).

Fig. 3 Laura's first video diary

As a junior scholar on the tenure clock, Laura's time is of utmost concern. There is a connection in her sentiments here that connects the feeling of tearing with time. Here she is reconciling that the tearing she was experiencing was connected with a sense of loss and lack of control over her most valuable resource—time. However, there is a yearning in her narrative as well, as she sought harmony while she is in the process ("I feel hopeful that the tearing will subside"). This yearning also leads her to take a cue from Anzaldúa (1987), adopting "a plural personality…in a pluralistic mode," where "nothing is thrust out, the good the bad and the ugly, nothing rejected, nothing abandoned. Not only does she sustain contradictions, she turns the ambivalence into something else" (p. 79). In this vignette, Laura was actively learning and developing the internal scripts (Robinson, 2023) to redirect her thinking away from binaries and toward "something else" altogether. Wrestling with whether or not to place a value judgment on the developmental process she is enduring was perhaps evidence of her figuring a new space, a "something else," as, "Figured worlds in their conceptual dimensions supply the contexts of meaning for actions, cultural productions, performances, disputes, for the understandings that people come to make of themselves, and for the capabilities that people develop to direct their own behavior in these worlds" (Holland et al., p. 60).

Figuring out *something else* requires that Laura develop the capability to "direct her own behaviors" within the context of her newly re-formed worlds. The development of this capability provides a different, more flexible objective to reach for; one that does not rely on an externally imposed image of "the perfect mom" or "the perfect scholar."

On the other end of the spectrum, Lynnette detailed the internal process of rescripting and refiguring her motherscholar identity, shifting boundaries to maintain her wellness, noting:

> Lynnette: For me being a motherscholar, I think I have benefited because I'm later in my career. Now having kids, I have a little bit more privilege of having tenure and having these things that protect me that I can shut off very easily at home. But in this transition, what I'm noticing in the [administration's office] and they're all women, but they don't shut off. When they're with families, they don't shut off. To the point where [our Dean] said, like, I need to figure out how to get them to shut off. But I don't operate like that. I operate that, [when] it is 3:30 on a Friday, I close my laptop. And I did not open it until I got here at 9:00 a.m., right? Literally did not open it – I left it in the car. I've created this new me.
>
> Laura: Do you think being a mother has forced you into that new me?
>
> Lynnette: Yeah. I…well, it's been stages. […] When I got tenure I told myself I'm going to… Sundays are mine. So I think I started the practice early but then once motherhood came, it was like, 'oh, no, I've gotten too far and worked too hard for these kids and this family.' So I'm saying that I guess what it means to be a motherscholar is going to be a shift for me. My kids are my priority. How do I not get sucked in [to work]? In a place that's supporting not getting sucked in. Right? I have a boss who's like, "I don't want you to operate like this" (Photoelicitation Interview 1, Laura and Lynnette, September 18, 2023).

Lynnette's narrative externally articulated the internal re-figuring and re-scripting of her professional boundaries, as she transitioned from faculty member to administrator. While the protections of tenure grant her additional flexibility over her time, the constant pull of being an administrator in a cultural context where other colleagues (who also have families) are "on call" further drives home the need for refusing to take on the role in this way. "How do I not get sucked in?," she asked. Her narrative suggests that she is in the process of figuring out how to step into this new terrain without losing the practices she put in place for herself for her own sustainability and wellness. She is in the process of figuring her world free from the paradox many motherscholars of Color face, asking "How does liberation from the particular determinations—the entrapments—of our cultural worlds come about through the tools shaped in those worlds for their perpetuation?" (Holland, 1998, p. 64). Her questioning exemplified the politics of Black womens' refusals, a decided "*see what we NOT gon' do…*" moment.

The introspection woven through this narrative was a purposeful action, and not solely reaction, to her new circumstances as she prepared for yet another life transition. These actions are about refusal, time, and reclamation; refusal to do the job, as is typically taken up, without care for all parts of the self; refusal to relinquish the precious time she had with her family, despite the pull to do so; and a reclamation of the notion that there are indeed other paths forward. She will not use "the tools shaped in those worlds for their perpetuation," or, to draw on our ancestor Audre Lorde (1984), the master's tools to dismantle the master's house. Stepping into these borderlands requires using other tools meant for our freedom, wellness, and liberation.

Conclusion

In this chapter, we aimed to tease out the tensions, liminalities, and affordances of being Black motherscholars. Using the conceptual frameworks of *the borderlands* and *figured worlds* allowed us to do this, giving shape and form to process our understandings of what it means for us to be Black motherscholars amidst the multiple pandemics of COVID-19 and rampant anti-Black racism. We found that adopting a mestiza consciousness/praxis (Anzaldúa, 1987), one in which being "town between ways" is viewed generatively, produced a sense of appreciation for the developmental process of *becoming* a motherscholar. Our visual duo-nkwaethnography has made visible and nameable the many choices we make as we figure our new worlds (Holland, 1998) on the borderlands of being a mother and scholar. As older mothers (we both birthed our children in our late 1930s/early 1940s), our identities have transitioned after spending more of our lives as scholars than mothers. What this transition has taught us is that there is great power in rejecting binaries and dualities that suggest we must be either mother or scholar. Rather, we have come to learn through this identity reformation process the posture and tools of the mestiza, the both/and. The tools we have acquired are the tools of flexibility, refusal, and non-duality.

Competing Interests

The authors have no conflicts of interest to declare that are relevant to the content of this manuscript.

References

Allen-Handy, A. (2021). Extracting life-giving strength from my roots: An endarkened feminist nkwaethnography of navigating tenure as a Black woman at a predominantly white institution. *The Journal of Intersectionality, 5*(1), 70–88. https://www.jstor.org/stable/48691457

Anzaldúa, G. (1987). *Borderlands/La Frontera: The new mestiza*. Aunt Lute Books.

Castro, C. (2023). Characteristics and perceptions of women of color faculty nationally. In Kristine de Welde & Andi Stepnick (Eds.), *Disrupting the culture of silence: Confronting gender inequality and making change in higher education* (pp. 173–178). Routledge. https://doi.org/10.4324/9781003444299-15

Charmaz, K. (2006). *Constructing grounded theory: A practical guide through qualitative analysis*. Sage Publications.

Choo, L. W. (2023). Photo elicitation interviews. In *Varieties of qualitative research methods* (pp. 383–387). Springer International Publishing AG. https://doi.org/10.1007/978-3-031-04394-9_59

CohenMiller, A. (2018). Creating a participatory arts-based online focus group: Highlighting the transition from DocMama to motherscholar. *Qualitative Report, 23*(7), Article 10. https://doi.org/10.46743/2160-3715/2018.2895

Crenshaw, K. (1989). Demarginalizing the intersection of race and sex: A Black feminist critique of antidiscrimination doctrine, feminist theory and antiracist politics. *University of Chicago Legal Forum, 1*(8), 139–167.

Dillard, C. B., & Bell, C. (2011). Endarkened feminism and sacred praxis: Troubling (auto)ethnography through critical engagements with African Indigenous knowledges. *Counterpoints., 379*, 337–349.

Fields, L. N., & Cunningham-Williams, R. M. (2021). Experiences with imposter syndrome and authenticity at research-intensive schools of social work: A case study on black female faculty. *Advances in Social Work, 21*(2–3), 354–373. https://doi.org/10.18060/24124

Gant, L., Shimshock, K., Allen-Meares, P., Smith, L., Miller, P., Hollingsworth, L., et al. (2009). Effects of photovoice: Civic engagement among older youth in urban communities. *Journal of Community Practice, 17*(4), 358–376. https://doi.org/10.1080/10705420903300074

Giddings, P. (1984). *When and where I enter: The impact of Black women on race and sex in America* (1st ed.). W. Morrow.

Goffman, E. (1959). *The presentation of self in everyday life*. Doubleday.

Gumbs, A. P., Martens, C., & Williams, M. (Eds.). (2016). *Revolutionary mothering: Love on the front lines*. PM Press.

Hemans, P. B., Lewis, P., & Osoria, R. (2020). The dual invisibility of mother-scholars of Color. *About Campus, 25*(2), 24–27. https://doi.org/10.1177/1086482220913702

Hill Collins, P. (2000). *Black feminist thought: Knowledge, consciousness, and the politics of empowerment*. Routledge.

Hines-Datiri, D., & Carter Andrews, D. J. (2020). The effects of zero tolerance policies on Black girls: Using critical race feminism and figured worlds to examine school discipline. *Urban Education, 55*(10), 1419–1440. https://doi.org/10.1177/0042085917690204

Holland, D. C. (1998). *Identity and agency in cultural worlds*. Harvard University Press.

Hooks, B. (1984). *Feminist theory: From margin to center*. South End Press.

Johnson, B. E. (2022). *Balancing academics and motherhood: Exploring role navigation with new mothers in counselor education doctoral programs.* ProQuest Dissertations & Theses.
Lapayese, Y. V. (2012). Mother-scholar: (Re)imagining K-12 education. In *Mother-Scholar* (1. Aufl., Vol. 85). SensePublishers. https://doi.org/10.1007/978-94-6091-891-9
Lorde, A. (1984). *Sister outsider: Essays and speeches.* Crossing Press.
Love, B. L. (2019). *We want to do more than survive: Abolitionist teaching and the pursuit of educational freedom.* Beacon Press.
Matias, C. E. (2022). Birthing the motherscholar and motherscholarship. *Peabody Journal of Education 97*(2), 246–250. https://doi.org/10.1080/0161956X.2022.2055897
McKenzie, L. G. (2022). *More than words: A photo-elicitation study exploring black motherhood in academia.* ProQuest Dissertations & Theses.
Robinson, S. (2023). Being beautifully rooted is a journey toward establishing emotionally healthy spirituality. In K. M. Dade & T. Parker (Eds.), *Black female perspectives from predominantly White institutions: Strategies for wellbeing in White spaces and beyond* (pp. 139–170). Lexington Books.
Schnackenberg, H. L. (2023). Motherscholar and MotherLeader: The More Things Change, the More They Stay the Same. In *Stabilizing and Empowering Women in Higher Education: Realigning, Recentering, and Rebuilding* (pp. 284–295). IGI Global. https://doi.org/10.4018/978-1-6684-8597-2.ch014
Spradley E., LeBlanc S. S., Olson Beal, H. K., Burrow L. E., Cross C. (2020). Proving our maternal and scholarly worth: A collaborative autoethnographic textual and visual storying of Mother-Scholar identity work during the COVID-19 pandemic. *Journal of the Motherhood Initiative, 11*(2), 189–209.
Turner, C. R., & Allen, K. R. (2022). "She's a friend of my mind": A reflection of Black sisterhood in academia. *Race, Ethnicity & Education,* 1–18. https://doi.org/10.1080/13613324.2022.2088724
US Department of Education. (2016). *The state of racial diversity in the educator workforce.* https://www2.ed.gov/rschstat/eval/highered/racial-diversity/state-racial-diversity-workforce.pdf
Williams, M., & Gore, A. (2019). *This is how we survive: Revolutionary mothering, war, and exile in the 21s century.* PM Press.
Young A. M. (2015). *Teacher, scholar, mother: Re-envisioning motherhood in the academy.* Lexington Books.

[illegible]

White Shadows: The Path to Awareness

Michele Turner

Abstract This piece recounts the author's journey as a Black mother navigating racialized experiences in undergraduate spaces. I challenge damaging narratives propagated by professors, like the belief that Black families inherently devalue education. In my master's program, I shifted from a conservative viewpoint to recognizing the systemic structures stacked against Black families. Internalised racism from my upbringing in predominantly white environments influenced my early beliefs. These beliefs were later challenged through enlightenment from advanced critical studies. Personal anecdotes illustrate how these experiences reshaped my approach to motherhood, fostering resilience and growth. This narrative offers insights into race, education, and personal transformation.

Keyword Educational inequity · Internalized racism · Personal transformation · Racialized experiences

"You two need to calm down," my sister said, her gaze piercing as she looked from me to my son. We had just toured The National Underground Railroad Freedom Center during our visit to a Cincinnati college when an argument broke out between my son and me. The topic was whiteness, and the debate became heated enough for my sister to step in. I don't remember exactly what sparked the argument, but I vividly recall the anger I felt: "How did I raise a son with so much internalized racism? Sending him to that white Christian school must have been a mistake. That's where he must have picked up all these misguided notions about Black people".

Later, I came to understand that what I witnessed in my son was not uncommon. Internalized racism, as psychologist David (2019) explains, is "the process by which individuals from marginalized racial groups adopt and believe negative stereotypes and attitudes about their own group, perpetuated by the dominant culture." This form of racialized self-perception can deeply affect identity development, especially in environments that subtly or overtly devalue Blackness. Scholars like Helms (2017)

M. Turner (✉)
Institute for Equity and Transformational Change, Madison College, Madison, WI, USA
e-mail: mturner6@madisoncollege.edu

C. R. Turner and M. L. Green (eds.), *Black Motherscholarship Within and Beyond the Academy*, https://doi.org/10.1007/978-3-031-99758-7_18

and Tummala-Narra (2016) emphasize that such internalization often begins in institutions like schools, where whiteness is centered as the norm and anything else is rendered inferior or invisible. My son's comments weren't just personal—they were the echoes of a system that had already begun shaping how he saw himself and his people.

His words stung because they reflected a mirror I wasn't prepared to face. As I reflected on the argument, I realized that my son sounded like I did when I was younger. Maybe it wasn't entirely the school's fault that he was so quick to defend white people while putting down Black people. I grew up in a family with my mom, dad, two brothers, and a sister in Milwaukee in a predominantly white neighborhood during the 1970s and 1980s. This was a time in which Milwaukee was deeply divided by racial segregation and systemic racism. In October, 1970, our family moved into a newly built house. There were no other Black families on our block which was no surprise because Milwaukee's discriminatory practices reached every area: housing, employment, and education. Redlining in Milwaukee had been enforced for decades, confining the majority of Black residents to specific neighborhoods on the North Side, and made it nearly impossible for Blacks to obtain mortgages or move into predominantly white areas. It was no wonder that we were the first Black family on our block.

I had very little interaction with Black people outside of attending church on Sunday mornings. All my friends at school and in my neighborhood were white, and we would walk together to the local public school. Surprisingly, my elementary school principal, Mr. Plumber, was Black. However, with Milwaukee public schools being segregated until I reached sixth grade and the majority of Black students attending underfunded schools with inadequate resources, I didn't have any Black classmates or teachers until the fourth grade. In fourth grade, we had a Black music teacher, Mrs. Washington, who would teach our class once a week. I still remember how she taught us to read music and introduced us to quarter notes and half notes. I thought she was so beautiful and smart and wanted to be like her, but she was only there for that one year. In fifth grade, there were two Black students in my class, and both of us were placed in what was then called the "Superior Ability" class, which was mostly made up of white kids.

I thought these kids were my friends until one day when the other Black girl went home for lunch and all the white girls decided to gang up on me. Somehow, I fought them off and then went inside to tell the teacher. I expressed my frustration and confusion, upset that my white classmates had attacked me. I told the teacher that I believed their actions were racially motivated. A couple of the girls cried, insisting they loved everyone and weren't racist. I recall being too mad to cry, but wanting to because I knew the only reason they attacked me was because of the color of my skin. I don't remember what the teacher said, just that she tried to console me while telling me that she didn't think they were racist. No parents were called, including mine; and no one apologized to me. We just went back to how we were after their tears, my anger, and the non-apologies. I quickly forgave them the next day; and we went back to being "friends".

Even though they claimed not to be racist, there were other indicators. I remember the jump rope songs we used to sing. One song that stood out was, "Chin, Chin China man, sitting on a bench, trying to make a dollar out of fifty-nine cents." As an adult, I looked the song up. It is a racist song from the 1800s; but at the time, of course, I didn't know that and sang along happily jumping rope. As a Black student, I joined in with the white children, singing what would now be considered derogatory songs about Chinese Americans —never thinking about how I would feel if they sang songs about Black people.

At the same time, my white friends felt comfortable telling me racist jokes about Black people because I was "not like the other Blacks;" so it seemed acceptable to them. I remember feeling so distant from other Black people that I wanted to marry a white man and was scared of Black men—despite having a loving Black father and uncles and no specific incident with a Black man that made me feel this way.

Navigating Desegregation: Reflections on Bias and Social Barriers in Junior High

In 1976, school desegregation was implemented in my city, coinciding with the year I began junior high school. This policy brought a noticeable shift in the student population, as many Black children from other neighborhoods were bussed to my school. Despite the increased diversity, my own social interactions remained limited, as I was enrolled in the "superior ability" classes, which were still predominantly white. I found myself hesitant to engage with the new Black students, largely due to my preconceived notions, unfamiliarity, and implicit biases. I was unacquainted with the cultural expressions and slang they used; and, in my own internalized racism, I mistakenly viewed these differences as deficits. My hesitation to interact with the Black students was influenced by a narrow and privileged worldview shaped by segregation and unequal educational opportunities. Upon reflection, I now recognize that my reluctance to connect was not merely about cultural unfamiliarity, but also a reflection of the systemic barriers and implicit biases that separated students along racial and socioeconomic lines.

This experience serves as a reminder of how segregation—whether de jure or de facto—can shape perceptions, limit opportunities for meaningful cross-cultural interactions, and reinforce racial divisions. My own internalized racism, fostered by the unequal social structures of that time, prevented me from seeing the new students as peers with equal worth and potential. Once, while walking down a hallway in junior high, a Black student stopped me and said angrily, "You think you're white and better than everyone else." I was surprised because I didn't know her. It disturbed me; but I just accepted that I didn't fit in with the Black kids and felt more comfortable with the white kids. I remember even saying that I got along better with white people than Black people. As a result, I adopted a perspective similar to my white counterparts, viewing me and my siblings as the "good" Black kids—different from and, in our minds, somehow "better" than the Black students.

Struggling to Belong: A High School Experience of Integration, Isolation, and Academic Achievement

While I was in high school, a race riot erupted. Even though Milwaukee schools were now legally integrated, it did not mean that everyone got along. Many of my white friends had moved out of the neighborhood. At that time I didn't know what white flight was. I just knew that my friends were moving to the surrounding suburbs and no longer attended our neighborhood school. At the time of the race riot, I was volunteering in the high school office and had a clear view of the chaos. I remember feeling scared and blaming the Black students for the violence—even though I didn't know and still don't know what triggered it. I recall thinking that things were fine until they started busing in the kids (Black) from the inner city—or as my white friends would say, "the core". My mother decided it wasn't safe for my twin brother and me to stay in that newly integrated school; so she transferred us to a parochial school where she believed we would be safer.

At the parochial school, we may have been "safe" physically, but not emotionally or psychologically. I never fit in at that school, with either the few Black students or the white students. I went from being an "A" student at the previous school to getting Cs in my new school. I would purposely miss the bus and arrive late to school, hiding under my hood with my head on my desk. No one cared enough to question why. I felt friendless and out of place. Every day for a year and a half, I begged my mother to take me out of that school. She finally relented and put my brother and me back in the school we had attended before, where the race riot had occurred.

When I returned to my former school, it was like I had never left. Students and teachers greeted me in the hallways as if nothing had changed. There were fewer white students and more Black students, but I never heard of any more violence. I got involved in various extracurricular activities; and my grades improved. Despite graduating near the top of my class, I received no academic guidance from the white counselors. A week before graduation, my white counselor called me into her office, handed me gold and green cords, and informed me that I was receiving academic honors and had qualified for the National Honor Society. She told me to wear the cords with my cap and gown at the ceremony the following week.

Finding My Path: Confronting Bias and Seeking Belonging Beyond High School

After graduating from high school, I had no idea what to do next. I wanted to go to college but didn't know where to start. I took a job as a nurse's aide in a nursing home and then enrolled in a community college to study commercial art. However, after a white instructor mocked my work in front of the class, I figured I wasn't ready for college and dropped out without officially withdrawing—leaving those grades on my transcript to this day.

Eventually, I ended up working at the Milwaukee County courthouse, where I saw firsthand how power dynamics played out. Most of the clerks/workers were Black; and the majority of the lawyers were white. While a few lawyers respected the clerks, many treated us like we were their servants and tried to order us around. The way we were treated was disturbing to me. I loved that one of my Black co-workers would always stand up to the lawyers and insist that they respect her. I never got to that point; but instead of standing up to them, I would keep my distance.

After two years, I left the courthouse to attend Jimmy Swaggart Bible College (JSBC) in Baton Rouge, Louisiana. I still had the mindset shaped by past experiences where I unconsciously leaned towards white people, and distanced myself from my own people. At that time, I believed that a religious setting would be different; I thought that there I would find a space based on unity and love. I expected Bible college to be a place where race wouldn't matter and where everyone would treat each other equally; but I quickly realized how naive I was. Baton Rouge was struggling with the same racist problems that Milwaukee was dealing with. In addition to that, the conservative white leadership of JSBC mirrored societal patterns and reinforced the marginalization of minority perspectives. In that space, racism was still very much present. Black students were expected to assimilate and experienced subtle and overt acts of racism, including stereotyping, exclusion and lack of sensitivity from peers and faculty. White students would frequently turn their faces away when I greeted them refusing to return my greeting. The head preacher delivered fiery sermons, claiming that Black people were cursed. He argued that this "curse" explained both the color of their skin and their current social circumstances. A major incident occurred when a white student song leader started dating a Black student. The leaders intervened, sitting him down and telling him that the Bible forbade interracial relationships. I was so hurt, angered, and confused by the hypocrisy when I know that the Bible says, "How can you say that you love God, but don't love your brother?" (John 4:20). Here were these Bible-toting Christians acting like Black people were lower than white people in God's eyes so they couldn't date or marry one another.

From Internalized Racism to Critical Race Theory: A Journey of Transformation

When I couldn't handle the hypocrisy anymore, my then-boyfriend and I left the Bible college. We married and started our family. Both of us unknowingly exhibited symptoms of internalized racism. We listened to conservative talk shows like Rush Limbaugh and his local counterparts and moved to the suburbs so that our children could attend "better" schools. I realize now that I had not abandoned my belief that we were the "good" Black family and that my desire to fit in with white people led us to move to the suburbs.

How did I go from that mindset to arguing with my son? For several years, I owned an in-home childcare program, which I closed when we had three children under the age of two. As our four children grew older, I felt they no longer needed me as much. After being a stay-at-home mom for a while, I decided to go back to school once the youngest started school. I discovered that some of my previous college credits could be applied toward a degree in Community Engagement & Education, which seemed perfect for me. Most of the courses were online; and one of the focus areas was childcare, in which I already had forty credits.

The program required additional credits in education policy and cultural diversity, with courses such as Community Issues, Policies, and Solutions; Communities and Neighborhoods in America; Cultural Foundations of Education; and Introduction to Community Action and Change. In these courses, I began to learn about the complexities of racism and understand why I felt uncomfortable in both worlds. I didn't feel like I fit in the white world and did not really feel like I fit in Black society. I felt a deep discomfort navigating between the two. In predominantly white spaces, I often felt out of place, as if I didn't truly belong. However, my interactions within Black communities also felt uneasy, as my life experiences kept me from feeling fully connected. This left me in a confusing space, where I felt disconnected from both cultural spheres, struggling to find where I fit.

When I first started taking college courses that addressed diversity and other race-related topics, all of my instructors were white. I quickly realized that just because they taught these subjects didn't mean they were fully aware or "woke" themselves. In one class, we read articles blaming the Black family for the so-called achievement gap—claiming that Black families historically don't value education, which explained why their children don't do well in school. In another class, Black neighborhoods were discussed derogatorily. Several of the classes promoted deficit views of people from lower socio-economic status and from marginalized cultural groups.

While taking those classes, I often felt frustrated—and sometimes outraged—by the biased views the white professors presented to students. I argued online with classmates who agreed with the instructors' perspectives and frequently wondered about my classmates' racial and ethnic identities. Since I couldn't know for certain, I found myself guessing based on their names. Even when the instructor intervened in our disagreements, it didn't help—they were the ones teaching these so-called facts. I was furious that students would leave the class with negative views of Black families; and I was angry at the instructors and researchers for perpetuating such harmful stereotypes.

To get my grades, I went along and gave the responses the instructors wanted. In one class, the end-of-year survey asked what we had learned. I wrote, "To say what the instructor wants you to say to get your grade." The instructor wasn't happy with that and emailed me about my comment. Since I had already received my grade, I ignored his email and made sure not to take any more of his classes.

One class was markedly different than some of the others. A class with Dr. Julie Kailin became a defining moment in my life. It completely shifted my worldview. Before that, I was still carrying the beliefs shaped by the conservative talk shows that I listened to, the news media, and the white people that I still hung around with who minimized or denied the reality of systemic racism. I had internalized these views, thinking that issues of race were largely isolated, exaggerated or part of the past. But Dr. Kailin's class, with its focus on antiracist education, shattered those illusions.

Her book, *Antiracist Education from Theory to Practice*, became a catalyst for my transformation. I devoured the text in just a week, highlighting every page as I began to learn about and confront uncomfortable truths about white America. The real turning point was the day Dr. Kailin showed us a video that chronicled the ongoing oppression of Black people, starting from Reconstruction through the 1970s. The footage was brutally honest about how white supremacy and systemic racism shaped every facet of Black life. It left me utterly devastated. It was like the foundation of everything I had believed up to that point crumbled beneath me.

Suddenly, I saw everything in a different light. The conservative talk shows I listened to, the neighborhood I grew up in, my Bible college experiences, and even the friendships I had—everything felt tainted by a false narrative. After watching the video, when Dr. Kailin asked us, "So how do you feel?" I could only answer with one word: hopeless. That feeling of despair was shared by other students of color in the room; but as we talked and discussed the video, I began to see Black people differently. We had survived despite centuries of intentional, systemic oppression—and that survival was a testament to our strength and power.

After that class, I walked to my car in silence, consumed by anger and resentment towards white people—feelings that were new and overwhelming. That anger stayed with me; but I eventually learned to channel it into something productive, something that drives the work I do today. That experience marked the moment when I could no longer ignore the truth. It fundamentally changed not just how I viewed white people, Black people, society as a whole and also myself. I became committed to fighting for justice and equity.

After that class, I continued working towards my degree, I completed the required courses and enrolled in every course related to race. My goal was to comprehensively understand racism and whiteness. When I was introduced to Critical Race Theory (CRT)—it resonated with me and captivated me like none other. CRT is a framework developed by legal scholars such as Derrick Bell, Kimberlé Crenshaw, and Richard Delgado that critically examines how race and racism are embedded within legal systems and social structures, arguing that racism is not merely individual bias but a systemic and enduring feature of American society (Crenshaw, 1995; Delgado & Stefancic, 2017). Working in childcare at the time, I was able to relate firsthand how the tenets of CRT applied to the treatment of Black childcare providers in my state. I could relate its tenets to other areas of my life—the courthouse, Bible college, and even my feelings that I had about myself as a Black American. CRT gave me language and context for experiences I had long struggled to articulate.

Breaking the Cycle: Confronting Internalized Racism and Creating a Legacy of Change

Looking back on my journey, I now realize how long it took me to recognize and confront my own internalized racism. Growing up in a predominantly white environment, I struggled with a sense of inadequacy, constantly feeling the need to prove myself equal to my white peers, even when my abilities surpassed theirs. I didn't know the term "internalized racism" at the time, but I fully embodied it. My experiences living in a predominantly white neighborhood, attending school with, and working alongside white people shaped my views of my own people and contributed to my internalized racism. Despite having positive Black role models, including my active father, I harbored an unfounded fear of Black men, influenced by media portrayals, my peers, and overheard conversations. I now understand that my son, growing up in a household where both parents struggled with similar issues, needed time and understanding—not just one conversation—to grasp the complexities of racism.

My college years taught me that diversity programs don't always translate to culturally responsive teaching, and that academic research often neglects the realities of Black families—instead blaming them for systemic issues that perpetuate inequality. Dr. Kailin's class and discovering Critical Race Theory opened my eyes to the pervasive nature of racism. It helped me understand how growing up in a predominantly white environment shaped my identity and influenced my internalization of negative racial perceptions. How could I have expected my son to navigate differently when he faced similar circumstances—growing up in a white-majority neighborhood, hearing negative discussions about Black people, and attending schools that perpetuated stereotypes? It's no surprise that our children seemed to be following the same path.

When my son challenged my concerns about white people, it forced me to confront my deep-seated biases and my own journey with internalized racism. Since then, my son and I have had many meaningful conversations about racism and internalized racism. We've discussed his experiences growing up in a white neighborhood, attending a predominantly white school, and his experiences as a young Black man in a society that marginalizes Black males. There were tears and anger as he shared how he had been treated in the schools we had paid for him to attend and in the colleges he chose to attend—tears because I was unaware of how he had been treated, and anger that I had no knowledge of those parts of his life and had not been there to intercede on his behalf. No mother wants her child to experience the pain that racism brings especially after dealing with it herself for a lifetime.

Now, as a Black motherscholar, the work I do is not just for me, but for my children, grandchildren, and all Black children—whether it is writing about bias in early childhood textbooks, teaching workshops on culturally responsive practices, or as a researcher leading a team of action researchers focused on the success and retention of Black students. I don't want them to face the same struggles I, my son, and so many others have had to endure. I don't want any child to have to struggle with internalized racism because of living in a white-oriented society where they are not valued and their Blackness is not celebrated. My scholarship is about creating spaces of belonging, promoting diversity, and striving for equity. It's about ensuring that every Black child, from birth through college, feels seen, valued, and understood. In my heart, I consider all Black children—my babies. My commitment to this work runs deep because I want to leave a legacy of change, where the next generation of Black children can thrive in ways we could only dream of.

Competing Interests

The author has no conflicts of interest to declare that are relevant to the content of this manuscript.

References

Crenshaw, K. W. (1995). *Critical race theory: The key writings that formed the movement*. The New Press.

David, E. J. R. (2019). *Internalized oppression: The psychology of marginalized groups*. Springer Publishing Company.

Delgado, R., & Stefancic, J. (2017). *Critical race theory: An introduction* (3rd ed.). NYU Press.

Helms, J. E. (2017). Racial identity theory and research: Contributions and challenges. In J. G. Ponterotto, Y. S. Foo, P. B. Pedersen, W. J. Lonner, & J. G. Draguns (Eds.), *Handbook of multicultural counseling* (4th ed., pp. 41–52). SAGE Publications.

Tummala-Narra, P. (2016). Conceptualizing racial trauma: Theoretical models and psychological impact. *Psychoanalytic Psychology, 33*(2), 263–273. https://doi.org/10.1037/pap0000069

We Ain't Going if She Can't Come with Me: An Auto-Biography of a Black Single Mama Who Walked Across EVERY Stage with Her Daughter

Daphanie N. Bibbs

Abstract With my daughter's arrival on August 31, 2015, I embraced motherhood. Yet, it wasn't until 2018 that I fully embraced single motherhood and queerness. Upon graduating in 2017, I hesitated to pursue graduate studies, fearing oppressive environments. Drawing from the wisdom of bell hooks, Patricia Hill-Collins (2022), and Simone Browne, I'll explore my experiences in anti-black educational spaces. Instances like being scrutinized for my pumping schedule or denied the joy of holding my daughter during graduation underscore these challenges. Using autoethnography, I examine my personal experiences as a Black single mother scholar navigating predominantly white institutions (Ellis, 2004; Holman Jones, 2005).

Keyword Autoethnography · Black motherhood · Queer Black mothers

> Seeing my mother cross the stage was wonderful. She became a teacher; and now I want to be a teacher. My mother is very fun. She is always there for me; and I am for her. Seeing her cross the stage every time is great. I'll be seeing it again in 2027, seeing her complete her journey is one for me! - Amiyah Bibbs, age 9 (Daughter of Daphanie N. Bibbs).

As a Black single and queer motherscholar navigating predominantly white educational spaces, I have encountered a multitude of challenges that have deeply impacted my academic journey. These experiences have ranged from being scrutinized for the timing of my pumping schedule to being denied the "simple" yet profound opportunity to hold my daughter during my graduation ceremony. These moments have not only tested my resilience but also shaped my sense of identity and belonging within the academic realm.

In this chapter, I delve into these personal experiences, offering a reflective examination of how such encounters have influenced my sense of self and my place within academia. Through this introspective approach, I aim to illuminate the intricate ways in which these challenges have intersected with my identity and aspirations. My hope

D. N. Bibbs (✉)
University at Buffalo, Buffalo, NY, US
e-mail: Daphanie@buffalo.edu

C. R. Turner and M. L. Green (eds.), *Black Motherscholarship Within and Beyond the Academy*, https://doi.org/10.1007/978-3-031-99758-7_19

is that this chapter will resonate deeply with readers, offering a glimpse into each stage of my journey. As you engage with my narrative, I invite you to reflect on the barriers and obstacles that persist within both private and public academic institutions. It is my sincere aspiration that this reflection will inspire a concerted effort to dismantle these barriers, fostering the creation of safe, inclusive spaces where motherscholars like myself are seen and valued—not just for our academic contributions, but also for our humanity, our wholeness, and our unapologetic presence in the scholarly community.

Stage 1: Internal Acceptance

Shortly after transferring from a university in Louisiana to one in Missouri, I was brimming with excitement about the new opportunities ahead. As an aspiring speech pathologist, I was eager to dive into my studies and explore the experiences awaiting me, particularly since I was now closer to my hometown of Chicago, IL. The spring semester began to highlight the many facets of my identity—both those I embraced and those I suppressed out of fear of judgment. Toward the end of that semester, I received the thrilling news that I had been accepted to teach abroad in South Africa. This opportunity felt like a significant step toward achieving my dreams and truly "becoming somebody." However, just a few weeks later, I discovered that I was pregnant. My emotions were a complex mix of excitement and denial.

I was extremely excited because, in the months leading up to my university transfer, I had often dreamed of holding a baby in my arms and felt a deep sense of joy at the thought. This vision was one among many; I had previously envisioned myself as a motivational speaker, a special education teacher, and eventually as Dr. Bibbs. Most of these dreams had begun to take shape, except for the last one. Yet, at the same time, I felt a sense of denial. At 20-years-old, still in college, and striving to establish myself professionally, I feared that my mother would be disappointed in my pregnancy and ultimately struggled with how this new reality would fit into my carefully laid personal and professional plans.

Embracing the Future Ahead

After digesting the news of my pregnancy, I visited the student health center on campus to inquire about counseling services for students. Immediately after sharing my story, I was met with several pamphlets outlining options of abortion and adoption by a non-Black male counselor. Proposing these services instead of listening first is one of the barriers Black mothers face. Adoption and/abortion shouldn't be the initial assumption of professionals who should have both the knowledge and skill set to foster independent decision-making at moments such as these. Although it was assumed that I was considering options of early termination instead of embracing the future ahead, I resisted and requested to speak to a counselor who identified as a woman in effort to experience another human who could potentially understand the future ahead and create a site of resistance and sense of "homeplace" (hooks, 1994) for my mental and emotional well-being. "Thankfully," the counselor I was assigned to, identified as a woman and was also pregnant at the time therapy sessions began.

As a result of her being extremely understanding of my circumstances, I began to trust my intuition and to lean into my ancestral power, which led to my entrance to the stage of internal acceptance. Accepting that I would be a young single mother also meant that I would go through periods of grief and loss. I always knew I would be successful in any profession I chose; but for the first time, I experienced doubt and engaged in negative self-talk. Could I really be as successful as I want to be and still be a "good mother?" was a question I posed to myself over and over again. Fortunately, my counselor allowed me to change my initial thoughts of therapy, learn to trust my own instinct, and unpack the underlying trauma that caused my fear of becoming a "good mother".

I gave birth to my daughter several months after completing a rigorous period of talk therapy, during which I had worked diligently to address my personal challenges and better understand myself. By the time my daughter arrived, I felt well-prepared to meet her needs and to honor both her needs and my own. I was confident in my ability to navigate the demands of motherhood while continuing to pursue my goals. Yet, amidst this new stage, I found myself grappling with a profound question: Who was I now? Was I still the same Daphanie who, with unwavering resolve, took the initiative to accomplish every goal I set for myself? The Daphanie who, driven by ambition and a clear vision, relentlessly pursued her aspirations with a determined spirit? I wondered if I was still the same Daphanie who had dedicated herself to earning a doctoral degree—a goal that required immense dedication and resilience. Could I still be that individual who had actively sought out every opportunity that would bring me closer to my dreams and align me with my true purpose in life?

Reevaluating My Identity

The arrival of my daughter brought about significant changes, both externally and internally. The responsibilities of motherhood introduced new challenges and priorities that sometimes made it difficult to see myself through the same lens as before. I was confronted with the task of balancing the demands of raising a child with the pursuit of my personal and professional aspirations. This balancing act required reevaluating my identity and understanding how to integrate my new role as a mother with my previously held ambitions. Despite these changes, I realized that while my circumstances had evolved, the essence of who I was remained intact. My core values and drive did not disappear; rather, they adapted to encompass my new responsibilities. I continued to be the person who strived for excellence, sought out opportunities for growth, and was deeply committed to my goals. The journey of motherhood did not diminish my identity but rather expanded it, adding new dimensions of strength, resilience, and purpose.

Ultimately, I came to understand that the Daphanie who once set goals and chased dreams was still very much present. She had simply evolved into a new version of herself—one who now embraced the multifaceted role of being both a dedicated mother and a passionate pursuer of her professional aspirations. This evolution was not a loss of identity but a testament to my ability to grow and adapt, integrating all aspects of who I am into a harmonious whole.

Stage 2: Discourse and Confusion from Those Who *Should* Support Me

Before going into labor, I spoke with my professor in an effort to let them know of potential changes and future work extension requests. I received messages from professors that seemed supportive and empathetic but was also met with various forms of resistance resulting in my return to class (in-person) two weeks after giving birth. I returned to class early out of fear of not being able to keep up with coursework and being viewed as "unproductive" by professors who voiced how challenging it would be to keep up if I were to fall behind and request more than one extension.

Resisting Hegemony

Upon returning to class, I shared with professors that I may need to excuse myself for pumping sessions. Many professors approved and acknowledged the need for me to leave class periodically while some professors shared grievances regarding the matter. Those grievances included: exiting the class frequently would be disruptive to the learning environment of students in class and would result in me missing content covered in class. I remember vividly being positioned to defend myself during class one evening when the professor, who was a woman, suggested I change my pumping schedule in order to prevent me exiting and re-entering the classroom environment.

On this particular evening of class, my then 4-month-old daughter was with me. She began to cry because she was hungry; so I decided to nurse her with my left arm and held my notebook and took notes with my right. This experience was particularly traumatic considering the entire class consisted of 20 students, 2 being Black and 1 being Black and a single mom (me). I was often propositioned with inquiries about if I had a husband and if I needed help— a matter of unsolicited surveillance, racism and lack of respect to my personhood, womanhood and motherhood. Hegemonic and heteronormative views of traditional family structures (a two-parent household) are idolized in mainstream media and lead to an overall perception that single parents

Fig. 1 Mommy and daughter share moments of Facetime during an evening class (2015)

often lead to bad or problematic parenting as well as that single-parent households are less "ideal" and/or less functional (Fig. 1).

Extraordinary Support

I have vivid memories of the extraordinary support I received from several professors during a challenging time in my life. Their efforts went far beyond mere academic guidance; they were deeply invested in ensuring that I felt comfortable and had everything I needed to succeed. One professor, in particular, went out of her way to help me balance my responsibilities as a parent and a student. During a particularly stressful period when I had a final exam to complete, she noticed that I had brought my baby with me. Recognizing the difficulty of the situation, she kindly took my baby into her arms and rocked her to sleep while I focused on finishing my exam. This gesture allowed me to concentrate fully on my work without the added worry of my child's needs.

Another professor demonstrated remarkable empathy and thoughtfulness in a different way. When he learned that I was unable to secure reliable childcare and would need to bring my daughter to class with me, he took it upon himself to make her feel special. He organized a small birthday party for her, complete with decorations and a cake, to celebrate her special day. This act of kindness not only brightened my daughter's day but also alleviated some of the stress I was experiencing. These experiences underscored the profound impact that supportive educators can have. They went above and beyond to accommodate my circumstances, demonstrating a level of understanding and compassion that was truly remarkable. Their actions made a significant difference in my academic journey, proving that with the right support, even the most challenging situations can be managed more effectively. I firmly believe that all professors should embody this level of empathy and dedication. Such support not only enhances the academic experience but also contributes to a more inclusive and understanding educational environment for all students facing similar challenges.

Upon completing my bachelor's degree, I approached the decision to pursue graduate school with a mix of nervousness and resolve. Concerned about facing another potentially oppressive educational environment while balancing my responsibilities as a mother, I opted to complete my first graduate degree remotely. This choice was driven by a desire to avoid feelings of being unwelcome or marginalized. As a Black single mother, I frequently encountered scrutiny and judgment rooted in hegemonic and Eurocentric views of motherhood. Many colleagues questioned whether I could achieve success as a single parent; and some even assumed I had a partner helping me, unable to believe that I could manage everything on my own. Despite these challenges, I persevered, demonstrating that the strength and resilience of single mothers can defy conventional expectations and pave the way for success on our own terms.

Stage 3: Acceptance and Embodiment of Intersecting Identities

I've viewed love as expansive and exhilarating since I can remember. Before I knew anything about queerness or LGBTQIA + communities, I felt that love shouldn't be tied to a specific gender but tied to those who you feel it from the most, whether that be woman or man. As I grew into my teens, I began to feel out of place and experienced confusion regarding the pressure for women to marry men and to live life traditionally. I even questioned who and what I was attracted to, resulting in my joining my highschool's GSA as an ally. Reflecting on my teenage years, I now understand I operated as an ally to the community as a shield to protect my authentic identity from judgment and scrutiny. I come from a semi-traditional family and so much of the teachings from my parents had a biblical context tied to it. Because of this, I assumed the way I viewed love between two human beings of the same or opposite sex was wrong and ungodly.

For years, I sought the kind of love and connection portrayed in the media, only to find myself feeling increasingly disheartened and empty. The idealized images and narratives of love seemed perpetually out of reach, leaving me with a profound sense of longing. It was only when I stepped into the role of motherhood that I began to find a new sense of purpose and fulfillment. Becoming a mother was a transformative experience that redefined my understanding of love and self-worth (Fig. 2).

In my journey as a mother, I made a heartfelt promise to myself: to show my daughter that she could be whoever she wanted to be and embrace whatever and whomever she chose. I wanted to create an environment where she felt empowered to explore her identity without constraints. As I settled into my role as a parenting student, I also embarked on a personal journey to explore my own sexual identity. This

Fig. 2 Amiyah and Mommy enjoying their last days in Indiana before moving to New York (2023)

exploration involved joining Facebook support groups and seeking out LGBTQIA-friendly clubs and associations on campus.

However, I soon noticed a significant gap in these spaces. While I found some level of connection and hope in these LGBTQIA communities, I realized that many members of these organizations were not mothers. This gap highlighted a crucial missing piece: the need for spaces that foster welcoming environments that go beyond traditional binaries and cater to the full spectrum of diverse identities. The absence of such inclusive spaces left me feeling that, while progress was being made, there was still a long way to go. There is a pressing need for greater inclusivity in all areas—more inclusive language, practices, and environments that make individuals who identify as queer feel seen and valued rather than dismissed and invisible (Fig. 3).

As I approach the completion of my PhD, I am eager to enter a new phase of my life focused on developing, advocating for marginalized beings, and simply being my authentic self. This next stage is not only about continuing my personal growth but also about creating and supporting spaces where my daughter, and others like her, can feel empowered to be their true selves. My goal is to contribute to a broader

Fig. 3 Mommy and Daughter a few weeks before year 1 of Phd Program begins (2023)

culture of inclusivity that allows all individuals, regardless of their identity, to feel embraced and celebrated.

Stage 4: Resistance - We Ain't Going if She Can't Come with Me

At the culmination of my Bachelor of Science in Special Education graduation in 2017, I was overwhelmed with a profound sense of accomplishment. After enduring sleepless nights and constantly facing judgment, the hard work I put into earning my degree finally paid off. The struggles I faced along the way seemed worth it; and I felt a deep sense of perseverance and achievement. I was eagerly looking forward to walking across the stage with my daughter by my side—a symbol of the journey we had shared. However, just before the ceremony, I was informed of a rule that only the graduate was allowed to walk across the stage to receive their degree. Initially, I felt a surge of disappointment and frustration. For the first time, I chose not to concern myself with others' opinions or what they might think. I decided that this was a moment too important to compromise on.

Moments before my name was called, my father, sensing the significance of the situation, discreetly handed me my daughter. With a mixture of determination and defiance, we walked together across the stage. My family, witnessing this act of resilience, rose to their feet and cheered me on. As I reached the podium to receive

Fig. 4 Amiyah walking across the stage with her Mommy (2017)

my degree, my eyes were filled with tears, and my heart swelled with an immense sense of pride. While many professors celebrated this milestone with me, some chose to distance themselves from this moment of personal triumph as they looked away and/or shook their heads in disgruntlement. This was a pivotal moment for me—it was the first time I resolutely declared, "I'm not going if she can't come with me!" The experience reinforced my belief in standing firm for what matters most, regardless of institutional constraints or external judgements (Fig. 4).

As my professional journey advanced, I maintained a determined stride in seizing every opportunity that came my way. My daughter frequently accompanied me—whether I was teaching, attending or presenting at national and international conferences, or participating in scholarly receptions. Despite the constant presence of my daughter in these academic settings, she often received praise for being "good" and not causing distractions. This praise, while seemingly positive, reveals a deeper issue within the culture of academia (Fig. 5).

The expectation that an eight-year-old girl should be commended merely for being quiet and unobtrusive in a room full of adults underscores a troubling aspect of the academic environment. This expectation mirrors the surveillance and discipline explored by Simone Browne (2015) in her critical work. Browne's scholarship highlights how marginalized individuals, including those who deviate from conventional norms, are subjected to intense scrutiny and pressure to conform. In academic

Fig. 5 Amiyah and Mommy before teaching a course on improving social studies Ed (2023)

settings, this translates to a surveillance of behavior that disproportionately affects those who are already marginalized, including scholars with children.

Moreover, Audre Lorde's (1984) contributions as a queer scholar provide further context. Lorde's work emphasizes the importance of acknowledging and embracing intersecting identities and experiences. Her critique of the dominant culture's exclusionary practices advocates for the creation of spaces that recognize and support the full spectrum of human experience. From Lorde's (1984) perspective, the pressure to fit within rigid academic/hegemonic norms often leads to the suppression of one's true self and the marginalization of those whose lives do not conform to traditional expectations. Not fitting into heteronormativity impacted my sense of belonging in a majority of the spaces my daughter and I occupied. Lorde's work brings voice to scholars like myself who both embody and acknowledge non-traditional paths to motherhood and the needed shadow work to discover the true you!

In this context, the need to coach my daughter to minimize her presence and only interrupt in emergencies reflects a broader issue within academia. It is disheartening that children must be molded to fit an adult-centric environment, which stifles their natural behavior and diminishes the opportunity for a more inclusive academic culture. Academia should not demand that children adhere to adult standards of conduct, nor should it penalize those who bring their whole selves, including their familial responsibilities, into their professional lives. If there were more spaces and events designed with students and professionals who have children in mind, such as family-friendly policies and inclusive practices, my daughter would not have to be restrained from simply being a child. Embracing this kind of inclusive change would not only align with Lorde's and Browne's critiques of oppressive norms but also foster a more humane and supportive academic environment for all—allowing other motherscholars to uphold a stance of resistance and sharing in solidarity that WE AIN'T GOING IF OUR CHILDREN CAN'T COME!

Competing Interests

The author has no conflicts of interest to declare that are relevant to the content of this manuscript.

References

Browne, S. (2015). Dark matters: On the surveillance of Blackness. *Duke University Press*. https://doi.org/10.2307/j.ctv11cw89p

Collins, P. H. (2022). *Black feminist thought: Knowledge, consciousness, and the politics of empowerment*. Routledge.

Dharani, M. K., & Balamurugan, J. (2024). The psychosocial impact on single mothers' well-being: A literature review. *Journal of Education and Health Promotion, 13*(1). https://doi.org/10.4103/jehp.jehp_1045_23

Ellis, C. (2004). *The ethnographic I: A methodological novel about autoethnography*. AltaMira Press.

Hine, D. C. (1989). Rape and the inner lives of Black women in the Middle West: Preliminary thoughts on the culture of dissemblance. *Signs: Journal of Women in Culture and Society, 14*(4), 912–920. https://doi.org/10.1086/494508

Holman Jones, S. (2005). Autoethnography: Making the personal political. In N. K. Denzin & Y. S. Lincoln (Eds.), *Handbook of qualitative research* (pp. 763–791). SAGE Publications.

hooks, b. (2014). Homeplace: A site of resistance. In *Yearning* (2nd ed., pp. 41–50). Routledge.

Lorde, A. (1984). *Sister outsider*. Crossing Press.

Interrogations of the Mythical Norm: Using Endarkened Poetic Inquiry to Queer Black Motherscholarship

Meghan L. Green

Abstract This chapter examines the silencing and marginalization of Black queer women faculty in higher education, particularly in the context of early childhood teacher education. Exploring the intersections of race, gender, and sexual orientation, I utilized endarkened poetic inquiry to critique the societal and institutional positioning of Black queer motherscholars outside of both Black heterosexual and white women's experiences. Through the lens of scholars such as Bailey & Miller (2015), Gumbs (2010), and Lorde (1984), who have long theorized about the intersections shaping the lives of Black queer femme-identified individuals, I seek to reflect on Lorde's notion of the "mythical norm" that continues to uphold dominant narratives. This chapter offers a personal and scholarly exploration of my lived experiences as a Black queer motherscholar and calls for a reimagining of higher education institutions toward a radical futurity that embraces these intersecting identities.

Keywords Poetic inquiry · Black queer feminism · Queer motherscholarship

Introduction

Audre Lorde (1984) conceptualized the marginalization of Black queer women in the liberation movements of the 1960s; and the idea of the "mythical norm" was born out of this reflective internal dialogue. Lorde (1984) described the weight that oppressed, marginalized communities shoulder by holding the responsibility to teach our oppressors about our lived experiences. What happens when we refuse to extend this olive branch and instead talk back to the very systems that belittle our existences? This concept resonated with me as a Black queer, neurodivergent motherscholar engaging with pre-service and in-service educators in a discipline that centers white, heterosexual, able-bodied ways of being and knowing. When I step into professional spaces in my discipline, I am reminded of my otherness. It sits on me and sometimes begs me to acknowledge its presence.

M. L. Green (✉)
Erikson Institute, Chicago, IL, USA
e-mail: mgreen@erikson.edu

C. R. Turner and M. L. Green (eds.), *Black Motherscholarship Within and Beyond the Academy*, https://doi.org/10.1007/978-3-031-99758-7_20

In this chapter, I hope to trouble the "mythical norm", specifically in early childhood teacher education, and present my truths for a (re)imagined possibility towards radical futurity as a Black queer motherscholar. To this end, the following question guided this endarkened poetic inquiry: *How have I used poetry to process my experiences as an early career Black queer motherscholar outside of the "mythical norm"?* I find myself struggling to be fully seen as an early career scholar in a world that prioritizes productivity over wellness even when folks in leadership express their beliefs in such ideals. There seems to be this unspoken agreement to look the other way when faculty express their concerns with the way things are. A common refrain keeps playing, "You are the only one telling us this, so you must be the problem." Feelings of isolation and disbelief creep in, and the choice becomes clear. As the only Black queer faculty member, I can decide to remain silent or leave the space entirely to protect my peace. Yet, it is sobering to realize that I was never standing alone outside of the margins.

You Were Never Alone: Black Queer Women's Experiences in Academia

Researchers have theorized for decades about how the intersections of race, gender, and sexual identity impact the experiences of Black queer femme identifying individuals in an array of spaces (Bailey & Miller, 2015; Glover, 2017; Gumbs, 2010; Gumbs et al, 2016; hooks & McKinnon, 1996; Hull et al., 1982; Lewis & Miller, 2018; Lorde, 1984; Smith, 2000). Glover (2017) argued that the silencing of Black queer women in institutions of higher education is the result of the intersections of race, gender, and sexual orientation. Black queer motherscholars' experiences are positioned outside of the margins of white women and Black heterosexual folks.

Truth-Telling from the Margins

There are some in academia who admonish individuals who speak publicly about the harms they have experienced within institutions of higher education. Referred to as *margin talk* by Lewis and Miller (2018), Black queer femme individuals' hushed testimonies provide insight into the ways we acknowledge each other's spirits in spaces that seek to diminish us. We are often told that our sexual identities should come second to racial solidarity to stand most effectively against patriarchal white supremacist regimes (Bailey & Miller, 2015; Glover, 2017; Morrow, 2023). This kind of ethnocentric heteronormativity does not serve us; it only pushes us further away from the Black feminist goals of liberation for all minoritized communities.

Quite often, our very presence upsets the tight restrictions white heteronormative binaries have placed on what is possible in academia and who belongs in these halls.

Being out as a Black queer professor is an act of testifying that boldly proclaims, "I'm the professor and I want you to get your life in here, to ensure that living your life is a possibility for you" (Lewis & Miller, 2018, p. 82). A sense of belonging is more than just a jovial feeling; it is an act that affirms the value of one's presence in a space. When I show up unapologetically as a Black queer professor, I am extending this affirmation to students of all gender and sexual identities and creating a learning community where every person is seen and celebrated. Over the last three years, queer and trans students enrolled in my courses have voiced their appreciation for my authenticity when sharing my truths. While the power of representation is not lost on me, I do feel the weight of tokenism. Black queer feminist scholars have routinely documented the troubles associated with being the sole queer faculty member of Color when institutional power structures favor students' comfort over the well-being and humanity of queer and trans faculty of Color (Bailey & Miller, 2015; Glover, 2017). My experiences as an early career Black queer motherscholar in early childhood teacher education are no different. I am often the first Black queer professor students have encountered in their post-secondary education. In a discipline steeped in epistemic violence against anyone from a minoritized background, I have encountered backlash from students and administrators alike when enacting a liberatory praxis (Broughton, 2022). Unfortunately, showing up whole often means positioning oneself as a target for the vitriol hurled at those right outside of the margins of the academy. Our survival in institutions of higher education is less about our individual successes and more about our collective possibilities (Gumbs, 2010; Morrow, 2023).

M(othering) Ourselves in the Academy

Black queer motherscholars have modeled authenticity by showing up unapologetically whole and practicing the kind of radical self-love that has sustained queer and trans communities for generations (Gumbs, 2010). We learned to nurture the most intimate parts of ourselves out of necessity and a desire to love in recognition of differences as opposed to in spite of (Lorde, 1984). In ivory towers that have long demonstrated their inability to love us back, Black queer motherscholars adhere to Lorde's (1984) call:

> Mothering ourselves means learning to love what we have given birth to by giving definition to, learning how to be both kind and demanding in the teeth of failure as well as in the face of success, and not misnaming either. (p. 169)

Morrow (2023) documented the radical ways that Black queer educators embodied Black queer joy as a means of thriving in the academy. Instead of focusing exclusively on our trauma responses, Morrow (2023) lifted the notion of *Black Queer Revolutionary Selfhood*—defined as a "demand for our humanity and the freedom to show up as our complete self, disavowing those who want us to assimilate or wish us dead" (para. 13).

Bailey and Miller (2015) reflected on their experiences as Black queer women teaching undergraduate students in the southern section of the United States. They focused on the emotions associated with their experiences in academia. After reading their powerful and transparent narratives, I realized that my own experiences were not figments of my imagination. I was not recklessly overreacting or assuming anything. This chapter is my battle cry and an expression of my lived experiences in spaces that often value only pieces of who I am.

Positioning

Intersectional Checklist:

- ✔ *Black*
- ✔ *Queer*
- ✔ *Femme presenting cis woman*
- ✔ *Mother*
- ✔ *Poet*
- ✔ *Tenure track faculty member*

When I was a freshman in college, I read Audre Lorde's (1982) "Zami: A New Spelling of My Name" for the first time. I felt a sense of belonging and kinship that I had never felt before. The text became a staple in my collection of prose and poetry by Black queer and trans artists. I had entered a new era of self-awareness as I consumed works by creative folks who lived and loved as I did. Folks who had always felt more comfortable just left of center—beyond the snug confines of a binary. I carried the lessons I learned from other Black queer and trans kindred spirits with me as I continued to graduate school and over the course of my twenty-year career as an early childhood educator. My appreciation of the nuances of my racialized and gendered identities grew as I started to value the fluidity of marginal galaxies. Instead of trying to place myself on one end or another on a binary scale, I embraced the messiness of both/and.

In the present inquiry, I offer my experiences in academia as a faculty member over the last three years. The shift from working primarily with young children to working with adults in higher education has been jarring at times. Before earning my doctorate, I taught pre-kindergarten to 4th grade for fifteen years and facilitated trainings on educator well-being and anti-bias and anti-racist early childhood education in the southwestern region of the United States (U.S.). I accepted a post-doctoral research position soon after graduating in May 2022. Accepting this position meant quickly relocating my family to the midwestern region of the U.S. I found myself immersed in an academic world that was a far cry from where I had spent the previous six years during my doctoral studies; and I felt wholly unprepared for the journey.

I had to leave my carefully curated Black queer and trans fictive kinship community behind to advance in my profession. Admittedly, I worried about the impact of this move on me and my children's well-being. My sons, ages 10 and 12 at the time, had grown up surrounded by a community of co-parents. Like other queer mothers, I have depended on fictive kinship communities and communal parenting for support, both during my doctoral studies and in my first years on the tenure track (Gumbs, 2016; Whittington, 2023). When I began my first year as an assistant professor of early childhood teacher education in July 2023, I once again looked to my community for support with mothering responsibilities. From depending on family members and friends to watch my sons while I travelled to academic conferences during the school year to requesting financial assistance for the boys' extracurricular activities, co-parenting as a Black queer motherscholar has always involved folks outside of my romantic partners. It is a communal act that includes a broad network of people in different spheres of my children's lives (Whittington, 2023).

The transition from a close-knit graduate school community to the publish or perish culture so prevalent in most research-intensive colleges and universities is often overwhelming to even the most prepared first year tenure track assistant professors (Bailey & Miller, 2015). Utilizing endarkened feminist epistemology and poetic inquiry, I sought to use the power of poetry to talk back to the mainstream discourse of higher education and to explore how I understand my positionality as a Black queer motherscholar inside/outside of academia. My constellation poems present my journey as a daughter of rural southwest Louisiana, a mother, an early childhood teacher educator, and an arts-based qualitative researcher in and along the margins of identity—just outside of the "mythical norm". Throughout the following chapter, I explore how I navigated this transition and enacted my vision of Black queer joy and Black queer revolutionary selfhood (Morrow, 2023).

Theoretical Frameworks

The present inquiry was grounded in Black queer feminism (Bonsu, 2018). Bonsu (2018) described Black queer feminism as a theoretical lens and praxis that draws upon both Black feminist and queer theories. As a Black feminist researcher, my work is guided by an understanding of self-definition and empowerment through cooperative means (Collins, 2000). Disrupting the binary of self or community means shifting my gaze towards ways to hold space for both. In the current work, I situate my personal experiences in the larger context of Black queer motherscholars across space and time.

Queer theory offers a fluid view of womanhood outside of the strict binary reproductions of race and gender (Cohen, 1997). Queerness is understood not as a description of one's sexual or romantic attractions, but instead as an act of interrogating the norm and introducing new possibilities (Cohen, 1997). Queer theorists reject heteronormativity as the standard and actively work towards radical freedom dreams rooted in revolutionary aims (Gumbs, 2016). Within the current chapter, I focus on the ways that Black queer feminism teaches us how to "[center] the voices and experiences of historically silenced and vulnerable groups within Black communities, including those that are queer, trans*, femme, poor, disabled, and undocumented" (Bonsu, 2018, p. 214). I applied a Black queer feminist lens to this inquiry by exploring how I have learned to mother myself within academia as a Black queer motherscholar in search of a brave space to call my own (Gumbs, 2010).

Endarkened Poetic Inquiry: Constellation Poems as Guides

Poetic inquiry as an arts-based qualitative research method seeks "to show embodiment and reflexivity, to collapse the false divide between body and mind, public and private…" (see Faulkner, 2018, p. 4). Endarkened feminist epistemology is understood as:

> How reality is known when based in the historical roots of Black feminist thought, embodying a distinguishable difference in cultural standpoint, located in the intersection/overlap of the culturally constructed socializations of race, gender, and other identities and the historical and contemporary contexts of oppressions and resistance for African American women. (Dillard, 2000, p. 662)

Through an artful blending of endarkened feminist epistemology (Dillard, 2000) and poetic inquiry (Cutts & Waters, 2019), I developed endarkened poetic inquiry (EPI) as a methodological framework that reflects Black women scholars' understanding of how the intersections of our identities impact our roles as educators and arts-based qualitative researchers. Cutts (2019) described *ars spirituality* as the embodiment of Black women's transformational knowing and being— describing Black women's poetry as "born of the spirit" (p. 917). Within EPI, this spiritual component is connected to Black women's embodied onto-epistemological traditions and is central to the inquiry process. EPI grants arts-based inquirers the opportunity to re-story the descriptive details of one's everyday life by honoring the complexity of memories and crafting poetic pieces that hold profound meaning through an intentional melding of self and communal relations to human and more-than-human imaginings.

Data Collection and Analysis

Black women's acts of conjuring have commonly been associated with the supernatural (Brooks et al., 2021; Harris, 2018; Pryse & Spillers, 1985). Our methods of storytelling are associated with otherworldly forms of signifying and testimony. Throughout this inquiry, I have relied upon my ancestral knowledge and ways of being. I have also trusted my intuition in ways that felt natural. Rejecting the positivist stance of objectivity, I embraced the opportunity to conjure new possibilities for inquiry with a research methodology that extended my understanding of the intangible (Brooks et al., 2021; Fearon, 2024).

Evans-Winters and Esposito (2018) noted, women researchers of Color should not be forced to adhere to the dominant notion of objectivity whereby our lived experiences are separated from our results and conclusions. My process was not linear or neatly defined. I rummaged through my previously shared public social media posts, text message exchanges with family and friends, emails, and private journal entries from June 2022 to January 2025 to find keywords, phrases, and sentences that captured my feelings in those moments. Then, I combined those found pieces into lyric poems "with a focus on my *self* to evoke emotional resonance with readers" (Quynh Phan, 2023, p. 2). After composing each constellation poem, I read the piece aloud and processed how it made me feel to activate the sacredness Dillard (2016) spoke of. By giving literal voice to each poem, I was able to hear the subtleties of each emotion I expressed and make necessary revisions based on how the piece resonated with me. Like constellations in a midnight sky, my emotions served as my guide towards something like a homeplace (Green, 2023).

Tales from the Multiverse

In this next section, my original poems are followed by narratives that provide more insight into how these pieces of my mosaic somehow fit together to inform how I made sense of my experiences. Within the following poems, I explicate themes around how I used poetry to make sense of my first years as an early career scholar. Since 2022, I have processed my experiences as a Black queer motherscholar through three lenses: (1) writing as catharsis; (2) writing as protection; and (3) writing as testimony.

Maiden, Mother, Crone: Writing as Catharsis

"Ode to (in)visible Struggles"
We smile to hide deep scars
Placed on hearts worn on our sleeves.
Scars that have scabbed over
And healed from the outside looking in.
They never heal though…not really.
They continue to fester behind smiles
Bright enough to light up any room.
Smiles that have cracked at the corners
And created more doubt than comfort.
They never bring comfort though…not really.
They provide a testimony for those
Who witnessed each slow death.
Deaths that seem surprising
And cause onlookers to question.

They never ask the right questions though...not really.

I was diagnosed with bi-polar disorder II when I was an undergraduate student. My mental health was always the specter that went bump in the night. It was also the thing people weaponized most against me when I stepped just outside what they considered appropriate or normal. Folks in academia continue to do the same thing. In the poem above, I grappled with the concept of visibility and (re)membering old wounds. As stated in lines 3 and 4—"Scars that have scabbed over/And healed from the outside looking in"— these wounds from the past appear superficially healed. Some of the scars I entered academia with were ones created by external calls for me to prioritize my head over my heart. Even though people around me praised the passion I brought to projects, they also recommended that I shield my emotions and focus more on logic. I felt like I was being asked to replicate the disembodied white supremacist, heteronormative stance Lorde (1984) cautioned against—"The white fathers told us: I think, therefore I am. The Black mother within each of us—the poet—whispers in our dreams: I feel, therefore I can be free" (p. 27). Through an intense exploration of my feelings, I discovered an appreciation for the beauty of things I had hidden away in myself.

My journey over the last three years has also included a struggle against externally (and sometimes internally) enforced binaries. I spent my first year as a faculty member establishing my voice in higher education. My turning point was the realization that I would be eaten alive if I continued to allow other people's comfort to dictate how I existed. When I transitioned away from my closest family and friends to join the tenure track, I wondered about the connections I would make with people in a new space. I was fortunate enough to build community with a few individuals who showed me grace and care as our bonds deepened. Despite these positive connections, however, I still felt at odds with the lack of Black queer and trans communal love and understanding. To truly embody a deep level of authenticity would mean taking off the masks I felt compelled to wear so often as a Black queer motherscholar. Moving forward, however, I have decided to be okay feeling everything at once and holding space for what it means to write as an act of catharsis—simultaneously letting go to hold on.

Green Thumbs and Numbness: Writing as Protection

"In My Mother's Eyes"
When the gods speak, heaven
Listens as a Black mother is forced
To bear the sorrow of burying her children.
Her world is ripped asunder as her
Steadfast dreams emphasize the
Interconnected nature of survival.
Crossing invisible borders,

She recovers her strength as the mold cools
And then shatters to reveal the final product:
the perpetuity of life for black people.

Alice Walker (2004) described Black women's search for our mothers' gardens as a metaphorical exploration of our foremothers' creative outlets. Her work has resonated with me as the daughter of a poet who often hid her words from the unforgiving eyes of onlookers. My first memories of poetry were inspired by my mother, and it was in her garden that I found the strength to express my emotions in lyrics and rhymes. Each word was a seedling buried just beneath the surface of rich black soil, waiting to eventually sprout into a poem. I wrote the poem above after reflecting on my mothering experiences and birthing loss. My oldest son, Zion Amir, passed away on December 11, 2007, due to my complications with what doctors referred to as an incompetent cervix. I remember holding his tiny body in the palm of my hand as he took just one faint breath. Carrying him had changed my life— "Her world is ripped asunder as her / Steadfast dreams emphasize the / Interconnected nature of survival". Just preparing to step outside of my personal little space to care for another human being had changed my life. His brothers still say his name because we honor those who transition from this space before we do. Even though my birthing loss occurred at least a decade before I ever entered academia, it still haunted me and shaped how I thought about my purpose as an educator and a scholar— "Crossing invisible borders / She recovers her strength as the mold cools / And then shatters to reveal the final product: / The perpetuity of life for Black people".

Morrow's (2023) conceptualization of Black queer revolutionary selfhood focused on Black queer and trans educators' methods of survival and thrival in academia. She noted the ways that Black queer and trans educators described their future goals and how those goals were tied to collective liberation. My freedom dreams have always involved people outside of my immediate circle. With the understanding and knowledge that I draw from the well of my foremothers, I see the completion of a circle created some time ago. As I read back through my memories on social media, I remembered the promise I made almost twenty years ago after the loss of my oldest son: I will always honor my child's memory through acts of love. I center communal care and responsibility in my role as a Black queer motherscholar as a means of putting forth Gumbs' (2016) vision of revolutionary mothering:

> To make visible the connections between a queer feminist of color practice and theory around mothering, intergenerationality and the future and what we see as the most crucial and challenging work of our time, the practice of mothering as an alternative building practice of valuing ourselves and each other and creating the world we deserve. (p. 31)

I believe that a queer vision of Black motherscholarship must be grounded in the collective well-being of Black folks across social identities. This understanding of queer mothering as liberation work guides how I approach my work in academia. Over the last three years, I have used poetry as a means of protection against academia's epistemic violence and spirit murder (Love, 2016).

Ode(S) to the Intangible: Writing as Testimony

"Revenge of the Bloodchild"
What happens if i give myself permission to be any iteration of who i am?
Yesterday, I wanted to be the bad bitch who colored outside of the lines with broken crayons.
Yesterday, I wanted to show everyone that the picture i intended to create is centered around folks who walk, talk, love, dance, sway, twerk, and bounce like I do.
Yesterday, I wanted every line in my drawing to bend to the right and curve in ways that defy the neatly prescribed notions of developmentally appropriate.
Yesterday, I wanted to forgive myself for every time I forced myself to bind my broken crayons with one thing or another in a feeble attempt to fix some perceived error.
A bit of tape here to protect the fragile feelings of alabaster others
A little drop of glue to cement the bonds of ebony onlookers
A slight wrapper switch to hide the names of unorthodox lovestyles
What happens if I give myself permission to be any iteration of who I am?
Today, I want to take all of my broken crayons and sit them in the sun to melt into an amalgamation of colors.
Today, I want to repurpose that mixture of colors into something new, something worthy of coloring a twisted image, outside of this world of small boxes and straight lines.
Today, I want to use this new crayon to create a space that tastes vibrant and feels loud.
Today, I want to forgive myself for every time I refused to see the beauty of those melted crayons and the potential they held for constructing a new world.
A world with soft pillowy spaces
A world big enough for the blurry edges
A world meant for the complexities of divergent minds
What happens if I give myself permission to be any iteration of who I am?
Tomorrow, I'll want to buy a new box of crayons and break them just for the hell of it.
Tomorrow, I'll want the opportunity to start over again on a new picture that suits my current mood.
Tomorrow, I'll want to design a gallery for the images that each of my alters created.
Tomorrow, I'll want to forgive myself for staring at the illustrations and imagining the stories behind them.
Stories of purpose and belonging
Stories of laughter and triumph
Stories of forgetfulness and fantasy

Most of the people I have encountered in academia seem to neatly compartmentalize and place their emotions into boxes and jars until they need them. I, on the other hand, do not. I am a colorful mess of everything at one time. I feel everything at one time. Lines 7 and 8— "Yesterday, I wanted to forgive myself for every time I forced myself to bind my broken crayons / With one thing or another in a feeble attempt to fix some perceived error" illustrate the tension I feel with my history of assimilation as a neurodivergent Black queer motherscholar. Every time I attempted to force myself into someone else's image of who I should be, I regretted not trusting the voice within. It became a cycle of apologizing for showing up fractured, yet whole, instead of standing firmly in my truth.

Recently, I received written communication from a heterosexual cisgender Black woman administrator in my organization with language that did not feel inclusive to me. When I privately responded to her message to voice my concerns about the erasure of queer and trans faculty members' gender and sexual identities, she provided the following response, "I should hope that whatever you are experiencing that makes you doubt so quickly and accuse so recklessly be resolved." Dismissing my concerns about the harm I was telling her I had experienced because of her words, she doubled down in her insistence that I had misunderstood her intent. This noted senior scholar reprimanded me, a Black queer junior scholar seeking a safe space, and proceeded to explain how I had harmed her by questioning her motives in the first place. Instead of offering a place of refuge in an already precarious institution, she proceeded to gaslight me and disregard my feelings. After this interaction, I felt extremely hurt and disheartened because of the hope I had placed on the potential of this relationship with a fellow Black motherscholar. The message I received was that my emotional response had no place in academia. I retreated into my writing and utilized it as a means of testifying against institutional silencing.

Discussion

As I considered the question guiding this endarkened poetic inquiry—*How have I used poetry to process my experiences as an early career Black queer motherscholar outside of the "mythical norm"?* —I thought about how my voice has shifted over time. Black queer joy and Black queer revolutionary selfhood are threaded throughout the pieces I crafted. Poetry has become my means of catharsis, protection, and testimony. As Morrow (2023) declared, "Those at the margins are constantly challenged to think about how we see ourselves, forced to consider and reconsider the essence of who we are" (para. 32). By examining how the intersections of my identity as a neurodivergent Black queer motherscholar impacted how others engaged with me, I also reflected on how those identity markers simultaneously worked together to influence my reaction to these external pushes and pulls. Mysticism, conjuring, spirituality, and sacredness are often weaponized against those of us who feel energies in the universe most innately (Brooks et al., 2021). This is why I developed endarkened poetic inquiry—to offer an arts-based methodological framework that stands against the institutional silencing of Black motherscholars. Poetry remains a constant guide and my way forward through the darkness as I exist in the world like a bell that reverberates the vibrations of everything around me,

Angela Davis (1994) urged us to remember the ways in which we, as Black women scholars, sometimes replicate the white, patriarchal, heteronormative harms of academia while defending our names against unwarranted slander. Respectability politics have never served our liberation goals and undermine abolitionist aims (Bailey & Miller, 2015). When reflecting on the interpersonal dynamics between Black women, Lorde (1984) questioned the reasons behind perceived animosity, "How often have I demanded from another Black woman what I had not dared to give myself—acceptance, faith, enough space to consider change? How often have I asked her to leap across difference, suspicion, distrust, old pain?" (p. 160).

Gloria Anzaldúa (1987) described the space that exists at the apex of multiple worlds as a borderland. For Anzaldúa, the borderland was both literal and figurative as she negotiated her existence as a mestiza, a lesbian, and a feminist. These intersections are understood as compliments of a whole being. As a queer Black neurodivergent cis woman, my intersections of identity influence how I cross a borderland that sometimes conflicts with my vision for the world. I often find myself questioning how to move in spaces where people only marginally understand my lived experiences. When I raise my voice as a scholar to advocate for other multiply marginalized folks like me, I wonder if my message gets lost in the waves of dissent from people who only share one of my intersectional identity markers? I ruminate on the following questions: (1) *How can I, as a Black queer motherscholar, exist beyond the borders others created to detain my spirit?;* (2) *Is the work of academia aligned with my dreams of building a liberated world filled with love, laughter, and light for Black communities?;* and (3) *Will the communities I love acknowledge my mothering labor and love me back?* These questions float around me like phantoms reminding me of how much these borderlands of race, gender, sexuality, and ability impact how I and so many of my sibling scholars step into academic work that honors the nuances of what it means for us to fluidly negotiate being seen and heard.

Rainbow symbolism has followed me around like an apparition threatening to disappear at the slightest mention of rays of sunshine. Yet and still, I hold onto this idea of blending colors together to make a bright spectacle that evokes feelings of joy and happiness. Rainbow colors are commonly associated with queer and trans communities, my community. My identity as a Black queer motherscholar goes beyond the expression of my sexual and romantic attractions. Just as Gumbs (2016) proclaimed, I am queer because I live outside of the parameters of the reality in which I was socialized. I am queer because I do not fit neatly into the boxes designed to hold someone like me who loves the company and energy of other queer individuals. I am queer because the glasses I wear have never been rose colored; they are stained with the colors that swirl together to create images that only seem distorted to folks who do not understand their purpose. I am queer by design. I am queer by definition. I am queer by birthright.

Conclusion

I have always considered writing to be a sacred act. It is more than a single act of defiance. Writing is life affirming. As a poet, I write because the words need to exist in a space outside of my head. I am always writing as if my life depends on it because, in most cases—it does. I write feverously because, as Dillard (2015) proclaimed, "...somebody needs to read those words to be alive, to be okay, to be enough, to heal" (p. 208). As I push forward in my tenure track journey and interrogate my identity as a Black queer motherscholar outside of the mythical norm, I acknowledge that my writing is cathartic, protective, and testimony.

Over the last three years, I have cultivated authentic, meaningful relationships with junior and senior colleagues within and outside of my institution who have helped me navigate this new journey away from my family and friends by providing emotional support and practical advice regarding academia's hidden curriculum. My hope is that this chapter can provide some comfort for other Black queer motherscholars who are starting their tenure track journeys. We deserve the chance to push against the binary of self-care versus communal care towards the homeplace of wholeness Lewis and Miller (2018) envisioned:

> For us, living free means we practice agency. We are persistent in loving ourselves and healing and make decisions about where we call home. We actively pursue our liberation and the liberation of our communities, knowing that we must be agents of transformation and liberatory praxis (p. 88).

I firmly believe that all junior faculty should be given advice on how to build community with colleagues at their institutions while respecting their values and ideals instead of being inundated with hyper-individualistic messaging pushing for more competition. This is especially important for Black queer motherscholars who enter the academy determined to (re)imagine community building outside of the mythical norm. I am accountable to the communities that raised me; and as I navigate all of these marginalized identities, I remember Lorde's (1984) words:

> It is necessary to teach by living and speaking those truths which we believe and know beyond understanding. Because in this way alone we can survive, by taking part in a process of life that is creative and continuing, that is growth. (p. 31)

This experience has been one of immense growth, and I cherish the opportunities to stop and reflect on how these margins have merged together to create a whole being.

Competing Interests The author has no conflicts of interest to declare that are relevant to the content of this manuscript.

References

Anzaldúa, G. (1987). *Borderlands/la frontera: The new mestiza.* Aunt Lute Books.

Bailey, M., & Miller, S. J. (2015). When margins become centered: Black queer women in front and outside of the classroom. *Feminist Formations, 27*(3), 168–188. https://doi.org/10.1353/ff.2016.0005

Bonsu, J. E. (2018). Black queer feminism as praxis: building an organization and a movement. *Black Women's Liberatory Pedagogies: Resistance, Transformation, and Healing Within and Beyond the Academy*, 211–224.

Brooks, K., Martin, K. L., & Simmons, L. (2021). Conjure feminism: Toward a genealogy. *Hypatia, 36*(3), 452–461.

Broughton, A. (2022). Black skin, White theorists: Remembering hidden Black early childhood scholars. *Contemporary Issues in Early Childhood, 23*(1), 16–31.

Cohen, C. J. (1997). Punk, bulldaggers, and welfare queens: The radical potential of queer politics. *GLQ: A Journal of Lesbian and Gay Studies, 3*, 437–465.

Collins, P. H. (2000). *Black feminist thought: Knowledge, consciousness, and the politics of empowerment* (2nd ed.). Routledge.

Cutts, Q. (2019). More than craft and criteria: The necessity of Ars spirituality in (Black women's) poetic inquiry and research poetry. *Qualitative Inquiry, 26*(7), 908–919. https://doi.org/10.1177/1077800419884966

Cutts, Q. M., & Waters, M. B. S. (2019). Poetic approaches to qualitative data analysis. In *Oxford Research Encyclopedia of Education.*

Davis, A. (1994). Black women and the academy. *Callaloo, 17*(2), 422–431.

Dillard, C. (2000). The substance of things hoped for, the evidence of things not seen: Examining an endarkened feminist epistemology in educational research and leadership. *International Journal of Qualitative Studies in Education, 13*(6), 661–681.

Dillard, C. B. (2016). Turning the ships around: A case study of (re) membering as transnational endarkened feminist inquiry and praxis for Black teachers. *Educational Studies, 52*(5), 406–423.

Evans-Winters, V., & Esposito, J. (2018). Researching the bridge called our backs: The invisibility of 'us' in qualitative communities. *International Journal of Qualitative Studies in Education, 31*(9), 863–876.

Fearon, S. (2024). Inquiry for social transformation: Black mother scholars redefining scholarly inquiry through black artistic expression. *Journal of Culture and Values in Education, 7*(3), 161–176.

Glover, S.T. (2017). "Black lesbians—Who will fight for our lives but us?": Navigating power, belonging, labor, resistance, and graduate student survival in the ivory tower. *Feminist Teacher 27*(2), 157–175. https://www.muse.jhu.edu/article/715994.

Green, M. L. (2023). "It's how you're delivering these messages": An examination of black women early childhood educators' liberatory practices through poetic inquiry. *Equity & Excellence in Education, 56*(4), 545–559.

Gumbs, A. P. (2010). *"We can learn to mother ourselves": The queer survival of Black feminism* (Doctoral dissertation).

Gumbs, A.P. (2016). M/other ourselves: A Black queer feminist genealogy for radical mothering. In A.P. Gumbs, C. Martens & M. Williams (Eds.), *Revolutionary mothering: Love on the front lines* (pp.19–31). PM Press.

Gumbs, A. P., Martens, C., & Williams, M. (Eds.). (2016). *Revolutionary mothering: Love on the front lines.* Pm Press.

Harris, L. J. (2018). Healing through (re) membering and (re) claiming ancestral knowledge about black witch magic. *Black Women's Liberatory Pedagogies: Resistance, Transformation, and Healing Within and Beyond the Academy*, 245–263.

hooks, B., & McKinnon, T. (1996). Sisterhood: Beyond public and private. *Signs, 21*(4), 814–829. Retrieved June 23, 2020, from www.jstor.org/stable/3175025

Hull, G. T., Bell Scott, P., & Smith, B. (Eds.). (1982). *All the women are white, all the men are black.* Feminist Press.

Lewis, M. M., & Miller, S. J. (2018). How does it feel to be a problem? A conversation between two feminist Black queer femme chairs. *Feminist Formations, 30*(3), 79–90.

Lorde, A. (1982). *Zami, a new spelling of my name*. Crossing Press.
Lorde, A. (1984). *Sister Outsider: Essays and speeches*. Crossing Press.
Love, B. L. (2016). Anti-Black state violence, classroom edition: The spirit murdering of Black children. *Journal of Curriculum and Pedagogy, 13*(1), 22–25.
Morrow, L. K. (2023). Toward our Black queer joy[ous] futures: To achieve[1] our freedom in the academy. *Theory, Research, and Action in Urban Education, 8*(1).
Pryse, M., & Spillers, H. J. (Eds.). (1985). *Conjuring: Black women, fiction, and literary tradition*. Indiana University Press.
Quynh Phan, A. N. (2023). "And I surrender to maternity": A poetic autoethnographic inquiry into juggling roles of a doctoral student mother during the pandemic. *Journal of Poetry Therapy, 36*(2), 172–181.
Smith, B. (2000). *Home girls: A black feminist anthology*. Rutgers University Press.
Walker, A. (2004). *In search of our mothers' gardens: Womanist prose*. Houghton Mifflin Harcourt.
Whittington, E. Y. (2023). 3 Re-imagining queer Black motherhood. *Refiguring Motherhood Beyond Biology*, 42.

Motherscholars in Community

Visionary Daughters: The Generational Shift from Mothering to Daughtering for Early Career Community College Faculty

Jamie Lulamae Moore

Abstract This chapter is a mixed methodology approach that considers the demands of care Black women face in their community college faculty positions, as related to mothering and daughtering metaphors. From 2018 through 2022, the California CC system adopted a variety of changes, including AB 705, the Call to Action and Vision for Success, which included new equity mandates. These changes created a call to leadership, which encouraged Black women faculty to take positions related to equity organizing, with no sustainable support for institutional change. To understand the emergent pressures on Black women faculty, this chapter considers personal healing, storytelling, and identity definition as an entry point to acknowledging this care work. This chapter engages in Black feminist autotheory, which centers self-definition to emphasize one's own humanity, often stolen from community college faculty in the larger conversation of higher education experiences. Identifying specific survival mechanisms as aligned with daughtering, this chapter recognizes how these skills enable a kind of care work that positions the daughter to be perceived as highly trusted and uniquely qualified. Can we reimagine the ways we deliver care and support that emphasizes sharing sustainable healing and learning practices with those in our spheres of influence?

Keywords Community College · Daughtering

Introduction

The blend of my early educational and cultural experiences helped define my multiple identities as teacher, daughter, and other-mother, priming me to move through future academic spaces with the spirit of giving service, people-pleasing, and speaking to injustice. Perhaps my earliest memory that lives at this intersection is standing at the front of a church congregation, reading the bio of our weekly Black American

J. L. Moore (✉)
College of the Sequoias, The Puente Project, Visalia, CA, USA
e-mail: jamiem@cos.edu

C. R. Turner and M. L. Green (eds.), *Black Motherscholarship Within and Beyond the Academy*, https://doi.org/10.1007/978-3-031-99758-7_21

History Maker from the bulletin. I was made speaker, scholar, and teacher by my Black church.

Right at the end of Sunday school, we'd see one of the deacons peeking into the windows of the classrooms to see if we were done with the session. Most of the kids shifted in their seats, not wanting to be picked to do anything during the main service. I wasn't loud enough to say "no," and not quick enough to run off to my parents when class ended. While we were often "Sister" or "Brother" addressing one another, I knew when I was addressed as "daughter," as the deacon addressed me, it was to ask for some act of service. I learned a daughter was knowledgeable and prepared for a task, but also lacked autonomy to choose whether or not to do a task.

Born and raised in northern California, my childhood was defined by my family's involvement in an insular Black Baptist church community in an otherwise primarily white and Latinx area. My father was Black and my mother is white, so we were not the typical family in that community, but my mother quickly became assimilated into these spaces and made herself daughter to Black elders of the church to learn how to raise Black children. I was raised deeply situated in Blackness as a primary identity, despite my biracial heritage. I was given books by Black writers and studied Black history at home and in community spaces. As an eldest daughter, my experience of taking care of siblings positioned me to be chosen to organize my peers, to tutor, and to lead student groups in primary and secondary school. It was in community college I found the first educational space where I felt autonomy over my own learning and the shift of expectation from taking care of others to tending to my own education. My classrooms reflected the diversity of my neighborhood, unlike the state university I transferred to in order to finish my bachelor's degree. Being a professor in a community college classroom gave me the space to use my educational and cultural training simultaneously, working with students I recognized and remaining connected to the issues of the local community.

I started teaching at 23-years-old, obtaining full time, tenure track status at 26, and tenure by 30. But with a service-minded perspective and my unconscious assimilation to my institution, my early burnout was inevitable. As one of the youngest professors on campus at the start of my career, I was treated as a novelty, but invited to the table(s) to give my perspective. It wasn't until the month before I was awarded tenure, I recognized how often those tables were turned on me; often I was invited into leadership for a failed effort to be blamed on me, (as related to my age, questions about my preparation, and "radical" leaning). I approached my work as heart work, aligning me with the practice of mothering as defined by Ross (2016) in the preface to *Revolutionary Mothering: Love on the Frontlines:* "Mothering, radically defined, is the glad gifting of one's talents, ideas, intellect and creativity to the universe without recompense" (p. xv). Studies of Black women being pushed into mothering positions "serve as a critical location to confront the massive loss and exploitation of intellectual workers in the academy. And there we find the invisibilized body, the sexualized, the gendered body, the racialized body, the underpaid body… and we find the servant body of both community and academic institutions" (Nzinga-Johnson, 2013, p. 17). I deeply felt and understood the experience of mothering, particularly in relationship with my students. Other professors and counselors constantly referred students to me—to my classes and my office hours, even if they were not in my classes. They primarily referred students of color, as well as any students they labeled as "problem students." More often than not, these were students who needed someone to listen and advocate for them after they had been pushed away from other campus services. This was tiring work, and especially so considering the heavy course load community college professors have to teach.

It was my interactions with colleagues and administrators that pushed my burnout over the edge. So much so, that I had a letter of resignation drafted before my tenure meeting. After multiple conversations with allies, (including the one other Black faculty in my department), I abandoned this letter and received my tenure. During this time, I was recognizing that my colleagues sought caretaking from me in a way that was different than the experience of mothering—perhaps due to the combination of my race, age, and career status. In our interactions, especially when I was in positions of leadership, there were active ways I was infantilized and disbelieved while also being asked to provide them emotional support. I learned that young community college faculty were the assumed informants to administration, and to no surprise, my diversity was viewed as a checkbox. In the surge of equity trainings and newly formed DEI committees, my work and the work of other Black women was visible, but it was still asked and expected. As I returned to graduate studies to understand what was happening to me and other young Black women in academia, my work aimed to reveal the pressure for Black women faculty to serve in newly created equity, student service, and curriculum leadership positions in the community colleges, dually asking Black women to solve the equity crises of the colleges and using them in a performative manner.

My research focuses on Black and Black-biracial women professors in community colleges for two specific reasons: (1) the experience of community college faculty is understudied, particularly the experience of Black women and how the responsibilities of community college differentiate them from those working in a research institution, and (2) the recent equity movements in the California community college system provide a unique opportunity to examine how Black women have been cajoled into roles of campus leadership, and while pushing for institutional change, have faced rejection from the institution (admin and colleagues) that force a reevaluation of their service to it. This context has created a revealing of and a reckoning with the roles of mothering and daughtering, (roles often veiled by false performances of praise, access to spaces of change-making, and calls to service).

In this chapter, I align my experiences with the voices of fellow Black women faculty to illustrate our position as daughters of the community college system and offer a reframing of that role that empowers us rather than serving as a catalyst to burn out. To do this, I will introduce my methodology, provide context to the recent equity movements of the California community college system, share interview excerpts from Black women faculty, and propose "visionary daughtering" as a method of maintaining selfhood in faculty leadership roles. Framing this work are my central research questions: (1) How have the recent changes in the California community colleges increased the expectation of care work from Black women faculty? (2)

Considering the metaphor of Black women as mothers in academia, does the visibility of this labor change the experience or perception of this care work? (3) How can daughtering as method provide insight to care work performed by early career faculty? (4) Can daughtering as theory provide a space for Black women faculty to find more agency in their professional service roles? Within these questions, I hoped to unpack how familial metaphors affect the performance of care work. As someone who felt deeply connected to providing care for my students, I realized I placed that value in care work because of my cultural training as a daughter. Considering the power in daughtering as method, I wondered if understanding daughtering in the context of community college faculty could help me reimagine my role and find a way to thrive.

Guiding Methodology

Black Feminist Autotheory

My initial motivation to engage in faculty research was to chronicle my own survival (or lack of it) and to analyze the conditions that brought me to this place of burnout. I adopted the term Black feminist autotheory as a descriptor of my primary methodology for several reasons: (1) autotheory allowed me to center storytelling and truth-telling—building theory from lived experience; (2) autotheory encouraged me to move beyond the assumed objectivity, often embedded in ethnographic practice, and instead present my experiences alongside/ connected to/ inextricable from the women I shared community with; and (3) autotheory reminded me of the rich literary lineage of Black feminist scholars writing themselves into academic record.

Generally, autotheory as method grounds institutional analysis with the personal while making space for the visioning of survival, care, and activism that is restorative and based in lived experience. Zwartjes (2019b) defines autotheory as "work that engages in thinking about the self, the body, and the particularities of one's lived experiences, as processed through or juxtaposed against theory—or as the basis for theoretical thinking. It strips the pretension of neutrality, of objectivity, away from the theorizing voice" (para. 3). Carving a space for themselves in a larger academic discourse, the autotheorist uses their experiences as the basis for developing new theories and exploring the complexities of and their connections to other theoretical arguments. This practice of thinking and writing critically about the self beyond the value systems of higher education institutions is rooted in the work of Black scholars defining ourselves outside of societal stereotypes (hooks, 2014) and claiming space in the academic conversation (Green, 2020). Autotheory as method for faculty narratives bends genre to claim an interdisciplinary space for Black feminist narratives to resist the systemic silencing of their voices.

While autotheory is connected and compatible with an ethnographic approach, in the context of Black feminist practice, the autotheorist presents not only a narrative of the self as relative to the community, but also incorporates community perspective to create a collective voice. The collective voice is essential to my understanding of self, especially in my cultural training as a Black daughter—something academia tries to train out of us. Black feminist autotheory explores identity formation in context of other women of color scholars, community knowledge, and institutional experience.

In her practice of Black feminist autotheory in "Need that Tastes Like Destruction: Lessons from (the) Lorde on the Occasion of Black Death and Dying," Terrion L. Williamson (2024) details her home-education and orientation into Black feminism as she draws a throughline between her observations of her mothers, her readings of Audre Lorde, and "felt life" of Black feminism. In her integration of Black feminism beyond the performative academic gestures, she writes, "when I began to reckon with care as foundational to black feminism rather than its mere byproduct I began to more readily embrace black feminism not just as a critical scholarly endeavor but as an essential framework for living what Ashton Crawley has beautifully theorized as 'otherwise possibility'" (pp. 270–271). Williamson theorizes that Black feminist autotheory practice emerges from the "fugitive lifeworlds of black women, girls, and nonbinary people for whom survival has always been precarious" (p. 271). It is within the practice of Black feminism and its intersection with autotheory that a space of reprieve can be carved, because this work not only holds the heaviness of what is at stake (our very livelihood, our aliveness), but also the vision for what a different future could be.

Enacting Black Feminist Autotheory

My first practice of Black feminist autotheory was engaging in personal writing that examined the academic interactions and faculty involvement that led to my burnout. I worked to build a literary practice, leaning on my training as a creative writer, that brought validity to the experimental nature of my reflective writing. This writing mostly took the form of critical memoir vignettes and poetry, beginning as a direct response to other Black women writers. I aimed to emulate Claudia Rankine's bluntness in *Citizen: an American Lyric*, as she describes her interaction with a white male colleague, asking herself "why [does he] feel comfortable saying this to me?" (Rankine, 2014, p. 6). In an early writing experiment, I responded section by section to Alice Walker's "The Taste of Grudge," building a hybrid text that was looking for definitions of the academic mother and daughter between the lines of Walker's defiance.

Black feminist autotheory as practice is intended to be an embodied experience, casting away the traditional ask of academia to be objective, (which is embedded in the history of autoethnography and its labeling of non-white narratives as "exotic") (Poulos, 2021, pp. 6–7). The centering of self and cultural ways of knowing—the refusal of neutrality—gave me a way to develop an academic voice that honored my authentic self as well as the legacy of Black scholarship that guided the work. Autotheory as method, "transgresses the borders around disciplines, [and] also around genres and mediums. Autotheory operates interstitially, in that inter-genre space the nonfiction field has slowly opened up to" (Zwartjes, 2019a, 2019b, n.p.). Each piece of writing felt like a distilled moment or container that I wanted to hold up to the light and share with Black colleagues, asking, "do you see what I see?" Zwartjes (2019a) argues that autotheory theorizes the plurality of self. This fracture of selves, (my inner self, my academic self, my daughter self, and all the space in between/overlapping), pushed me to take the next step into refining this method through dialogue with other Black women faculty.

Collaborative Theory Making

Concurrent with my personal writing practice, I began informal conversations with other Black women faculty about the themes that were coming up in my writing. A driving motivator to seek out this dialogue was that I was the only tenured Black woman faculty in my entire college district. Thus, these conversations happened with faculty in neighboring towns and college districts, as well as with Black women across the state that I met through professional networks. Over tea dates, phone calls, and video sessions, I brought the seeds of my personal theory-making to these trusted peers and we planted them in the soil of our shared testimonies. We returned to conversations, comparing notes how we saw mothering or daughtering show up in our interactions with other faculty and students. Before engaging in any formal qualitative research, it was these check-ins, vent sessions, and collaborative inquiries that encouraged me to be deliberate about adapting this methodology in a way that allowed me to place our narratives alongside each other, similar to the way that in our dialogues with each other, we begin to collaboratively theorize and answer each other's questions through our experiences.

As I moved to the next step in my research, I designed a formal interview process that sought to honor this collaborative definition building and collaborative theory-making. In fall 2022, I interviewed thirteen Black women faculty currently working in California community colleges (CCCs) to see how they defined their care work, how this caregiving had shifted with new equity-focused legislation in the CCCs and to see if they connected with my feelings of burnout. To begin, I asked them to write a short narrative that described a recent moment of providing care to someone in their campus community and how it represented the kind of work they found themselves doing, (including if that work was voluntary or asked of them). As we reviewed those narratives together, we highlighted key words and phrases, creating a word cloud that outlined their methods of care work and the pressure that motivated their actions. As we settled in on what care work looked like in their professional life, I shared my working definition of daughtering in the context of faculty roles. I asked each faculty how they felt their care work aligned or differed from this definition, and how their experience might contribute to a deeper understanding of daughtering. While many knew of and connected with the metaphor of mothering, many early-career faculty found a deeper resonance with the term daughtering and expressed interest in understanding how daughtering as method/praxis could help them gain more agency.

Daughtering as Method

In *Black Feminist Qualitative Inquiry*, Venus Evans-Winters (2018) explains, "daughtering implores us to decode words and tolerate the pain of other people's interpretations of our tresses, bodies, language, behaviors, dispositions, [and] personalities," and argues that "daughtering is not passive. In fact it is quite subversive, watchful, and clandestine for the sake of survival. We are socialized to read in between the lines" (p. 138). Daughtering as theory in relationship to faculty roles asserts that Black women, (often socialized into caregiving by family, communities and society at large), are often subject to and actively aware of persistent stereotypes and their labor is no longer "invisible." While "mothering" is the metaphor that is most discussed as a descriptor of the care work of Black women in academia, there is a generational divide with younger Black women faculty who did not have to be "the first" or the trailblazers on their campuses. They face similar pressures with a twist of ageism. Daughters in academia exist in continually oppressive institutions that demand care work for access to professional privileges, despite the increased visibility and discourse of this labor. They are asked to the table and also are infantilized when they present an idea that does not align with workings of the system. Recognizing daughtering provides the opportunity for faculty to be strategic in the ways care is acknowledged, critically discussed, and used as a catalyst for change.

For the purposes of this research, my definition of daughtering borrows from Venus Evans-Winters, who explains that "much of our understandings of the social world are shaped by our experiences as daughters in an anti-black and anti-girl world. Daughtering influences our approaches to data theory, analysis, and representations of our observations and lived experiences" (Evans-Winters, 2018, p. 27). Daughtering is a set of social survival skills that inform one's point of view and positionality. These survival skills can vary depending on the atmosphere someone grew up in but can often manifest as acts of intentional or unintentional care work. Specific to a Black and Black-biracial context, my definition of daughtering includes the cultural training to be secret-keepers and supplanters in our family units and communities, which then replicates in the workplace. These skills enable a kind of care work that positions the daughter to be perceived as highly trusted, responsible, highly intelligent and uniquely qualified.

My contribution to Evans-Winters's theory is the framing of daughtering in the community college context through two specific skills. Daughtering as secret-keeping asks Black women faculty to call on their training as observers and confidants to understand and hold sensitive information and to use discernment to be strategic with that information (which can affect their care work). As a secret-keeper, I planted myself in the faculty break room when I was a brand-new professor, listening to the gossip, complaints, and celebrations of the faculty around me. From observing, I learned the language of the campus community and the buzz words that got my department riled up. As my presence became more familiar, I was invited into these conversations or folks would reveal their frustrations of the day as they refilled their coffee—information that became helpful for me to navigate the social landscape of the department.

Daughters as supplanters asks Black women faculty to be constantly prepared to assume roles beyond their identity, roles that often end up superseding their identities, for the illusion of voice and power. One example of this is an experience I share with one of my interviewees—same role, different colleges. In fall 2020, as our colleges scrambled to assemble performative diversity committees in response to the increased attention of police brutality after the murder of George Floyd, we both served as chairs of these committees. We both experienced becoming the "Equity Experts" of our campuses, as informal narratives about who we were and what our work stood for began to circulate among our colleagues. These narratives were positive and negative, depending on who did the telling and how they felt the equity work affected them. Early in the equity-responsive work, administration used these roles to paint us as authority figures on campus, but as the steam ran out on making systemic change, we both experienced a change in that narrative. For me specifically, my role as equity chair meant I was now seen as a barrier to other faculty requests and an auditor of others' work, (which meant I shifted from being pushed to advise campus groups to being distrusted). The interviewee shared that her campus management called a major campus goal, "her equity project" which they said failed because of the committee's poor planning, discrediting her leadership abilities rather than admitting the college's ineptitude to make change. In these supplanting roles, without time and energy to reflect on where we could build agency, we only had the illusion of voice and leadership.

In the community college context, it is important to understand how recent shifts have affected a system-wide call for an increased dedication to professional service. This has only deepened the pressure for Black women at these institutions to perform care work, both for students and the overall campus community.

Context of the California Community Colleges

The California community college (CCC) system situates itself as the ultimate higher education space for service as it is the most visibly mission driven sector of California's higher education system, serving over 1.8 million students across 116 campuses. While the offering of certificate and vocational programs means that the community college is still portrayed as a "lower" class of college, (implying both the education quality and the socioeconomic status of the students it serves), the discourses around student debt, the economic struggles of a larger section of the population, and the high success rates of student transfers in the California State University and University of California systems have made community college a more attractive option for students. A point of pride for the CCC system is the diverse student body, with one example of this being that "92% of California's 116 community colleges are considered Hispanic-serving institutions" (Cuellar et al., 2023).

For a system that serves the most diverse students, our faculty and staff demographics do not match our student demographics. This metric is an important one to consider when thinking about who is providing students with the culturally competent care that is critical to the success of historically excluded students. In the CCC system, 57% of tenured or tenure-tracked faculty are white, 19% are Hispanic, 12% Asian, and 5% are Black, (with some unspecified and others under 1%) ("Faculty and Staff Demographics Report"). The temporary or adjunct staff demographics mirror the full-time faculty demographics. This means that Black women faculty are often isolated or alone in our campus districts. Beyond my full-time appointment, my college district has three part-time Black women faculty across disciplines. Between professors, counselors, and athletic coaches who may teach physical education courses, we have 7–10 Black men.

With its historical focus on remedial education, there has been, (and continues to be), an equity crisis within community college academic programs, with Black and Latinx professors at the forefront of the push to eliminate remedial courses that force students to take up six units before qualifying for a credit level course. Remedial courses defined the community college experience for many students until recently. Flawed placement tests funneled students into courses one, two or even three steps below transfer-level courses that qualify towards their associates and bachelor's degrees. Remedial courses could delay a student's timeline to graduation by years, stretching a traditional four-year degree into a six- or seven-year journey. Many studies over the years demonstrated that remedial courses were not effective in preparing students for further education and in fact, they "actually hinder degree completion: just over 30 percent of community college students placed in remedial courses completed a degree, certificate, or transfer in six years, compared to 70 percent of students placed directly in college-level courses" (Ed Trust West, n.d., para 2). The hindering of academic progress also had a specific racial and economic effect, with a disproportionate amount of Black, Latinx, and Indigenous students being placed in remedial courses, (sometimes even by self-selection because of the lack of academic counseling, by default for lack of placement test or ineffective, biased academic counseling, or lack of availability in required courses). According to research by Education Trust-West, "almost 90 percent of Black and Latinx students were enrolled in at least one remedial course across California Community College campuses (CCC) in 2009"[1] (Ed Trust West, n.d., para 2).

[1] Perhaps important to note is that a majority of these remedial courses (in my observations) are taught by faculty of color and by part-time faculty. A load of remedial courses was my first full-time teaching assignment, which I didn't question at the time because I was working with the most diverse students on campus, which allowed me to feel an ease and safety with my students about my own identities. Although most of my colleagues and professional community agreed with the research on the way these courses harmed student progress, there was still a sense of loss of the community they created and the fear that our white colleagues would be unprepared to serve these students (which, for the most part proved to be true). When taught by part-time instructors, these

Assembly Bill 705, passed by the California governor Gavin Newsom in 2017, finally addressed this fundamental course placement inequity, forcing the CCC system to create accelerated pathways to transfer courses, change course placement measures, and in most cases, eliminate remedial courses altogether to provide universal access to transfer level courses. While compliance with this new law has taken time and looked different at each campus, in 2020, the Public Policy Institute of California (PPIC) proclaimed, "one of the most immediate and notable outcomes of AB 705 has been the dramatic improvement in equitable access to college composition" (Cuellar Mejia et al., 2022, para 12).

In June 2020, the California community college chancellor's office released the Call to Action. This document was meant to address the two important sociopolitical shifts in higher education at the time. Firstly, it considered the movement to online learning, which necessitated deeper conversation about equity and access as the nation adapted to the COVID-19 pandemic. Secondly, it answered the call for higher education institutions to respond to the increase of police brutality upon and murders of Black and Brown youth. The Call to Action is a pivotal document in shifting the social atmosphere and faculty pressures within community colleges, which leaned on the metaphor of each campus as a "community college family." The document declared, "we cannot say that we are equity champions and be afraid of having open dialogue about structural racism" and suggested that "campus leaders must host open dialogue and address campus climate" (California Community College Chancellor's Office, 2020, paras. 1–4).

This work was followed by a revised diversity, equity and inclusion plan as well as the updated Vision for Success, which outlined seven commitments from the CCC system to reach its "full potential" and "meet workforce needs" in a way that is student ready (California Community College Chancellor's Office, n.d., p. 1). Demonstration of this work was tied to funding, linked to reporting systems, and coded (while vaguely) into campus strategic plans. While innovative in its vision and necessary in its reach for accountability, the Call to Action, (and subsequent CCC system wide documents), relied on terms like "student equity," "diversity" and "inclusion" that were not collectively defined. The focus of this work was also specifically in service to only one institutional group, students, a priority of any higher ed institution, but does not target the systemic oppression experienced and put into action by faculty and staff. This framing created immediate conflict and burnout in the rapid pursuit of this call.

To enforce these new measures and to further the restrictions on offering remedial courses, a follow-up bill, Assembly Bill 1705 was passed on 2022, to "to maximize the probability that students will enter and complete transfer-level coursework in English and mathematics within a one-year timeframe of their initial attempt in the discipline" (California State Assembly, 2022, para. 2). At the time of this writing, AB 1705 is continuing to shift / correct placement measures and course offerings across the CCC system. From a faculty perspective, these legislative changes not only mean

---

students who are more likely to need more attention, who are more likely to be first-generation, have the least amount of time with their instructors.

shifts in literal course offerings but also indicate a shift in how we meet, support, and retain students in our classes. Aligning these documents together—to fully embrace the equity imperative of our moment—means tangible curricular reform, especially reform that centers the perspective, needs and assets of historically excluded students.

With the expectation of serving every student at the core of the mission of all community colleges, the system is in a moment of public reckoning as they realize this is not what they have been doing. This reckoning includes an important moment of self-awareness from faculty, many of whom were not as teachers in their graduate programs (Robinson & Hope, 2013), and thus must remedy the fact that they do not know how to best serve historically excluded students. While many white faculty and student service professionals continue to rely on connecting students to faculty and staff of color to provide deeper-level support, the entire community college system is turning to its historically marginalized faculty to step into leadership roles to foster change (even as the system is not built for and is unwilling to enact lasting change). A consequence of rushing this equity work meant placing an undue burden on Black daughters who, in the cultural training of care work, knew how to manage both the service to white (and other assimilated POC) colleagues in their painful racial awakenings, and provide complex emotional care to students.

Black Women's Care Work in the California Community Colleges

With the context of the recent developments in the CCC system, the pressure and significance of this social, political, and legal moment becomes clearer, specifically how it builds upon previous equity work to uniquely position Black women to take on an undue amount of involvement in equity changes, (willingly or unwillingly). In "I'm Not Your Mama, Do Your Work: The Black Female Academic as Surrogate Mother," Tokeya C. Graham (2013) provides prospective on the professional load of Black community college faculty:

> The type of work I do at the community college is undervalued because it is viewed as being 'natural.' I teach 5 courses in a semester (not including advising and committee work) and simply do not have the time to dedicate more service hours to meet all of my students' needs. …However, I feel pulled in that direction that puts the student, and by association, the institution first. …Without the college taking ownership for its responsibility to the students, I serve as an undercompensated triage agent…I am a small part of the wheel doing a major part of the labor. And due to this, I become complicit in my own undoing (p.118-119).

Graham knows her work is indispensable to her students and her voice is necessary for advocating for equitable change for students and faculty alike. However, as she excels in this work, (and realizes how she is perceived, as an expert in care), she feels forced into this identity. While in reflection, Graham rejects any connection to the maternal metaphor in her professional role, the nature of the community college and its students makes it difficult for her to find a balance and establish boundaries that allow her to maintain a healthy separation between care for her family and her professional duties. Graham's perspective serves to spotlight the precarious professional location of Black women faculty in community colleges: culturally competent practitioners whose perspectives are necessary to equitable change, but who may risk their personal and professional wellness by being in leadership positions. However, as Graham rejects these labels completely in her professional identity, I sought to understand my cultural connection to the term "daughtering" alongside the narratives of other Black women faculty and to interrogate why we felt both activated and tethered to these identities.

Family Metaphors as a Trigger of Care Work

The family metaphor serves as an important trigger of care work, reasserting and shifting power dynamics in every interaction. One definition of care work in the context of CCC Black women faculty is the relationship to and acts of service for anyone outside of the self, but especially for people outside of the homeplace. To survive within academia, many of us try to create homeplace in the spaces we have domain over in our institutions: our classrooms, our offices, or student success centers. Homeplace, as bell hooks (1990) reminds us, can be a site of resistance or cultural rebellion. It can be a space of sharing cultural currency. Alongside other aspects of daughtering, there is also the creation of homeplace, which "was not simply a matter of Black women providing service; it was about the construction of a safe place where Black people could affirm one another and by doing so heal many of the wounds inflicted by racial domination" (hooks, 1990, p. 384).

I use the term "care work" to do two things. First, to signal the tenderness of the word "care", often saved for the service of the ones we love, or to even just express an aspect of love. Embedded in "care" is not only (gaining and exerting) the knowledge of what is needed to provide the circumstances for someone's well-being, but also the attentiveness and intention of doing something right to mitigate harm. It is the utmost duty of a daughter to care—and to be able to have quietly and without complaint learned what it is to provide the appropriate care for each individual or unit demanding it. Secondly, to bring up the obligation and responsibility of the word "work," which is primarily meant to refer to the physical, emotional, and mental toll that providing care can take, but also to remind the reader that work is not optional for most.

Existing in a workplace, having to provide for the self and family, means exposure to spaces that are not only the site of racial aggression, but become spaces where care is required of us because of stereotypes Black women face. For me, for Graham, and the participants of my research, the family metaphor elicits a deeper somatic and cultural response, tied to the sense of responsibility instilled by family and community values, and creates a false equivalency of these values to our required service to the institution. When my college president took the cue of the chancellor and used "college family" as an address in campus-wide emails, it knotted something in my stomach. The family role I was most familiar with, and felt the urge and responsibility to respond as, was daughter. Consciously and unconsciously, I wondered what it could mean to be daughter to the institution, especially as the allegiance to the role felt tied to my employment and financial security.

Reflecting on how I was triggered by the family metaphor, before I was awarded a sabbatical in Spring 2021, I had spent the last several years coordinating a student cohort transfer program, chairing our Equal Employment Opportunity (EEO) Committee, developing new EEO training for the district, serving on several hiring committees (including chairing one), counseling leaders of other hiring committees, designing and delivering an equity-responsive professional development summer training for faculty, and chairing our newly formed Diversity Equity and Action Committee. While I had all this notable leadership on campus, my work was continually cast as "radical" and "woke," which resulted in threats (personal and professional) from members of the campus community. At the same time, I was in weekly conversations with campus administration to support the development of equity language and received lengthy emails from colleagues asking for emotional support/validation of their racial equity journeys. I often carried fear for my personal safety in campus spaces (and beyond). In the spirit of Black feminist autotheory, I sought connection, validation, and authority to speak truth to this experience in community with other Black women faculty.

Interview Results

Taking Care of Students

From the interviews, two main themes emerged, the first of which is taking care of students. There was some complexity to this theme, as the interviewees did not feel resentful about the care that they provided to students, rather, they took pride and felt connected to the students they were able to create bonds with. However, there was a sense of hesitation and/or questioning when that care is the expectation, (especially when students are recommended to them by other colleagues), and when it is clear students don't receive that level of care elsewhere. One example of this comes from the interview with a professor at a large college in central California. Professor A is a full-time, tenure-track faculty who was new to her campus at the time of the interview. She shared:

> I've been told on multiple occasions by multiple faculty and students that I'm too nice. I find that very mind boggling. I think to myself: do y'all want me to be mean? Is there something in my persona that on the one hand [says] we want you to coddle our students and bend over backwards, but at the same time you're too nice? I said if y'all want me to be less nice, then tell me exactly where I can cut corners to where it does not reflect poorly on me.

While Professor A had generally positive feelings about her interactions with her colleagues, this line of questioning made her wonder why she was constantly being sent students (both by colleague recommendation, and peer word of mouth). She felt connected and motivated by her student engagement and her positive impact not only on campus culture, but student completion. While Professor A expressed a desire to be in conversation with her colleagues about her techniques, as an early career faculty and one that was new to the community college system, she was not approaching those conversations from a sense of arrogance or expertise, but rather as a bid for connection with her colleagues and an opportunity to share what to her felt like inherent knowledge. Her care work came from a place of deeply understanding and caring about her students, especially students of color, and she questioned if her colleagues shared that depth. This questioning signaled that wonder of whether she would be credited for what she shared because while there was a rapport among colleagues, there did not seem to be a sense of intentional community building with students, which is exactly what she was trying to establish.

Care Work in Many Forms

Professor T, a part-time faculty member with twenty years of experience teaching at a midsize Central California college, shared the movement between recognition of mothering and daughtering roles in her care work. Speaking from a different generation, she had to do some of the pioneering work on her campus as the first and only Black woman in her department. However, coming from generations of family who worked in education, Professor T's care work was an expression of her being a daughter to this legacy. She shared the personal impact of the work from this perspective:

> It's hard because sometimes I feel like I overstep and become more involved with people than I need to be. I have pro and cons [about my care work]—I feel like I'm creating better opportunities for [students] and in my life I feel fulfilled in terms of what I've accomplished. Like, in terms of being able to touch all these different generations of people—I always get moms and sisters and brothers and cousins and boyfriends saying, "oh yeah I want to take your class."

Her care work and commitment to her students manifests in several ways. She is involved in many service roles on campus, hoping that she can always point students to the right resources as well as help develop new ones. She also makes herself available for students beyond class time, even as adjuncts at her college are only compensated for a few office hours a semester, depending on budget. Even as she fluctuates between feeling like mother and daughter in her professional spaces, Professor T demonstrates the service-oriented perspective of daughter in her active engagement in all campus activities and feeling unfinished in her work.

Learning Personal and Professional Boundaries

Professor S, who works as a part-time professor at a midsize community college and as an articulation officer at a large community college, both in Central California, shared a building pressure on her as she is still early in her career. She is highly aware of the stereotypes of Black women in academia, and perhaps because of her mixed employment status, reflected on doing a lot of work to actively disprove stereotypes, even at a personal health cost. She explains:

> It's easy to lose yourself. You begin not to say "no". You just take things on, even if it's overwhelming or you know you're burning the candle at both ends. I don't want to always be the center voice or that person that everybody goes to, but it seems that even if I don't want to do it, I'll end up doing it.

Professor S did not feel like she had the agency in either of her positions to assert boundaries or not perform extra duties. Particularly in her roles as articulation officer, she found herself forced into extra work by colleagues who did not follow procedures she shared, or she had to make herself constantly available to explain things and fix things for them. As an early career professional, opportunities often feel tied to this performance of perfection.

With about thirty years of experience in higher education, and the last twenty of those working in community colleges, Professor P felt intimately familiar with struggling to be seen in her departments while also being asked to perform labor for colleagues and administration. Her reflection provides insight to understanding of the hot and cold receptions Black women professors receive from colleagues. After many years of feeling like the "village caretaker" she argued:

> And as Black women at the community college, especially in leadership positions, they make their own assumptions of us, and it could be based on how you look, how you carry yourself. At my community college we are very invisible or if we are in a position of leadership, people do not want us to be successful, and they do everything that they can to [challenge us].

Professor P shared staying late at work on a regular basis and feeling like her care/work was never acknowledged by her colleagues. An important thing that Professor P pointed out in her interview is that during the Covid-19 pandemic, when virtual meetings with students and colleagues entered her home space, she felt like she had no safe space from performing this care work other than her bedroom. Rather, as Botts-Ward (2022) says in her autotheory practice, "we learn that these bodies are the safest homes we've ever known, even in all of their precarity." Now as she begins to reassert boundaries, she must also work to reclaim the spaces where she feels like she gets reprieve from these expectations.

Mothering Versus Daughtering

As I analyzed these responses in my graduate work, the generational divide in relationship to mothering/daughtering roles became clear, and I found myself wondering how a long-term view of these pathways to burnout could open up space for a reimagining of these roles. While part of me still questioned the familial language of mother/daughter, my own experience and that of the interviewees taught me the feeling of cultural indebtedness to the legacy of mothering and daughtering was essential to finding empowerment and connection between our experiences.

From that long-term view and considering the generational attachment to the terms mother or daughter, I gathered several key understandings. For the early career participants, many felt they entered the profession with the expectation of being stereotyped and working against bias. Like me, as they were building their professional identities they watched (and participated in) critical changes to the institutional culture. The metaphor of daughtering resonated in multiple ways: it acknowledged the service they found themselves performing for the college, it honored the legacies of the elders in their home community and campus communities that they felt connected to, and it signaled a shift in awareness of their care work as campuses became more literate in equity language. For the mid-to-late year folks, like Professor T, beyond how students perceived her age, the resonance of the mothering role was also tied to her legacy of service to the institution—including the years it went virtually unacknowledged. Of my participants, around four more strongly identified this way, while seeing parallels to my proposed theory of daughtering in the CCCs context. Each of these participants had served as "firsts" in some way, first Black faculty (at all) or first Black faculty in a specific leadership position. They shared the experience of feeling deeply undervalued by the campus community. Between the mid-career folks, like Professor P, there was a clear focus on the self and healing journeys as they navigated how to assert new boundaries in their professional lives. Both of these categories felt unwavering commitment to their students and a sense of purpose in their teaching roles, rather than other leadership positions.

Conclusion: Visionary Daughtering

Daughtering defined through secret-keeping and supplanting provides us insight to the skill and cultural training that Black women bring to faculty roles. Acknowledging how these traits and skills are useful in the academic space allows us to imagine how to transform them into skills that feed our visions for autonomy and freedom in these spaces. Transforming the tension of secret-keeping to storytelling creates the movement towards visionary daughtering. The ontology of daughtering does not go away, in fact the continued embodiment of this role is crucial to the ability to do the visioning. Stepping into the identity of visionary daughters is the recognition of the skillset of cultural daughtering and the active transformation and/or reframing of these skills to restore agency, belonging and humanity to the daughtering person.

The term visionary daughtering comes from the mind of Alexis Pauline Gumbs, specifically a talk she delivered to Michigan State University in 2016 titled: "Visionary Daughtering: An Intimate and Intellectual Activist Archive."[2] Gumbs grounds the talk in June Jordan's guiding theory of "love is life force," signaling to her the healing energy that is possible with intergenerational connections. She defines daughtering "as work, a form of labor and a specific positionality that defines a variety of social and discursive relationships," which this work has outlined within the faculty context (Michigan State University 2016). Visionary daughtering in praxis is the intentional choice of care work that serves to restore my humanity and ability to radically imagine my potential, while continuing to honor the traditions that shaped me. In order to honor that legacy, any care work provided as a visionary daughter is informed by and trusts my embodied knowledge, my epistemology, and is sensitive to the communicative power of my dreams.

To be a visionary daughter is not measured by the extroverted, traditional modes of leadership. It is not solely in the speaking up, the fighting for a place at the table, or the protest. Rather, the visionary reclamation of the role of daughter is the self-care embedded in acknowledging the power we possess from our cultural background, lived experiences and community connections. It is in the modeling of boundaries, the assertion of voice, the mentoring of each other. Most importantly, it is in the ability to step back from the center of conflict and burn out to use our observational and care work skills to imagine new possibilities for our educational, community, and personal spaces.

I hesitate to frame visionary daughtering in a way that can be understood and palatable to our institutions, as something that can be taken and processed into a DEI recommendation; visionary daughtering belongs to the Black women faculty working to stay alive. I also reject the idea of creating or contributing to a survival guide to academia. Visionary daughtering asks us to push aside the prescribed notions of being in academia and undo the parts of our assimilation we can reach by holding our core values over the values of the institution. Our institutions will never value this kind of personal work or invest in our wellness when the system is predicated on our unwellness. The system relies on "healing" or wellness sessions that distract us from the self, our cultural wealth, and ways of knowing. Rather, they want to redirect us to the "why" of our work: why we care so much about our students, why service is necessary to build a strong campus community. This evades the naming of the system's expectations and abuses. As with the co-optation of "imposter syndrome," I do not offer visionary daughtering to the institution as a phrase for them to hollow out and individualize the experience of suffering or self-care.

What I offer to the institution is the opportunity to commit to spaces where community can be built, sustained, and funded. It is rare in the community colleges to have affinity spaces or activities—often it is a fight to even create those spaces for students

[2] With deep gratitude to Dr. Yomaira Figueroa for locating the recording of this session to help this research.

beyond categorical programs. There needs to be an investment in faculty professional development that is not solely tied to teaching, but rather focuses on retention strategies that value cultural wellness and knowledge. Faculty mentorship is vital to this as well, which can create spaces and relationships where faculty feel safe to express the difficulties of professional identity development and ask questions about and challenge campus culture. Spaces and time to build these community connections give partners to Black women faculty to collaborate with in new visions for our professional identities and ways to exist in institutional spaces.

The act of visioning asks to move forward, to step into vulnerability with the belief that you will gain a resilient strength by not hiding behind the superficial armor. Visionary daughtering can take the assumed labor of daughtering and "transform it into revolutionary potential, right at the site where bondage is supposed to be produced" (University of Michigan, Gumbs, 2015). This role of daughtering asks: can we reimagine the ways we deliver care and support (to the people and spaces we chose to) that emphasizes sharing sustainable healing and learning practices with those in our spheres of influence?

Competing Interests

The author has no conflicts of interest to declare that are relevant to the content of this manuscript.

References

Botts-Ward, R. (2022). On self-making and black girl interiors. *ASAP Journal*. https://asapjournal.com/transmedial-autotheories-5-healing-at-home-on-self-making-and-black-girl-interiors-ree-botts/

California Community College Chancellor's Office. (2020). *Call to action*. https://www.cccco.edu/-/media/CCCCO-Website/Files/Communications/dear-california-community-colleges-family

California Community College Chancellor's Office. (n.d.). *Vision for success*. https://www.cccco.edu/-/media/CCCCO-Website/Files/Workforce-and-Economic-Development/RFAs/19-300-001/appendix-d-vision-for-success-a11y.pdf

California State Assembly. (2022). *AB 1705*. https://leginfo.legislature.ca.gov/faces/billTextClient.xhtml?bill_id=202120220AB1705

Cuellar, M., Garcia, G., Nunez Martinez, M., & Bencomo Garcia, A. (2023). Building capacity for equity and servingness across California's Hispanic-serving community colleges. *USC Race and Equity Center*. https://static1.squarespace.com/static/62c4ba2609f6370427726636/t/64e3fc4108a23457e70a9415/1692662859454/Report%2B4%2BHSCC-spreads-small+%281%29.pdf

Cuellar Mejia, M., Rodriguez, O., Johnson, H., & Alesi Perez, C. (2022, August). Community college English in California's new era of student access. *Public Policy Institute of California*. https://www.ppic.org/publication/community-college-english-in-californias-new-era-of-student-access/

Ed Trust West. (n.d.). *Racial equity in remedial education.* https://west.edtrust.org/racial-equity-in-remedial-education/#:~:text=And%20yet%2C%20almost%2090%20percent,the%20California%20State%20University%20(CSU)

Evans-Winters, V. (2018). *Black feminist qualitative inquiry: Writing a mosaic of our daughter's bodies.* Routledge.

Graham, T. C. (2013). I'm not your momma, do your work: The Black female academic as surrogate mother. In S. Nzinga-Johnson (Ed.), *Laboring positions: Black women, mothering, and the academy* (pp. 111–123). Demeter Press.

Green, N. (2020). The re-education of Neisha-Anne S. Green: A close look at the damaging effects of 'a standard approach,' the benefits of code-meshing, and the roles allies play in this work. *Praxis: A Writing Center Journal, 14*(1).

hooks, b. (1990). Homeplace: A site of resistance. In *Yearning: Race, gender, and cultural politics* (pp. 382–390). South End Press.

hooks, b. (2014). Keeping close to home: Class and education. In *Talking back: Thinking feminist, thinking black.* Routledge.

Michigan State University. (2016). Dr. Alexis Pauline Gumbs, visionary daughtering: An intimate and intellectual activist archive [Video]. YouTube. https://www.youtube.com/watch?v=dBp8RVzPW8M

Nzinga-Johnson, S. (2013). Introduction: Extending the boundaries. In S. Nzinga-Johnson (Ed.), *Laboring positions: Black women, mothering, and the academy* (pp. 1–32). Demeter Press.

Poulos, C. N. (2021). Conceptual foundations of autoethnography. In C. N. Poulos (Ed.), *Essentials of autoethnography* (pp. 3–17). American Psychological Association.

Rankine, C. (2014). *Citizen: An American lyric.* Graywolf Press.

Robinson, T., & Hope, W. (2013). Teaching in higher education: Is there a need for training in pedagogy in graduate degree programs? *Research in Higher Education Journal, 21.* https://files.eric.ed.gov/fulltext/EJ1064657.pdf

Ross, L. (2016). Preface. In A. Gumbs, C. Martens, & M. Williams (Eds.), *Revolutionary mothering: Love on the front lines* (pp. ix–xiv). PM Press.

Williamson, T. (2024). Need that tastes like destruction: Lessons from (the) Lorde on the occasion of black death and dying. *Feminist Studies, 19*(2–3), 260–277.

Zwartjes, A. (2019a). Autotheory as rebellion: On research, embodiment, and imagination in creative nonfiction. *Michigan Quarterly Review.* https://sites.lsa.umich.edu/mqr/2019/07/autotheory-as-rebellion-on-research-embodiment-and-imagination-in-creative-nonfiction/

Zwartjes, A. (2019b). Under the skin: An exploration of autotheory. *Assay Journal, 8*(1). https://www.assayjournal.com/arianne-zwartjes8203-under-the-skin-an-exploration-of-autotheory-61.html

We All We Got! Kinship as Resistance: Reimagining the Academy Through Black Women's Othermothering

DeLisha Tapscott

Abstract This exploration of Black women scholars highlights the significance of fictive kinship and othermothering practices as crucial tools for resiliency, community-building, and resistance in academia. It reveals the intertwined struggles of navigating scholarly pursuits while simultaneously confronting institutionalized barriers, emphasizing the need for communal ties. Through a blended autoethnographic approach, it focuses on how Black women forge bonds similar to family, fostering emotional and intellectual sustenance amidst systemic othering. This research advocates for inclusive policies and practices that integrate the principles of these relational dynamics, acknowledging the unique experiences and labor undertaken by Black women in fostering equitable and emboldened spaces.

Keywords Othermothing · Fictive kinship · Higher education · Womanism · Intersectionality · Afrocentric feminist epistemology · Othering

Introduction

> She is a friend of my mind. She gather me, man. The pieces I am, she gather them and give them back to me in all the right order. (Morrison, 1987, pp. 272–273)

Morrison's words capture the essence of what it means to be held and seen—fully and without reservation. These words frame the connections that sustained me through the most challenging moments of my academic journey. In those moments when my breathing quickened, it was my sisters who held me close like my mother would, telling me, "We will make it through this." Even though we had no connection through blood, I credited my success to theirs and moved through the walls of academia, holding onto them for dear life. The walls around us were disingenuous and uninviting, casting doubt at each turn that our Black bodies belonged. Extending our love for one another, we practiced caregiving beyond biological boundaries. Moving

D. Tapscott (✉)
Purdue University, West Lafayette, IN, USA
e-mail: delisha@delishatapscott.com

C. R. Turner and M. L. Green (eds.), *Black Motherscholarship Within and Beyond the Academy*, https://doi.org/10.1007/978-3-031-99758-7_22

through these academic walls, we leaned into each other. We utilized the core principles of womanism and Afrocentric feminist epistemology by implementing strategies of resistance that were once born out of survival and ultimately transitioned into kinship rooted in love. During a global pandemic, we virtually held each other as we navigated the newness of an online doctoral program focused on organizational leadership. Our program, which claimed to focus on social justice, included only three faculty members of color during our time there. While we, the only four Black women in our cohort, were nominally welcomed into the space, the institution's actions often conveyed the opposite, implicitly suggesting that race should remain unspoken.

The Formation of Our Black Cohort—Finding Unity in Isolation

In the early stages of our doctoral journey, it became evident that the institutional environment was not designed to support us. While we initially only interacted during classes and group activities, our online immersion event, meant to unify the cohort, only magnified our feelings of isolation and exclusion. Behind the scenes, utilizing technology, we began connecting, validating each other's experiences, and recognizing the need for a space where our voices could be heard without dismissal. Our decision to form a Black cohort was born out of necessity, a collective understanding that we could only succeed if we supported each other. What began as individual frustrations evolved into a sanctuary of shared strength. Through our bond, we created a foundation of care and accountability, ensuring that no one would have to navigate this journey alone.

Within this space of shared strength and solidarity, individual acts of courage further defined our collective resistance. In practice, each of us had a hand in exemplifying how our kinship became both a shield and a rallying cry as she confronted systemic inequities head-on.

Takiah's Commitment to Sisterhood and Justice

As we navigated our program, Takiah exemplified the bravery required to confront inequities head-on, demonstrating how our kinship became both a shield and a rallying cry. While pregnant and navigating the demands of teaching in a racist school environment, she faced blatant bias from a faculty member who dismissed her concerns about the curriculum's lack of inclusivity. Rather than retreat, Takiah challenged this faculty member during a live session, using her lived experience to underscore the curriculum's inadequacies. Her boldness, coupled with our support behind the scenes, forced a broader conversation about whose voices and narratives were being centered in the program. Takiah's courage reaffirmed our commitment to advocacy and set a precedent for future cohorts to demand better.

It was here that we fostered community while feeling isolated and marginalized by an institution that neither held us nor guided us to safety (Collins, 1998; Maseti, 2018). We shared our voices and collective wisdom and framed our kinship to highlight our interdependence and intersectional narratives (Holland, 2017). While only three of us held biological mothering roles outside our institution's walls, we each became mothers to one another, ensuring that we were well-fed physically, mentally, emotionally, and spiritually (Maseti, 2018).

Whose Mother Are You?

Being raised in the Black community, one comes to learn that the idea of a chosen family is not new; however, the concept has been coined throughout the teachings of Black queer scholars, noting the necessary cultivation of family when facing spaces where dual exclusion is present (Cohen, 1997; Smith, 1983; Stack, 1974). For Black women, chosen family has often been utilized as a survivalist technique, especially those experiencing a sense of othering within the walls of predominantly white institutions (Cohen, 1997; hooks, 2018; Lorde, 1982; Smith, 1983). In this piece, I describe higher education institutions as spaces where whiteness and white dominance co-create the notion of othering as they uphold the marginalization of Black women scholars, rendering them invisible or fundamentally different (Cohen, 1997; Collins, 1990a; hooks, 1981; Lorde, 1984).

Fictive kinship and othermothering practices have been crucial for Black women in academia, enabling them to nurture resiliency and academic persistence (Collins, 1998; Grant & Ghee, 2015). The labor involved in developing and maintaining these supportive networks—often through acts of care, mentorship, and advocacy—is largely deemed invisible. This labor includes the emotional and intellectual effort required to forge connections with other Black women while simultaneously navigating the complexities of institutional racism and sexism (Crenshaw, 1989). These practices of othermothering are often leveraged as resistance to these barriers (Guiffrida, 2005). I define othermothering as the act of nurturing, protecting, and supporting others beyond biological ties. It acts as a survival strategy recognized and valued by Black women and Black motherscholars as an essential component in the communal and mentoring roles in raising Black women scholars (Collins, 1990b; Stovall, 2022).

Through this research, I advocate envisioning and enacting transformative futures that dismantle oppressive structures to foster equitable and inclusive spaces. Explicitly, this work explores the following question:

- How do Black women scholars utilize othermothering and fictive kinship practices to simultaneously navigate the interconnected pressures of scholarly pursuits while forming a resistance against institutionalized barriers?

Grounded in Womanism (Maparyan, 2012; Phillips, 2006; Walker, 1983) with Afrocentric feminist epistemology (AFE) as a foundation (Asante, 1998; Collins, 1998) and Intersectionality at its core (Cho et al., 2013; Crenshaw, 1989; Hancock, 2016), this chapter underscores the importance of voice and collective wisdom while illuminating the duality of the experiences of Black women scholars by highlighting the transformative power of Black women scholars and motherscholars' fictive kinship and othermothering practices in academic spaces (Collins, 1990a, 1990b; Crenshaw, 1989; Walker, 1983).

To ground myself in these frameworks, it was important to ground this narrative in my lived experiences. To do so, I turn to my sister scholars—Takiah, Tiffeni, and Jewell—whose stories illustrate the power of kinship, othermothering, and collective action in navigating and resisting the systemic barriers we faced.

Reflections on Kinship Through My Sister Scholars

When I think about our journey through my doctoral program, I see the strength, grace, and complexity of the women who became my anchors. Each of them, in their own way, showed me what it meant to stand firm in a space that was not built for us.

For me, Tiffeni was a grounding force; within her, she carried the weight of wisdom and experience. When I think of her, I think of her work as a librarian. If I had to define her, I would describe her as Black with a capital B; her life's work focuses on pushing back against an educational system that seeks to silence narratives. Through her, I learned about the power of knowledge and how to wield my voice with purpose. See, Tiffeni did not just navigate spaces—she claimed them, showing me that power does not always have to be loud but must always be intentional. Her ability to tie our present struggles to the resilience of the past reminded me that we belonged, even when our academic institution tried to make us feel otherwise.

Next, there was Jewell. She had a quiet but energetic strength that emerged in powerful ways. Throughout our program, I watched her navigate the demands of a job she no longer wanted, a beautiful relationship, and the dual responsibilities of her own health and her mother's health with a resolve that inspired me. Within the program, she refused to back down in the face of those who sought to silence us. Jewell reminded us that our voices matter, even when they tremble. She taught me to push through uncertainty and claim space, even when it felt uncomfortable.

Then, there was Takiah, the embodiment of persistence. A mother of young children, she spent much of our program pregnant while working in a racist school environment that constantly tested her resolve as a teacher. However, she never faltered in using her voice to challenge the inequities around her. Takiah showed me what it meant to balance personal struggles with a relentless commitment to justice. Her courage reminded me that the fight is not just for us but for the generations that come after.

Last but certainly not least, there was me. A wife, caretaker, and mother of two, battling depression and anxiety while carrying the weight of working in a DEI role in a climate post-Breonna Taylor. The role itself drained me as the organization was more interested in diet-DEI principles than in making lasting changes. I often felt like I was holding my breath, juggling life, work, and the program's intensity. However, these women sustained me. Through their voices, their actions, and their unwavering belief in us making it, I found the strength to keep going. Together, we built something that felt sacred—a space where we could pour into each other, hold each other, and remind each other that we deserved to be here.

Grounded Within: Fictive Kinship and Othermothering

This piece centers Black women, who hold me steady and guide me spiritually as I write. Built on diverse frameworks, it embeds Blackness and honors the unique experiences of womanhood, community, care, and resistance. Fictive kinship and othermothering have supported my journey and shaped this work.

While these kinships are often labeled as "fictive" due to the absence of blood ties, the term itself fails to capture the depth and significance of these relationships. Referring to them as fictive can unintentionally diminish the profound connections and emotional bonds they embody, framing them as less real or substantial (Carby, 1987; Stack, 1974). As an only child without siblings, I have built my community and family through intentional relationships with people who entered my life without any prior ties. These individuals often hold greater importance to me than some blood relatives, as they represent my chosen family, who sustain me in ways that traditional kinship cannot.

Similarly, the concept of othermothering expands the idea of care and family, offering a level of support and nurturing akin to a mother's love (Guy-Sheftall, 1995; James, 1993). Relationships like those with my sister scholars reflect this dynamic, providing not just guidance but a depth of care that goes beyond simple connection. Together, fictive kinship and othermothering illustrate how Black women create profound systems of care and support rooted in love and sustained through intentional community-building. Table 1 distills these concepts, offering a clear framework for understanding their cultural roots, personal significance, and collective impact.

Methodology & Framing: Centering Kinship and Voice

Data Collection

This chapter adopts a blended autoethnographic approach rooted in my lived experiences as a Black woman scholar navigating a predominantly white academic institution. Autoethnography allows me to center my personal narrative while simultaneously exploring the transformative role of relational dynamics—specifically fictive

Table 1 The role of fictive kinship and othermothering in building community and resistance

CONCEPT	DEFINITION	CULTURAL CONTEXT	PERSONAL REFLECTION & IMPACT
FICTIVE KINSHIP	Social bonds and relationships are formed through cultural and social acknowledgment, not based on blood or legal ties (Billingsley, 1992; West & Fenstermaker, 1995).	In Black communities, kinship often transcends biology, with terms like "auntie" and "cousin" used to signify chosen family connections (Chatters, 1984; Nelson).	As an only child, I create family through intentional relationships. These bonds, often stronger than those with blood relatives, sustain and ground me, offering a chosen family that becomes essential to my well-being. This Serves as a foundation of emotional and psychological support, enabling resilience and creating spaces of belonging that challenge exclusionary systems.
OTHER-MOTHERING	Extends the maternal role beyond biological mothers to include community members who provide care, guidance, and nurturing (Griffin, 2004; Harris, 2019).	Rooted in the ethos of "it takes a village," othermothering fosters collective care, often forming bonds through shared intersectional experiences of race, gender, and class.	During my doctoral journey, othermothering manifested through acts of care—texts, care packages, and celebrations—reflecting a deep commitment and nurturing solidarity bonds. This Foster's sanctuary and resistance within exclusionary spaces, providing tangible care and advocacy that enable persistence and collective empowerment among Black women scholars.

kinship and othermothering—in fostering persistence and acts of resistance. This methodology integrates personal recollections, a review of our digital archive in GroupMe and text messages, and reflections on shared experiences with my sister scholars—Takiah, Tiffeni, and Jewell. These relationships served as a lifeline during moments of systemic exclusion and isolation, anchoring me in spaces of care, support, and advocacy.

Data Analysis

Rather than generalizing their stories, I reflect on these bonds' deep personal and collective significance in our lives. The voices of my sister scholars are woven throughout the narrative, appearing in vignettes and shared reflections that highlight how our relationships enabled us to resist institutional barriers and envision new possibilities within the academy. These vignettes provide tangible examples of how our kinship served as both a means of survival and a foundation for systemic change. By bridging the personal and collective, I position kinship and community-building as essential tools for reimagining academic spaces through the stories and lived experiences of my sister scholars and me.

Theoretical Frameworks

To do this, I engage in three interconnected frameworks: Womanism, Afrocentric Feminist Epistemology, and Intersectionality. Together, they highlight how fictive kinship and othermothering enabled us as Black women scholars to persist and resist within predominantly white institutions (Ogunyemi, 1985; Phillips, 2006).

- Womanism emphasizes survival, care, and resilience (Collins, 1998; Walker, 1983). Previously, during my doctoral program, I wrote about our bond and how it allowed us to lean "into each other out of fear of losing more than just ourselves" (Sylvester, 2022, p. 2). Our sanctuary created resistant capital (Yosso, 2005), capturing our perspectives and resources. This capital enabled us to develop strategies that supported our navigation of a racialized environment (Maparyan, 2012; Sylvester, 2022). My sister scholars and I embraced these principles, forming a virtual refuge to support one another emotionally, celebrate successes, and share strategies for resistance.
- Afrocentric Feminist Epistemology (AFE) amplifies storytelling, shared knowledge, and cultural wisdom to resist dominant narratives in white-dominated spaces (Collins, 1998; Weems, 1993). My sister scholars and I used storytelling to empower ourselves and center our voices. Through Afrocentric feminist epistemology, our fictive kinship became a network of shared knowledge, and othermothering reflected communal care (Collins, 1998; Holland, 2017).
- Intersectionality emphasizes how race, gender, and other identities interact with systems of oppression. For Black women, academic challenges must be examined through their combined impact (Ahmed, 2012; Crenshaw, 1989, 1991). Within my doctoral program, this intersectional framework was essential to understanding the compounded pressures we faced as Black women. Our identities shaped not only how we were perceived but also how we were treated by faculty, peers, and institutional structures. Microaggressions, such as being labeled "too emotional" or "too aggressive," were not just acts of racial bias or gender discrimination but were situated at the intersection of both (Dickens et al.,2023; Sylvester, 2022).

Visualization

It was essential to create a visual showcasing the dynamic and interconnected nature of Black women and Black motherscholars' mutual support, as illustrated in Fig. 1. This model demonstrates how these frameworks work together to create a foundation of intersectional kinship within academic communities.

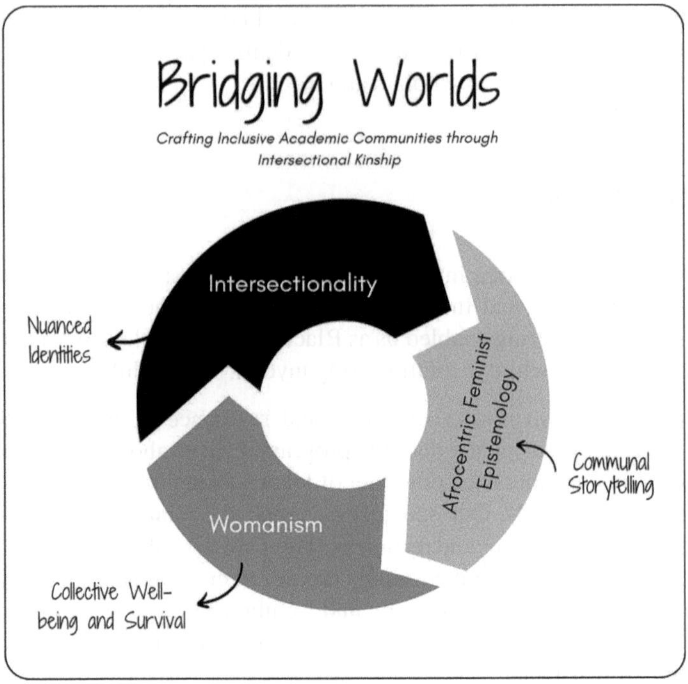

Fig. 1 Bridging worlds: crafting inclusive academic communities through intersectional kinship

Grounding this work in these theories amplifies the cyclical nature and holistic approach, which calls for an improved understanding and continued evolution of practices within academic spaces.

Architects of Resistance: Constructing Networks of Othermothering and Kinship

When I began writing this piece, I thought of a term that would encompass how we, as Black women scholars, were the designers of our own space: architects of our resistance. This term reflects how we intentionally and strategically created spaces of care, advocacy, and survival within an academic system that often excludes us. As architects, we used our collective creativity and determination to construct support networks through othermothering and fictive kinship. These spaces became both a refuge from harm and a foundation for challenging the inequities we faced. Our resistance was not incidental; it was purposeful, rooted in our shared experiences, and focused on reimagining what it meant to persist and thrive in an environment not designed for us.

In May 2020, during the global pandemic, I met my sister scholars for the first time as we began our doctoral program. Out of about ten Black students in our cohort, we became the only four left, as others had left the program for various reasons. At first, we didn't know each other well, only connecting during classes or group activities. However, during a multi-day virtual immersion meant to foster community and introduce us to the program's values, our shared feelings of exclusion became impossible to ignore. One session focused on the Enneagram, a personality framework described as a tool for self-awareness and growth. When we challenged its lack of intersectionality and pointed out how it centered on whiteness while erasing other experiences of color, the presenter dismissed our input entirely. As we tried to press the issue, the program's dean silenced us by brushing off our concerns in front of our peers. At that moment, those interactions intensified months of feeling unseen, making it painfully clear that this program was not designed to include or value us.

Despite not knowing each other well, we found ourselves leaning on one another during that experience. Behind the scenes on Zoom, we messaged each other, affirming what we felt was valid and offering support in real time. Together, we strategized how to respond, determined not to let them erase us. In that moment, what started as shared frustration turned into the foundation of a bond. Afterward, we decided to meet outside of class to build deeper connections and create the support system the program failed to provide.

Not long after, the dean called us into a meeting. Instead of addressing the harm done or validating our experiences, he made the conversation about himself, referencing his identity as a white gay man with Black children as if that provided a semblance to our identities and experiences. He then shifted the focus onto us, asking for suggestions on how to improve the program for students of color. His request for our unpaid emotional and intellectual labor was frustrating, especially in a program that claimed to center social justice but left us to fill in the gaps.

We left that meeting angry, exhausted, and questioning whether we should even stay. The program clearly was not built for us, and it showed in every interaction. However, leaving didn't feel like an option. We were the first in our families to pursue doctoral degrees, and quitting was not something we were willing to accept. Instead, we turned inward, building strength through each other. Together, we created a space where we could thrive, even when the program refused to hold space for us.

From that moment on, we dealt with one thing after another, including a racist and sexist teacher, a diversity, equity, and inclusion course that did not address inequities as they were happening, and countless instances of microaggressions from our cohort members. While we left those moments in tears and with our hearts in pain, what came from them was the birth of our sister circle—a sanctuary for four Black women from varying places. A librarian, a teacher, an analyst, and a director at a nonprofit, varying ages and statuses, came together to commit to holding each other through this. We came together out of necessity and of understanding what it felt like to hold isolation and frustration in the centers of our chests in a space that seemed indifferent, if not somewhat hostile, to our presence.

Taking a Stand Together

Our collective efforts to confront institutional wrongs reached a defining moment when we decided to take action against a faculty member's harmful behavior. His actions, rooted in both racism and sexism, created a toxic classroom environment where students felt silenced and uncomfortable. He often made disparaging comments during lectures that exposed his biases, emboldening others to reveal their own discriminatory beliefs. These dynamics made the space unbearable, as his dismissive attitude toward our pushback, whether out of obliviousness or indifference, only reinforced the harm. His behavior, which had been an ongoing issue before we joined the program, had gone unchecked until we spoke up. Further showcasing that we were forced to do what the university would not. Meeting with the equity team at our university, we shared detailed accounts of his actions and their impact on our learning environment. This collective effort led to his departure, a powerful example of how speaking truth to power can create change. This moment highlighted how systemic oppression impacted us while demonstrating how our collective voices could disrupt harmful norms and demand accountability.

Although we started as strangers, we quickly embraced othermothering practices, caring for one another as if we were sisters despite not being blood-related. These bonds of care soon evolved into providing each other with the guidance needed to navigate the program and ensure we could all succeed. We would schedule our classes with each other in mind. Thursdays from 7 to 10 pm became our night. We would ensure that it worked for all of us when it was time to sign up for classes so that we could have each other's backs. If it did not work for us, we switched to a time that would. If someone was sick, one or two other sisters were always present to stand at attention. It was like we were standing arms linked with each other, bracing ourselves and blocking for one another in moments of distress. Sundays became our time to replenish the energy we had spent. We used that time to talk about the foolishness of our live sessions, work on our homework, or get thought partners for our dissertations. We would advise each other on where to look for sources, how to track our information, and chat about what was happening with us outside of coursework. That time was our necessary sanctuary, where we built a sisterhood that held each other accountable through moments of doubt and triumph.

As a recent doctoral graduate, I look back on the experiences of my sister scholars and me. In the beginning, I genuinely believed we were hopeful, thinking that reaching this level of success surely would have afforded us some sense of belonging, acceptance, and sustenance, but it just was not that. As architects of resistance, we built community and connection, holding and nurturing each other as mothers would their children. While there were fleeting moments of hope, our experience was primarily defined by what we could create with the limited materials we were given. For me, this journey was both exhausting and beautiful. We carved out spaces where whiteness had no place, transforming kinship and othermothering into necessary acts of survival. While we voluntarily chose to love and care for each other, our coming together was born out of necessity; these bonds were forged as both a refuge and a resistance, demonstrating how survival often necessitates intentional community-building in spaces where exclusion is the norm. I wish we could have had the opportunity to build these bonds naturally out of want rather than need, nurturing each other freely rather than out of necessity. I often wonder what our time would have been like if we had an environment that saw and heard us and came prepared to love us to the extent we needed it. However, even in that exhaustion and frustration, we remained the architects of our resistance, which became a reminder of our strength and what academia could be if it created space for us to belong without resistance.

Building Resiliency and Community Through Invisible Labor

What I have come to realize is that through our kinship, we created supportive networks that stretched beyond academic guidance into foundational practices focused on emotional and intellectual growth. In other words, no one could tell us we would not make it as long as we had each other. Our destinies became linked, our sanctuary spaces became birthing grounds for collective boundary setting, and our practices reshaped the landscape for those who came after. While we used our bodies to absorb the racism, sexism, and colorism we experienced, we crafted resilience strategies that pushed back against our institution's lack of support. Admittedly, these strategies were not always healthy. The weight of constantly pushing back against systemic oppression often left us emotionally and physically drained. However, through the power of our bond, we cultivated a collective understanding: we were not only making it out alive and intact, but we were also laying a foundation for others to thrive.

Emotionally, we were worn out, but our support of one another validated our experiences. As Black women in higher education, we were all too familiar with the pervasive feelings of isolation and alienation that stemmed from being overlooked and undervalued within academic spaces (Collins, 1998). These shared experiences deepened our kinship practice, enabling us to nurture and pour into one another. It ultimately extended beyond itself into moments of solidarity and mutual respect for what we had given to our process. This sense of care was crucial to our emotional validation and advancement (Buckingham, 2018). Our collective mothering also supported us in pushing our narratives to the forefront and forcing the university to center our needs, whether they wanted to or not. In a way, we could assert our intellectual and professional identities within this predominantly white institution, moving ourselves into the center of what felt like a storm. Still, instead of our house being brittle and broken, we repaired it each time with steel (Davis, 2011).

Standing on Business with an Unyielding Voice

Jewell's quiet but unwavering resolve reminded us of our shared purpose, especially in moments when her insights were unfairly overlooked. During a critical group project, Jewell's contributions were consistently ignored by her peers. Frustrated but undeterred, she confided in us. Together, we strategized to amplify her voice in the next meeting. When Jewell spoke, we redirected the group's attention to her insights, affirming her points and challenging the dismissive dynamics at play. This was not just about ensuring her contributions were acknowledged; it was about dismantling the stereotypes that rendered Black women's voices invisible. Jewell's strength, supported by our collective advocacy, demonstrated the transformative power of our bond.

Conclusion: Imagining a Radical Future for Academia

The concepts of othermothering and fictive kinship offered us a way to respond strategically to the institutional barriers we experienced. We used these practices to advocate for institutional reforms that included the removal of certain professors, consideration of the literature we reviewed within our coursework, and opportunities to work directly with the school on a bias-focused task force. We wanted to see the change and knew it would not happen under the institution's timeline. While we recognized this was not our responsibility, we did not want what happened to us to happen to anyone else if we could help it. In my first academically published piece, I decided to publish a journal article about our experiences that detailed the creation of our sanctuary space, the burden of our resiliency, and the lessons I learned from being a part of an archaic institution that sought to promote change and inclusion but practically missed its mark (Sylvester, 2022). Within this piece, I relived the impacts of exclusive spaces while also suggesting radical change by utilizing bell hooks' (1994) Love as a Practice of Freedom and Brooks's (2017) Critical Theory of Love to focus on liberation. While this commentary highlighted our struggles, it ultimately acted as a catalyst for shifting this work above and beyond our sisterhood, stretching out into other cohorts to ensure they would not experience the same.

Ultimately, much of our labor remained invisible to peers, faculty, and the broader academic community—those who benefited from our contributions without acknowledging them. This labor included mentoring other students, advocating for institutional change, and creating spaces of care and support, all while meeting the demands of our academic responsibilities. These efforts went unrecognized because they fell outside traditional measures of academic success (Richie, 2012). Our outspokenness as Black women further compounded this burden. Both students of color and white students often relied on us to address inequities or advocate for changes, looking to us for leadership but rarely stepping forward themselves. The weight of these expectations, combined with limited institutional support, left us navigating both personal struggles and systemic challenges, often at great personal cost.

For Black women scholars, this lack of recognition exacerbates systemic inequities, undervaluing the emotional and intellectual labor we contribute while expecting us to carry the burden alone. These contributions, critical to the academic community, are dismissed or overlooked, taking a toll on our professional growth and well-being. While my sister scholars and I completed our degrees, this journey was not without challenges. By the end, we felt a sense of relief but also abandonment by the university, as if it was just as ready to move on from us as we were from it. Though we excelled in our dissertation work, the atmosphere surrounding us was heavy, a reminder of the isolation we endured and the lack of institutional support we longed for.

Towards the end of our time, we felt they were just as done with us as we were with them, and while we were excelling in our dissertation work, the air around us was thick. It was as if, even in the end, we were being seen as the problem that needed to be pushed away rather than the women who could have supported drastic programmatic changes. While never spoken, the tension around our presence was always a cloud, and with every moment that passed, the more we pushed through the program, the more we leaned into one another because there was no one else who could hold us up but ourselves.

While reflecting on my past experiences, I find it essential to dream forward into a future that radically reimagines academia, not just for Black women and Black motherscholars but also for those who navigate intersecting roles as faculty members, administrators, and mentors within these systems. Reimagining these structures requires academic environments and scholars to embrace transformative change through policies, practices, and research. This vision challenges existing norms, integrating Black women's collective care, cultural knowledge, and communal resilience into the fabric of academia.

For this vision to thrive, institutions must prioritize:

- **Transformative Leadership**: Empower Black women to shape policies and practices, centering their voices as experts in decision-making.
- **Equitable Resource Allocation**: Fund research, mentorship, and wellness initiatives that reflect Black women's lived experiences and needs.
- **Leadership and Representation**: Embed cultural knowledge and collective practices into academic communities to cultivate authentic inclusion.

As a Black woman and recent doctoral graduate, I cannot proudly hold this title without committing to changing the system that excluded me. My strength to persist came from the unwavering support of Takiah, Tiffeni, and Jewell, who stood beside me. Together, we provided care in a space that often felt hostile and unwelcoming. Beyond traditional caregiving roles, we became confidants, mentors, and advocates, sharing resources, supporting each other's work, and creating a sanctuary where we could simply be…us.

Additionally, our intersectional kinship gave us the agency to create a bond as strong and as valid as those we were related to by blood. We celebrated our wins; we held each other during our frustrations and talked each other down from our fears. We codesigned a safe haven—a sanctuary—a radical resistance to help us persist in our scholarly pursuits. Therefore, this research is a continuation of the efforts taken by four Black women scholars who dared to dream of something different than we experienced. By dreaming and advocating for change, this piece hopes to be a part of imagining what it means to enact a radical future that institutionalizes the practices and principles of othermothering and fictive kinship, hoping to utilize them no longer to survive, but that they become a standard component of thriving.

Competing Interests The author has no conflicts of interest to declare that are relevant to the content of this manuscript.

References

Ahmed, S. (2012). *On being included: Racism and diversity in institutional life.* Duke University Press.

Asante, M. K. (1998). *The Afrocentric idea.* Temple University Press.

Brooks, D. (2017). *Critical theory of love: Reflections for liberation.* Routledge.

Buckingham, D. (2018). *Invisible labor: A mixed-method study of African American women and their emotional labor in the academy* (Electronic Theses and Dissertations 849). https://egrove.olemiss.edu/etd/849

Carby, H. V. (1987). *Reconstructing womanhood: The emergence of the Afro-American woman novelist.* Oxford University Press.

Cho, S., Crenshaw, K. W., & McCall, L. (2013). Toward a field of intersectionality studies: Theory, applications, and praxis. *Signs: Journal of Women in Culture and Society, 38*(4), 785–810. https://doi.org/10.1086/669608

Cohen, C. J. (1997). Punks, bulldaggers, and welfare queens: The radical potential of queer politics? *GLQ: A Journal of Lesbian and Gay Studies, 3*(4), 437–465. https://doi.org/10.1215/10642684-3-4-437

Collins, P. H. (1990a). *Black feminist thought: Knowledge, consciousness, and the politics of empowerment.* Routledge.

Collins, P. H. (1990b). Black feminist thought in the matrix of domination. In *Black feminist thought: Knowledge, consciousness, and the politics of empowerment* (pp. 221–238). Routledge.

Collins, P. H. (1998). The social construction of Black feminist thought. *Signs: Journal of Women in Culture and Society, 14*(4), 745–773. https://doi.org/10.1086/494543

Crenshaw, K. W. (1989). Demarginalizing the intersection of race and sex: A Black feminist critique of antidiscrimination doctrine, feminist theory, and antiracist politics. *University of Chicago Legal Forum, 1989*(1), 139–167.

Crenshaw, K. W. (1991). Mapping the margins: Intersectionality, identity politics, and violence against women of color. *Stanford Law Review, 43*(6), 1241–1299. https://doi.org/10.2307/1229039

Davis, A. Y. (2011). *Women, race, & class.* Vintage.

Dickens, D., Hall, N., Farmer, M., & Johnson, N. (2023). Diary study on microaggressions, identity shifting, and mental health among Black women in STEM graduate programs during COVID-19: The mediating role of perceived supervisor support. *Journal of African American Women and Girls in Education, 3*(1), 10–30.

Grant, C. M., & Ghee, S. (2015). Mentoring 101: Advancing African-American women faculty and doctoral student success in predominantly White institutions. *International Journal of Qualitative Studies in Education, 28*(7), 759–785. https://doi.org/10.1080/09518398.2015.1036951
Guiffrida, D. (2005). Othermothering as a framework for understanding African American students' definitions of student-centered faculty. *Journal of Higher Education, 76*(6), 701–723. https://doi.org/10.1353/jhe.2005.0041
Guy-Sheftall, B. (1995). *Words of fire: An anthology of African-American feminist thought.* The New Press.
Hancock, A. (2016). *Intersectionality: An intellectual history.* Oxford University Press.
Holland, N. E. (2017). Beyond conventional wisdom: Community cultural wealth and the college knowledge of African American youth in the United States. *Race, Ethnicity and Education, 20*(6), 796–810. https://doi.org/10.1080/13613324.2016.1150823
hooks, b. (1981). *Ain't I a woman: Black women and feminism.* South End Press.
hooks, b. (1994). *Teaching to transgress: Education as the practice of freedom.* Routledge.
hooks, b. (2018). *All about love: New visions.* HarperCollins.
James, S. M. (1993). A possible Black Feminist link to social transformation? In S. M. James & A. P. A. Busia (Eds.), *Theorizing black feminisms: The visionary pragmatism of Black women* (p. 45). Routledge.
Lorde, A. (1982). *Zami: A new spelling of my name.* Crossing Press.
Lorde, A. (1984). *Sister outsider: Essays and speeches.* Crossing Press.
Maparyan, L. (2012). *The womanist idea.* Routledge.
Maseti, T. (2018). The university is not your home: Lived experiences of a Black woman in academia. *South African Journal of Psychology, 48*(3), 343–350. https://doi.org/10.1177/0081246318792820
Morrison, T. (1987). *Beloved.* Knopf.
Ogunyemi, C. O. (1985). Womanism: The dynamics of the contemporary Black female novel in English. *Signs: Journal of Women in Culture and Society, 11*(1), 63–80. https://doi.org/10.1086/494200
Phillips, L. (2006). Womanism: On its own. In L. Phillips (Ed.), *The womanist reader* (pp. 19–22). Routledge.
Richie, B. E. (2012). *Arrested justice: Black women, violence, and America's prison nation.* NYU Press.
Smith, B. (1983). *Home girls: A Black feminist anthology.* Kitchen Table Press.
Stack, C. B. (1974). *All our kin: Strategies for survival in a Black community.* Harper & Row.
Stovall, W. (2022). *Yes, it's for us: An examination of Black othermothering as a framework for cultural brokering for African American students and families* (Doctoral dissertation). California State University, Sacramento.
Sylvester, D. (2022). Against all odds: Reflections from a "scary" Black woman. *Dialogues in Social Justice, 7*(1), Article R1337.
Walker, A. (1983). *In search of our mothers' gardens: Womanist prose.* Harcourt.
Weems, C. H. (1993). *Africana womanism: Reclaiming ourselves.* Bedford Publishers.
Yosso, T. J. (2005). Whose culture has capital? A critical race theory discussion of community cultural wealth. *Race, Ethnicity and Education, 8*(1), 69–91. https://doi.org/10.1080/1361332052000341006

DeLisha Tapscott, Ed.D., is a writer, researcher, and social change agent with a background in organizational leadership and management. Her research examines the intersectional experiences of identity negotiation and Black women within white-dominant spaces. With a focal point on Black women, she believes that "Black women and their stories are ignored and often become whispers in the background, like ghosts in the night," As a facilitator, she has spoken and written about social justice, the experiences of Black women within society, and intersectionality at various venues, such as Harvard University, Texas A&M University, and the University of Maryland. She is passionate about using her talents and platforms to speak up against injustices impacting the Black community and to inspire others to become catalysts for change.

Beyond Surviving: On Black Motherscholars Thriving in Wellness

Tiffany S. Wiggins, Regina Gavin Williams, and Jemilia S. Davis

Abstract Black mother scholars experience a multitude of challenges in their efforts to successfully integrate the needs and demands of their dynamic lives. From unsupportive workplaces to dual oppression, feelings of isolation to being an on-demand caregiver, their journeys are complex and often untold. Grounded in Black Feminist Thought, the authors share a collaborative autoethnography on their nuanced realities as Black women faculty, practitioners, and mothers. Drawing on the IS-Wel model, they not only illuminate their individual narratives of survival in the pursuit of wellness, belonging, and leading, but also reimagine a world where they and their sistren thrive.

Keywords Black feminist thought · Autoethnography · IS-Wel model · Wellness & belonging

Introduction

In the context of systemic barriers and individual struggles, Black mothers in the United States confront unique and complex challenges that often go unnoticed. Black mothers experience different pressures due to the history of labor participation, discrimination, and social pressures to work outside the home to provide for their families (Collins, 2022; Dow, 2019). The statistics are telling: eighty-five percent of Black mothers serve as either co- or primary breadwinners while

T. S. Wiggins · R. G. Williams
North Carolina Central University, Durham, NC, USA
e-mail: rwill233@nccu.edu

J. S. Davis
University of North Carolina at Chapel Hill, Chapel Hill, NC, USA
e-mail: tsw@unc.edu

J. S. Davis
e-mail: jemilia_davis@unc.edu

C. R. Turner and M. L. Green (eds.), *Black Motherscholarship Within and Beyond the Academy*, https://doi.org/10.1007/978-3-031-99758-7_23

committing significant time and energy to developing and maintaining their homeplace (Coleman-King et al., 2022; Glynn, 2016; hooks, 1990). This labor intensifies as Black mothers navigate the dual oppression of racism and sexism while simultaneously protecting their children from discrimination and countering negative messaging (Garland McKinney & Meinersmann, 2023). These high levels of mental, physical, social/emotional, and financial labor can have significant tolls on the health and well-being of working Black mothers (Woods-Giscombé, 2010).

As Black mothers who are faculty members in the academy, we recognize these challenges through our lived experiences. Our positionality reflects what Patricia Collins defines as the Black woman's standpoint—a unifying perspective informed by the intersectional oppression of race and gender (Collins, 1989). From this standpoint, we explore our experiences as Black motherscholars, examining how we navigate and resist a workplace environment with a legacy of exclusion and labor exploitation that targets our intersectional identities. The structure and systems that comprise most U.S. colleges and universities frequently position us to establish our own sense of work-life balance, reinforcing a gender hierarchy that fails to foster family- or life-friendly work environments in academia (Anderson et al., 2014; Berheide et al., 2022).

While documenting Black motherscholars' barriers remains crucial for driving institutional change, we deliberately shift our gaze toward the possibilities of thriving in these spaces. Inspired by Audre Lorde's powerful declaration that "caring for oneself is not self-indulgence, it is self-preservation, and that is an act of political warfare" (Lorde, 1988), we define thriving as making intentional progress toward holistic wellness—a state that encompasses our mental, physical, emotional, and spiritual well-being. Through a collaborative autoethnographic approach, we blend Myers and Sweeney's (2004) Indivisible Self (IS-Wel) model with Patricia Hill Collins' Black feminist thought (2022) to examine our experiences in the academy. This integrated framework allows us to provide voice and truth to the nuanced lives of three Black women at the intersection of faculty expectations, practitioner roles, and parenting demands. By sharing our individual and collective journeys toward wellness, we contribute to the cultural heritage of Black feminist thought while inviting other motherscholars to join us in reimagining an academic context where thriving, not just surviving, becomes our collective reality.

The Motherscholars

We are Tiffany, Regina, and Jemilia—the three sister scholars and co-authors of this chapter, whose individual journeys in womanhood, motherhood, and scholarship have become beautifully intertwined through shared experiences, professional paths, and intentional community building. Our paths converged through a beautiful tapestry of professional connections, mutual friends, and shared commitments to supporting Black mothers in academia. Our paths first crossed individually—Regina and Jemilia as colleagues at the same institution during Jemilia's doctoral studies, Tiffany moving to North Carolina years later to step into Regina's former role, and all of us connecting through *Melanin Mommas*—the local Black mom group founded by Jemilia and Regina. These intersecting journeys blossomed into a powerful sisterhood that embodies the wellness and community we advocate for in this chapter. Together, we represent different experiences of Black motherscholarship while sharing a common vision for thriving in academia.

Tiffany: I am an assistant professor of higher education administration at a mid-sized public HBCU in North Carolina, where my 15 years of experience as a higher education practitioner-scholar inform my teaching, research, and praxis. My journey as a Black motherscholar began in my late 20s as a new mom to my only daughter while working as an undergraduate student advisor at a university in Washington, DC. Early experiences of balancing city life, student-facing work, and high child-care costs taught me invaluable lessons about the power of community and self-advocacy—ultimately deciding to return to my hometown in Virginia for a career reset and family support. Over a decade later, having earned a Ph.D. and navigated multiple personal and professional transitions, I am a single mother, successfully co-parenting across state lines, raising a Black young woman to embrace her inherent brilliance and beauty. This journey deepened significantly when my relocation to North Carolina in 2019 connected me to a transformative sisterhood of Black women, many working within academia. My scholarship focuses on Black women's lived experiences across the academy, paralleling my evolution in understanding holistic wellness and collective care. Having moved through various institutional contexts—from PWIs to HBCUs, from staff to faculty roles—I developed a keen understanding of how institutional structures can nurture or hinder our wellness journeys. My commitment to mentoring Black women emerged from my own experiences and was strengthened by the realization that my daughter was watching how I treated myself, managed stress, and built community. This awareness and the power of genuine sisterhood in academia fuel my dedication to modeling holistic wellness as personal practice and resistance against systems not designed for us to flourish.

Jemilia: I am a clinical assistant professor and program director for an undergraduate major at a public, large, predominately white institution in a small southeastern city. Being raised by parents who migrated from Jamaica for education, the daughter of a college professor and administrator, my deep commitment to education and the opportunity it espouses to provide began at a young age. Today, it has translated into three education degrees and 15 years of experience across public education sectors with the hope that I am doing my part to promote equitable success for the next generation. The joy of my work is being in the classroom, co-constructing knowledge around leadership practice, and elevating diverse voices in scholarship and practice. My scholarship emphasizes leadership practices that foster equitable participation in organizations, especially in higher education institutions. My identity as an educator directly influences my parenting style as a mom of two. I spend time fostering my sons' love for reading at the library and volunteering at my oldest son's elementary school. During a challenging diagnosis of secondary infertility, I developed a deep commitment to my holistic wellness by prioritizing daily activity and routine therapy appointments, emerging as a fierce advocate for physical and mental health among my family and friend groups. I find my strength on walks listening to my favorite podcasts, in pages penned by my favorite Black women authors, on lunch dates with my husband, and in sister circles that accept my silence in group texts or frequent voice notes while shuttling from place to place.

Regina: I am an assistant professor of counselor education and the director of the career counseling program at a mid-size HBCU in a southeastern urban city. I am also a licensed clinical mental health counselor, national certified counselor, and qualified supervisor working part-time in private practice supporting adults experiencing a range of mental health concerns. My research has focused on the adult self-sufficiency and mental health of youth in foster care, with a secondary research focus on the intersection of career development and diversity. After becoming a mother of two, the first of whom I experienced a traumatic birth, I strive to advocate for improving the birthing outcomes of Black mothers. I feel strongly about supporting the perinatal mental health of Black birthing mothers, recognizing that many of us suffer from mood disorders in silence, both during the pregnancy and postpartum periods. I hope to create spaces for healing and community for Black mothers and Black motherscholars alike, in the same way I have benefitted from my village.

Theoretical Grounding

Black Feminist Thought

Black feminist thought is an intellectual tradition that emerged from the U.S. context, which often exploits our labor, denies us access to rights and privileges, and controls the narratives surrounding our images (Collins, 2022). Building on the foundational work of scholars like bell hooks, who challenged traditional feminist theory's neglect of Black women's experiences, and Angela Davis, whose analysis of Black women's labor and resistance shaped our understanding of intersecting oppressions, this tradition continues to evolve through contemporary contributions (Davis, 1983; hooks, 1981). Black feminist thought is characterized by six features: a shared but evolving consciousness among Black women; the recognition of individual responses to common experiences; a commitment to social justice as a critical social theory; a call to action for Black women intellectuals; the flexibility to adapt to changing contexts; and an unwavering embodiment of a humanist vision (Collins, 2022). Despite attempts to silence the voices and experiences of Black women, we find strength in the rich legacy of Black women intellectuals who validate our experiences and inspire us to take action. The discussions within Black feminist thought on Black motherhood, particularly advanced by Patricia Hill Collins and developed by scholars like Jennifer Nash and Alexis Pauline Gumbs, highlight how our experiences are influenced by the controlling images of a selfless matriarch who embodies immense strength in facing adversity (Collins, 2022; Gumbs et al., 2016; Nash, 2018).

As an act of resistance, we explore our journey towards holistic wellness and invite our sister motherscholars to do the same—redefining this very controlling image that has historically oppressed Black women economically, politically, and ideologically in today's context.

Throughout our study, we recognize our place in the academy as an outsider-within holding identities that our institutions were not built to uplift, acknowledge how intellectual activism prompts us to do what is right by our wellness beyond survival, and wrestle with controlling images that historically prioritize our labor over our wellness (Collins, 1986; Judie & McClure, 2023; Wilder & Osborne-Lampkin, 2013). These tenets are intuitively ingrained in our conversations and approach to making sense of our experiences in this research. Our research aims to add ourselves to those deserving of love, care, and joy in a career field that acknowledges that we often give this to our students, colleagues, and institutions but do not receive the same in return. It informs how we approach the gifts of faculty life as Black motherscholars while acknowledging the challenges shaped by the power and oppression that impact our journey.

The Indivisible Self (IS-Wel): An Evidence-Based Model of Wellness

Myers defined *wellness* as living in a way that centers optimal health and well-being, which consists of integrating mind, body, and spirit to live a fulfilling life in both human and natural communities (Myers, 2000; Wallace, 2019). In this regard, Myers and Sweeney (2004) developed the Indivisible Self evidence-based model of wellness (IS-Wel) as a foundation for better organizing the principles of wellness found on the Wheel of Wellness (Myers, 2000). Myers and Sweeney utilized the work of Adler (1954) and positive psychology to form the IS-Wel model, which includes one higher-order, uni-dimensional factor (total wellness), five second-order factors (Essential Self, Creative Self, Coping Self, Social Self, and Physical Self), and 17 third-order wellness factors which make up each of the second order factors. The model also includes contextual variables to understand how environmental factors might impact an individual's development (Bronfenbrenner, 1999; Myers & Sweeney, 2004). In this context, the IS-Wel model helps individuals identify the areas of wellness that are both important to them and the areas they want to improve or change (Myers & Sweeney, 2007). The five second-order factors are explained herein.

Five second-order factors. The *Essential Self* includes self-care, spirituality, cultural identity, and gender identity components, emphasizing a sense of purpose, meaning, and hope to live a fulfilling life. With these four components, Myers and Sweeney (2004) discussed the importance of having a sense of purpose, meaning, and hope to live a fulfilling life. The *Creative Self* consists of five components: emotions, control, thinking, work, and positive humor (Myers & Sweeney, 2004). These components speak to the attributes each person shapes in their efforts to form a unique place within their social interactions (Myers & Sweeney, 2004). The *Coping Self* consists of stress management, self-worth, realistic beliefs, and leisure. These components address the need to regulate our reactions to life happenings and reduce the negative impacts of these events (Myers & Sweeney, 2004). The *Social Self* consists of the components of friendship and love. Myers and Sweeney (2004) addressed the importance of friendship and love in enhancing one's quality and longevity of life and positively impacting one's mental health. Finally, the *Physical Self* consists of the components, exercise and nutrition, which research shows tend to be two essential aspects of an individual's holistic well-being and attributes to one's life longevity (Myers & Sweeney, 2004).

The IS-Wel model has been frequently used to examine wellness across the lifespan and within various populations (Avera et al., 2015; Clarke et al., 2016; Manning, 2017; Seguin et al., 2018; Spurgeon & Myers, 2010). Research further noted that conceptualizing wellness through the values of African American culture (e.g., collectivism, family, racial/ethnic pride, community, etc.) while examining the impact of various social factors (e.g., discrimination and racism) on the strengths of the African American lived experience is essential (Constantine & Sue, 2006; Wallace, 2019). Likewise, the IS-Wel model serves as a conceptual foundation for exploring strategies that may aid Black motherscholars who desire to work towards holistic wellness and belonging as they navigate their multiple roles.

An Integrated Approach

Further, to examine our experiences as Black women in the academy in concert with our desires for holistic wellness as mothers, Fig. 1 showcases how we integrated Myers and Sweeney's (2004) IS-Wel model with Collins' (2022) Black feminist thought, creating a conceptual model that centers our unique positionality and lived experiences. This integrated approach illustrates how the five second-order factors of wellness interact with the key tenets of Black feminist thought, acknowledging both the institutional barriers we face and our capacity for self-definition and intellectual activism both within academic spaces and as a members of broader society.

Methodology

We chose collaborative autoethnography to explore the complexities of our identities and experiences as Black women striving for professional success within the academy, a balanced lifestyle as a present mom, and personal fulfillment through holistic wellness practices.

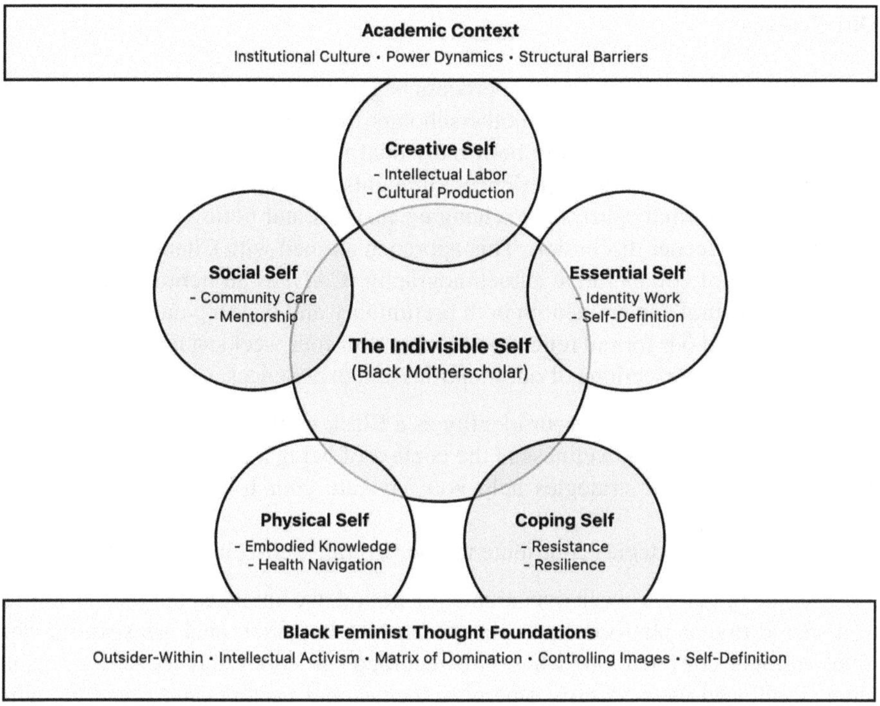

Fig. 1 Integrated IS-Wel model & Black feminist thought framework

Collaborative Autoethnography

Collaborative autoethnography (CAE) guided our research and discovery in a way that aligned with our values and approach toward learning. Its collaborative approach resonates throughout the qualitative research method, inviting us to engage in self-reflection and community learning that reflects the way many Black women engage in and exchange intellectual thought to combat bias in seemingly progressive moments like Black social and political thought, feminist theory, and heterosexism (Collins, 2022). Chang et al. (2013) highlight that CAE is "self-focused, context-conscious, researcher-visible, and critically dialogic" (p. 22). These characteristics informed our process as we engaged in self-writing and reflection, then connected as a group twice to make meaning of our experiences. Our chapter reflects this in our positionality statements and embedding information about the context in which we live as Black motherscholars.

Our Process

Our collaborative autoethnographic process began with a commitment to document our lived experiences as Black motherscholars through systematic self-reflection. Over two weeks, we engaged in both individual writing and voice note documentation, capturing our daily experiences, thoughts, and activities. Our group chat served as an informal space for exchanging insights and noting contextual events that warranted deeper discussion. This approach aligned with Chang et al.'s (2013) understanding of collaborative autoethnography (CAE) as an iterative process that encourages natural engagement in both preliminary and ongoing data collection.

We structured our formal reflection process over four weeks, guided by questions that probed the intersections of our identities and experiences:

- What experiences define your identity as a Black mother-scholar?
- How do you envision wellness in the context of being a Black mother-scholar?
- What resources or strategies help you navigate your role as a Black mother-scholar?
- How do these strategies contribute to your overall well-being and sustainability?

After the initial two-week documentation period, we uploaded our journal entries to a shared digital platform and convened for an in-person analysis session. This ninety-minute conversation, which we recorded on Zoom and transcribed using Otter.ai, allowed us to identify emerging themes and explore unresolved thoughts collectively.

The subsequent phase of our process involved focused individual tasks, including writing positionality statements and reflecting on practical strategies for maintaining wellness in our daily lives. Two weeks later, we reconvened to analyze both our shared and unique experiences, examining the distinct factors that influenced our academic challenges and successes. Our final analysis phase involved reviewing the journal entries and meeting transcripts, employing both traditional coding methods and AI-generated recording summaries to validate our primary themes. This chapter emerges from this rigorous process of deep self-reflection and community labor, drawing from our journal entries, in-person discussions, and informal communications. Through CAE, we amplified our voices and perspectives as Black motherscholars. This methodological approach illuminated our nuanced experiences, demonstrating how prioritizing wellness enables us to navigate our complex lives with wholeness and sustainability.

Narratives of Three Black Motherscholars

Through individual reflections, shared dialogue, and experiences, we identified key reflective moments in balancing our identities with expectations, prioritizing self-care, and rebounding from challenges.

Balancing Act of Motherhood and Faculty Life

One of the first themes to emerge from our conversation was the complexities of balancing our professional aspirations with our responsibilities as mothers and how we leveraged our unique positionality as faculty to contribute positively to our wellness. To balance motherhood and faculty life, we made decisions about our boundaries to ensure that we could do the work but not at the cost of our home life, strengthening our *essential self*. We recognized the autonomy and flexibility we achieved as motherscholars working in academia allowing us to lean into our *creative self*. This platform is also an example of developing a creative outlet to provide community and support for Black motherscholars, while also contributing to our assets as academic professionals. This tending to the creative self reflects the literature which states that creative women appreciate diverse creative acts (Reis, 2002).

We also nourished our *social self* when we celebrated a counter-narrative that emerged against the controlling images of Black women in academia, illustrating that we do not have to choose between family and professional success. We emulated ways to make our faculty life work for us and marveled when others found their way.

During our conversations, Jemilia referenced where her allegiance lies between the academy and her household saying, "I will work hard for our undergraduate students, but I never want it to tip the balance where my kids feel neglected. I want my children to talk about me more deeply than the undergrads I work with". While teaching gives her a sense of purpose and strengthens her *essential self*, she prioritizes her children as the prime benefactors of her trained expertise in learning and human development. In a fixed-term role traditionally assigned with the majority of teaching labor, she likens her experience to the legacy of labor exploitation where more Black women are in non-tenure track roles committed to teaching responsibilities than in research-focused roles that contribute to Black intellectual thought (Schneider & Bichsel, 2024). Acknowledging the context in which she works, she chooses to whole-heartedly commit to her teaching practice while setting personal boundaries. Black feminist thought characterizes these actions as how Black women may give the illusion of conformity by working hard while also boundary-setting as a form of resistance (Collins, 1990).

Tiffany reflected on her desire to supplement her faculty income and pursue her interests through grant awards and consulting projects while still enjoying her work as a faculty member and mentoring students. For example, Tiffany noted:

> That's the part of being a faculty member that I do enjoy…you can be creative, you can create this life. It's not just teaching and [conducting research] and mentoring students…If I want to write a book, cool. If I want to be a speaker, [only] if I want to…I love that aspect of it. So I think for me when I think about what's next it's really more so, how do I continue to create this life and world where everything is kind of flowing together in alignment, while also getting paid?

As Black women scholars interconnect the emotions, control, thinking, work, and positive humor within their *creative* selves, several of these components arose as a desire to balance our scholar and mother identities. Tiffany also demonstrates her commitment to defining a life that she wants that aligns with the inherent flexibility of her faculty role, particularly in an online asynchronous graduate program. As an outsider within, she recognizes the flexibility that faculty life can bring and leans into this understanding to tap into her *creative self*, thus benefiting her household (Collins, 1986).

Examples of success stories emerged within the weeks we were tasked to reflect on our experiences. One success story was the selection and installation of Dr. Karrie G. Dixon as the 13th and second female Chancellor of North Carolina Central University, a local HBCU in the NC Triangle. Close to home, with shared identities and crossed professional paths, we all shared the collective joy of her accomplishment in our various group chats. Regina articulated the renewed energy she felt from seeing Dr. Dixon effectively juggling multiple identities, "Knowing how much of a hands-on mom she is and still getting to this level, it's refreshing to know movers and shakers are doing both and accomplishing the dream while being attentive to their kids." We all felt the power of self-definition when this Black motherscholar achieved her professional goals while maintaining her reputation as a present and invested mother. Rather than the controlling image of a matriarch who is painted as one who self-sacrifices with no personal gain outside of the success of her children and community, we see someone who has remained committed to success as both a mother and professional. Her ascension to leadership redefined Black matriarchy in higher education and inspired us.

A Daily Negotiation of Academic Motherhood and Self-Care

Though our positive experiences integrating our personal lives with our work lives positively impact our emotions and behaviors to live full and healthy lives, this balance is not without its challenges. We recalled how we negotiated our duties as a Black mother in pursuit for the academy with self-care on the balance. Across our data, there were instances where we remembered the conversations that stuck with us and informed our next step. Our labor seemed tilted toward the academy and our children more than caring for ourselves, a familiar paradox that informs our common experiences as Black women. Because of the legacy of exploiting our labor, we are often not privileged to engage in self-care activities that would in turn, preserve our *spiritual self, physical self,* and *coping self.*

Tiffany reflected on a personal struggle of managing her PhD studies while raising her young daughter and being a full-time college administrator. She recounted, "Every time I opened my laptop, she knew…it was like, 'Mommy, mommy, mommy!' I started to get frustrated and had to remind myself that it wasn't her fault. I had to adjust my schedule to do work after she went to bed." Meanwhile, Jemilia discussed the critical decision to prioritize her education and family over a full-time job, emphasizing the financial and emotional toll it took. She shared a poignant memory: "I remember telling my therapist, 'I'm about to make this big life decision, so I figured I might as well get some added emotional support.' And she said, 'I don't think that's the reason why your son will go to therapy when he's older; it's not going to be because you decided to work on your doctorate.'" Tiffany and Jemilia both tapped into their *coping self* to manage their stress as they both wrestled with whether their actions were feeding into any negative stereotypes of Black women for their children.

When Regina reflected on facing challenges in finding a position as she settled into the idea of starting a family as a newlywed, Regina referenced her *spiritual self*.

> I just need to get something stable, that's going to allow me to have a meaningful career that I'm going to enjoy. I was an interim in a position that I applied for, I was like, let's just roll this out, whatever happens, like, God is going to have to lead it...I kept applying for positions here and there in academia, just to see where I landed, and I finally landed somewhere. And it was like, Lord, thank You for the miracle; I just did not think it was going to happen, where we would both settle into careers and feel satisfied with that and have an opportunity to raise a family.

Even when using strategies that tap into the strengths of our coping and spiritual selves, we recognized that we wrestled with society's expectations and the sacrifices we felt we needed to make. The living contradiction of choosing a method towards upward mobility and deeply loving our families felt like an either-or, making our joy when we struck a balance or saw someone else do so that much more gratifying.

Community Support as a Wellness Strategy

There was a collective agreement that emphasized that the resources and strategy we find the most rewarding on our journey as Black motherscholars have been engaging in a community. In alignment with Black feminist thought, we sought intellectual connections with the next generation, sister circles, and community organizing groups who all contribute to empowering Black women. Black feminist thought sets a standard for the collective work around humanism and empowerment, calling our thought to promote action and improved outcomes for everyone around us. It was clear that access to these communities nurtured our *creative self, social self,* and *physical self.*

We discussed our intentionality in supporting other Black women scholars, both in their pursuits to obtain a faculty position and in their retention of those academic roles. For instance, Regina noted that upon entering her doctoral program, she found her "doc sista village," which consisted of Black women who helped her navigate the academic challenges of her program, attend professional conferences, and network for employment opportunities. Meanwhile, in 2018, Tiffany created *Black Girl Mentor*, an online community of practice that centers mentorship for, by, and amongst Black women and girls—a project birthed from her personal mentoring experiences and her dissertation research on the mentoring relationships of Black women higher education professionals. Today, Black Girl Mentor has a reach of almost 3000 supporters across its podcast listeners and social media followers. Jemilia fondly remembers deciding to host the first *Melanin Mommas* brunch when she and Regina invited friends and colleagues to enjoy time to reconnect and affirm each other in our motherhood journeys.

As Black women and scholars, we discussed how we often feel isolated in environments not designed for us or choose to operate in isolation as protection from the world's biases and uncertainties. We further reflected on the importance of standing firm in our identities as Black women scholars despite facing marginalization and the gatekeeping we have experienced in academia. Being in a community with other motherscholars and Black intellectuals provided an opportunity to resituate our experiences in a context that dismisses the importance of creating community spaces that are affirming, life-saving, and soul-nourishing.

Across our examples, we tended to our *creative self* and *social self*, friendship appeared to be a critical component of our self-care and community support as Black motherscholars. The themes of community and collectivism among our trusted circles of friends, family, other Black women scholars, and Black mothers appear to be critical to both our personal and professional joy, as well as acclimation and retention in our academic spaces. For example, Tiffany reflected on receiving her first full-time professorship and how other Black women scholars reached out to her to offer support and resources as she acclimated to her new role, as well as how welcoming it felt to be surrounded by this spirit of collectivism. Further, our conversations centered around the idea and need to form coalitions specifically for Black women in academia to increase the representation and success of those who are also mothers in the academy.

Implications & Future Directions: Thriving Reimagined

Communing through this collaborative approach was fueled by our desires to be free in our bodies and work, to create a home and village where our children can thrive, and to model how our sistren may also engage in reflective practice that inspires change. Our contributions are an act of *intellectual activism*, utilizing our expertise in research and academic writing for an opportunity to inspire new action to support holistic wellness for Black motherscholars. Given the multiple roles Black motherscholars hold, it is essential to engage in holistic wellness practices that aid us in overcoming and navigating any barriers we may experience. As *outsiders within*, our commitment to our students and the academy cannot be prioritized over our wellness benefits, longevity, and our own families, as has been done in the past (Collins, 2022). In utilizing the five second-order factors as a framework from Myers and Sweeney's IS-Wel Model (2004), we can reimagine an environment that would holistically support Black motherscholars.

Creative Self

Higher education institutions need to create a work environment that is conducive for Black motherscholars to meet the academic demands of their institutions without compromising their wellness needs which might be accomplished through tending to one's *creative self.* For Tiffany, *Black Girl Mentor* became a way to hone her creative energy, while Jemilia enjoys book clubs like *Well-Read Black Girl* that highlight Black women writers who she incorporates in leadership classes, and Regina invests her time in creating communal spaces for Black mothers to learn and heal. One research study noted that creative women appreciate diverse creative acts (e.g., work, interests and hobbies, home tasks, friendship and personal relationships, etc.) and tend to have a creative output that is more diverse (Reis, 2002). An example of tending to the *creative self* was evident in a research study by Watson et al. (2024) in which a collaborative poetic autoethnography methodology was utilized to explore the mentorship experiences of Black women doctoral students who attended predominantly white institutions. This illustrates the creativity Black women can engage in (i.e., poetry) as an effort to express their challenges and resilience within academic spaces (Turner & Green, 2023). Another study by Sobande and Wells (2023) utilized a longitudinal exchange of poetry to explore the experiences of Black women early career academics. These examples illustrate how Black women can utilize creativity to express the challenges they experience, as well as to engage in community building and liberation.

Black motherscholars can align with their *creative selves* by engaging in virtual sanctuaries and communal spaces where they can meet regularly, both online and in-person, to exchange ideas and to provide support to one another. These efforts could include virtual writing and research retreats, collaborative research groups, and social media collectives that transcend geographical boundaries, creating a global community of solidarity and support. Making academic sabbaticals and grant funding readily accessible can give Black women and Black mothersscholars alike, an opportunity to tend to their creative self. Leaning on each other is a tradition of Black feminist thought, connecting theory to action to redefine how we see ourselves by surrounding ourselves with the diverse perspectives across Black women collectives whether in books, mentoring groups, or social spaces.

Coping Self

Our abilities to manage stress, recognize our self-worth, and the importance of engaging in leisure is an essential component in the survival and thriving of Black motherscholars. In recognizing our self-worth, it is important to stand firm in our identities as Black women scholars. In this regard, active engagement in culturally responsive therapy and coaching can support Black motherscholars in improving any negative mental health symptoms they have experienced. For Regina, providing mental health counseling, conducting research within counselor education, and training counseling students as a professor are all part of her life's work. Jemilia highlighted how her therapist's response to her concerns about the impact of going back to school full-time on her son provided her with meaningful support. This affirmation of her choice to prioritize self-care sparked a discussion about the importance of continuing to prioritize self-care to maintain energy and motivation while balancing multiple identities. In addition to engaging in therapy, Tiffany also benefits from the support of coaches to help her make forward progress in various areas of her life, including career/business, fitness, health, and parenting; as a result of her deep work in therapy and coaching, Tiffany, as a single primary parent, prioritizes solo travel and child-free vacations each year to rest and reconnect with herself.

Jones (2020) noted that Black feminist therapy could be utilized as a culturally relevant therapeutic approach in helping to move "Black women's life situations from a model of pathology to one of wellness" (p. 26). Resources like the *Therapy for Black Girls* (2024) directory offer a curated list of therapists who specialize in supporting the specific needs of Black women, some of whom utilize a Black feminist therapeutic framework that recognizes the Black women's standpoint and the contextual circumstances that create health disparities (Sanford, 2018). Furthermore, Black motherscholars can manage their stress by minimizing the number of academic obligations that they take on to balance their time commitments better. The research noted that having policies that permit caregivers more flexible time outside of the workplace to care for their families can help support the whole person in and outside of work (Coleman-King et al., 2022). Such policies can encourage Black motherscholars to only lend their time and talents to research and work projects that they feel are of most value to them and to have this decision supported by their academic departments.

Black feminist thought emphasizes the importance of knowledge validation and sharing within communities of Black women, making mentorship a vital expression of this theoretical framework (Collins, 2022). While mentorship serves as a critical component in illuminating one's self-worth and managing stressors (Kelly & Fries-Britt, 2022), the limited representation of Black women in academia has created an inequitable burden, requiring them to shoulder a disproportionate share of mentoring responsibilities (Watson et al., 2024). This reality reflects what Black Feminist scholars have long identified as the "outsider within" status of Black women in academia, where they are simultaneously essential to and marginalized within institutional structures. Drawing from Black Feminist principles of collective consciousness and reciprocal relationships, mentorship models must be reimagined to honor both communal knowledge production and the lived experiences of Black motherscholars. This reimagining manifests in revolutionary mentorship approaches where knowledge exchange is bidirectional and power hierarchies are intentionally dismantled through mentorship circles or collectives (Colclough, 2023; Cupid, 2020; Wiggins, 2017). In these spaces, each member serves as both mentor and mentee, embodying the Black Feminist principle of lifting as we climb. Moreover, meaningful allyship through sponsorship becomes another expression of this collective approach, where advocates actively amplify the work of Black motherscholars, ensuring their intellectual contributions are recognized and valued in spaces where they have historically been excluded.

Social Self

The journey of Black motherscholars is uniquely challenging, marked by the dual pressures of academic and maternal responsibilities within a context often fraught with systemic racism and gender biases. To thrive, Black motherscholars must cultivate a profound sense of belonging, which involves "the feeling, belief, and expectation that one fits in the group and has a place there, a feeling of acceptance by the group, and a willingness to sacrifice for the group" (Macmillan & Chavis, 1986, p. 10). Black mothers have gained belonging and social support from multiple sources such as family, friends, significant others, spiritual communities, and parenting groups (Bryant et al., 2024). Tiffany, Regina, and Jemilia found the collaborative autoethnography process as a culturally relevant methodology that was grounded in their budding friendship and sisterhood in the academy. Answering the call to write for this was in response to other sister scholars nudging us in this direction just as Black women intellectuals have done to contribute to Black feminist thought.

The term *village* has deep roots in Black communities, describing the networks that support and nurture Black mothers and their children (Bryant et al., 2024). These support systems echo the traditions of maroon communities, where enslaved people created autonomous spaces of resistance and mutual care (Thompson, 2006). Today's Black motherscholars continue this legacy through sister scholarship—intentional communities of support and intellectual kinship that sustain our academic and maternal work (Anckle, 2021; Shilling et al., 2021). In reimagining our villages, we create both formal and informal networks that serve as contemporary maroon spaces, where we share experiences, collaborate, and practice radical care for one another.

Reimagining belonging for Black motherscholars involves innovative and transformative strategies that go beyond traditional approaches. By building radical support networks, engaging in revolutionary mentorship and sponsorship, integrating holistic wellness practices, advocating for transformative institutional change, and embracing intersectionality in new ways, Black motherscholars can create environments where they feel deeply valued and included. These reimagined strategies not only enhance their academic and personal well-being but also enrich the broader academic community, fostering a more inclusive and equitable landscape for all. If one is already part of a sister circle or counterspace for Black women, they can welcome other Black motherscholars who may, too, benefit from the balm of sisterhood.

Physical Self and Essential Self

Exercise and nutrition as forms of self-care are important components of our overall health and well-being as Black motherscholars. There is overwhelming evidence that maintaining consistent exercise and a healthy diet positively impact one's life longevity. Black motherscholars can prioritize their exercise and nutrition (i.e., physical self) by joining fitness communities specifically created for Black women to be accountable for one another in achieving their health and wellness goals. Jemilia has actively promoted and engaged with groups like GirlTrek (2024) to support Black women walking 30 min daily towards healing and liberation while learning about the historical context. During the pandemic, the walking podcasts captured her through the group's intellectual activism promoting holistic wellness in the physical and essential self. Tiffany discussed engaging in more physical activity, such as signing up to work with a personal trainer and utilizing the real-time metrics of her new smart ring to manage stress and prioritize her overall health. This is particularly important as we reflected on the stressors we experience as busy motherscholars with little time to engage in wellness. Engaging in these activities sets an example for wellness that is emphasized uniquely by our role as mothers and furthers the wellness goals of the next generation we raise in our homes (Collins, 2022). Our act of resistance in finding ways to incorporate wellness activities for our physical and essential self defies the controlling image of a selfless matriarch and fuels us to live longer lives for sustained impact in our homes and on our campuses.

Conclusion

Our narratives are a testimony to the resilience and brilliance of Black motherscholars as we navigate complex realities while authoring our own stories of success. While the academy often falls short in providing the support we need to thrive, Black feminist thought affirms our experiences and emphasizes the importance of holistic wellness in the face of injustice (Collins, 2022). Drawing on Lorde (1988) and Hersey's (2022) wisdom that self-preservation and rest are forms of resistance, we envision a world where Black motherscholars are celebrated, not tolerated; where our voices transform the academy, not merely complement it; and where we are simply whole and well. We invite you to join us in co-creating this reality—one where Black women thrive as scholars, leaders, and mothers. Our future depends on it.

Competing Interests The authors have no conflicts of interest to declare that are relevant to the content of this manuscript.

References

Adler, A. (1954). *Understanding human nature*. Fawcett. (Original work published 1927).

Anckle, S. (2021). Sisterhood & scholarship while black. *Aphra Behn Online, 11*(1), 0_1–3. https://doi.org/10.5038/2157-7129.11.1.1265

Anderson, C. D., Mattley, C., Conley, V. M., & Koonce, D. A. (2014). Community colleges and the reproduction of gender in the academy: Experiences of women stem faculty. In V. P. Demos, C. W. Berheide, & M. T. Segal (Eds.), *Gender transformation of the academy* (pp. 41–62). Emerald Group Publishing Limited.

Avera, J., Zholu, Y., Speedlin, S., Ingram, M., & Prado, A. (2015). Transitioning into wellness: Conceptualizing the experiences of transgender individuals using a wellness model. *Journal of LGBT Issues in Counseling, 9*(4), 273–287. https://doi.org/10.1080/15538605.2015.1103677

Berheide, C. W., Watanabe, M., Falci, C., Borland, E., Bates, D. C., & Anderson-Hanley, C. (2022). Gender, type of higher education institution, and faculty work-life integration in the United States. Community, *Work & Family, 25*(4), 444–463. https://doi-org.nccu.idm.oclc.org/10.1080/13668803.2020.1776220

Bronfenbrenner, U. (1999). Environments in developmental perspective: Theoretical and operational models. In S. L. Friedman & T. D. Wachs (Eds.), *Measuring environment across the lifespan: Emerging methods and concepts* (pp. 3–28). American Psychological Association.

Bryant, L. S., Leath, S., Billingsley, J., & Moseley, S. (2024). "She has a village": The intergenerational benefits of social support networks for Black mothers and daughters. *Psychology of Women Quarterly, 48*(3), 390–410. https://doi-org.nccu.idm.oclc.org/10.1177/03616843241233289

Chang, H., Ngunjiri, F., & Hernandez, K.-A. C. (2013). *Collaborative autoethnography* (1st ed.). Routledge. https://doi.org/10.4324/9781315432137

Clarke, P. B., Adams, J. K., Wilkerson, J. R., & Shaw, E. G. (2016). Wellness-based counseling for caregivers of persons with dementia. *Journal of Mental Health Counseling, 38*(3), 263–277.

Colclough, K. (2023). *The role of mentorship in the advancement of Black women in higher education administrative roles* (Order No. 29999239). Available from ProQuest Dissertations & Theses Global (2777787319). https://www.proquest.com/dissertations-theses/role-mentorship-advancement-black-women-higher/docview/2777787319/se-2

Coleman-King, C., Brown, T., Haynes-Thoby, L., & Dowie-Chin, T. (2022). "Reclaiming our time": Black mothers cultivating the homeplace during times of crisis. *Journal of Social Issues*. https://doi.org/10.1111/josi.12570

Collins, P. H. (1986). Learning from the outsider within: The sociological significance of Black feminist thought. *Social Problems, 33*(6), S14–S32. https://doi.org/10.2307/800672

Collins, P. H. (1989). The social construction of Black feminist thought. *Signs, 14*(4), 745–773. http://www.jstor.org/stable/3174683

Collins, P. H. (2022). *Black feminist thought: Knowledge, consciousness, and the politics of empowerment*. Routledge.

Constantine, M. G., & Sue, D. W. (Eds.). (2006). *Addressing racism: Facilitating cultural competence in mental health and educational settings*. Wiley.

Cupid, S. (2020). *"It felt like home:" Exploring practices and mentoring experiences among Black doctoral women and Black faculty women in sister circles at Mid-Atlantic universities* (Order No. 27958146). Available from ProQuest Dissertations & Theses Global (2409166905). https://www.proquest.com/dissertations-theses/felt-like-home-exploring-practices-mentoring/docview/2409166905/se-2

Davis, A. Y. (1983). *Women, race, and class*. Vintage Books.

Dow, D. M. (2019). *Mothering while Black: Boundaries and burdens of middle-class parenthood*. University of California Press.

Garland McKinney, J. L., & Meinersmann, L. M. (2023). The cost of intersectionality: Motherhood, mental health, and the state of the country. *Journal of Social Issues, 79*(2), 596–616. https://doi.org/10.1111/josi.12539

GirlTrek. (2024). *GirlTrek: Healthy Black women and families*. Retrieved October 25, 2024, from https://www.girltrek.org/
Glynn, S. J. (2016). *Breadwinning mothers are increasingly the U.S. norm*. Center for American Progress. Retrieved from https://www.americanprogress.org/issues/women/reports/2016/12/19/295203/breadwinning-mothers-are-increasingly-the-u-s-norm/
Gumbs, A. P., Martens, C., & Williams, M. (2016). *Revolutionary mothering: Love on the front lines* (1st ed.). PM Press.
Hersey, T. (2022). *Rest is resistance: A manifesto* (1st ed.). Little, Brown Spark.
hooks, b. (1981). *Ain't I a woman: Black women and feminism*. South End Press.
hooks, b. (1990). *Yearning: Race, gender, and cultural politics*. South End Press.
Jones, L. V. (2020). *Reenvisioning therapy with women of color: A Black feminist healing perspective*. NASW Press.
Judie, B., & McClure, S. M. (2023). Patricia Hill Collins's on intellectual activism: The expansion of our field of perspective. In *The future of American higher education* (pp. 227–237). Routledge.
Kelly, B. T., & Fries-Britt, S. (Eds.). (2022). *Building mentorship networks to support Black women: A guide to succeeding in the academy*. Routledge.
Lorde, A. (1988). *A Burst of Light: Essays*.
Macmillan, D. W., & Chavis, D. M. (1986). Sense of community: A definition and theory. *Journal of Community Psychology, 14*, 6–23.
Manning, J. (2017). *Changes in health resulting from the "Internship Process" in a cohort of professional psychology doctoral student applicants* [Doctoral dissertation, Sam Houston State University].
Myers, J. S. (2000). The wheel of wellness, counseling for wellness: A holistic approach to treatment. *Journal of Counseling & Development, 78*, 251–266.
Myers, J. E., & Sweeney, T. J. (2004). The indivisible self: An evidence-based model of wellness. *Journal of Individual Psychology, 60*(3), 234–245.
Myers, J. E., & Sweeney, T. J. (2007). *Wellness in counseling: An overview*. American Counseling Association. https://www.counseling.org/resources/library/ACA/Digests/ACAPCD-09.pdf
Nash, J. C. (2018). *Black feminism reimagined after intersectionality*. Duke University Press.
Reis, S. M. (2002). Toward a theory of creativity in diverse creative women. *Creativity Research Journal, 14*(3/4), 305–316. https://doi-org.nccu.idm.oclc.org/10.1207/S15326934CRJ1434_2
Sanford, T. (2018). Applying a Black feminist framework to explain Black women's health disparities. *The Classic Journal*. https://theclassicjournal.uga.edu/index.php/2018/04/27/applying-a-black-feminist-framework-to-explain-black-womens-health-disparities/
Schneider, J., & Bichsel, J. (2024, April). *Representation and pay equity in higher education faculty: A review and call to action*. CUPA-HR. https://www.cupahr.org/surveys/research-briefs/representation-and-pay-equity-in-higher-ed-faculty-trends-april-2024/
Seguin, T. C., Bjornsen-Ramig, A. L., Blount, A. J., & Dinkel, D. M. (2018). A wellness approach to investigating student veterans' career goals. *Health and Kinesiology Faculty Publications, 53*. https://digitalcommons.unomaha.edu/hperfacpub/53
Shilling, A., Leddy, S., & Miller, L. (2021). Sister scholarship: A métissage manifesto for decolonizing the academy. In E. Lyle (Ed.), *Sister scholars: Understanding issues of identity as women in academe* (pp. 21–31). Brill Sense.
Sobande, F., & Wells, J. R. (2023). The poetic identity work and sisterhood of Black women becoming academics. *Gender, Work & Organization, 30*(2), 469–484. https://doi-org.nccu.idm.oclc.org/10.1111/gwao.12747
Spurgeon, S. L., & Myers, J. E. (2010). African American males: Relationships among racial identity, college type, and wellness. *Journal of Black Studies, 40*(4), 527–543.
Therapy for Black Girls. (n.d.). *Find a great therapist for Black girls in your area*. Retrieved October 25, 2024 from https://providers.therapyforblackgirls.com/
Thompson, A. O. (2006). *Flight to freedom: African runaways and maroons in the Americas* (1st ed.). University of the West Indies Press.

Turner, C., & Green, M. (2023). "My representation is performative": Black women's reflection of academia through collaborative autoethnographic poetic inquiry. *Journal of African American Women and Girls in Education, 3*(1), 31–48.

Wallace, D. (2019). *Examining perceptions and sensemaking of wellness among African American women who manifest the archetype of the strong black woman.*

Watson, V. T., Smith, F. A., & Gooden, C. (2024). Stitching narratives: Poetic autoethnography of Black women's mentorship in academia. *Cultural Studies/Critical Methodologies, 24*(3), 204–209. https://doi-org.nccu.idm.oclc.org/10.1177/15327086241226922

Wiggins, T. S. (2017). *An interpretive phenomenological analysis of the lived experiences and mentoring relationships of Black women student affairs administrators* (Order No. 10684973). Available from Ethnic NewsWatch; ProQuest Central; ProQuest Dissertations & Theses Global (2029125066). https://www.proquest.com/dissertations-theses/interpretive-phenomenological-analysis-lived/docview/2029125066/se-2

Wilder, J., Jones, T. B., & Osborne-Lampkin, L. (2013). A profile of Black women in the 21st century academy: Still learning from the "outsider-within." *Journal of Research Initiatives, 1*(1), Article 5.

Woods-Giscombé, C. L. (2010). Superwoman schema: African American women's views on stress, strength, and health. *Qualitative Health Research, 20*(5), 668–683. https://doi.org/10.1177/1049732310361892

Dr. Tiffany S. Wiggins is a Clinical Assistant Professor of organizational learning and leadership at the University of North Carolina at Chapel Hill. As an experienced practitioner-scholar, Dr. Wiggins's work centers identity, community, and wellness within academic and organizational contexts. Specifically, she explores the dynamic personal and professional experiences of Black women across the academy, the effectiveness and impact of mentoring relationships across the lifespan, and contributing factors of success for graduate and doctoral students. She is the founder of Black Girl Mentor, a community of practice that champions mentorship for and by Black women and girls, an ICF-certified coach who operates Noire Coaching & Consulting, and serves as a board member for *Cohort Sistas* and *NASPA Center for Women.* Beyond her professional and scholarly pursuits, her most important role is devoted mother to her teenage daughter.

Dr. Regina Gavin Williams is an Assistant Professor of counselor education and director of the Career Counseling program at North Carolina Central University. She is a licensed clinical mental health counselor (NC), qualified supervisor (NC), national certified counselor, and a licensed school counselor (GA). Her research focuses on the college and career readiness, adult self-sufficiency, and mental health of youth in foster care, with a secondary research focus related to the intersection of career development and diversity. Her role as a mom inspires her advocacy work on the community stakeholder advisory board for a UNC-Chapel Hill study entitled, ACURE4Moms.

Dr. Jemilia S. Davis is a Clinical Assistant Professor and Program Director for the Human and Organizational Leadership Development undergraduate major at the University of North Carolina at Chapel Hill. She enjoys learning alongside current and future leaders through courageous conversations and meaningful experiences that develop critical leadership skills. She is an active scholar-practitioner who examines the role of senior leadership in organizations and the influence executive leader perspectives, practices, and policies have on promoting equitable success for historically excluded communities. She does life partnered with her best friend and their two little loves who call her mom.

Blackademic Mamas in Chat: Using Endarkened Feminist Epistemology to Explore How Black Mothers Navigate Academic Socialization

Sacha Sharp, Brooke Harris Garad, and Kristina Johnson Yates

Abstract Inspired by bell hooks' *Sisters of the Yam* (2014), we developed a Black Academic Mamas group, called Blackademic Mamas, to support one another socially, emotionally, and professionally. Through the group, we sustain our sisterhood via text chat, brunch dates, and by attending our children's various social and school-related events. We share resources, strategize, and lean on one another to help process experiences as parents and academic professionals. For this chapter, we draw from endarkened feminism (Dillard, 2019) to discuss how our Blackademic Mamas group, specifically the group texts, provides a model for scholars seeking to create supportive spaces for successfully navigating their personal and professional lives.

Keywords Black motherhood · Queer motherhood · Endarkened feminism · Sista circle · Text chat

Introduction

The National Center for Education Statistics (2022) reports that four percent of faculty at postsecondary institutions are Black women. The Centers for Disease Control (2022) estimates Black women are three times more likely to die from pregnancy-related causes compared to white women. These data represent how we as Black women and mothers need support systems to navigate spaces and overcome challenges experienced in society. In other words, to be well we need one

S. Sharp (✉)
Indiana University School of Medicine, Indianapolis, IN, USA
e-mail: sachshar@iu.edu

B. Harris Garad
Butler University, Indianapolis, IN, USA
e-mail: bharrisgarad@butler.edu

K. Johnson Yates
Indiana University – Indianapolis, Indianapolis, IN, USA
e-mail: kridjohn@iu.edu

C. R. Turner and M. L. Green (eds.), *Black Motherscholarship Within and Beyond the Academy*, https://doi.org/10.1007/978-3-031-99758-7_24

another. Unfortunately, Black mothers are often defined by the white heteronormative culture that relegates us to being tokens or wholly ignored (Dow, 2019). Moreover, Black women in higher education are also socially, physically, and psychologically affected by de facto segregation prevalent on predominantly white institutions (PWI) campuses (Fries-Britt & Kelly, 2005; Ohito, 2021). These challenges are present even prior to factoring in our status as mothers. Therefore, exploring how we create spaces to exist authentically is necessary for Black women mothers as we navigate academic socialization in higher education.

For this chapter, we use endarkened feminist epistemology (Dillard, 2019) as a conceptual framework to discuss how our Blackademic Mama text chat serves as a sister circle that allows us to better navigate the challenges associated with academic socialization. We work from this Black feminist framework to link realities of socially constructed identities, such as race and gender, to historical and present-day oppression experienced by heterosexual and queer Black women (Dillard, 2019). Further, we engaged sista circle methodology (Johnson, 2015) as a means for data collection, and used bell hooks' *Sisters of the Yam* (2014) as a tool for guiding our discussion.

In this chapter, we will offer examples of challenges consistent with our identities as Black mothers—navigating the realities of queer, heterosexual, interracial, and transnational marriages—who are raising our children in predominantly white spaces, while also navigating similar spaces as professionals in academia. We begin by offering our positionality as members of this research team, friends, and scholars to better contextualize the challenges we face. We then offer a literature review around topics relevant to academic socialization for Black mothers, and the need for counterspaces.

Positionality

We are Black women and mothers who are positioned both as researchers and participants for this study. We are also descendants of ancestors who were forcibly brought to the United States through the Transatlantic slave trade. Therefore, we offer perspectives as Black women who must negotiate systems of oppression in an American context, understanding how white supremacy is deeply rooted in the foundation of this country.

Sacha is a heterosexual mother of three, who is in an interracial marriage with a white man and is agnostic toward religion, aspects of her being that influence her research and perception of the world. She serves as a faculty member in a professional school at a Research 1 institution of higher education. Brooke refers to herself as a "scholarmama," acknowledging how motherhood influences her work as an educational researcher. Her international, interfaith, multilingual marriage with an Afar man from East Africa also significantly shapes her worldview and ways of being.

Kristina is a Black lesbian wife, mother, daughter, friend, ex-Christian dreamer. These central parts of her identity shape her internal conceptualization of self and external interactions with the world.

Academic Socialization for Black Women

Black women in the academy face institutional racism, sexism, and a lack of support structures essential for our social and emotional well-being (Patterson-Stephens et al., 2017). While not an exhaustive list of oppressive experiences, scholars identify how oppression negatively impacts Black women, threatening our place in the academy by undermining our academic progress, diminishing our sense of belonging, and increasing stress and mental health concerns (Ellis, 2001; Grant, 2021; Porter et al., 2020). For Black mothers, navigating race, gender, and sexuality in the academy is often fraught with complexity. As Black women and scholars, our identities and histories significantly influence our parenting. These influences manifest in the values we instill, the challenges we face, and the communities we build to support our families. According to Dow (2019), Black mothers described a lack of belonging, a need for community, and a tax related to overcoming the financial hardships manifested through racialized oppression. Researchers also found that Black mothers need to build community with other Black women who share similar experiences (McLean & Mentor, 2019).

For Black queer women, research still has much to uncover regarding our experiences and progress within the academy (Bradley, 2020; Duran, 2019). That said, the paucity of literature confirms that for students and faculty alike, Black queer women face feelings of isolation, complex moments of oppression, instances of homophobia, and outsiderness even among racial solidarity (Bailey & Miller, 2015; Patton & Simmons, 2008). Because of these challenges, Black women mothers from various identity backgrounds often engage counterspaces that are specifically designed to allow self-expression, validation, and affective community (Solorzano et al., 2000). Counterspaces can be campus culture centers, church environments, or other community organizations (Patton & Harper, 2003). Consistently, sister circles as a counterspace are organic environments that are more accessible for Black women faculty and mothers and have proven to exist as sustainable spaces that include peer mentorship, resistance strategies, and healing practices (Garrett et al., 2022; Grant, 2021; Lane et al., 2022; Palmer, 2021; Patton & Harper, 2003; Porter et al., 2020).

Conceptual Framework: Endarkened Feminism

To provide a lens for conceptualizing and making meaning of the depth of Black academic motherhood, we turn to endarkened feminism (Dillard, 2000, 2006, 2019). Endarkened feminism is an epistemology that centers Black women's ways of knowing and being. An endarkened feminist framework represents a departure from the problematic and under- examined language, approaches, assumptions, and epistemological starting points frequently found in academia and educational research. Similar to how language shapes how we see, understand, and describe our worlds, Dillard (2006) advocates for culturally engaged explanations of being human within educational research, preferring: (1) the culturally-rich terminology of endarkened feminism where the "enlightened" conceptualizations of white feminism fall short, (2) relationship-rich research with space for subjectivity, and (3) culturally engaged and community-oriented work.

By engaging in endarkened feminism, we do not separate our academic work from the work of building our communities. We do not prioritize/idolize objectivity and distance where friendship is fruitful both for the spirit and the scholarship. We embrace our responsibility to engage in the work of co-creating and pulling other sisters into affirming spaces that will help us navigate life and the professoriate. Therefore, when we as Black mothers in higher education come together to create space for mentorship and friendship, we are practicing an ideological belief that these reciprocal relationships make us better scholars, teachers, mothers, and holistic human beings (Dillard, 2019). We are disrupting the status quo of doctoral studies and the professoriate, and actively modeling a different way of doing things. As we articulate in the subsequent methodology section, an endarkened feminist framework also emphasizes the value of studying ourselves and telling our stories to make space for our ways of being and knowing in research.

Methodology

In addition to using endarkened feminism (Dillard, 2019), we used sista circle methodology (Johnson, 2015) to explore our experiences as Black mothers engaged in chat. Sista circle methodology is derived from the concept of sister circles, or spaces designed to foster a sense of belonging and serve as a supportive and nurturing environment where Black women come together to share experiences, offer encouragement, develop self-definitions, and build community (Johnson, 2015). Sista circle methodology is a qualitative research method that goes beyond focus groups allowing researchers to become active participants in the data production for their research study (Johnson, 2015). Sista circle methodology allows for an iterative research process that centers Afrocentrism for the purpose of disrupting the Eurocentric values that often exist in other research methods. Tenets of sista circle methodology include communication dynamics, centrality of empowerment, and researcher as sista scholar (Johnson, 2015).

Communication dynamics is the first tenet of sista circle methodology and we use it to embrace the unique style of communication, nonverbal cues, and digital visualizations Black women use when in community with one another (Johnson, 2015). Centrality of empowerment is the second tenet rooted in the understanding that Black women are the purveyors of Black womanhood, and we are constantly negotiating and shaping our realities as we engage dialogically (Johnson, 2015). The final tenet is researcher as sista scholar and highlights the importance of the researcher being connected to the research beyond leading the conversation and providing analysis (Johnson, 2015). Consistently, we used sista circle methodology to prioritize the exchange of information that happens organically when we as researchers share our own personal experiences while becoming part of the research (Johnson, 2015; Lacy, 2017). By examining our text message conversations, we can better understand ourselves and how our experiences have helped us unlock deeper meaning and healing.

Setting and Data Collection

We established our Blackademic Mamas text chat in the summer of 2021 after attending an in-person brunch. The group began with four members, three of whom worked at one public institution of higher education in the midwest, while the other worked at a private institution in the same city. Over time, two more women were invited to the group based on their identities as Black mothers in academia. There are currently six members of the text group; however only three members came together for this paper with permissions from the others.

The intention of Blackademic Mamas was to build community as Black women and mothers navigating academia. We agreed to attend monthly brunches, host playdates for our children, and chat with one another via text messages to work through academic and personal challenges. Using text messages became an integral feature of our group because our busy schedules made it difficult to meet in-person. Through texting, we stayed connected and could share in-the-moment details about experiences we found relevant to the group. Moreover, the text message conversations allowed topics to span an undefined amount of time, therefore allowing us to offer nuance and complexity to the conversation we did not otherwise get with in-person communications.

Within two months of establishing this group, Brooke recommended that we read *Sisters of the Yam* (hooks, 2014) to foreground our experiences and allow for the development of a true sisterhood. We all agreed since we were familiar with hooks' work, and we felt we were doing a *Sisters of the Yam* collective intuitively. We decided using the book could guide our conversation and was also a way to structure our engagement given we didn't originally know each other that well. Moreover, because Brooke had experience with participating in this type of engaging community through her graduate studies, we were excited by the recommendation and the possibilities presented.

Similar to the approach taken for our text group, we used *Sisters of the Yam* to guide our data collection for this study. Firstly, each researcher found quotes from the *Sisters of the Yam* that we believed would align with the types of conversations had in the Blackademic Mamas text group. The quotes served as the material basis for our text message content analysis (Mertens, 2014). Using the quotes, we were able to search through our text messages and find content relevant to the academic socialization and motherhood to formulate categories for analysis. We had several discussions about the quotes most salient to us and how the text conversations identified have shaped our sisterhood. After multiple rounds of conversation and reflection, we identified three quotes that were used in our data analysis. Those quotes will appear in our findings. We concluded that the quotes could be organized in two domains, (Un)Masking and Healing, with the overarching theme of building community seen as driving each interaction.

Data Analysis

In addition to performing the content analysis, we continuously engaged endarken feminism to undergird our synthesis of the data found in our text messages. Endarkened feminism helped us make additional meaning of the text, which we further analyzed through conversations held via Zoom and through text message for the purpose of this research. We were able to highlight new understandings of old discussions and reflect on how our perspectives may have changed or remained the same. These conversations were iterative and inclusive of all members of the Blackademic Mama chat, as they happened spontaneously. Although the conversations were designed to produce this paper, they also served as a means for deepening the sisterhood between us via the chat.

Findings

To represent our findings, we highlight the specific quotes from *Sisters of the Yam* used to identify text chats from our group. We then provide a snapshot of the text message exchange identified for analysis. Finally, our analytical reflections are provided in between each section, a synthesis designed to highlight our meaning making process and to depict how we built and sustained our group. The themes derived from our analysis are about (un)masking and healing. Concerning (un)masking, we discuss the oppressive ways society makes us mask as Black mothers, but also how our Blackademic Mamas community promotes unmasking within the group and in public spaces. Finally, healing is the section where we use the Blackademic Mamas group to embrace the ways we heal and overcome the challenges associated with socialization in the academy.

(Un)Masking

We selected two quotes from *Sisters of the Yam* (hooks, 2014), that represent our experiences with (un)masking. The first quote states, "Justifications for 'wearing a mask' is obvious when we consider the circumstances of living in conditions of legal racial apartheid, where [B]lack folks had so little recourse with which to address wrongs perpetrated against them by white [people]" (hooks, 2014, p. 13). The second quote reads, "Collective unmasking is an important act of resistance (hooks, 2014, p. 16). We understand these quotes to be related to the practice of authenticity and the ability to either show up as our truest selves or conceal our identities for protection from the structures of gendered racism and homophobia that continue to oppress us.

Using Fig. 1, we highlight a sample text chat from the Blackademic Mamas group that we believe is consistent with conversations about masking and unmasking. The text message highlights a conversation about being available to our students in authentic ways. We then had conversations about what it meant to be authentic, and the risks we take when exposing our true selves in academic settings.

Through additional reflection and analysis, we found this conversation was particularly meaningful for Kristina, who expressed unease around the academy and other spaces she occupied because of her identity. She desired authenticity and believed unmasking required a level of vulnerability reserved for those who would reciprocate. She shared how in the academy, Black scholars have questioned her ability to authentically engage around issues of race because she is married to a white woman. Her lesbian identity often came into question when her research focus on Black queer girls did not align with the heteronormative expectations of girlhood in the Black spaces. Because the Blackademic Mamas group is composed of women who are

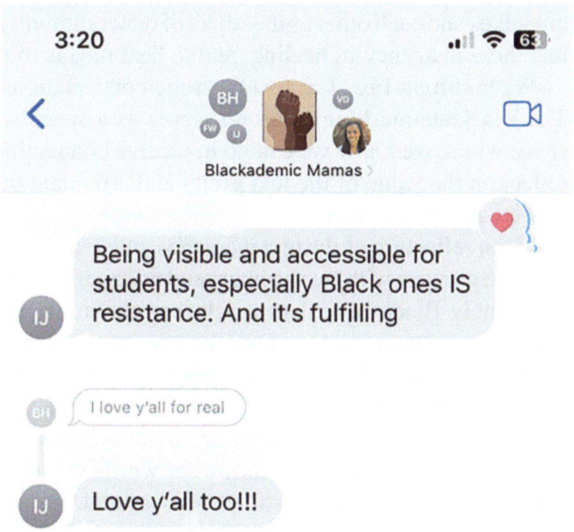

Fig. 1 Texts about un(masking)

primarily married to men, Kristina had moments where she shielded her sexuality as a protective strategy, albeit complex. While the group continued to offer her guidance, mentorship, and solidarity, duality remained. Unmasking for Kristina continues to be contextual. That said, the digital environment in which the Blackademic Mamas group exists allows author three to negotiate the complexities on her own terms.

Sacha also shared how masking and unmasking was a daily process because of her role as a diversity leader in her department. She discussed having to navigate promoting authenticity for her students of color when Eurocentric ideals of professionalism were in direct contrast. Moreover, Sacha expressed similar but markedly different concerns with presenting authentically in Black spaces because she is married to a white man and raising biracial children. Although navigating heteronormativity is not a salient process for Sacha, she identified with issues around race and the gatekeeping strategies that include questioning her Blackness, that she often experienced when doing diversity work. The Blackademic Mamas group served as a space where she could process her feelings of what being authentically Black meant. The validation received from members of the group via text helped support that meaning making process.

Healing

Regarding the theme of healing, we identified a quote that read, "In self-healing, Black women can identify that voice within themselves and begin to replace it with a gentle, compassionate, caring voice. When we see the positive results in our lives, we are then able to extend the generosity we give ourselves to others" (hooks, 2014, p. 28). Reflecting on this quote, we understood that we must first give grace to ourselves and each other as members of our community to truly heal. We acknowledge that there is agency in healing, and to heal means to positively pour into ourselves.

We highlight Fig. 2 as text message conversations tied to our healing processes. The Blackademic Mamas group serves as a space where we can be vulnerable. A space where we know we can go to receive connection and validity. We consistently reflect on the value of the text group and articulate our appreciation for sharing this space with one another.

Upon reflection of the text messages, quote and past conversations, Brooke shared how she grew up with two brothers and no sisters in her family of origin. She acknowledged how Black feminism taught her about sisterhood, and how she parents her daughters with the same values she tries to forefront in her friendships because she thinks sisterhood should be affirming without rivalry. She found the Blackademic Mamas group to be a tangible reflection of the Black feminist values she espoused as a mother and friend, and how those values are rooted in healing. Brooke asserted, "if each sister in the text group knows her worth and understands that there is more than enough love, success, and shine to go around, these sister spaces would be healing

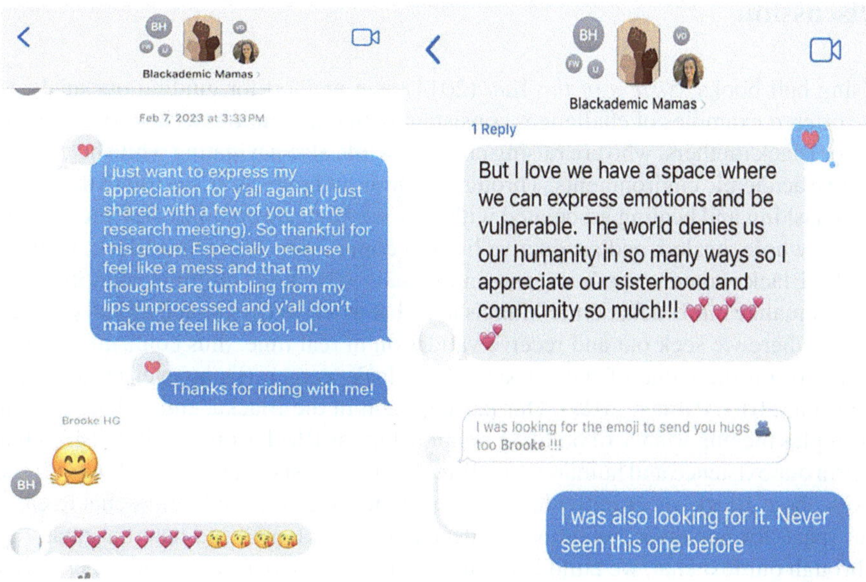

Fig. 2 Text messages about appreciation and healing

and affirming." Moreover, Brooke understood that through engaging in critical self-reflection and healing work, members of the group could avoid the judgment and condemnation that Black women are often relegated to.

Kristina found the Blackademinc Mamas group was a space where she was free to talk about her joy, success, failure, and fear. She determined if she was cautious to make connections with Black women no matter their sexual orientation, she was cautious to connect with herself. Indeed, she saw herself through the women in the Blackademic Mamas group. Kristina elaborated by sharing how her experiences with Black women have historically been fraught with tension and energy that caused her to grow weary. It stemmed from her upbringing in the church. As a Black lesbian, and human who always presented queer to others, her identity was a problem in many spaces. To Kristina, the Blackademic Mamas are a group of Black women who have embraced parts of her that have historically been judged and condemned. The connections developed in Blackademic Mamas fostered a type of nuance that helped Kristina heal and be a better person, mother, scholar, and friend.

Discussion

Using bell hooks' *Sisters of the Yam* (2014) as a method for guiding our analysis, we offered examples of challenges consistent with our identities as heterosexual and queer Black mothers, who are raising children while also navigating white heteronormative academic environments. Through analysis and reflection, we found themes of (un)masking and healing associated with how we navigate complexities and attempt to live whole, healed, and productive lives in community with other Black women.

As Black women, mothers, and individuals who hold multiple identities, we conceptualize our Blackademic Mamas text chat as a sister circle and digital counterspace where we seek out and receive validation in real time, thus confirming extant literature on the value of these spaces for Black women (Dunmeyer et al., 2023; Johnson, 2015; Palmer, 2021). Our participation in the Blackademic Mamas group examples the importance of building relationships as Black women relationships that affirm our existence and humanity (Collins, 2000). Consistent with Hutchings (2023) work about Black queer individuals, we used the Blackademic Mamas chat to carve out space for ourselves, intentionally decentering whiteness and heteronormativity. Through our text chat, we build community based on shared values and experiences; however, we also acknowledge and embrace our differences, appreciating that we are not a monolith.

Our group holds space for intersectional identities and tensions related to navigating the academy because of the respect we have for one another. We help one another interrogate biases and do not shame one another; instead, we provide grace to one another allowing for healing and authenticity (Cooper, 2015). Our research is consistent with literature that highlights the various resistance strategies Black women use to overcome the negative experiences within the academy (Love et al., 2023; Palmer & Udoh, 2024). We recognize that we have more to learn about each other and ourselves, but we commit to doing so in the spirit of community and celebration.

Implications

In this paper, we offer insight into the importance of having research that affirms us as Black women and mothers. There is a dearth of research that explores the multiple identities Black women hold—most notably queer identities and motherhood, and how we navigate academia. This paper highlights how Black queer women may navigate Black women relationships with trepidation and can experience some difficulty if not allowed the space to be their authentic selves. Moreover, we highlighted the importance of being intentional with joy and grace for ourselves, and how that translates to community building and respect for other Black women. As an implication of this work, we encourage more research that explores the experiences of Black mothers and Black women who hold queer identities. We also encourage research that specifically explores marginalized identities within the Black women community so as to understand the nuances that can come with the multiple identities Black women hold. We should not simply state that Black women are not a monolith, we must also honor their different voices and experiences by centering the ways we are not monolithic in our research.

Implications of this work also include a model for how Black women can use digital environments to develop supportive networks when the Black women representation does not exist on their campus. Our Blackademic Mama text chat is an example of how we as Black women mothers with different intersectional identities can still lean on one another to problem solve and navigate academia. Consistently, more research is needed to understand the various technologies Black women use to sustain sisterhoods designed for navigating academic socialization when there are so few Black women on PWI campuses.

Conclusion

For this chapter, we used endarkened feminism and sista circle methodology to explore the ways we as Black women and mothers navigate academic socialization. Using *Sisters of the Yam* (hooks, 2014) as a guide, we identified text messages from our chat for reflection and analysis. This chapter advances what is known about the experiences of Black women doctoral students and faculty members by providing first-hand accounts of how we use our Blackademic Mamas text group as a resource for academic survival. According to hooks (2014, p. 45), "we are not raised to believe living well is our birthright." We often consider our survival rather than believing we deserve to thrive. Upon reflection and through our engagement in Blackademic Mamas, we build community with intentionality to bring about our healing and authenticity with inclinations towards thriving. Through community such as Blackademic Mamas, we understand that together we can achieve what it means to live well.

Competing Interests The authors have no conflicts of interest to declare that are relevant to the content of this manuscript.

References

Bailey, M., & Miller, S. J. (2015). When margins become centered: Black queer women in front and outside of the classroom. *Feminist Formations, 27*(3), 168–188.

Bradley, R. R. (2020). In search of community: The experiences of Black queer women in college. *Journal of Student Affairs, New York University, 16*, 24–33.

Centers for Disease Control and Prevention. (2022). W*orking together to reduce black maternal mortality*. https://www.cdc.gov/healthequity/features/maternal-mortality/index.html

Collins, P. H. (2000). *Black feminist thought: Knowledge, consciousness, and the politics of empowerment*. Routledge.
Cooper, B. C. (2015). Love no limit: Towards a Black feminist future (in theory). *The Black Scholar, 45*(4), 7–21. https://doi.org/10.1080/00064246.2015.1080912
Dillard, C. B. (2000). The substance of things hoped for, the evidence of things not seen: Examining an endarkened feminist epistemology in educational research and leadership. *International Journal of Qualitative Studies in Education, 13*(6), 661–681.
Dillard, C. B. (2006). *On spiritual strivings: Transforming an African American woman's academic life*. SUNY Press.
Dillard, C. B. (2019). To experience joy: Musings on endarkened feminisms, friendship, and scholarship. *International Journal of Qualitative Studies in Education, 32*(2), 112–117.
Dow, D. M. (2019). *Mothering while Black: Boundaries and burdens of middle-class parenthood*. University of California Press.
Dunmeyer, A. D., Shauri-Webb, K. R., & Muhammad, G. G. E. (2023). "We are not broken": Using sista circles as resistance, liberation, and healing. *International Journal of Qualitative Studies in Education, 36*(7), 1248–1265.
Duran, A. (2019). Queer "and" of color: A systematic literature review on queer students of color in higher education scholarship. *Journal of Diversity in Higher Education, 12*(4), 390–400.
Ellis, E. M. (2001). The impact of race and gender on graduate school socialization, satisfaction with doctoral study, and commitment to degree completion. *The Western Journal of Black Studies, 25*, 30–45.
Fries-Britt, S., & Kelly, B. T. (2005). Retaining each other: Narratives of two African American women in the academy. *The Urban Review, 37*(3), 221–242.
Garrett, S. D., Williams, M. S., & Carr, A. M. (2022). Finding their way: Exploring the experiences of tenured Black women faculty. *Journal of Diversity in Higher Education, 15*(3), 225–238.
Grant, J. (2021). No, I'm not crazy: A Black feminist perspective of gaslighting within doctoral socialization. *International Journal of Qualitative Studies in Education, 34*(10), 939–947.
hooks, b. (2014). *Sisters of the yam: Black women and self-recovery.* South End Press.
Hutchings, Q. R. (2023). For me, us, our community: A kiki methodology of black queer storytelling. *Departures in Critical Qualitative Research, 12*(4), 6–28. https://doi.org/10.1525/dcqr.2023.12.4.6
Johnson, L. S. (2015). *Using sista circles to examine the professional experience of contemporary Black women teachers in schools: A collective story about school culture and support* (Doctoral dissertation). University of Georgia.
Lacy, M. C. C. (2017). *Black graduate women's self-defining process using media and sista circle methodology* (Doctoral dissertation). University of Georgia.
Lane, T. B., Patterson-Stephens, S. M., Perez, E., & Pierre, D. F. (2022). Examining relationships that matter: A qualitative study of Black women in doctoral education. *Journal of African American Women and Girls in Education, 2*(1), 27–46.
Love, B. H., Templeton, E., Ault, S., & Johnson, O. (2023). Bruised, not broken: Scholarly personal narratives of Black women in the academy. *International Journal of Qualitative Studies in Education, 36*(10), 2229–2251.
Mertens, D. M. (2014). *Research and evaluation in education and psychology: Integrating diversity with quantitative, qualitative, and mixed methods.* Sage.
McLean, A., & Mentor, M. (2019). A seat at the table: Womanist narratives of Black mothers in doctoral programs. *Taboo: The Journal of Culture and Education, 18*(1), 18–39.
National Center for Education Statistics. (2022). *Characteristics of postsecondary faculty. Condition of education.* U.S. Department of Education, Institute of Education Sciences. Retrieved May 31, 2022, from https://nces.ed.gov/programs/coe/indicator/csc
Ohito, E. O. (2021). Some of us die: A Black feminist researcher's survival method for creatively refusing death and decay in the neoliberal academy. *International Journal of Qualitative Studies in Education, 34*(6), 515–533.

Palmer, D. (2021). *I got a lot to be mad about: Sista circles as a counterspace for black women doctoral students* (Doctoral dissertation). Indiana University.
Palmer, D., & Udoh, E. (2024). Removing the veil of whiteness in qualitative research using sista circle methodology. *International Journal of Qualitative Methods, 23*, 16094069241278160.
Patterson-Stephens, S. M., Lane, T. B., & Vital, L. M. (2017). Black doctoral women: Exploring barriers and facilitators of success in graduate education. *Higher Education Politics & Economics, 3*(1), 157–180.
Patton, L. D., & Harper, S. R. (2003). Mentoring relationships among African American women in graduate and professional schools. In M. F. Howard-Hamilton (Ed.), *New directions for student services. Meeting the needs of African American women* (Vol. 104, pp. 67–78). Jossey-Bass.
Patton, L. D., & Simmons, S. L. (2008). Exploring complexities of multiple identities of lesbians in a Black college environment. *Negro Educational Review, 59*, 197–215.
Porter, C. J., Green, Q., Daniels, M., & Smola, M. (2020). Black women's socialization and identity development in college: Advancing Black feminist thought. *Journal of Student Affairs Research and Practice, 57*(3), 253–265.
Solorzano, D., Ceja, M., & Yosso, T. (2000). Critical race theory, racial microaggressions, and campus racial climate: The experiences of African American college students. *Journal of Negro Education, 69*(1/2), 60–73.

Sacha Sharp, Ph.D. (she/her) is Vice Chair for Strategic Engagement, Director of Medical Education Innovation, and Assistant Professor of Medicine in the Department of Medicine at Indiana University School of Medicine. She is also Adjunct Assistant Professor in the program of Africana Studies at IU- Indianapolis. Dr. Sharp earned her PhD at IU Bloomington with a higher education focus in the Department of Education, Leadership, and Policy Studies. She also earned a master in education and human development from the George Washington University.

Brooke Harris Garad, Ph.D. (she/her) teaches in the College of Education at Butler University where she prepares undergraduate students to excel in elementary education settings. Dr. Harris Garad completed a doctorate in Education from The Ohio State University where she focused on equity studies in education and qualitative and culturally relevant research. Dr. Harris Garad has worked with preschoolers to graduate students, but teacher education is at the heart of her research and professional experience.

Kristina Johnson Yates (she/her) is studying urban education within the School of Education at Indiana University- Indianapolis. She earned her Master of Social Work from Indiana University with a concentration in child welfare and obtained her undergraduate degree from the University of Florida with a bachelors in Family, Youth, and Community Sciences. Johnson Yates comes from a black feminist perspective that intersects the foundations of a career in social work with the intricacies of higher education. As a black, queer mother, Johnson Yates is empowered by connections made with other black mothers who exist in academic spaces.

Index

C. R. Turner and M. L. Green (eds.), *Black Motherscholarship Within and Beyond the Academy*, https://doi.org/10.1007/978-3-031-99758-7

MIX
Papier aus verantwortungsvollen Quellen
Paper from responsible sources
FSC® C105338

If you have any concerns about our products,
you can contact us on
ProductSafety@springernature.com

In case Publisher is established outside the EU,
the EU authorized representative is:
Springer Nature Customer Service Center GmbH
Europaplatz 3, 69115 Heidelberg, Germany

Printed by Libri Plureos GmbH
in Hamburg, Germany